CHILDREN
with
MENTAL
RETARDATION
A Parents' Guide
Edited by
Romayne Smith, M.A., CCC-SLP

WOODBINE HOUSE • 1993

Published by Woodbine House, 5615 Fishers Lane, Rockville, MD 20852,
Toll Free 800/843–7323.

Copyright © 1993 Woodbine House, Inc.

Cover design and illustration by Lili Robins

Library of Congress Cataloging-in-Publication Data

Children with mental retardation : a parents' guide / edited by Romayne Smith.
   p. cm.
  Includes bibliographical references and index.
  ISBN 0–933149–39–5 : $14.95
  1. Mentally handicapped children—United States. 2. Mentally handicapped
children—United States—Family relationships. 3. Parents of handicapped
children—United States. I. Smith, Romayne.
HV894.C48 1993
649' .152—dc20   90–50258
                             CIP

Manufactured in the United States of America

10 9 8 7 6 5 4 3 2 1

Table of Contents

Acknowledgements

I would like to thank the many people whose time, energy, and sincere interest in children with mental retardation helped to make this book a reality. First, my gratitude goes to the chapter authors for their many months of hard work and patience. Next, I owe a special thank you to the professionals from many disciplines who contributed their thoughts and suggestions: Dr. Eugene del Polito and Laura Klingler, audiologists; Laura Jacob, Sharon Anderson, Joan Simon, and Laurie Benjamin, occupational therapists; Mindy Toby, Jacqueline Strickland, and Carol Schuman, physical therapists; Kathy Porter, special education teacher; Dr. Patricia O. Quinn, developmental pediatrician; and Sue Okun and Nick Girardi, school principals who shared their thoughts about mental retardation and its impact on the children in their schools. Thanks are also due to Celia S. Feinstein at Temple University for her insight into the changing terminology in the mental retardation field. I am, of course, especially indebted to the families who gave their time, experience, and encouragement so that others might learn from them, and to those who have shared glimpses of their family lives by allowing us to publish photographs of their children.

Finally, I thank my husband, who encouraged and endured and never said no when I needed a sounding board.

Introduction

By Romayne Smith, M.A., CCC-SLP

I work with many parents who are just learning about their child's mental retardation. I have seen how much anguish, pain, and confusion they go through in the beginning, and how desperately they search for support, information, and guidance. And for many years, I have wanted to do something to help ease these parents' entrance into the world of mental retardation. This book is my attempt to do just that. It is designed to provide insight and information to parents like you: parents of young children with mild to moderate mental retardation. Parents of children with severe or profound mental retardation may also find some information in this book of interest—specifically, the chapters on medical, legal, assessment, and advocacy issues. But the chapters dealing with family life, daily care, and education will likely be of limited use.*

To introduce you to most of the major issues that you face, I have included chapters written by two types of experts: professionals from various disciplines whose job is to help children with mental retardation and their families make the best of a tough situation, and parents who have learned to cope with the challenges and changes that mental retardation brings to a family. These chapter authors provide background information on different facets of raising a child with mental retardation, plus practical strategies to help you help your child achieve his or her potential.

The authors of this book cover a lot of ground—from the evaluation process, to coping with your feelings about the diagnosis, to helping your child succeed at home, at school, and in the community. In the end, I hope all this information will help you see that having a child with mental retardation is *not* an unmanageable predicament, although I realize that it can feel that way at times. In

---

* In 1992, the American Association on Mental Retardation adopted new terminology to describe the different degrees to which mental retardation can affect people. Using this terminology, the book's intended readership is primarily parents of children with mental retardation who need intermittent to limited support, and secondarily parents of children who need extensive to pervasive support.

fact, mental retardation is only one small part of your child's make-up. It doesn't really define who your child is or is becoming. Like all children, your child has a distinctive personality and a vast array of interests and abilities. He has a lot to give as his own unique member of your family and of the community. I hope this book will show you that mental retardation will not keep him from becoming a loving and lovable part of your life.

Throughout the book, you will find passages in bold-face print. These are statements made by real-life parents of children with mental retardation who have been through what you are going through. By sharing their feelings, experiences, and advice, these parents offer support and a parent's perspective on the information presented in each chapter. They also offer the knowledge that you are not as alone as you might think.

Because it would be impossible to cover everything you need to know in one book, this book includes resources to help you track down additional information. There is a Reading List with descriptions of books and periodicals that can provide further information about the topics discussed in each chapter. There is also a Resource Guide to national and state organizations that can supply you with information, support, and other kinds of help. The Glossary includes terms used in the text, as well as some you may encounter in dealing with medical and special education professionals. You may also find it helps when you are trying to explain things to friends and family members.

In this era of political correctness, a few notes about word usage are in order. First, the personal pronouns "he" and "she" are used alternately by chapter to refer to children with mental retardation. I did not want to imply that all children with mental retardation are either male or female, and constantly using "he or she" to refer to a child can be cumbersome. Second, throughout the book I have consistently used the term "mental retardation" rather than such variations as "mentally challenged," "cognitively challenged," "mentally handicapped," or "mentally impaired." I did this for three reasons. First, "mental retardation" is the "official" diagnostic term presently used by the American Psychiatric Association to describe this particular developmental disability. Second, "mental retardation" is the label you are most likely to hear from medical and special education professionals. Third, "mental retardation" is a very specific term for a very specific disability—when you read it, you know what it means, avoiding the confusion caused by more general terms such as "developmental delay." I realize that "mental retardation" is not everybody's favorite terminology for the condition, but I did not choose to use it with the intention of hurting, insulting, angering, or demeaning anyone. I hope no offense is taken where none was intended.

When you have finished reading this book, I hope you will find yourself with the information and courage you need to handle a role you have probably not chosen: being the parent of a child with mental retardation. It's tough, but it can be done. Thousands of families can attest to that. Everyone involved with this book wishes you and your family all the best as you go about your lives.

One

=== ❈ ===

What Is
Mental Retardation?

Chahira Kozma, M.D., and Jeremy S. Stock, Ph.D.*

If your child has been diagnosed as having mental retardation, understanding what that diagnosis means for him and for you is crucial to helping him lead a full and rewarding life. Unfortunately, there are many misconceptions about mental retardation. You may have heard, for example, that children with mental retardation are incapable of learning, or that they never grow up. These outdated notions linger on, even though they have been proven wrong.

This chapter helps to clear up the misconceptions. It explains what mental retardation is and is not, and discusses in a general way what to expect for your child. It also answers many questions parents commonly ask about the diagnosis and causes of mental retardation.

The planning for care of children with special needs has changed quite dramatically over the past decade. In past years, parents were encouraged to choose residential placement or institutionalization for children with most types of special needs. The

* Chahira Kozma, M.D., is an Assistant Professor of Pediatrics at Georgetown University Medical Center in Washington, D.C. She is a clinical geneticist and a developmental pediatrician, and currently works in the Child Development Center at Georgetown University Hospital. Dr. Kozma has conducted several research activities in the field of mental retardation and has presented her results during national conferences on mental retardation/developmental disabilities. In addition, she has published several articles in the field of genetics and dysmorphology. Jeremy S. Stock, Ph.D., a clinical psychologist, is a Clinical Assistant Professor in Pediatrics at Georgetown University Hospital Child Development Center. She participates on interdisciplinary teams to evaluate children with developmental disabilities and infants who are at high risk for developmental disabilities. She has a part-time private practice.

recent trend, however, has been for children to be kept at home with their families and have their needs served within the community. For this reason, it is important for parents to have a good understanding of their children's special needs in order to be strong advocates for their children. Since the enactment of federal laws requiring that local communities provide special services for children, parents have an even greater need for knowledge about their children's condition and the services which must be provided by the educational system. With this knowledge, parents can communicate effectively with the teachers, physicians, psychologists, and therapists who play such an important role in their children's lives. By making sure that they understand their children's needs, parents can better help them develop to their own individual potential. The chapters that follow will help you build on the foundation this chapter provides, giving you the information you need to ensure that your child receives the care and services best suited to his unique needs.

What Is Mental Retardation?

Mental retardation is a type of developmental disorder. A developmental disorder is a condition that appears early in life and has a life-long effect on the way an individual grows and acquires skills, or *develops*. Mental retardation is the most common developmental disorder, affecting about 2 to 3 percent of the population. It often occurs in combination with other developmental disorders such as cerebral palsy, autism, and epilepsy. This chapter describes mental retardation as viewed on its own; Chapter 9 discusses other childhood disorders that can be associated with mental retardation.

In 1992, the American Association on Mental Retardation (AAMR) developed a very specific definition of mental retardation, which reads:

> *"Mental retardation" refers to substantial limitations in present functioning. It is characterized by significantly subaverage intellectual functioning, existing concurrently with related limitations in two or more of the following applicable adaptive skill areas: communication, self-care, home living, social skills, com-*

*munity use, self-direction, health and safety, functional academics,
leisure and work. Mental retardation manifests before age 18.*

This long definition means that a
child with mental retardation performs significantly below his age
level in two areas: 1) *intellectual
functioning,* or intelligence; and 2)
adaptive functioning, or the ability to
act independently and get along in
social situations. Remember that the
diagnosis of mental retardation
depends on the assessment of both
intelligence and a person's ability to
function socially and independently
compared to other people of the same
age and culture. How much mental
retardation affects a child's abilities
in these areas varies widely. That is,
one child's development may be affected by mental retardation to a relatively mild degree while another
child's development might be affected more significantly.

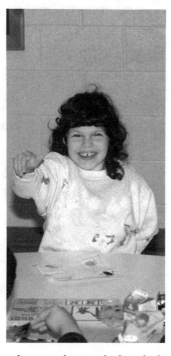

Perhaps the best way to understand mental retardation is in
relation to normal development. As a developmental disability,
mental retardation means a significant and lifelong impairment in
development—for example, in the acquisition of language, thinking, self-help, social, and other skills. It does not mean, however,
that development and learning is impossible. Rather, mental retardation means that the *rate* of development is slower than in a child
with normal intellectual and adaptive skills. The *individual* rate of
development for that child is critical to understanding how rapidly
that child will learn. For example, for every year that passes, a child
with mental retardation might make the same amount of progress
as a child without mental retardation would make in six months.
Consequently, at eight years of age, this particular child might have
the skills of a typical four-year-old. At this rate of development, you
might expect the child to function like a ten-year-old at twenty years

of age and a fifteen-year-old at thirty years of age. In reality, however, children develop most of the skills they need to function as adults by age sixteen to eighteen. That is, *skill development* usually reaches a peak at around age sixteen, although everyone—with and without developmental problems—continues to learn throughout their lives. Therefore, in the example of a child whose development seems to progress at about half the normal rate in early childhood, it is likely that he would function about like an eight- or nine-year-old as an adult.

Although learning may be slower, children with mental retardation can and do learn. Within the broad limits set by their mental retardation, these children have tremendous potential. With the right kinds of help at school and at home, children with mental retardation can master many of the same skills as other children. And like everyone else, they can continue to learn and grow all their lives.

How much *your* child will be able to learn depends on many factors, ranging from the degree of his mental retardation to the educational services he receives. As with any child, you simply cannot predict how much he will be able to achieve eventually. However, you certainly can help him reach his potential and enjoy the highest quality of life possible.

Our daughter has a little neurological damage, but there is nothing anybody can do about it. We know she's got mental retardation; we know she's going to learn at a slower rate. But she is learning. It's not like she is at a standstill.

I don't notice that Scott's different as much when he's by himself. It's when he is with other kids that he seems to be different sometimes. He doesn't talk and they do; he doesn't walk. . . . I mean, I see another child who's two-and-a-half or three years old and walking and talking normally and things like that, and I think, "Well, I guess he _is_ slow or he _is_ different." But usually we just see the daily progress he makes and don't compare.

※

Before Beth was born, I didn't have a very clear idea of mental retardation at all. I just thought that there was the typical "look" and that people with mental retardation didn't speak all that well.

Making a Diagnosis of Mental Retardation

If your child has been diagnosed with mental retardation, it means that tests have shown that his intellectual and adaptive functioning is below average. To understand your child's diagnosis, you therefore need to know what experts mean by intelligence and adaptive functioning, as well as how functioning in these areas is measured.

What Is Intelligence?

The experts who consider what intelligence really is have never reached an absolute agreement. However, there is a broad understanding of what is meant by the term. Intelligence means the ability to gather and make sense of the information that surrounds a person in the world, to act on it, and then to use it in other situations to make sense of new experiences. In order to function in the world, people must be able to put many different intellectual skills together. We must be able to pay *attention* to the world around us, *remember* what we have experienced before, *abstract* or pull out the important information, use it to *problem solve*, and then *generalize* or apply what we have learned to new situations. How well someone does all these things together determines how intelligent that person is considered to be.

Intelligence is measured by widely used and well-recognized tests (commonly called *IQ tests*). These tests have been developed and standardized and revised for many years. They are reliable (get the same kinds of results each time) and valid (actually measure what they are designed to measure). For the most part, they measure the underlying skills which predict how well a child is likely to learn from his environment, especially at school. Therefore, these tests help to predict which children may have difficulty learning the things they need to be able to function independently in the world. The results of intelligence tests are called *intelligence quotients* or *IQ's*.

Intelligence tests are constructed in such a way that the average (mean) score is 100. Although 100 is the mean score on an IQ test, people who score somewhat above or somewhat below 100 are still considered to function in the "average" range. Often, scores between 80 and 119 are considered to be within the average range of intelligence. More than two-thirds of all people taking IQ tests score in this range. Scores between about 70 and 79 are regarded as being in the borderline range between average intelligence and mental retardation; and scores below about 70 to 75 are generally considered to be in the mentally retarded range. About 2 to 3 percent of people score in this range. Figure 1 shows the relative numbers of people who score in the average, below average, and above average range on tests of intelligence.

Figure 1—Range of Human Intelligence

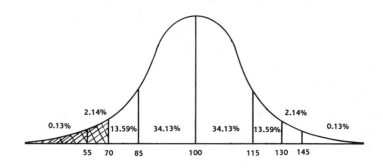

What Is Adaptive Functioning?

As pointed out earlier, below-average intelligence is only one part of what is required for a diagnosis of mental retardation. The other part is a finding of below-average *adaptive functioning.*

The term adaptive functioning means all those skills that are necessary for independence in daily living. Adaptive skills include all the abilities to interact socially, communicate, and take care of personal needs. Abilities include activities of daily living (dressing, feeding, grooming, and toileting); communication skills (both understanding and expressing language); socialization (with peers, family members, and within the community).

As a child develops more independence in adaptive functioning he masters more advanced skills. For example, a two-year-old with average adaptive functioning might be expected to understand the safety rule that it is dangerous to touch something hot. Later, a child should understand traffic rules such as looking both ways before crossing the street. Likewise, a child's communication skills generally progress from simply letting his mother know that he is hungry to very sophisticated levels of reading and writing. Usually, a child's adaptive functioning levels are fairly similar to levels of cognitive abilities, except when other factors such as physical or sensory impairments further complicate independent functioning. For example, a child who has cerebral palsy in addition to mental retardation may have more trouble acquiring self-help skills such as toothbrushing and grooming, due to movement limitations.

Adaptive functioning, like IQ, is gauged by comparing your child's abilities with those of other children his age. For example, how do your child's abilities to eat independently or to answer the phone compare with the norm for his age? To evaluate adaptive functioning, a psychologist interviews parents and teachers about the adaptive behaviors a child shows at home, and checks off achievements on a standardized checklist. Chapter 4 explains tests of adaptive functioning in more detail; Chapter 2 provides more information about the adaptive functioning of children with mental retardation.

What Is Mental Age?

Although you will generally hear your child's intelligence described in terms of an IQ score, you may also occasionally hear it described in terms of *mental age (MA)*. Mental age is the age at which an *average* child would receive the same number of items correct as your child does on a particular test or checklist used to assess young children's development. That is, if your five-year-old performed the same number of tasks correctly as the average three-year-old would, he would be considered to have a mental age of three. Tasks on such a test might include: sorting like and unlike objects; putting objects in sequence; and matching, identifying, and naming pictures and objects.

In the past, this idea has been broadened to assume that a child with a chronological age of five and a mental age of three is going to act like, seem like, and be like other children who have both chronological and mental ages of three years. This idea holds up only in the most general way. For example, if your five-year-old has a mental age of three years, then you might expect his attention while you are reading to him to be *more like* that of a three-year-old. However, mental retardation doesn't just affect the rate at which children learn, but also their pattern of strengths and weaknesses. Therefore, your child might not have all the comprehension of stories that a normally developing three-year-old would. In other words, his attention may be more like that of a three-year-old, but his comprehension of concepts may not. So do not rely too heavily on the idea of mental age when trying to understand what your child may or may not be able to do. Instead, it is better to understand overall mental age as an *average* of a pattern of strengths and weaknesses. Therefore, it is important to know more about your child's profile.

Old and New Ways of Describing Mental Retardation

There is no single best picture of children with mental retardation. Like children who are developing normally, children with mental retardation develop in a unique way, with different patterns of strengths and weaknesses. In addition, just as there is a wide range in what is considered normal development, there is also a wide range of development among people with mental retardation.

Over the years, professionals have used different classification systems to describe these differences in the way mental retardation can affect an individual's functioning. In 1992, a new classification system was introduced by the American Association on Mental Retardation. You may, however, continue to encounter the old classification system for some time, both in reading older publications on mental retardation and in dealing with professionals who have not yet switched to the new system. For this reason, both the old and the new classification systems are described below.

The Old Classification System

Until 1992, children with mental retardation were customarily diagnosed as having a particular level or degree of mental retardation based on their IQ scores. That is, a child's mental retardation was classified as either mild, moderate, severe, or profound. Children with IQ scores roughly from 50 or 55 to 70 were considered to have mild mental retardation. Children with scores from 35 or 40 to 50 were considered to have moderate mental retardation. Children with IQs from 20 or 25 to 35 or 40 were said to have severe mental retardation, and those with scores below about 20 were said to have profound mental retardation.

Using this classification system, about 85 to 89 percent of all people with mental retardation fall into the mildly retarded range, while another 6 to 10 percent are in the moderately retarded range. Only about 3 to 4 percent of people with mental retardation score in the severe range, and about 1 to 2 percent in the profound range.

In the past, these classifications were mainly used to determine what level of education or training would best suit a child's capabilities. For example, schools usually expected children with mild mental retardation to be able to learn "academic" subjects such as reading and arithmetic more easily than children with moderate mental retardation. Schools usually expected to spend more time teaching daily living skills such as toothbrushing and dressing to children with severe mental retardation than they did to children with moderate mental retardation.

The New Classification System

The AAMR's new system for classifying levels of mental retardation is based not on IQs, but on an individual's unique strengths, weaknesses, and needs for special supports. The intent is to describe more accurately the variability in the way different people with the same IQ score can function. That is, under the old system, two children who scored in the moderately retarded range were generally assumed to have roughly the same potential for learning. However, the new system is intended to recognize that capabilities and performance can vary widely between two children who score in the same range.

Another difference is that, under the old system, most children were classified as having the same degree of mental retardation all their lives, because they usually scored in the same range on IQ tests all their lives. The new system, however, is based on the assumption that "most people with mental retardation will improve their functioning with effective supports, allowing them to live more productive, independent, and integrated lives." (AAMR, 1992). Consequently, the new system allows the description of a person to change over time as that person improves his abilities to get along in the world.

The new system classifies people not by their IQs, but by the amount of support or help they need to get along in their environment. Therefore, the new classification system gives a more accurate and comprehensive picture of that individual. The four levels of support are:

1. Intermittent: does not require constant support, but may need support on a short-term basis for special occurrences, such as help finding a new job.
2. Limited: requires certain supports consistently over time, such as with handling finances or may need time-limited support for employment training.
3. Extensive: needs daily support in some aspects of living, such as long-term job support.
4. Pervasive: requires constant, high-intensity support for all aspects of life.

What to Expect from Your Child

Perhaps you are wondering what effect your child's level of mental retardation might have on his future learning and independence. Generalizations are difficult to make, because each child with mental retardation is unique. For a number of reasons, one child may learn skills better and more rapidly than would be expected just based on his level of mental retardation, whereas another may not quite live up to expectations. Yet many professionals *do* have at least general expectations for children based on their level of mental retardation. Here are some very *general* ideas of how mental retardation may affect your child.

Children whose IQs range in the high 50s and the 60s are often not diagnosed until the preschool years. These children often achieve early social skills, as well as movement skills such as sitting and walking pretty much on schedule. They may not appear to be significantly different from other children until they are expected to learn more advanced cognitive skills in school. With appropriate educational help, eventually they can often master academic skills up to about a sixth-grade level, although it takes them longer than average to learn these skills. Most people with mild mental retardation are capable of eventually developing sufficient social, vocational, and self-help skills to be able to live and work in the community, either independently or semi-independently.

Children whose IQs range from the high 30s to the low 50s are likely to be diagnosed by late infancy or preschool age. They are more likely than children with milder mental retardation to have early delays in learning movement skills, and are more likely than children with higher IQs to have cerebral palsy or other physical disabilities. In addition, they usually have delays in language and social skills. With special education and speech and language therapy, however, most children with this level of mental retardation make good progress in communication, social, and self-care skills in the preschool years. With special education, they usually can master academic subjects at about the second- to fourth-grade level, and can make excellent progress in learning social, self-help, and employment skills. As adults, they can usually perform meaningful work in the community or in a sheltered "workshop" setting, with or without support or special help. Most can live successfully in group homes or other living arrangements in the community, where they have the advantages of both independent living and supervision.

Children whose IQs range from the high 20s through the 30s are usually diagnosed at an early age, due to significant difficulty with movement and language skills. Their eventual progress depends heavily on the physical difficulties they experience. With help, especially with more recently developed technologies and techniques, they can learn some speech skills and communicate their wants and needs. While academic skills such as reading and writing are difficult, they often can learn community survival skills such as recognizing street signs. In school, instruction often focuses on self-help skills such as hygiene, as well as vocational training. As adults, they frequently can work with supervision in community jobs or in special shops. Many can also perform many necessary daily activities themselves, usually with supervision.

Children whose IQs fall below about 20–25 make up the smallest percentage of children with mental retardation. They have considerable difficulty making developmental progress in most areas. Many have physical limitations and may need complete custodial or nursing care. With intensive training, they often can learn some self-help and communication skills, depending on the hearing, vision, movement, or other problems that may accompany their mental retardation. In adulthood, many can perform some simple jobs and live in supported community settings, although they continue to require intensive supervision and help.

How Mental Retardation Affects Intelligence

As discussed earlier, intelligence includes attention, memory, abstract thinking, problem-solving, and generalizing. Mental retardation may impair all of these skills, but some of these areas are usually more impaired than others. Understanding the strengths and weaknesses your child is likely to have is crucial. With this knowledge, you will be able to have more appropriate expectations for your child's day-to-day behavior. You will know in which areas your expectations should be the same as for another child of the same mental age, and you will be able to save yourself and your child the frustration of expecting too much in other areas.

The sections below further explain some of the main areas of intelligence and discuss how mental retardation can affect them.

Attention

Attention is the ability to focus on something and keep that focus over time. In order to learn, people need to pay adequate attention to what they see, hear, and feel, and be able to shift their attention easily from one thing to another when needed. The human brain is generally set up so that, as a child becomes more familiar with the world, he learns to attend to only the important information amid the constant barrage of information from his senses.

Children with mental retardation frequently have attention problems, which can be of several different types. Often they cannot attend for long enough or to several things one right after the other. You may notice that your child with mental retardation becomes overloaded with information more quickly than his brothers or sisters. You may need to give him directions slowly, one at a time. You may find that he doesn't get as much out of an experience as other children because his capacity to take it all in is more limited.

Distractibility is another common attention problem in children with mental retardation. Distractibility occurs when a child's brain doesn't filter out enough information or discriminate between what should and shouldn't be let through for further processing. As a result, your child may have trouble settling his attention on something and keeping it there for a while. Perhaps he can't sit still long enough to finish hearing a story or doing a puzzle. He may litter your house with games that he pulls out and starts but leaves undone as his eyes and ears latch onto something else. This is not to say that he *never* stays with an activity: some things have intense enough interest to hold his attention. But particularly when learning new skills at school, where he will need to focus on something difficult, paying attention may be very hard for him. If focusing attention is a serious problem for your child, he may have attention deficit hyperactivity disorder (ADHD) in addition to mental retardation. ADHD is discussed in Chapter 9.

Some children with mental retardation over-focus their attention. They have a hard time shifting their attention from one thing to the next. If your child has this problem, it may seem as if he doesn't hear you call when he is playing, watching TV, or looking at a book. Children who are over-focused have trouble making transitions: it is hard for them to stop doing one thing and move on, even to something they like. For example, they may have difficulty tearing themselves away from a picture book to watch a favorite video. These children may also focus on small details without getting the "big picture." For instance, a child who is fascinated with insects might focus only on the picture of a bee in a farm scene, disregarding the meaning of the whole picture.

When a child repeatedly focuses his thoughts on the same thing, or repeats an activity over and over, he is said to be *perseverating*. For example, he may get "stuck" on the idea of lawn mowers or Daddy's blue Toyota, and think or talk about them endlessly. Some children who perseverate make movements that seem purposeless. For example, they may continually flap their hands or spin the wheels on a toy car. A child might make these movements to comfort himself, or he might make them to entertain himself (sometimes referred to as *self-stimulation*). Of course, all children have favorite activities, songs, stories, and so forth that they enjoy doing or hearing over and over. A child is only thought of as perseverative if he *cannot* vary the way he performs an activity, cannot move on to a new activity without a great deal of prodding, or feels as if he *must* carry out the behavior.

Perseveration poses learning problems when it prevents a child from learning something new or prevents him from behaving in a more appropriate manner. Although most children who perseverate will continue to perseverate all their lives, with guidance they can learn to work around their perseveration. For example, they can learn to shorten the amount of time they perseverate on an activity or thought before going on to something else.

Finally, children with mental retardation may be overly sensitive to information coming from their senses of touch, balance, or movement. This over-sensitivity can distract a child from attending to more important parts of the experience. For example, your child might be so bothered by the tag in his new pajamas that he can't attend to what daddy is saying, or so anxious about maintaining balance on his bike that he can't attend to what's up ahead. These types of sensory problems are covered in Chapter 2. Chapter 6 discusses teaching strategies that are useful in working around attention problems in general.

Memory

Memory is the ability to hold onto, store, and then retrieve information that has been learned. It is what enables your child to recognize macaroni and cheese as something he has seen, eaten, and liked before. Memory stores information that arrives through all of the senses. For example, visual memory helps your child recognize the macaroni, and memory for how it tastes makes him want to have some. Auditory memory is involved when your baby responds to your voice or when your child asks for a familiar song and then sings along with it.

Poorer memory is assumed to account for at least some of the difficulties that children with mental retardation have in learning something new. For example, it may take your child longer than another child his age to memorize the "Pledge of Allegiance" or the national anthem. In general, however, memory is often less affected in children with mental retardation than are other components of intelligence. That is, children with mental retardation tend to remember about as well as other children of their same *mental* age. This rule does not always hold, however. In children who have experienced some specific neurologic brain injuries, the areas of the brain in charge of memory may be damaged, causing more serious memory problems.

Abstract Thinking

Abstract thinking—or the ability to grasp concepts, principles, or processes that cannot be experienced directly through the senses—is typically among the weakest areas for children with mental retardation. Children with mental retardation typically think in very concrete terms—it is easier for them to think about something they have actually seen, felt, or touched than it is for them to think about abstractions. For example, seeing how things are related—how they are the same or different—will probably be difficult for your child. Thus, your child might readily identify a dog or a cat, but have trouble understanding that they are both animals or pets.

Abstract thinking is the cornerstone of learning. Without the ability to make mental relationships, a child cannot move on to higher levels of thinking and problem solving. For example, a child with mental retardation may have learned to read the words "Boys" and "Girls" and yet may continue to go into the wrong bathroom. A higher level of reasoning is required to understand why those words are on the door and to make the connection between their own gender and which door they should enter.

Seeing patterns among things is crucial for reading and arithmetic skills. The abstract understanding of time, space, and quantity lead children to be able to perform arithmetic operations and function more independently in the physical world. Understanding the "hows" and "whys" of rules leads to social judgment and the perspective-taking needed for more sophisticated social relating. Difficulties in abstract reasoning skills, *beyond the level predicted by a child's mental age*, are a hallmark of mental retardation. For example, if you have been told that your eight-year-old child has a mental age of five, he is likely to have more difficulty with abstract reasoning skills than a typical five-year-old. Understanding this specific weakness in your child may help you set appropriate expectations.

Problem Solving

Children problem solve when they figure out how to use a stick to reach a toy that is out of reach, open a jar, or find the face of their father when playing peek-a-boo. At more sophisticated levels, problem-solving requires abstract reasoning skills to understand and apply mathematical concepts or to solve interpersonal problems. While children with mental retardation have difficulty solving problems, this area of intelligence more closely parallels mental age. In general, you can expect your child to solve day-to-day problems at or near his mental age level. However, you should not expect him to be able to figure out more complex problems on his own without specific instruction.

Generalization

Generalization is the ability to apply what has been learned through experience to new situations. For example, if a child has learned to summon help at home by calling for mom or dad, and then figures out that he can summon help on the school playground by calling for a teacher, he is generalizing. Like abstract reasoning, generalization is a "higher-order" process and is a particular weakness in children with mental retardation. For example, your child might solve a puzzle by trial-and-error, eventually hitting on the strategy of finding all the straight-edged pieces to make the border, but when he goes on to a new puzzle (or even a new piece), he may not understand that he can re-use his successful strategy. He may instead go back to trial-and-error problem-solving. For this reason, your child may need to be taught the same skill many times in many different but similar situations. For example, even though your child may have learned how to turn the light off and on, he may not be able to generalize that knowledge to turning on and off an electronic toy. Instead, he may need to learn the skill anew each time he encounters a switch.

Generalizing abstract ideas is particularly difficult for children with mental retardation, even when their mental age is taken into account. Thus, a child with mental retardation who has a mental age of three may know the word "empty" for his cup when he's drunk his milk. But he may not generalize the use of the word "empty" for the cup before the milk is poured, his toy box when the toys are out, or the tub when the water is gone. He may need to learn the word again for each specific situation. In contrast, a three-year-old without mental retardation may figure out on his own how to use the word more generally by referring to his tummy as "empty" when he is feeling hungry.

As the preceding section discusses, children with mental retardation may share some similar patterns of intellectual strengths and weaknesses. When compared to normally developing children of the same mental age, children with mental retardation have more difficulty with more complex thinking processes such as abstract reasoning and generalization. Their attentional skills and memory, however, are more comparable to those of other children of the same mental age. There are other factors, however, that can affect the learning ability of a child with mental retardation. These factors include personality traits such as temperament and motivation, as well as physiologic factors such as medical conditions, sensory strengths and weaknesses, and motor skills. In other words, your child may learn and achieve more or less than might be predicted based on his level of mental retardation alone.

===== ✳ =====

We think he's bright, we think he's gorgeous, but we do not think that he's going to be brilliant. On the other hand, unless I see him playing alongside other kids, I have a very hard time thinking of him as mentally retarded. It just seems to me that he has problems with his speech and is very slow.

===== ✳ =====

The biggest difference we noticed in the beginning was that our baby was not really alert to what was going on.

===== ✳ =====

She was very, very rigid in the feeling that everybody had to be home when it got dark. It's just within the last year that her big sister has been able to go on overnight stays without our daughter getting very upset over the fact that we aren't all together.

For the longest time, there were certain things that had to be done in the "proper order" during the day, or had to be done in a certain place or position. For example, when our son was real small, he would take his little cars and line them up in a row. If you walked by and made one of those cars move a fraction of an inch, he went crazy. He wanted that line right there, in perfect order. Also, he would never <u>build</u> with building blocks; he lined them up. Even when the psychologist would try to get him to build stacks, he'd just line them up like a train, no building. He was like that with most of his life at that point. I mean, everything had to be done a certain way, and if you deviated from that, he couldn't handle it. He did not like change at all.

Our son can certainly understand things that can be demonstrated, but if you just explain something to him, he has difficulty grasping it. This goes for even relatively simple concepts like "under" and "over." If you were just to say to him, "It is under the table," he would get confused. He would go look on the table when the shoe was under the table. He would hear "table," and that would be the only thing out of the whole sentence he would understand.

One difference between Ricky and other kids is his inconsistency. Sometimes Ricky will not be able to do something—read or write a word, add some numbers, or type something on the computer—that I have seen him do several times before. Sometimes he can't answer a question that I know he knows (or has known) the answer to. My other kids seem to retain what they know. Maybe Ricky gets derailed by slightly different situations or contexts in which questions are asked. Maybe sometimes how he is asked trips him up. That is a very noticeable difference between Ricky and other kids.

Will My Child's Diagnosis Change?

Hearing the diagnosis of mental retardation is extremely painful for every parent. Whether accurate or not, most parents have a picture or idea in their mind of what "mental retardation" implies.

Often that picture is a bleak one, extreme or exaggerated. It is painful to put your child into the picture in your mind. However, whatever you imagine the future to hold for your child, only time and your child can show you what his potential truly is. As you adjust to the diagnosis as a family, it may help to remember that your child is exactly the same precious and special person he was before you heard the words "mental retardation."

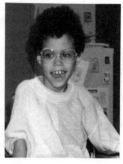

Chapter 3 discusses some of the emotional reactions parents often have to the diagnosis.

Often parents wonder whether their child will outgrow mental retardation or whether the diagnosis might change over time. Unfortunately, mental retardation is a lifelong developmental disability. Assuming that your child has been correctly diagnosed, he can be expected to keep that diagnosis all his life. More importantly, however, he can also be expected to learn and make progress throughout his life.

Before children are diagnosed as having mental retardation, they are often given other labels. For example, when infants or preschoolers show delays in development, medical, psychological, or educational professionals may tentatively diagnose them as having "developmental delays." There are several reasons that this diagnosis may be used early on and "mental retardation" diagnosed later. First, it was believed in the past that the tests used to measure intelligence did not produce accurate results when used with young children. It *is* important, however, that tests be administered only by professionals experienced in working with young children. Another reason professionals may use the diagnosis of developmental delays is that they realize that they should wait for a psychological evaluation to confirm what they suspect. Often, professionals use this label because they know that your child needs special educational and therapeutic help, but will not be eligible for this help unless he is diagnosed as having a specific disability. Most often, professionals diagnose developmental delays because they do not yet know whether your child will catch up to his age peers with special help or will continue to demonstrate delayed development. Finally, some professionals may tell you that your child has developmental delays because they don't want to be the one who breaks the news that your child does, in fact, have mental retardation.

If, in the past, your child was considered to have developmental delays, professionals were leaving open the door for the possibility that he might catch up in at least some areas of development. They were saying that the reasons for your child's delays or the permanence of those delays were not known. A diagnosis of mental retardation implies a more permanent diagnosis. Your child is not expected to catch up and may even fall further behind in comparison to other children his age. However, he can and should still make tremendous progress and learn many new skills in most areas.

Still, you may wonder whether your child actually has a learning disability rather than mental retardation. A learning disability, after all, seems more manageable, less overwhelming and incapacitating over the life span. Very rarely, however, is a learning disability mistaken for mental retardation. When a child has a learning disability, he makes less progress in one or more very specific areas of development than he would otherwise be expected to make, but overall has an average IQ. That is, he might have trouble with writing or math, but achieve at or above average in all other areas of development. Children with mental retardation, on the other hand, have lower than average skills across a broader range, with overall intelligence measured in a below-average range.

I was never exposed to adults with developmental disabilities. So I figured that you just shed them as you got older. I felt that if I could hurry our son along, that would be nice.

How Does the Brain Cause Mental Retardation?

How the brain performs its vital functions is one of science's deepest mysteries. We still do not know enough about how the brain ordinarily works to pinpoint how it works differently in children with mental retardation. Research into brain chemistry, structure, and operation continue, and eventually the brain will yield up many of its secrets to scientists. Some basic information is known, however, and is reviewed in this section. For you, understanding how your child's brain or its operation may differ is important to understanding how mental retardation will affect his life.

How the Brain Ordinarily Works

The brain is the center of the human nervous system. It is responsible for receiving all the information coming in from the world around us, as well as the information from other organs within the body. In addition to receiving this information, it also interprets the information in the following ways:

- decides what is and is not important;
- compares information coming in to information already in memory to determine whether the incoming information is new or familiar.
- sends information from the initial receiving areas to other areas of the brain, depending on what needs to happen—for example, store the information in memory, react in some way, continue to process further;
- orders other body parts such as muscles to initiate voluntary movements.

Figuring out how the brain does these things is an area of fast-growing research. This research is being furthered by new technology that allows scientists to "see" brains working while people are performing various tasks. So far, they have learned that higher-level thinking or cognitive tasks use several areas of the brain at once. Understanding how different areas of the brain interact seems to be the key to understanding how the brain governs behavior and thought.

Although we don't yet understand how the brain performs its more sophisticated functions, we do understand how it works at a basic level:

The brain is a collection of billions of nerve cells. It operates as an electrical system. One group of nerve cells generates electrical impulses. These impulses are relayed by chemical reactions to receiving ends of nearby nerve cells. The impulses keep being relayed along organized tracts or pathways. Relays coming into the central nervous system (from the eyes or ears, for example) keep going until they end up in the part of the brain that evaluates information from that source. After the information is analyzed, outgoing relays keep going until they trigger an appropriate response elsewhere within the brain or body—whether it be producing an emotion, making an arm move, or focusing attention.

The development of the brain is very complex. During the development of the nervous system, nerve cells are generated, migrate (move) to their intended locations in the brain, connect to each other, and differentiate (or become specialized for their particular function). Much of this process occurs before birth. In fact, when the fetus is four months old, all of the basic brain structures are in place. Internally, however, changes related to cell maturation continue to occur and the brain continues to mature for some years after birth. For example, a process called "myelination" or "myelinization" continues into early adulthood.

During myelination, a protective covering develops around bundles of nerve cells (fibers) which all have the same function. For example, there are bundles that process visual information and bundles that tell the muscles in the legs to walk. Nerve cells that are myelinated are more efficient transmitters of electrical impulses than bundles that are not myelinated, or not completely myelinated. So, the older a child becomes, the more efficiently his brain transmits messages from one area to another.

The fact that the brain takes so long to mature is the reason that an infant's or child's experiences can influence later development. Even in these early years, different parts of the brain have practice or experiences that lead to paths being laid down from one area of the brain to others. Scientists believe that learning depends on the ability of electrical impulses to build these paths and then make the paths more distinct by using them and re-using them. For children with mental retardation, the process of laying down the paths may take longer and be more difficult.

How Your Child's Brain Is Different

The word "mental" in the term "mental retardation" refers to the fact that the function of your child's brain has somehow been impaired. Many times this impairment may be at a very basic level. For example, there may be more or fewer nerve cells than usual in a given area of the brain, or cells that should be in one location may end up in a different location during your child's prenatal development. In other cases, there may be some damage to nerve cells. For many children, whatever has gone awry may never be known.

Some physical differences in the brains of children with mental retardation have been discovered. For example, scientists have found abnormalities in the cells of the cortex, where the centers of higher cognitive and mental processes are located. These abnormalities occur within the regions of the cells that receive or transmit the electrical impulses. The variations are in the number and size of those regions or in the spatial arrangements among cells' connections. In some cases of severe mental retardation, there has been incomplete migration of nerve cell bodies.

Another difference in the brains of many people with mental retardation appears to be in the division of work among areas of the brain. The human brain is divided into two halves, called hemispheres. As children grow and develop, each hemisphere ordinarily takes over certain functions. For example, in most right-handed people, the left hemisphere is where language is processed and where sequential reasoning goes on (for instance, the kind of logical thinking that goes into understanding such problems as if a=b and b=c, then a=c). The right hemisphere performs visual-spatial processing—for example, by allowing you to mentally picture each room of your house or to figure out where a puzzle piece goes. The functions of the hemispheres are the same in most left-handed people, although in a small percentage of left-handed people they are reversed. Each hemisphere also governs the motor control of the opposite side of the body. That is, the left hemisphere controls movements on the right side of the body, and vice versa.

Scientists have found that in children with mental retardation, differences between the functions of the two sides of the brain are not as clear-cut. Sometimes there appears to be no difference in functioning, or if there is, the difference occurs later in life and is less distinct. In other words, it seems that the brains of people with mental retardation are less well-organized in the ways they go about processing and responding to information. For example, your five-year-old with mental retardation may still not always use the same hand to pick up his spoon, use a marker, or brush his teeth.

In years to come, researchers will undoubtedly discover other differences in the brains of children with mental retardation. The problem with current data is that until the last two decades or so, research into the neurological basis of mental retardation was very general. Researchers reported what they found in the brains of adults and older children and didn't really look at the brains of younger children. Also, research often lumped all people with mental retardation together, regardless of the cause of their mental retardation or its degree. In addition, scientists generally performed their research on people who had been institutionalized and had therefore not received all the education and experiences that would have benefitted their functioning.

Our son hasn't had a dominant side that much. Over time he's become more of a right-hander, but for the longest time, if you gave him a ball to throw or whatever, he would be as likely to try it with his left hand as with his right.

Some Known Causes of Mental Retardation

By now you have probably been cautioned not to blame yourself for somehow having caused your child's mental retardation. That is easy enough for professionals to say to parents. Most parents, however, do go through a period of feeling somehow at fault for their child's mental retardation. Remember, though, unless you drank alcohol heavily or used drugs during pregnancy, it is highly unlikely that you did anything to cause your child's mental retardation.

What, then, causes the differences in the brain that result in mental retardation? Researchers have identified hundreds of causes, ranging from genetic and prenatal factors, to complications during birth and infancy. Many more causes will likely be discovered in the future. At present, researchers are unable to identify the cause of mental retardation in up to 75 percent of children. In other words, more than three-quarters of all parents never learn the reason for their child's mental retardation.

Scientists categorize the known causes (*etiologies*) of mental retardation according to when they occur during development—from preconception (before the egg is fertilized) through the early childhood years. Below are the broad categories they use to categorize the origins of mental retardation:

PRENATAL (occurring before birth)

   A. Genetic
      1. Inherited Genetic Causes
      2. Noninherited Genetic Causes
   B. Early alterations of embryonic development
      1. Specific syndromes (e.g., Williams syndrome)
      2. Multiple congenital anomalies/mental retardation (multiple birth defects)
   C. Other Prenatal (Acquired) Causes
      1. Alcohol/illicit substances/other drugs (prescribed medications)
      2. Maternal infections
      3. Other maternal health conditions
   D. Pregnancy problems

PERINATAL (occurring around the time of birth)

   A. Fetal oxygen deprivation (difficulties getting oxygen to the brain)
   B. Prematurity

POSTNATAL (occurring after birth)

   A. Infections
   B. Head Injuries
   C. Tumors
   D. Lead Poisoning
   E. Unknown factors

The sections below explore these types of causes in more detail.

═══ ❋ ═══

They did a complete work-up on our daughter at the pediatric endocrinology center. They did genetics and some x-rays. They did everything they could at that point in time. They found nothing that explained why our daughter is retarded. They just found all the physical anomalies we already knew about.

Prenatal Causes

GENETIC CAUSES

In this category, the cause of a child's mental retardation can be traced to a genetic problem. A genetic problem means that sometime during the prenatal period, something went wrong with the child's genes or with the chromosomes. Genes, or the DNA materials the genes contain, are the blueprint that determine or

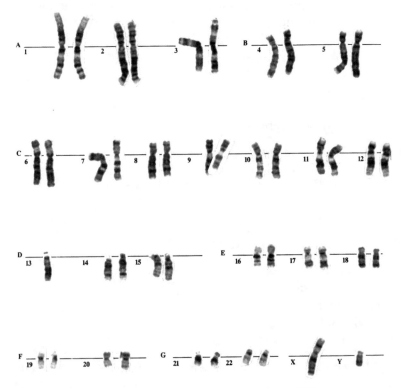

The karyotype or chromosome complement of a normal male (46, XY).
Courtesy of Dr. Jeanne Meck.

influence physical and personal characteristics such as eye and hair color, height, and intelligence. The chromosomes are microscopic, rod-shaped bodies that are present inside every cell of the body and contain the genes or the hereditary materials. Each human cell contains forty-six chromosomes, or twenty-three complementary pairs. Twenty-two pairs are called autosomes and one pair is called the sex chromosomes. Females have two X sex chromosomes and males have an X and a Y chromosome (see figure 2). Germ cells (the mother's egg and the father's sperm) contain twenty-three chromosomes only—one half of the required set of forty-six. At fertilization, the embryo receives forty-six chromosomes, half contributed by the mother's egg and half by the father's sperm.

Inherited Genetic Causes

Some genetic problems that cause mental retardation are inherited. That is, the background for these conditions is present in one of the parent's genetic make-up, and can therefore be said to exist prior to conception. For example, a parent may pass on a chromosome with an abnormal gene, or pass on too many or too few chromosomes. Some inherited causes of mental retardation include tuberous sclerosis, fragile X syndrome, Hurler syndrome, Tay-Sachs disease, and phenylketonuria (PKU).

Fragile X Syndrome. Fragile X syndrome is one of the leading inherited cause of mental retardation, affecting approximately 1 in 750 males and 1 in 1,250 females. The condition results from the presence of an abnormal or defective gene (the fMR-1 gene) on the child's X chromosomes. This abnormal gene leads to weakness of the structures of the X chromosome, which can be seen as a "break" or fragile site under the microscope. Because the defective gene is on the X chromosome, the condition predominately affects males. Since females are born with two X chromosomes, one from each parent, their normal chromosome can mask the effects of the abnormal one. Girls are therefore usually unaffected or mildly affected by the fragile X gene. In contrast, males, who have one X and one Y chromosome, have no back-up for the affected X chromosome, and are therefore more susceptible to the effects of the abnormal gene.

The majority of affected males have some degree of mental impairment, ranging from learning disabilities to severe mental retardation. Most tend to cluster in the mild to moderate range of mental retardation. About one-third of females affected by the abnormal gene have learning disabilities or mild mental retardation. Problems which are also commonly seen include sensory impairments, hyperactivity, attention problems, and self-stimulating behaviors and difficulties with social interaction. Delayed speech and language development also occur frequently and are often the first indication of a problem that leads to a diagnosis.

Children with fragile X can have a number of distinctive physical characteristics. These include large head (*macrocephaly*), prominent forehead, large testicles (*macroorchidism*), tall face, large ears, and prominent chin. Physical problems may include double-jointedness, low muscle tone, flat feet, and occasionally heart murmur. Ear infections (*otitis media*) are also common.

Other Inherited Causes. Other examples in the inherited category of causes of mental retardation include hereditary chromosomal abnormalities in which the child is missing or has an extra chromosome. In these cases, one of the parents, who shows no signs of having a disability, has what is called a "balanced rearrangement of chromosomes." This term means that a fragment of one chromosome has been transferred to another chromosome. This parent has a risk of having a child with an *un*balanced chromosome abnormality. That is, the child could inherit the chromosome that is missing a fragment *or* the chromosome that has extra genetic material, and end up with a pattern of chromosomes that upsets development and leads to mental retardation and physical anomalies.

Although only a small portion of children with mental retardation have this type of problem, it is very important to identify those that do. The reason it is important to identify these children is that parents who have one child with this type of inherited condition are at risk of having other affected children. A genetic counselor can discuss with parents the chances of recurrence and the availability of prenatal diagnostic tests.

Noninherited Genetic Causes

A frequent and important cause of mental retardation is the *sporadic* occurrence of major changes in the *germ cells* (egg and sperm that go on to develop into an embryo). *These are the genetic causes of mental retardation that are not inherited.* The genetic material originally supplied by each parent is normal, but then—during the early stages of cell division of the germ cells or of the fertilized egg—an error in separation, recombination, or distribution of chromosomes occurs. Chromosomal problems during early cell divisions are very common. The majority of these chromosomal problems, however, are not compatible with life. That is, most of the time that this type of chromosome abnormality happens, the fetus does not live long enough to be born. Types of chromosomal abnormalities that *are* compatible with life and that result in mental retardation include Down syndrome, Trisomy 13, Trisomy 18, and cri du chat syndrome.

Down Syndrome. Down syndrome (Trisomy 21) is the most common noninherited genetic cause of mental retardation, occurring in about 1 in 700 live births. Down syndrome is caused by an extra copy of chromosome number 21 in the cells of the body. In the majority of cases of Down syndrome, the extra chromosome results from "nondisjunction"—a faulty distribution of chromosomes in the mother's or father's germ cells, leading to the presence of forty-seven, rather than the normal forty-six, chromosomes in the fertilized egg. Nobody knows for sure what causes the nondisjunction that leads to Down syndrome, but advanced maternal age frequently appears to play a role. Although many younger woman have babies with Down syndrome, the risk of having one goes up sharply among mothers in their later thirties and forties. Some scientists believe that hereditary factors, excess radiation, and thyroid problems may also be possible causes of Down syndrome.

Down syndrome most often results in mild to moderate mental retardation, although some children with Down syndrome have more severe mental retardation and a few have normal or near-normal intelligence.

Besides affecting intelligence, Down syndrome may also cause one or more of the following physical characteristics: eyes that appear to slant upward, a small nose with a flat bridge, a small mouth with a shallow roof, small ears that may be set lower than usual on the head, smaller than average hands and feet, and low (floppy) muscle tone. Other conditions often associated with Down syndrome include: heart defects, intestinal malformations, hearing and vision impairments, underactive thyroid (hypothyroidism), and

instability of the upper two vertebrae. These medical complications can usually be cured or improved if diagnosed and treated promptly.

Conditions such as fragile X syndrome and Down syndrome that are characterized by a specific combination of signs and symptoms are classified as "syndromes." The Resource Guide at the back of the book lists organizations that can provide additional information on the causes, incidence, symptoms, and diagnosis of many mental retardation syndromes.

The doctor put it into layman's terms. He said that a pregnancy is like a very intricate blueprint of a building, and the fetus goes on its nice little path to build this house just right. He said that somewhere around the third week, our daughter went off the track and there was no turning back. It was nothing we did; it just happened and we've got to live with it. That was one of the best visits I ever had, because I needed somebody to tell me that I didn't screw things up during labor or something.

=== ※ ===

Our pediatrician suggested that I go see a geneticist, all the way back then. I said, "Why, why do you want me to see him? What is 'genetic'?" He said that was where they took a history of your family. He was very apologetic. He didn't want to come right out and tell me that maybe there was a real problem or syndrome.

Early Alterations of Embryonic Development

A congenital malformation (birth defect) is an abnormality in function or structure of any organ that appears during fetal development. Doctors have long known of the link between such malformations and mental retardation. Children with birth defects, or congenital anomalies (differences), commonly have physical symptoms or characteristics that indicate that there may be an underlying problem with brain development. These physical traits include abnormal hair pattern, small or large head, abnormal eye or ear shape, and abnormal creases of the hands. In the majority of children, diagnostic tests of the brain reveal normal structure. The differences in the brain are most likely more subtle than current tests can detect, but may include differences in the layering of the cortex or in the migration of brain cells. When similar physical and mental differences occur in a recognizable pattern that has occurred time and again with other children, a child with these traits may be diagnosed with a particular syndrome, or be assigned to a specific diagnostic category (for example, Williams syndrome, Cornelia de Lange syndrome, Sturge-Weber syndrome). More commonly, however, children with multiple anomalies and mental retardation do not fit recognizable patterns and are frequently referred to as having "Multiple Congenital Anomalies/Mental Retardation" (MCA/MR).

Other Prenatal (Acquired) Causes

There are a number of environmental influences, or *teratogens*, that can cause mental retardation and other abnormalities in a developing fetus. A teratogen is any chemical or physical substance that may cause physical or functional problems in the developing fetus. Examples of teratogens include alcohol; illicit drugs; prescribed medications; toxins (poisons) such as lead and mercury; maternal infections; and maternal metabolic conditions such as diabetes.

Exposure to teratogens does not always cause fetal defects, nor does it always cause the same type of defects. How teratogenic exposure affects the developing embryo depends on factors such as the stage of pregnancy when exposure occurred, the genetic make-up of the fertilized egg, genetic and environmental factors in the mother, and the type and dosage of the teratogen itself. Exposure during the first two weeks of pregnancy either results in spontaneous abortion or has no effect at all. Exposure during weeks three through twelve is likely to result in the abnormal growth and development of body organs or parts. Later exposure may cause abnormal functioning of organs, although they may appear outwardly normal. Little is known about how teratogens affect the fetus, but they usually cause cell death, alter tissue growth, and interfere with the development of the form and structure of various organs and body parts.

Fetal Alcohol Syndrome. Fetal Alcohol Syndrome (FAS), which can affect children whose mothers drank alcohol during pregnancy, is one of the most common conditions caused by teratogenic exposure. In fact, FAS is presently the leading cause of mental retardation in the western world, occurring in an estimated 1 in 500 to 700 births.

The amount of alcohol needed to cause FAS varies from person to person. Full blown or classic FAS is most likely to occur when mothers drink moderate to high amounts during pregnancy. Doctors have not found a safe drinking level for pregnant women. In addition, studies have shown that excessive drinking is dangerous at every stage of pregnancy. Whenever drinking stops, chances for having a healthier baby improve.

Children with FAS have a combination of physical, behavioral, and mental birth defects, including:

1. Below average growth rate before and after birth. Babies born with FAS are usually small at birth and usually do not catch up as they get older. Studies have shown that babies born to women who stopped drinking during pregnancy tend to be larger and have better growth rates than babies born to women who drank throughout pregnancy.
2. A characteristic facial appearance. Usually children with FAS have widely spaced eyes, a short upturned nose, flat philtrum (the ridge that runs between the nose and upper lip), and a thin upper lip. Occasionally, they also have cleft lip and palate, hemangiomas (birthmarks made up of clusters of blood vessels), and differently shaped ears.
3. Central nervous system or brain impairment. Mental retardation is the most common and serious disability associated

with fetal exposure to alcohol. Children with FAS usually have a mild degree of mental retardation, although some have normal intelligence and some have more severe mental retardation. Hyperactivity, attention problems, speech and language difficulties, and behavioral problems are also common.

Children with FAS may also have many other abnormalities, ranging from heart defects and eye problems to muscle tone and joint problems. Children who have one or two, but not all of the signs above are said to have Fetal Alcohol Effects (FAE).

Maternal Infections. Some children develop mental retardation as the result of exposure to their mother's infections, either before or during birth. Ironically, pregnant women who have these infections may show no symptoms at all, or only mild symptoms. Depending on the stage of development of the fetus, however, the infection can be disruptive enough to cause mental retardation, as well as other problems such as vision and hearing disorders. On the other hand, the infection may cause no harm at all, or may cause problems that are less severe than mental retardation. In other words, one type of infection may produce a wide spectrum of problems, ranging from mild to severe.

At present, nobody knows exactly how prenatal infections disrupt the development of the fetal nervous system. Researchers have, however, identified a number of infections that can lead to mental retardation, including cytomegalovirus (CMV), rubella, measles, chicken pox, syphilis, toxoplasmosis, hepatitis B, coxsackie virus group, and acquired immune deficiency syndrome (AIDS).

Cytomegalovirus (CMV) is the most common congenital infection. The virus is widespread and most women develop immunity to the virus by age thirty. Fortunately, while many fetuses are exposed to CMV, few have obvious damage from the infection. A fetus is most at risk if it is the first time the mother has been infected with CMV. While pregnant mothers with CMV infection show no symptoms, the disease can result in widespread damage to the fetus. Affected infants can be born prematurely with low birth weight. Neonatal signs of infection include skin rash, jaundice (yellowish discoloration of the skin), and large liver and spleen. The CMV can damage the brain tissue, causing small head size (microcephaly), small eyes, hearing impairment, and cerebral calcifications. Ninety percent of newborns with CMV have no symptoms at birth. Of these children who have no symptoms at birth, a very few will later show signs of congenital infection, most commonly hearing impairment, but also sometimes mental retardation.

Rubella, commonly known as German measles, is another infection that has mild effects in children and adults, but can cause severe damage to a developing fetus. The most severe disabilities occur if the mother is infected during the first few weeks of pregnancy. Effects on the brain of the fetus can be devastating, resulting in mental retardation, cerebral palsy, microcephaly, seizures, and other problems. Affected infants are also small at birth, and tend to have congenital heart defects, small eyes, and difficulties with other body organs. Fortunately, mass immunizations of children and susceptible women have almost eradicated birth defects resulting from Rubella.

Another virus that often produces devastating disease in the newborn is Herpes Simplex. It is a common venereal disease, and after CMV, it is the most common viral infection in pregnant women. Newborns contract the disease from their mothers during birth, rather than before birth. It is most often acquired when the mother has active herpes in the genital region. Babies who are severely infected with the herpes can sustain damage to all organs of the body, including the brain. They may develop mental retardation, microcephaly, seizures, and sensory impairments. About .03 to 0.3 babies per thousand are infected with herpes at birth.

Toxoplasmosis is another infection that may cause mental retardation. Toxoplasmosis is caused by a parasite that is common in warm-blooded animals, especially cats. Humans only get the disease by coming in contact with the feces of infected animals or by eating undercooked meat. Adults often show no symptoms at all. The danger that a pregnant woman will pass the infection on to a fetus is greatest during the first trimester. Infected infants may be born with low birth weight, anemia, jaundice, and a large liver and spleen, as well as hydrocephalus (an excess of cerebrospinal fluid in the brain), microcephaly, and calcifications in the brain. Later signs of congenital toxoplasmosis include mental retardation, seizures, cerebral palsy, and a disease of the retina that can result in blindness.

Other Maternal Health Conditions. Many other maternal factors besides infections are potentially harmful to a developing fetus. Some of these may increase the risk of mental retardation. For example, maternal conditions such as diabetes, high blood pressure, and heart and thyroid diseases can increase the likelihood of premature birth, intrauterine growth retardation, and developmental problems. Also, obstetrical complications such as incompetent cervix and uterine fibroids carry the risk of prematurity, which can result in mental retardation and other disabilities, as discussed later in the chapter.

Toxemia, a complication of pregnancy most common among teenage mothers and mothers over thirty-five, can lead to several problems that may result in mental retardation. This condition appears to affect the kidneys, causing varying degrees of water retention, protein in the urine, and high blood pressure. Toxemia carries a significant risk of prematurity, intrauterine growth retardation, and abruptio placenta (see next section). All of these conditions increase the risk that the baby will be born with mental retardation or other developmental disabilities.

RH incompatibility is a maternal-related condition that was once a significant cause of mental retardation. Today, medical treatment has to a certain degree eradicated it as a cause. Because the potential for problems must be promptly recognized in order to prevent them, however, it is worth discussing.

The RH factor is a minor blood group (the "positive" or "negative") attached to the four major blood types (A, B, O, AB). A woman with RH negative blood may have an infant with RH positive blood if the father has the RH positive factor. If minute amounts of blood from the infant enter the mother's circulation, which usually occurs at the time of delivery, they are recognized as foreign by the mother's system, and her body reacts by developing antibodies to the RH positive factor. During any subsequent pregnancy with a fetus with the RH positive factor, maternal antibodies pass to the fetal circulation. The antibodies then destroy the red blood cells of the fetus, cause severe anemia, hypoxia (oxygen deprivation), and neonatal complications. As discussed below, hypoxia can lead to brain damage and mental retardation. RH Incompatibility can be treated today by use of the medication RhoGAM, an antibody injection, immediately after the first and all subsequent deliveries.

Perinatal Causes

Sometimes a fetus's brain develops normally, but is injured or impaired when the baby is delivered. Most often, this kind of brain damage occurs when the flow of oxygen to the baby's brain is interrupted or impeded. A loss or decrease of oxygen can damage brain cells by causing a build-up of carbon dioxide in the blood and tissues, low blood sugar (hypoglycemia), and other disturbances in the body's metabolism.

Placenta Previa and Abruptio Placenta

Mental retardation can sometimes result from problems with the placenta, the organ that supplies the fetus with nourishment. The two major problems that can develop are placenta previa and abruptio placenta.

In placenta previa, the placenta extends over the cervical opening of the uterus, rather than being attached in the usual location about two-thirds of the way to the top of the uterus. If the condition is not diagnosed before the woman goes into labor, the placenta tears as the cervix opens and bleeding occurs. Mental retardation may then result from poor oxygen supply to the fetus's brain.

Abruptio placenta involves the early detachment of the placenta from the wall of the uterus before the baby is born, resulting in a decrease in the oxygen supply to the brain. The detachment may be caused by high blood pressure, a short umbilical cord, or physical injury, and can also be induced by smoking or snorting crack or cocaine. The next section explains how insufficient oxygen can result in mental retardation.

Lack of Oxygen

When the blood stream is carrying insufficient oxygen to an area of the body, it is known as hypoxia. When the oxygen supply to an area of the body is completely cut off, the condition is known as anoxia. When either condition occurs in a child's brain, it can lead to mental retardation. Whether mental retardation results depends on the location and size of the area deprived of oxygen, the length of time it is affected, the resulting cell death due to hypoxia or anoxia, the unavailability of glucose, the build-up of toxins, and the infant's age, weight, and health. Less serious episodes of anoxia or hypoxia might result in learning disabilities, or no noticeable developmental problems at all.

During labor, a number of problems can cause hypoxia or anoxia. If the mother's pelvis is too small to allow passage of the baby's head, she may have a long and difficult labor and the baby may have an intracranial hemorrhage (bleeding in the brain) or sepsis (blood infection). If the mother's uterus contracts too forcefully or too weakly or slowly, it can interfere with fetal blood circulation, leading to hypoxic brain damage or abruptio placenta. Brain damage can also result if the fetus's umbilical cord prolapses (precedes the fetus down the birth canal), blocking the flow of blood through the cord to the child and causing hypoxia or anoxia. Breech birth (birth of a baby with its legs or buttocks first) can also lead to oxygen deprivation, brain trauma, and other problems that can lead to mental retardation because a fetus is more likely to have its head become entrapped in the pelvic opening when it is born in a breech presentation. Babies who did not develop normally in utero are more likely to be born in the breech position.

In addition to causing mental retardation, hypoxic or anoxic episodes occurring around birth can result in *cerebral palsy*. This is a condition that interferes with control of movement, balance, and posture. Chapter 9 discusses cerebral palsy in detail.

Prematurity

A premature infant is defined as a child born at or before the 36th week of gestation, one month before the expected date of birth. There are a number of maternal and fetal factors that contribute to prematurity, including adolescent pregnancy, poor nutrition, inadequate prenatal care, toxemia, twinning or multiple births, multiple previous pregnancies, weak cervix of the uterus, and congenital malformations of the fetus. Compared to full term infants, premature babies have a greater risk of developing significant complications. Among these problems are *respiratory distress syndrome* (a lung disorder with symptoms including labored, grunting respiration and poor oxygenation of body tissues and room air), *apnea* (a condition in which breathing periodically stops), chemical or metabolic imbalances (such as low blood sugar, low blood calcium and magnesium), and jaundice. Premature babies have a fragile network of blood vessels that supply the brain. These vessels are sensitive to changes in oxygen and pressure, such as those that occur with respiratory distress syndrome, metabolic complications, and their treatment. Premature babies typically develop bleeding in parts of the brain. Severe hemorrhages into the brain tissue can lead to cerebral palsy and mental retardation. Hydrocephalus is another complication that occurs in higher frequency among premature babies who suffer from brain hemorrhages. In hydrocephalus, there is an excess of cerebrospinal fluid, the liquid that fills the brain cavities. Treatment for this condition includes using drugs to decrease the production of cerebrospinal fluid. If this is not effective, a shunt will be placed surgically to drain excess fluid from the brain. With proper treatment, the majority of children do well, although a significant percentage will develop intellectual and motor disabilities. If untreated, hydrocephalus can produce progressive brain damage and lead to serious medical complications.

Postnatal Causes

As explained earlier in this chapter, mental retardation may begin anytime before a child is eighteen. A child can be born with average or above intelligence, but then suffer damage to the brain that results in mental retardation. It is important to realize that not *all* brain damage causes mental retardation. Some children who receive brain injuries recover completely. Others sustain more lasting effects, but do not have the pervasive effects that would be diagnosed as mental retardation. For example, a child's speech and language skills might be permanently impaired as the result of a brain injury, but he might eventually regain his skills in other areas. A child is considered to have mental retardation rather than a brain injury *only* when he has lower-than-average skills in all areas of development as a result of the injury.

Infections

A variety of infections can affect young infants after birth and can cause brain damage and mental retardation as a result. One such disease is viral meningitis. This is an infection that attacks the covering of the brain and spinal cord (the *meninges*), causing inflammation. Several different viruses can cause meningitis, or it can be a complication of viral diseases such as mumps, measles, chicken pox, and sepsis—a bacterial infection spread by the bloodstream throughout the body. Meningitis is a serious disease for people of any age, but in infants it can result in permanent brain damage. This brain damage, depending on its severity, can cause mental retardation.

Some infections can enter the nervous system and cause encephalitis. Encephalitis is an inflammation of the brain tissue itself, and can be as devastating to infants as meningitis. Encephalitis can be contracted directly, or can be a complication of mumps, measles, chicken pox, herpes viruses, and other rare viruses.

Head Injuries

Mental retardation can result if an infant or child is in an accident in which he suffers a serious head injury or great enough loss of blood to reduce oxygen in the brain. Automobile accidents are the most common cause of severe head injuries, but head injuries may also be caused by falling downstairs and fracturing the skull, falling out of a crib or window, and the like. Physical abuse, including shaking children, can also cause enough brain damage to lead to mental retardation.

Tumors

Tumors are relatively rare in children. However, brain tumors that put enough pressure on surrounding tissues to damage the cells could lead to permanent brain damage. If the brain damage affects a large enough area, mental retardation can result.

Lead Poisoning

Lead poisoning in children is a serious public health problem. Lead poisoning develops most often when a child repeatedly licks, eats, or inhales chips of lead-based paint. Other unusual sources of lead poisoning include juice stored in improperly lead-glazed earthwares, drinking water stored in lead-lined cisterns, and food cooked in lead-soldered vessels. When the level of lead in the body builds up over the course of many months, it can cause lethargy, anemia, seizures, brain damage, and even death. Once lead poisoning is diagnosed, medications can help the body eliminate the excess lead. Treated children, however, may still have developmental delays or mental retardation.

Why Does My Child Have Mental Retardation?

As mentioned above, it is often impossible to determine the cause of a child's mental retardation. But most professionals believe it is important to at least *try* to determine why a child has mental retardation. Here are some reasons:

If it is found that your child's mental retardation is due to a particular syndrome or condition, there will be information available on the typical development and medical problems of children with that condition. This means that teachers, therapists, doctors, and parents will be able to anticipate difficulties and treat them accordingly. For example, if your child is determined to have fragile X syndrome, you would know that the doctor should check for possible seizures and hearing and vision problems. If the doctor discovered any of these problems, he or she could plan a treatment program that would prevent any of the problems from further impeding your child's development. Likewise, if your child has Williams syndrome, you would know that your child may have attention deficit disorder and may therefore behave impulsively. If school personnel are aware that your child is not intentionally misbehaving, but, rather, that it is very difficult for him to focus his attention, sit still, and think before acting, they are more likely to react with understanding instead of annoyance.

If you are planning to have other children, you will probably also want to know what your chances are of having another child with mental retardation. If the cause of your child's mental retardation is known, a physician or geneticist can counsel you about the risk of recurrence. He or she can also tell you whether brothers and sisters and others in your extended families are at increased risk. For some genetic causes of mental retardation, scientists know exactly what percentage chance there is that future children will also be affected. If your child was premature, doctors may also be able to predict the chances of having another premature baby, depending on the cause. If you are one of the many parents who have a child with mental retardation due to an unknown cause, it certainly leads to tough decisions about having additional children.

Determining the Cause

Several professionals play major roles in diagnosing mental retardation and in determining the cause of a child's mental retardation. The first two professionals parents are likely to encounter specialize in diagnosing mental retardation. They are the clinical psychologist and developmental pediatrician. The developmental pediatrician is a medical doctor who specializes in diagnosing and working with children with developmental disabilities. A psychologist is a professional trained to understand how the human mind works and to evaluate human behavior. Depending on where you live, you may see one of these professionals or both. They will carefully evaluate your child through tests, interviews with parents, observation, and examinations. They will then explain their diagnosis or recommend further testing to pinpoint the cause.

If further testing is needed to determine the exact cause of your child's mental retardation, you might be referred to a clinical geneticist or a neurologist. A clinical geneticist is a medical professional with special knowledge about heredity and genetic conditions. The geneticist will examine your child carefully for any signs and symptoms of genetic conditions, and obtain a detailed family pedigree to look for evidence of hereditary disorders. He or she will then order diagnostic tests that are tailored to your child's history and physical characteristics.

Genetic testing is a relatively new area of science, and has proven extremely useful in pinpointing the causes of many conditions. The most common genetic testing technique is *karyotyping* or chromosome analysis. In karyotyping, a geneticist takes a blood sample (usually) or skin sample (rarely) and then cultures—or grows—the sample in a petri dish. Once it has grown, the geneticist is able to isolate the individual chromosomes and arrange them according to their size. The geneticist then examines the chromosomes under a microscope for any abnormalities. This examination can reveal many genetic conditions, such as Down syndrome.

For some genetic conditions, karyotyping fails to accurately reveal the cause. For these conditions, an even newer technique, called *molecular testing*, is used. Molecular testing can probe deeper than karyotyping and reveal conditions that karyotyping cannot reveal. Conditions that molecular testing is used to diagnose include Prader-Willi syndrome and fragile X syndrome. Molecular testing allows for prenatal diagnosis and accurate genetic counseling.

If your child has already been diagnosed with a known syndrome, a geneticist or genetics counselor can give you information about your child's genetic condition and the ways it might affect his health and development. Genetics professionals may be able to add to what you already know about any developmental problems your child may be encountering. They may also be able to tell you of any physical or behavioral problems that may arise as your child gets older. Finally, if you are planning to have another child, they can help you determine the risk of the genetic abnormality occurring again in your family. They can also advise you about any prenatal tests that may be available.

Depending on your child's condition, neurological testing may be necessary to determine the cause of his mental retardation. The neurologist is a medical doctor who specializes in diagnosing and treating disorders of the central nervous system—the body system that includes the brain and the nerves traveling up and down the spinal cord to and from the brain.

The neurologist will evaluate your child's nervous system through an examination performed in his office, a developmental clinic, or a school. The neurologist will check your child's reflexes, muscle tone, motor skills, and coordination. He or she will also briefly examine your child's vision and hearing, and often observe whether your child's speech, social behavior, and behavior control are appropriate for his age.

The neurologist may prescribe a number of tests. The one most frequently performed is the EEG (electroencephalogram). This test graphs the electrochemical energy patterns of the nerve cells in the brain to look for seizure activity. Electrodes are placed at various points on your child's scalp to detect this energy. The test isn't painful, but your child must be very quiet and still for an extended time. Consequently, the test is usually done on children when they are sleeping. Your child may be given some medication to help him sleep through the procedure. Two other tests that may be used are the CT Scan and the MRI (Magnetic Resonance Imaging). Both of these techniques provide pictures of the brain—the CT Scan through x-rays, and the MRI by making use of the brain's magnetic energy. CT Scans are commonly used, but the newer MRI technique is not as widely available.

Neurologists use these tests to look for evidence of abnormal structures or functions in the brain which might contribute to delayed development. For example, they look for malformations or missing parts in the brain and evidence of trauma, such as scars or areas of dead tissue. Sometimes these diagnostic tests don't yield any information that explains your child's mental retardation. Nevertheless, they are important because they rule out any disease or condition requiring medical attention.

Before our second kid was even born, I made an appointment to take him to one of the neurologists that a lot of the kids were going to. I just wanted to make sure he was OK.

━━━ ✳ ━━━

Our son's CAT scan came out within normal limits. The MRI was within the normal range, too. But the EEG showed that he had a lesion on the left-hand side of his brain, and they figured that that was probably from birth.

━━━ ✳ ━━━

When I was seven months pregnant with our next child, my obstetrician said that he thought the baby was going to be too small. I was really neurotic. He said, "Well, why don't you go and maybe get a sonogram next week?" I said, "I'm not waiting twenty-four hours." We called right

away to schedule the appointment. I remember running for that sonogram. The obstetrician was wrong; Kim was fine.

I finally had to go to the geneticist because I wanted to know if this was something genetic. Is this something my other daughter has to worry about? Is this something my sister should worry about? I just wanted to get to the bottom of the story. The geneticist said that something probably went wrong around the third week of conception. So it wasn't something that happened at delivery, but it probably wasn't inherited, either.

The History of Mental Retardation

Parents of children with mental retardation are often subjected to other people's reactions to their child's condition. There are as many attitudes toward mental retardation as there are people who react to your child. Perhaps by examining a little of the history of mental retardation, you might better understand some of these different attitudes and how they evolved. Society's attitude continues to change. Therefore, with a glance toward the past and a little education, it may be possible to improve attitudes in the future.

Undoubtedly, there have been people with mental retardation since the beginning of the human race. Until fairly recently, however, little was understood about the nature and causes of mental retardation. Because so little was known about the condition, society often reacted to mental retardation as it did to any other unknown—with fear and prejudice. In ancient Greece and Rome, for example, infants with obvious disabilities, including mental retardation, were often killed at birth. By the Middle Ages, however, churches in Europe were beginning to set up places for the care and protection of children with disabilities. However, many children with disabilities were still put to death or used for others' entertainment.

In the Renaissance, greater value was placed on human life, so using death as a "treatment" for mental retardation and other disabilities began to fall out of favor. Yet even as scientific knowledge grew, society as a whole continued to consider children with mental retardation as less than human. In fact, in the last half of the nineteenth century, Charles Darwin's ideas about evolution and natural selection were used to justify the continued mistreatment of people with disabilities. People with mental and physical disabilities came to be viewed as "throwbacks" who were not as highly evolved as other people. According to some people's views, allowing individuals with mental retardation to mix freely with other members of society interfered with the process of natural selection. Consequently, institutionalizing people with mental retardation became a popular method of keeping them away from the rest of society. Also in the name of "natural selection," about half the states in the United States eventually passed laws condoning the practice of sterilization. (Many states still have sterilization laws on the books, but these laws are rarely invoked.)

Although misunderstanding about mental retardation was usually the rule, a few enlightened thinkers in every age recognized the potential of people with mental retardation. In the early nineteenth century, for example, Jean Marc Gaspard Itard became one of the first to concentrate on the education of children with mental retardation. Itard was influenced by the philosophy of John Locke, who believed that the environment is the sole determinant of a person's development and knowledge. In turn, Itard influenced the work of two other nineteenth-century pioneers in special education: Maria Montessori in Italy, and Edouard Seguin in France and the United States. Many of Seguin's ideas sound strikingly modern even today. For instance, he believed in individualizing instruction and in beginning instruction at the child's present level of development. So, although institutionalization *was* widespread in the U.S. by the late nineteenth century, there were both good and bad institutions. There were institutions designed only to segregate people with disabilities for the good of society, and there were institutions that aimed to benefit their residents through appropriate training and activities.

At the beginning of the twentieth century, Alfred Binet in France developed the first intelligence tests. He intended the tests to be used in determining which children in the public school system would need specialized instruction. At about the same time, public school classes for children with mental retardation also were opened in the U.S. Here, too, intelligence tests were used to diagnose mental retardation in a standard way. Henry Herbert

Goddard devised a system for classifying mental retardation based on mental age. Under Goddard's system, those with mental ages (MA) of less than two years were classified as "idiots"; with mental ages of three to seven, as "imbeciles"; and with mental ages of seven to twelve, as "morons." Although Goddard didn't intend these terms to be hurtful, they were later used to perpetuate negative stereotypes about people with mental retardation.

In the 1930s and early 1940s, researchers began to demonstrate the effects of environment on intelligence. They found that some environments were more conducive to learning, and that the right kinds of stimulation could increase scores on intelligence tests. Eventually, their research led to the finding that removing a child from his home, particularly during the early years, could prevent the child from developing to his full potential. Still, until the 1970s, institutionalization was quite common. Doctors routinely recommended immediate institutionalization of newborns born with conditions associated with mental retardation. Many children with mental retardation languished in facilities where the lack of loving attention and appropriate instruction guaranteed them bleak, unfulfilling lives. And until the 1950s, many school systems in the U.S. provided little special education for students with mental retardation. Children who lived with their families either didn't attend school at all, or were placed in regular education classrooms, whether or not they could benefit from them.

At last, school systems began to bow to the pressure put on them by parents of children with special needs. Beginning in the 1940s and 1950s, these parents had been organizing themselves and working for improved educational opportunities for their children. In 1950, the Association for Retarded Children (later called the Association for Retarded Citizens and now simply the ARC) was formed, giving parents added clout in advocating for their children's rights. Gradually, states began passing laws requiring local school districts to provide special education for all children who could benefit, including children with the most profound mental retardation.

The outlook for children with mental retardation brightened even more during the presidency of John F. Kennedy. When JFK took office in 1961, he established the "President's Panel of Mental Retardation." This board persuaded the federal government to provide money, mandates, and models for obtaining and expanding services for people with mental retardation.

Finally, in 1975, the federal government passed a landmark special education law: Public Law 94–142 (since renamed the Individuals with Disabilities Education Act, IDEA). This legislation required that all children with disabilities receive an education tailored to their unique learning needs and that schools no longer segregate them from other children unless absolutely necessary. Thus, the law gave children with disabilities unprecedented opportunities to learn and to become contributing members of society. Since then, additional laws have given children with disabilities an even better chance to participate in mainstream society. IDEA, Part B and Part H, require that special educational and therapeutic help be provided for infants and preschoolers with disabilities, and the Americans with Disabilities Act of 1990 prohibits discrimination on the basis of disabilities in just about every public arena. Chapter 8 discusses all these important disability laws in detail.

Over time, society is going to have to learn better ways of dealing with children with mental retardation—of helping them function in a normal environment. Eventually, systems everywhere are going to have to adjust their programs to benefit children who once were just institutionalized.

Growing up, I was not exposed very much to people with mental retardation. I remember when I was in junior high, I used to walk home past this one girl who was not in school. Every day when I walked by, she used to say, "You have long hair." I remember feeling very uncomfortable. I was a little afraid of her, and I'm sure that nobody was particularly friendly to her. Now, when I think back, I know that she obviously had a lot of potential—she could relate to others and all—but she just had nothing to do all day long. Then, when I was in college, I took Abnormal Psychology and went on a field trip to an institution. And that was our education in Abnormal Psychology. At that time, they were still using the classifications of "idiot" and "imbecile" and all that. It wasn't that long ago. It was pretty sad. Now that my kid is in the category of "mentally retarded," I figure I'm going to try to change people's thinking. I mean, how dare they use those words? It's all part of getting involved.

Conclusion

Obviously, mental retardation can affect your child's life in many ways. As with any child, however, it is usually impossible to predict today what your child will be able to do tomorrow. Some children with mental retardation learn academic skills in school and good work skills through on-the-job training, and eventually go on to live and work independently in the community. Other children have a harder time picking up skills and managing on their own. One thing is clear, however: all children with mental retardation have a much better chance than ever before of achieving their potential. Today, children are identified as having developmental delays much earlier than they used to be, even if they don't receive an "official" diagnosis of mental retardation until later. They start receiving special educational help earlier, and the help they receive is usually more effective than in the past. In addition, schools are required to work closely with parents in educating children with mental retardation, so you will have a great deal of influence over what your child learns and how well he learns it.

As you learn more about mental retardation, you will become a better advocate for your child. You will be able to ask useful questions of the professionals who work with your child and push for the services he needs. Together, you and your child will explore and push the limits of his potential. As a family, you will continue to learn new skills and ways of coping. As society continues to broaden its attitudes toward mental retardation, as educational and other services continue to improve and expand, and as you give your child your support and motivation, your child's future will continue to brighten.

═══ ※ ═══

I don't see him constantly as handicapped. If anything, I think, "Wow, isn't he doing well."

═══ ※ ═══

It's a shame in a way that there's all this negative stuff connected with mental retardation, because you still end up with a beautiful child.

═══ ※ ═══

I had contact with retarded kids when I was growing up in a small town. I was never one to pick on them, even though I was one of the rugged kids on the block. I had a friend who always said, "If I have a retarded kid, I'm going to put her on a roller coaster with no seatbelt," and I never laughed. I didn't think that was funny. I think about that sometimes. Today that guy's got two beautiful children, just like I have three beautiful children, but one of mine happens to be retarded, that's all.

REFERENCES

The American Psychiatric Association. *Diagnostic and Statistical Manual of Mental Disorders (Third Edition - Revised) DSM-III-R.* Washington, DC, 1987.

Batshaw, M.L., Perret, Y.M. *Children with Disabilities: A Medical Primer.* Baltimore: Paul H. Brookes Publishing Co., 1992.

Blackman, J.A., Ed. *Medical Aspects of Developmental Disabilities in Children Birth to Three. A Resource for Special Service Providers in the Educational Setting.* Iowa City: University of Iowa. Division of Developmental Disabilities, 1983.

Crocker, A.C. "The Causes of Mental Retardation." *Pediatric Annals* 1989. 18:623–35.

Crocker, A.C., Nelson, R.D. "Mental Retardation." In Levine M.D., Carey W.B., Crocker, A.C., Gross, R.T., Eds. *Developmental-Behavioral Pediatrics.* Philadelphia: Saunders, 1983: 756–70.

Hagberg, B., Kyllerman, M. "Epidemiology of Mental Retardation: A Swedish Survey." *Brain and Development* 1983. 5: 441–9.

Mental Retardation - Definition, Classification, and Systems of Supports. 9th ed. Washington, DC: American Association on Mental Retardation, 1992.

Schaefer, G.B., Bodensteiner, Y.B. "Evaluation of the Child with Idiopathic Mental Retardation." *Pediatric Clinics of North America* 1992. 39: 929–43.

Sattler, J.M., *Assessment of Children.* 3rd ed. San Diego: Jerome M. Sattler, Publisher, 1988.

Two

☸

Development and Mental Retardation

Gerard A. Gioia, Ph.D.*

When your child has mental retardation, it may seem as if every other child in the world is passing yours by. Your neighbor may have a child the same age who is racing around the house, while your child can barely sit up on her own. Your sister's child may be talking a blue streak, while yours does not even say "Mama." These differences in the way your child grows and acquires skills, or *develops*, can be traced directly to her mental retardation.

Although mental retardation *will* affect how your child develops, that does not mean she will not develop. It only means that she will take longer than usual to learn the skills and behaviors she needs to get along in the world. And it means that she won't reach the same level of learning that she would if she did not have mental retardation. But, with the right kinds of help from parents and professionals, children with mild to moderate mental retardation can surpass your expectations.

This chapter focuses on the developmental process. It explains what is meant by "development," what the "normal" rates of development are, and how children with mental retardation develop. More importantly, it points out some of the many ways you, the parent, can help to optimize your child's development.

* Gerard A. Gioia is a pediatric neuropsychologist. He is the Director of the Division of Pediatric Psychology and Neuropsychology at Mt. Washington Pediatric Hospital in Baltimore, Maryland.

What Is Development?

Development is a complex process of growth and change that is still only partially understood. Basically, it is the process through which children acquire a variety of skills and abilities that allow them to understand and function in their world. For example, they learn to sit up, ride a bike, and color; to say "Mama," speak in sentences, and talk about their experiences; to feed and dress themselves and make friends. In short, development is what enables a child to progress from complete dependency on others for her well-being to the point where she is able to take care of many or most of her own needs.

How well and how quickly your child develops depends on several factors. These include her inborn potential to learn, as well as the types of experiences that help shape that potential. For example, before your child can learn to speak, she must be able to make sense of and imitate the speech she hears. She must also have experiences that motivate her to learn to speak: adults who talk to her, give her models to imitate, and don't always understand her so that her speech attempts have to become more accurate.

For many years, experts disagreed on whether a child's development was due to the biological capacities she was born with (nature) *or* to stimulation from people and things in the environment (nurture). Most developmental experts now agree that *both* elements are crucial to a child's optimal growth. Thus, although there is little you can do to change your child's innate abilities to learn, you can still have a profound effect on the rate and quality of her development.

What Is "Normal" Development?

Development occurs in stages. It usually takes place in an orderly, sequential fashion with later-developing skills building upon earlier skills. For example, children most often babble first and then speak in single words before learning to combine words into sentences. Children also generally crawl before taking steps independently. Likewise, most children first master basic cognitive concepts such as cause and effect—for example, shaking a rattle or banging a toy on the table to get a sound. Then they learn to solve complex problems—for example, using a stick to obtain a toy that is out of reach or figuring out how to operate the cassette player.

Most children reach specific developmental goals, or *milestones*, in approximately the same order. This makes it possible to set general guidelines for the ages when milestones are normally achieved. For example, most children learn to take their first independent steps between nine and sixteen months of age; to use words to communicate their desires between one to two years of age; and to consider different ways to solve a problem between three and five years of age.

Obviously, children can develop skills at somewhat different ages and still be considered to be developing "normally." As explained earlier, this variability is due not only to the varying abilities with which children are born, but also to outside influences that can impede or encourage learning. Children who are developing normally can also learn skills faster in some areas than in others. For example, one child may take her first steps at ten months of age, but not speak her first words until thirteen months of age. Another child may say her first words at ten months, but not take her first steps until fourteen months. Each set of skills is within "normal" developmental limits, although the two children clearly have very different ways of interacting with their worlds. "Normal" development simply means that a child is achieving skills during the same age *ranges* that most other children do.

To determine whether a child is developing normally, professionals such as psychologists, physicians, educators, and early intervention specialists look at whether her rate of acquiring skills falls into the normal range. Chapter 4 explains how development is evaluated.

Although children with mental retardation do not develop skills at the same rate as other children do, they do develop them in the same general sequence. This means that a knowledge of normal development can serve as a framework to help you see your child's differences. If you recognize your child's differences, you can then give her the help and guidance needed to reach most milestones. For children with mental retardation, as for all children, later (more complex) skills generally build on earlier (simpler) skills.

TABLE 1—Milestones of Normal Development

Age	Cognition	Language
6 months	Actively explores environment. Reaches for and handles objects.	Babbles ("gaga"). Knows own name. May recognize "no."
1 year	Can hold objects in mind for brief period of time. Interest in simple cause-effect relationships.	Understands about ten words. Says first words.
18 months	Able to solve simple problems by using tool to get desired result.	Enjoys nursery rhymes and picture books. Knows 10-20 words. Uses familiar phrases such as "what's that?" and "come here."
2 years	Can hold objects and thoughts in mind for longer periods of time. Can label experiences. ("Daddy go work") Can infer cause from effect and vice versa.	Vocabulary comprehension increases rapidly. Begins to combine words ("doggy ball"; "bubbles gone"). Speech intelligible to others about 65% of time.
3 years	More sophisticated problem-solving and reasoning, but still tied to personal experience. (Can operate VCR after watching parent use.)	Understands complex sentences ("You may go to Jeremy's house if we get home in time"). Asks many questions; can take several turns talking, staying on a topic. Speech intelligible to others about 80% of time.
4 years	Continues to make progress in problem solving.	Uses 4-7 word sentences. Uses language to convey experiences. Understands spatial concepts such as "above" and "between," and knows numbers up to about 4 and several colors. Is capable of making all or nearly all speech sounds
5 years	Can think through and solve problems with less reference to self and based more on objective experience (fixing a toy that she hasn't watched others fix before).	Understands many time and number words (before, after, yesterday, tomorrow, more, most, a few). Can accurately count to 10 or 12. Is learning alphabet and days of the week. Begins using threats ("I'm going to tell Mom") and insults ("You're a dork"). Further refines pronunciation of later acquired sounds (often r, l, th, j).

Table 1 (Continued)

Social	Play	Motor
Laughs aloud. Smiles at self in mirror. Recognizes and prefers familiar voices.	Bangs objects. Solitary, repetitive play.	Sits alone steadily. Can hold objects between the thumb and palm. Transfers toy from one hand to another.
Cooperates in mutual activities such as rolling ball, getting dressed with adult.	Repeatedly does same actions with familiar objects (hugging and kissing doll).	Can stand alone and take several steps independently. Is able to pick up small objects between thumb and forefinger. Scribbles with marker on paper. Holds a spoon.
Imitates familiar activities (reading book, sweeping).	Carries special toy. Begins to substitute one object for another (pretend). Plays simple games (peek-a-boo, throwing ball to parent).	Walks independently, seldom falling. Walks up stairs with adult help. Throws a ball. Builds a 3-block tower. Begins to keep lips closed while chewing.
Understands self as different than others. Social independence (may venture out on social situation without parent by side or insist that parent be present.) Possessive of toys.	Play is more symbolic (can pretend doll is baby). More active play. Plays side by side, but not with other children (parallel play).	Runs well without falling. Walks up and down stairs independently, holding rail. Can kick a ball and turn door knob. Drinks from cup without spilling. Bites through soft-medium foods and begins true chewing.
Better able to coordinate own needs with others' and to take turns. Begins to play in a group of 2-3.	More creative in play with emphasis on why and how. Likes to dress up in costumes, play act cartoon characters.	Rides a tricycle. Jumps short distance. Puts shoes on. Builds a 9-block tower.
Can play with other children with beginning cooperation (takes turns; plays games that require turn-taking).	Same as social skills. Very dramatic.	Walks downstairs one step per tread. Can stand on one foot for 4-8 seconds. Can copy a cross symbol. Can dress self except for tying shoelaces.
Can play cooperatively with others in groups of 2-5. Understands needs of other children and doesn't always insist on own needs. Forms stronger friendships; becomes competitive.	Makes elaborate structures with blocks. Plays games by the rules.	Skips, alternating feet. Ties shoelaces. Can copy a square and a triangle. Cuts fairly accurately with scissors.

The Areas of Development

During the course of development, children learn many different types of skills and behaviors. For convenience, child development experts often group similar skills into what are called *developmental areas*. For example, all skills having to do with communication are grouped into one developmental area, and all skills having to do with thinking or problem solving are grouped into another. One way the developmental process can be divided is as follows: 1) cognitive abilities; 2) language and speech skills; 3) gross motor skills; 4) fine motor skills; 5) social-emotional skills; 6) play skills. To give you an idea of expectations for normal development in each of these areas, Table 1 provides an overview of skills usually achieved by a particular age.

Cognitive Development

Your child's cognitive abilities are what are ordinarily called thinking capacities—her ability to understand concepts, pay attention, remember, and reason. In general, cognitive abilities allow your child to understand, organize, and make sense of her world.

Cognitive development begins in the first days of life when children begin to learn about the nature of objects, people, and events in their environment. They learn, for example, that they can get milk from a nipple and that when they are on their stomachs they get a different view than when they are on their backs. Generally, however, an infant less than a year old has little capacity to *hold* any information in her mind. Only toward the end of the first year do most infants begin to grasp the concept of object permanence— that is, that something continues to exist even if it's out of sight at the moment. This marks the beginning of the child's ability to think symbolically about her world, which is critical for all later cognitive abilities. Examples of how infants explore these new concepts about the world include the games of peek-a-boo and hide and seek. An infant enjoys the momentary absence of a parent's face in peek-a-boo because she is able to briefly hold the idea in her mind and then become thrilled when the face does indeed return visually.

Throughout the first year of life, an infant develops a basic understanding of cause-effect relationships—for example, if she hits a hanging object, it will move. As they become more physically active, children take a keener interest in cause-effect situations and will purposely seek them out—for example, by repeatedly rolling a ball to an adult in order to have it rolled back. Or they may observe how they are able to get a sibling or parent to react by their own actions. For example, they may repeat a facial expression that made family members laugh.

As children enter their second year of life, they become more capable of holding information about objects, words, places, activities, and people in their minds and of using this information to solve problems. In contrast to eight-month-olds, who typically do not remember a toy if it is taken away, children can now search for a toy recently hidden. At eighteen months to two years of age, children can begin to anticipate the consequences of their own and others' actions. These advances in thinking abilities enable children to understand the world in more depth. They also prepare them to play more independently and creatively with people and things in their environment. For example, the child may independently construct a tower of blocks to knock over, or pretend to feed a doll.

Over the next few years, children become increasingly inventive. They develop the ability to pretend and may enjoy dressing up as someone other than themselves. They can creatively re-combine thoughts and activities in novel, inventive ways. For example, they might playfully recombine words to a song to make a unique, humorous rendition. At the same time their imagination soars, their thinking and behavior continue to be very much bound to their own experiences. They usually cannot create ideas that go beyond their direct experience until they reach the age of six or seven. So, for example, preschoolers and kindergartners might play Batman or dentist or spaceman, but would not introduce a unique variation such as spaceman dentist. This is because they cannot imagine how being a dentist in space would be different than being one on earth, even though they know what both dentists and spacemen do.

Throughout her childhood, the normally developing child continues to develop a longer attention span; improves her ability to think abstractly about objects, ideas, and experiences; learns to be more flexible in reasoning and problem-solving; and can learn and remember information that is increasingly complex. Older children learn to ask the question "what if?" and think through possible scenarios without having to act them out. This makes for a much greater ability to deal with problems independently and creatively. These advanced cognitive abilities allow older children to become increasingly independent in all activities.

Language and Speech Development

In ordinary conversation, we sometimes blur the distinctions between the words "speech" and "language." But the two words are not really synonymous. To understand how children develop the ability to communicate, it is important to understand the distinctions between these terms.

Speech is the process of producing sounds and combining them into words to communicate. Language, on the other hand, is any system of rules for combining sounds into words and words into sentences. English and Spanish, for example, are languages that are spoken and written, while American Sign Language is a language that consists of gestures. Most people are eventually able to use a combination of speech, written symbols, and gestures for communication.

Learning how to communicate with others is crucial to a child's eventual independence. In the process of developing communication skills, children must first learn to understand language and then to use language to convey information to others. The ability to understand spoken words, gestures, or written symbols is called *receptive language,* while the ability to use language to put thoughts into words is called *expressive language.*

Until about ten to twelve months of age, most children are *preverbal.* That is, they are unable to use meaningful words to communicate. This does not mean, however, that they are incapable of communicating. Quite early in life, they are able to communicate their needs by cries, coos, and other sounds; facial expressions; and gestures and body language such as turning away from an adult when they have lost interest in playing. Infants frequently practice preverbal speech sounds such as cooing in the first several months, and repetitive babbling ("da-da's") beginning at about six months. By their first birthday, they use long strings of syllables that parents usually think of as "jabbering." At this point, they usually respond to familiar words and some short phrases.

In the second year of life, a child's vocabulary develops rapidly. She understands more and more short sentences and responds to questions. Around the age of twenty months, the child starts joining two words together to express herself ("Mommy milk!"), and by two years she is identifying photos and pictures in books. This signals a more complex level of language usage. In the third year, children continue to comprehend and use increasingly complex language in conversation. For example, they can understand and create sentences with five or more words. By now, children can usually use language to understand and bring order to their world. That is, they can ask questions about things that puzzle them and put solutions to these problems into words. And by the age of four or five, they can use language in fairly sophisticated forms to convey their experience and needs. For example, they can easily describe the events of their day or use language to persuade their parents to buy them a toy.

Motor Development

Motor skills allow children to explore their surroundings and act upon their world. These skills are usually divided into two basic types: gross motor skills and fine motor skills. Gross motor skills involve large muscles of the body such as those in the legs, arms, and abdomen. Examples of gross motor skills include walking, crawling, and sitting. Fine motor skills use smaller muscles in the hands, face, and eyes. They include such skills as using finger and hand movements to eat and draw, and making mouth movements to chew and speak.

During the first year of her life, a child usually reaches several important gross motor milestones. Generally, she learns to control head movements between three and five months of age; can hold herself in a sitting position by five to ten months; and experiments with pre-walking movements such as stepping, pulling to stand, standing alone, and cruising on furniture between seven and twelve months. A child often takes her first independent steps toward her first birthday. But she can walk as early as nine months or as late as fifteen to sixteen months and still be considered within the "normal" range. During her second and third years, the child becomes more skilled at walking (sideways, backwards, up and down stairs) and running. She also develops climbing and jumping skills and the ability to kick, catch, and throw a ball. These skills all draw on her steadily increasing strength, balance, and coordination. As the preschooler learns to ride a tricycle and masters even more complex skills, her ability to explore her world independently and creatively continues to grow.

Paralleling the development of gross motor skills is the development of fine motor skills. During her first year, an infant makes considerable progress in controlling hand and finger movements. She learns to reach for and grasp large objects such as blocks, and then smaller, pellet-sized objects such as bits of cereal. In her second year, she learns to use tools such as pencils and crayons in play. Between two and four years, she practices early drawing and writing skills, learning to make increasingly sophisticated and coordinated strokes. By the time she is three to five, she can usually copy simple designs such as circles, squares, and triangles. Also around this age, she learns to use scissors, and to fasten and unfasten buttons, snaps, and zippers on clothing. At five, she can begin to tie her shoelaces.

At the same time children are learning to make skilled hand and finger movements, they are also learning to make the skilled mouth movements needed to speak and eat. Skills involving muscles in and around the mouth are called *oral-motor* skills. In the beginning, children don't produce very intelligible speech sounds because the muscles of the face and mouth are not strong and coordinated enough. Through the preschool years, their articulation of sounds continues to improve, although certain sounds (l, r, th) may still not come out quite right. By the age of five, most children easily articulate the majority of sounds used in speech, so that their conversation is usually completely intelligible.

Eating skills develop hand in hand with speech skills. During just the first year of life, children progress from suckling liquids to biting, munching, and swallowing a variety of tastes and textures of baby and table foods. By about the age of twenty-six months, children usually have a complete set of baby (primary) teeth. Therefore, by about the age of two, a child generally eats almost all the same foods her family does, with the exception of very hard or tough foods that might choke her. From two to three years of age, children learn to refine the movements of their jaw, lips, and tongue by biting and chewing foods. Gradually they learn to move these parts of their mouth more efficiently, with smaller movements, and more independently of one another. All these developments not only improve their eating skills, but also their ability to produce additional speech sounds and longer words and sentences.

Social-Emotional Development

As they develop social-emotional skills, children learn appropriate ways of interacting with and responding emotionally to others. They learn, for instance, not to take someone else's toy without asking. These abilities depend on a child's growing awareness and acceptance of herself as an individual and of her own separateness from others.

Young infants are not able to view themselves as separate from the external world. Gradually, they learn that they are individuals with certain interests and needs. But they still cannot always separate their own needs from others' needs. Thus, a child may demand to have a snack immediately, even though her parent is busy with something else. As their social skills increase, children learn to delay the immediate gratification of their needs and take in the reality of the situation (for example, waiting ten minutes for a snack). Children generally learn to coordinate the demands of others through cooperation between the ages of two and five.

Throughout the preschool years, children gradually learn to understand the thoughts, feelings, and behaviors of others and to socialize more effectively. Occasionally, they go through periods in which they have trouble balancing their own needs with those of others. For example, toddlers often consider their toys as prized possessions and have great difficulty sharing them. With experience and support, though, children learn to share and to understand that other people's needs are important, too.

To fit into society, a child must also mature emotionally. Here development is linked to the child's inborn *temperament,* or emotional style. According to child development experts, temperament is what determines how easily a child learns to handle the emotional demands of the outside world. Some children are said to have "easy" temperament styles, while others are "difficult" or "slow to warm up." Children with an "easy" style have less difficulty adapting to stress and can usually handle a wide range of situations. Children with "difficult" temperaments tend to react to stresses more quickly or strongly. For example, they may be more upset if asked to stop playing and get ready for bed. How well a child is able to handle stress becomes especially important in later childhood. If a child can deal with stress and manage anxiety appropriately, she can normally work out a more effective solution to a problem than a child who becomes more anxious.

Also important is the match between the child's and the parents' temperaments. The better the match, the better the ability of the child to learn appropriate ways to handle stress and anxiety. This match can also affect the bond that develops between parent and child. For example, an "easy" parent with an "easy" child is more likely to have a satisfying parent-child bond than an "easy" parent and a "difficult" child. It may be more difficult for a parent to feel close to a child who is frequently irritable with others.

Although a child's temperament is largely determined before birth, another important aspect of emotional development is not. Self-esteem, or a child's acceptance of her strengths and weaknesses and confidence in her abilities, is something that is learned. As infants and children attempt to master tasks over the course of development, the positive or negative feedback that they receive affects the way they view their competence and self-worth. Children who feel like successes more often than they feel like failures tend to develop good self-esteem. This enables them to approach new situations with confidence, and to persevere when frustrated.

Play

Play is more than just a recreational activity for preschool children. It is also a way children learn about the world and use combinations of skills in many developmental areas. For example, when a child learns to take turns when playing a board game, she is practicing social-emotional and language skills. When she puts a jigsaw puzzle together, she exercises cognitive and fine motor skills.

Play skills reflect development in cognitive, language, motor, and social-emotional skills. Just as other areas of development follow predictable stages, so too do play skills. For instance, a young infant is still quite self-centered, so she focuses on solitary, repetitive play activities such as banging two toy cars together. By two years of age, she is willing to play side by side with other children, but doesn't usually join in their play. In this type of *parallel* play, two children might each play in the same sandbox, but not really interact with each other. At three, children begin to play games *with* other children, but their play is still not completely two-way in nature. For example, two children might talk to each other and share equipment while playing in the sandbox, but each build their own separate sand castle. Around the age of four or five, children are finally able to cooperate fully with others during play. They understand other children's needs and share more equally.

The development of cognitive abilities and the development of play skills are also related. As mentioned above, an infant's first attempts at play are quite repetitive and unimaginative. Later, as the child learns to think about objects and ideas in symbolic ways, her play becomes more creative and inventive. She can, for example, imagine that a stick can substitute for a rocket. As her ability to symbolize increases, the three-year-old delights in pretending to do what she's seen others do, either in person or on TV. She can also make believe without props—for example, pretend she's washing the dog or playing a guitar. In the role of herself, she may also pretend that she is doing something she has done before—for instance, going to the zoo, visiting an amusement park, having a birthday party. The older preschooler can play still more imaginatively, taking on the roles of a variety of characters in an elaborate fantasy world. She may act out activities she has not personally done, but has observed on TV or read in a book—for example, going on a safari to see jungle animals.

How Developmental Areas Are Related

For purposes of discussion, development *can* be divided into the areas described above. But in real life, many developmental skills cannot be so neatly pigeonholed. That is, many real-life skills depend on development in more than one area. For example, playing Follow the Leader takes both communication *and* motor skills. Likewise, communicating in multi-word sentences involves not only language skills, but also speech skills. To feed herself, a child must first have the gross motor skills to hold her trunk steady while she makes fine motor movements—reaching, grasping, chewing—with her hands and mouth. She must also have the sensory development to know how hard to grasp a utensil or hold a piece of food so that she neither drops it nor crushes it. And to behave appropriately in a variety of social situations, a child must have the cognitive abilities to understand what is expected of her, the social and emotional maturity to actually *do* what is expected of her, and the language skills to understand what is said to her and to express herself.

Obviously, progress in each area of development is closely linked to progress in other areas. By the same token, if a child is delayed in one or more areas of development, other areas are also likely to be affected. For example, if a child's motor development is delayed because she has cerebral palsy, she will have problems physically exploring her world. This reduced contact and experience could contribute to delays in cognitive development. If, for example, she could not use her hands to turn a handle or open a container, she might have more trouble learning about cause-effect relationships. Likewise, if she couldn't move well enough to keep up with other children's play, she might have greater difficulties in social development.

Adaptive Behavior

The end result of development is not just acquiring isolated skills. It is being able to use these skills to function independently and successfully in the real world. For example, the goal of learning cognitive skills such as addition and subtraction is not just to be able to pass math tests in school, but to make practical use of those skills in balancing a checkbook, figuring out how much change is owed, or calculating how much carpet to buy for the living room floor. The goal of learning to make speech sounds is not just to combine them into words, but to be able to hold meaningful conversations, ask strangers for directions, place an order in a restaurant, or use the telephone to report an emergency. This ability to cope independently and effectively in the interpersonal world is known as *adaptive behavior*.

Adaptive behavior is often divided into three types:

1. Personal self-help skills. These include skills and abilities needed to manage immediate personal needs—eating, toileting, grooming, dressing.

2. Community self-sufficiency skills. These include behaviors that enable an individual to look after her own well-being and social relationships within the community. Examples are the abilities to: handle and budget money; shop; look after one's own safety; tell time; drive a car or take public transportation; vacuum, wash dishes, wash floors, and do other domestic activities; and communicate appropriately with others.

3. Personal-social responsibility. These behaviors include personality traits and skills usually considered necessary to succeed in the community. Initiative, perseverance, responsibility, and the ability to socialize and use leisure time effectively are important examples of this type of adaptive behavior.

Just as there are "normal" rates for developing in other areas, there are also "normal" rates for learning adaptive behavior. No one expects a child to know how to apply her skills and to function as self-sufficiently as an adult does. Instead, children are expected to use their skills at a level appropriate to their age. For example, a three-year-old with adaptive behavior appropriate for her age would be able to drink from a cup, dress and undress with only a little help from parents, and use the toilet with some independence. She would also understand basic safety measures—for example, that she should avoid hot stoves, use caution around strangers, and stay out of the street. She would have at least a  general understanding of the function of money. In addition, she would be able to adapt to social situations and communicate her needs to others at a level appropriate for her age. A twelve-year-old with appropriate adaptive behavior would be able to apply basic academic skills in daily life activities—for example, to figure out if she has enough money to buy a video game she wants. She would also be able to use appropriate judgment and reasoning in most situations she is likely to find herself in. For example, she would know not to step off the curb when the "don't walk" signal is flashing, and that she shouldn't let a stranger in the house if she is home alone. And she would demonstrate social skills appropriate to her age. For example, she would know how to behave appropriately at a slumber party, but not at a job interview.

If somebody comes to the door and says, "Where is Mr. Jones, the principal, I would like to kill him with this rifle," our daughter would say, "Oh, he's in room 210." So, she definitely has some problems with judgment and using her skills more appropriately.

When Development Doesn't Go As Expected

Although there is great variability in development, there *are* earlier and later limits to what is considered "normal" development. Statistically, 68 percent of all children develop skills within the average range, while 16 percent fall above and 16 percent fall below normal limits. Approximately 2.2 percent of all children develop at a rate significantly above average, while the same percentage of children develop at a rate significantly below average. Children with mental retardation make up this latter category. Mental retardation, in fact, is called a "developmental disability" because the child does not develop in the same way as usual. As Chapter 1 explains, children with mental retardation have delays in all developmental areas. They make progress at a rate that is significantly slower than is expected of children their age. Often, too, they do not learn skills as well as other children.

Just as the development of children who don't have mental retardation varies, so does the development of children with mental retardation. Although all children with mental retardation develop more slowly, there are differences in the rate of development between one child and another. There may also be differences in the order in which children with mental retardation achieve developmental milestones. The eventual endpoint of development for any one child cannot be predicted, although that endpoint will probably not be the same as for a child who does not have mental retardation. Mental retardation will likely narrow the range of activities your child will eventually be able to do as an adult.

Before your child was diagnosed, you probably had at least some vague concerns about the rate at which your child was learning new things. Perhaps she didn't start talking as early as an older sibling or show as much interest in playing with toys recommended for children her age. As Chapter 3 discusses, your emotions likely seesawed wildly as you tried to assure yourself that nothing was wrong, despite evidence to the contrary.

Even after your child was diagnosed, you may have denied that she had mental retardation. Denial is actually a perfectly understandable reaction. Your disbelief could be supported by the variability in what is considered "normal" development. You might have thought that the diagnosis was wrong and that your child would soon catch up. Sympathetic family members, friends, or professionals might also have convinced you that your position was justified, perhaps by sharing the story of one child who proved all theories wrong. ("I have a friend who didn't start talking until age three and she's a corporate executive now!")

Accepting that your child's potential will always be different than most other children's can be heartwrenching. But facing up to this truth can also be the best thing you ever do for yourself and your child. Even though children with mental retardation do not achieve quite so much so quickly as other children, they *can* make tremendous developmental progress. They can also continue to learn all their lives. And just as with other children, it is difficult to predict precisely how far they will be able to go. What is known, however, is that children with mental retardation need more help than usual in reaching their eventual potential. And the earlier they begin to receive the right kind of help, the more likely it is that they will achieve everything they are capable of. This is where you, as a parent, come in. As later chapters explain, you play a vital role in making sure that your child has the best possible learning experiences at home, at school, and in the community. To help you understand what your child's special learning needs may be, the next section explains how childrden with mental retardation typically develop.

The Development of Children with Mental Retardation

Just as in "normally developing" children, there are two factors that affect how children with mental retardation develop. First, the child's inborn biological and neurological capacity set the *general limits* for the rate and eventual endpoint of development. That is, a child with mild mental retardation will develop more slowly than a child with "normal" intelligence, but more quickly than a child who has moderate or severe mental retardation. Second, environmental factors such as the type and amount of stimulation a child receives at home and at school play a key role. For example, an infant with mild mental retardation who receives regular and appropriate language stimulation beginning early in life will be more likely to develop effective language skills than a child who receives little regular language stimulation.

Obviously, there is a great deal of variety in the rate and quality of development among children with mental retardation. But there *is* one important similarity. Children with mental retardation usually develop more slowly in all areas—cognitive, language, motor, social-emotional, play, adaptive behavior, and sensory abilities—than other children their age.

The sections below explain how children with mental retardation typically develop in each area. The examples are meant only to highlight the general issues in each developmental area and do not represent the only ways that a child may develop. Because of the complexity of development in all children, it is not possible to provide exhaustive examples.

Lots of retarded children are just like Alex, just like him. They have little things about them that are different from most kids. There's always at least one thing that's different about them. We've noticed this about the kids in Alex's class.

A large part of her development is like taking a standard child's development and stretching it out another 50 percent. It's like prolonging the childhood.

Your Child's Cognitive Development

Your child's thinking and reasoning abilities will not develop in the same way as they would if she did not have mental retardation. This is because mental retardation affects cognitive abilities in several primary ways. Chapter 1 discusses these difficulties in detail, but briefly, they include:

1. A slower rate of learning. Children with mental retardation take longer to master new information and skills, and require more repetition and reminders to learn.
2. Attentional difficulties. Children with mental retardation have more trouble focusing their attention, as well as shifting it to new activities.
3. Problem-solving difficulties. When confronted with a problem, children with mental retardation usually have more trouble understanding the nature of the problem and are less active in finding possible solutions. For example, if a four-year-old without mental retardation cannot reach a toy on the table, she will usually seek other means to get it. But a child with mental retardation may persist in reaching without considering other ways of solving the problem.
4. Less critical thinking. A child with mental retardation is less likely to realize that several facts are inconsistent. For example, your child may hand over her lunch money to an older child on demand without considering possible consequences.
5. Limited abilities to think abstractly. Children with mental retardation tend to think concretely—to be bound to the immediate situation. For example, they may have trouble envisioning what the consequences of something they do or do not do today will be tomorrow.
6. Difficulty storing and retrieving information. Your child may have less information in her memory than she would if she did not have mental retardation, as well as more trouble recalling information that is in her memory.
7. Difficulty *generalizing*. This means your child will have trouble applying something she has learned to do in one situation to a new situation. For example, if your child has learned to use the toilet in your bathroom at home, she may

be at a loss as to how to use a toilet in a friend's house where the tissue is in a different place.

In general, the greater the level of mental retardation, the more exaggerated these problems. For example, a child with very mild mental retardation may have each of these cognitive difficulties to a mild degree. A child with moderate mental retardation will probably have greater difficulty with all of these skills. In addition, certain causes of mental retardation may affect cognitive abilities in certain ways. For example, fragile X syndrome often causes attention deficit problems and perseveration. Children with Williams syndrome may have hyperactive or impulsive behavior, but also relatively good memories.

All of these differences in your child's cognitive abilities will definitely affect how she learns and how much she is able to learn over the long term. For example, because she learns more slowly and has a shorter attention span, she will need to be taught skills through frequent, short teaching sessions. And because she has difficulty thinking abstractly, she will need to be taught in relevant, real-world situations. That is, she will learn how to use a computer best by using it herself, rather than by watching someone demonstrate its use, and she will learn how to handle money by buying items in a store, rather than by adding figures with pencil and paper. Chapter 5 provides more information on effective teaching methods for children with mental retardation.

In the end, just as with other children, your child's cognitive abilities will place some limits on what she can achieve. Exactly what those limits will be may not be apparent for some time, or they might be apparent early on. For example, if your child has a great deal of trouble solving everyday problems, it may be obvious when she is quite young that she should not aim for a job where she needs to make decisions on the spot. On the other hand, you may not know for many years whether your child will be able to get a driver's license. She may learn to read street signs and understand basic traffic regulations, but you may not know whether she has the capacity to study and remember everything in the test booklet until she tries. Likewise, your child may be in her early twenties before it is clear whether she can think critically enough to live on her own with a roommate, or whether she would be better off with more supervision. As discussed in the sections below, cognitive difficulties also affect learning in other areas, particularly language and social skills.

It's weird. She has an incredible memory for things she's seen before. She remembers events and things like that. It isn't always relevant and it doesn't always matter, and sometimes I wish she would just stop talking about it. It's like she's kind of free-associating.

We've got this computer program called "Super Solvers." If you sit down and read the clues to him, he can do all of the <u>processing</u> and <u>figuring out</u> and give you the right answer. So the comprehension and putting it together is there. It's just the act of reading that's real difficult for him.

Nancy's cognitive differences stand out in greatest contrast to her siblings'. As I watch her struggle to learn words, numbers, and writing, her brothers seem to just soak up this information naturally, without one-tenth the effort Nancy must exert to learn the same things.

=== ✳ ===

I wish my son wouldn't just go spacey sometimes. I know he's thinking about something there inside himself. But I feel like other people see him

like that and think "He's really out of it," and then just write him off. That embarrasses me and makes me hurt for him.

======= ※ =======

He has a fascination with science and nature. He likes watching nature programs and a lot of science and technology programs. Obviously, he doesn't understand everything and he doesn't have the correct vernacular to go with everything, but he understands the basic workings.

======= ※ =======

Sometimes Ricky is so "on," so completely focused, learning so easily that I am amazed by how smart he is. If he could only be that way more often. Ricky has good days—when he is turned on by what he is learning—and days when he is uninterested and dull. I do not know how to get him to be turned on to learning all the time or if that is possible for him (or anyone else for that matter). Also, some things he learns really turn him on. I remember when he learned to use a calculator, it just clicked for him; he really liked it and learned so fast and easy. It also matters how he is taught. Ricky is stimulated by learning from <u>his</u> world—he learns to read stories from his life faster than academic stories. He learns to add money from a fast-food menu faster than from a sheet of numbers that have no inherent meaning for him.

Your Child's Language Development

Children with mental retardation frequently have speech and language problems. Some of these difficulties are due directly to limited cognitive abilities. For example, because of problems with attention and memory, your child may have trouble remembering and attending to what words mean and how they sound. Or she may have trouble learning and remembering how to make a word plural or how to use words to describe something that happened in the past.

Many children with mental retardation also have physical problems that make speech production more difficult. For example, children with Down syndrome often have lower muscle tone in the face and mouth, and a smaller, shallower mouth, all of which can make it harder to articulate words. Children with fragile X often have low muscle tone, too, and may therefore have trouble articulating words clearly and precisely. Children who have cerebral palsy may also have muscle tone problems in the face, as well as problems using the muscles in the trunk needed for proper breath control. And as Chapter 9 discusses, children with mental retardation are more likely to have hearing impairments, which can lead to problems with articulation.

Because of cognitive and physical difficulties, children with mental retardation frequently take longer to reach speech and language milestones. For example, a child with mild mental retardation may say her first words at two years of age, rather than at around one year of age, and may combine two words around her third or fourth birthday, rather than her second.

The degree of your child's mental retardation will determine how quickly she picks up language skills, as well as how close to "normal" her speech and comprehension will eventually be. In general, though, you can expect that she will learn to say and understand words at a slower rate. Even when she is very familiar with words and sentences, she will probably be less efficient at comprehending them. For example, even though she may have understood the names of colors for a year, when asked to pick up "the green key," she may sometimes pick up the yellow one simply because it is closest to her. Anybody can make these kinds of mistakes, but they will happen to your child more frequently because she processes language and organizes her response less efficiently and accurately.

Your child will also have more difficulty learning to use and understand words that describe abstract concepts—for example, time concepts such as "yesterday" or "next week" or concepts that are relative such as "bigger" or "younger." In general, the more concrete the concept, the earlier your child will learn it. That is, if a concept relates to something that is easily seen or experienced, your child will find it easier to learn. For example, "broken," "dirty," and "hot" are all relatively easy words for most children with mental retardation to learn.

Your child's eventual ability to understand more complex sentences and to create her own sentences will depend on the degree of her mental retardation. It may also depend on the cause of her mental retardation, as mentioned at the beginning of this section. Generally, the milder a child's mental retardation, the sooner she will develop receptive and expressive language skills, and the more sophisticated her language skills will eventually be. But remember, language development also depends on other factors, ranging from the amount and types of speech therapy and other help your child receives, to the encouragement and practice she is given at home, to her own desire and motivation to communicate effectively. Many children with moderate mental retardation learn to communicate in complete, although sometimes ungrammatical sentences, while others use one- or two-word utterances to make their needs known. See Chapter 5 for information on how speech and language therapy can strengthen your child's communication skills.

When I go out and no one else can understand him or I go to pick him up at the nursery school and I hear the other kids say things like "Mommy, the puppet lady was here today," I think, "Gee, my son knows everything you know, kid, he just can't say it." But it bothers me. I've gotten to the point where I brag about him knowing his alphabet, because I want people to know that he's smarter than he seems because of his poor speech.

His ability to pick out important sounds or signals from the background noise isn't that good. If you're in a crowd out in a public place, you need to be within arm's reach of him because he can't hear you call him. He can also get overloaded if there is a lot of information coming in all at once.

She had a lot of ear problems, first of all. So she didn't even start speaking until she was almost four. We just attributed her slowness to ear problems.

She didn't make a sound for a year while she was turning over and crawling and standing up, but not walking. It was quite a while before she talked.

I wish my daughter's tongue didn't just hang out—she looks so dull. That's what I'm afraid others are thinking, anyway.

In the last few months, my son and I have communicated a lot better. It's really neat that we are able to communicate and know that he knows he is communicating with us and that he understands what we say. He's not a "thing," he's a "people" now.

Your Child's Motor Development

Problems with motor development can take a variety of forms, depending upon the cause of mental retardation. For some children, underlying neurological problems can significantly affect motor skill development. For example, children with cerebral palsy may have significant problems with *muscle tone*—the amount of tension or resistance to movement in their muscles. Muscle tone may be excessively tight and not allow muscles to move smoothly and easily. Or it may be so "floppy" that movements take a great deal of effort and are hard to control. Children with Down syndrome or fragile X syndrome may also have this second problem, especially in the early years.

Even when they don't have specific neurological problems, children with mental retardation are often slower at achieving early motor milestones such as sitting, walking, using a spoon, and scribbling with a crayon. And when they do master motor skills, their movements may be more awkward or uncoordinated. For example, children with mental retardation usually need extra help learning to throw and catch a ball, balance on one foot, cut with a pair of scissors, or tie shoelaces. One particularly important difference is the way some children with mental retardation hold pens and pencils. Their grasp is termed "immature" because they hold pens and pencils in their fist rather with their fingers and thumb. Because they often have some problems with controlling their fine motor skills, it is harder for them to write legibly. The letters they write tend to be larger and less well-formed than other children's.

Another way children with mental retardation may differ is in their motor planning—how their brains plan when and how to move, and decide which limbs move first, second, and third, and how to position their bodies. For example, catching a ball requires motor planning to coordinate bringing hands together close enough (but not too close) to catch the ball just as it arrives. Or, following a set of directions such as "Walk over to the swing and put one leg over it," can be difficult at first because it requires planning a lot of separate but coordinated movements. Some of these motor and coordination problems are connected to the sensory problems some children with mental retardation have. These problems are discussed later in this chapter.

As in other areas of development, children with mental retardation usually do not "catch up" completely with other children in motor skills. However, with the right kinds of intervention, they will make progress and learn motor skills throughout their life. Consequently, most people with mild to moderate mental retardation do  learn to do most of the motor skills they need to function independently or semi-independently as adults. They usually do not become all-star athletes, but they often truly enjoy and feel proud of the motor skills they can do, like swimming, running, and team sports. Chapter 5 provides information about how occupational and physical therapists can help your child maximize his motor abilities.

His hand-eye and motor coordination aren't that hot. He's done a lot better in the past year or so, but for the longest time he had problems catching a ball, kicking the ball properly. If he was playing baseball or something, he had a hard time hitting the ball. He gets frustrated a lot.

━━━ ※ ━━━

We had taken childbirth classes and, of course, everybody gets together after the babies are born. We had the reunion when Betsy was four months old. So we had the babies lined up in their baby seats, and our daughter was the only one with her head leaning off to the side because she couldn't hold her head up.

═══ ✳ ═══

With eating, it was natural for her to use either hand. Whatever side the fork landed on, that's the hand she would use.

═══ ✳ ═══

Our son was happy, but he was sort of like a blob. He had no tone, no gross motor strength. Now I know what it is called. My friend would take her little boy and kind of balance him on his legs, but my son would just kind of tilt over. I guess the biggest thing was that he wasn't sitting. He couldn't get up from a lying to a sitting position, either.

═══ ✳ ═══

He's really good at mechanical things and putting things together. I think it's because he's a very visual child, extremely visual. Even when he was a very young child, he was able to watch me manipulate the stereo or something and then do that himself almost instantaneously.

Your Child's Sensory Abilities

Because mental retardation, by definition, affects all areas of development, it stands to reason that sensory-related development can also be impaired in children with mental retardation. A child with mental retardation may have trouble taking in, processing, or responding to information from any one or more of the many senses—sight, hearing, touch, taste, smell, and the senses of movement, body position, and gravity. This, in turn, will affect development in other areas.

Some children with mental retardation have difficulty processing touch sensations. They may be overly sensitive to being touched on certain parts of the body, or may find certain textures of food, clothing, lotions, floor surfaces, etc., upsetting to the touch. They may cry if they are made to wear a hat or long pants, or refuse to let anyone brush their teeth. When children deliberately avoid types of touch that are tolerable or enjoyable to most other people, they are said to have *tactile defensiveness.*

Tactile defensiveness can interfere with development in a variety of ways. If your child does not like to be touched lightly by others, she may shrink away from hugs or pats from adults. This kind of reaction may discourage people from spending time with her, and as a result, she may have fewer opportunities to learn social or language skills from them. Her social-emotional development could also be delayed if she avoids playing with other children because they may bump her, grab her hand, or otherwise make her feel insecure and uncomfortable.

In addition, children with mental retardation may have trouble learning feeding skills if they have *oral tactile defensiveness (hypersensitivity)*—that is, if they dislike touch in and around their mouth. Some children with this problem dislike foods with certain textures, tastes, or temperatures. For example, they may refuse to eat mashed potatoes, yogurt, or anything else with a smooth texture. Other children may refuse all meats or all fruits and vegetables. Still others will accept only a particular brand of food they like. If they are forced to eat something they do not like, children with this hypersensitivity may gag. Needless to say, oral tactile defensiveness can make mealtimes highly stressful for both children and their parents.

Children with mental retardation may be hypersensitive to other sensations as well. For example, sudden movements or loud sounds may bother your child more than you would expect. Then again, she may be undersensitive (hyposensitive) to other sensations. For example, she might not be able to feel a light touch on her skin. Or she might not be able to keep track of what's in her mouth unless it has a strong taste or is very textured, or unless she overstuffs her mouth.

Children with mental retardation may also have problems related to difficulty with their senses of movement and balance. For example, they may have low muscle tone—that is, their muscles have more flexibility or "give" than usual. Low muscle tone is especially common in children with fragile X or Down syndrome. Low muscle tone can affect development in several areas, depending on the parts of the body that are affected. For example, if your child has low muscle tone in her trunk, she may be unable to sit upright for long periods during circle time at school. She may expend too much effort sitting up to pay attention to what the teacher is saying, and will have to work harder to remain in an upright position while she is using her arms and hands to write, use scissors, or do other fine motor activities.

Children with mental retardation may also have trouble learning fine motor skills such as fastening and unfastening buttons and zippers because they have problems telling where their hands are in relationship to their body. Or they may not be able to gauge their body's reaction to gravity or know how to keep themselves upright when fast compensations are required. This may make it harder for them to learn to walk on uneven surfaces, easily sit down in a chair, or jump into the air and land on their feet. Feeling insecure and uncertain about movements obviously does not help a child develop feelings of competence or independence. On the contrary, it can make a child very fearful or irritable.

He ate baby food pretty well up until a certain point, but after a while it just became "don't get near me with that. I won't have anything to do with that." He never had a thing to do with mashed potatoes. That went flying. His favorite foods right now are French toast, hamburgers, hot dogs, French fries. He's only gotten to the point of eating meat like hamburgers and hot dogs within the past couple of years. He's always liked macaroni and cheese and spaghetti. He runs in real cycles with foods. French toast and waffles he has liked for a long time. He does not like eggs.

She doesn't like anything in her mouth. We just found out in the last couple of years that she has what is called a hypersensitive tongue. So she likes things that are fairly solid in texture. She won't have anything to do with anything mushy.

He doesn't like to be touched a lot—not by people, not by things. And he doesn't like his pants to be up around his stomach or too tight. He pushes them down below his belly button. He doesn't like them on his waistline.

Back before Brian was a year old, I thought, "He's going to die on us because he's going to choke." He has that much trouble even with taking children's aspirin. He hates the flavor. Maybe he is doing it on purpose or whatever, but to me, he's not a bratty kid acting up, but somebody who is really frightened. The coughing and inhaling at the same time scares me to death. I called the Emergency Room one time because I thought it had gone into his lungs and I wanted to know.

Your Child's Social-Emotional Development

Children with mental retardation usually acquire social skills more slowly than other children. For example, a five-year-old with mental retardation may act like a younger preschooler, clinging to her parents instead of joining in to play with other children. Once she does begin to play, she may prefer to play alongside other children, rather than *with* them. And she will not be as adept at negotiating with other children to get her own way—for example, to play the game that she wants to play. Because children with mental retardation do not act like other children their age, other children may sometimes avoid them. This may be especially a problem if your child has behavior difficulties such as hyperactivity, impulsiveness, aggressiveness, excessive shyness, unusual movements, or distractibility. Obviously, if other children avoid your child, it can compound her difficulties in developing social skills. She may have fewer opportunities to socialize with children who behave appropriately, and therefore, fewer opportunities to learn how to behave appropriately herself.

Children who score in the mild range of mental retardation may be aware of the differences between their skills and those of other children. They may realize that others are making fun of them or shunning them, although they may not know exactly why. This can lead to negative feelings of self-worth. It can also cause them to stay on the sidelines or to be very quiet when they are around normally developing children. This, in turn, reduces their opportunities for developing social skills appropriate for their age. Of course, not all children with mild mental retardation are aware of ridicule and subtle rejection. Many are happy to be included in other children's play in any way, and feel good about themselves no matter how they are treated.

With plenty of practice and appropriate models, most children with mild to moderate mental retardation can learn appropriate social skills for many situations. At home, they learn to say "please" and "thank you," to share, and to ask before borrowing someone else's belongings. At school, they learn how to play appropriately with their classmates (how to start playing with another child, how to maintain the play, and how to solve problems that occur in play); how to take responsibility for their behavior and for their belongings; and how to follow the rules of a game so they can participate. In the community, they learn how to behave appropriately in stores, restaurants, buses, and other public areas.

Because of their cognitive difficulties, though, people with mental retardation never quite become as socially adept as they would otherwise. For example, because of problems with critical thinking, your child may always be more gullible than others. She may spend her money for an offer that most people would recognize as being "too good to be true," or fall for a mean-spirited practical joke. She may also have difficulties knowing *when* it is appropriate to act a particular way. For example, your child may have learned how to start a casual, friendly conversation, but may not realize that the time to start a conversation is not while she is supposed to be working, but during lunch break. In addition, she may have other difficulties during common social contacts, including talking inappropriately to strangers, saying things in a coversation that seem to come "out-of-the-blue," saying the same thing several times in one conversation (perseverating), difficulty maintaining the appropriate body distance, and trouble reading a person's cues to know when a conversation is ending.

===== ✳ =====

She is very outgoing and friendly, but people could take advantage of her too. She is not very discerning. She needs support. I don't know if she'll be able to handle money differently in ten years. But at this point, she would pay $10,000 for something that costs $10.

===== ✳ =====

When she was two years old, she was very happy, but it was difficult to make her laugh. She just didn't seem to see the humor in funny faces. Sometimes she would go into hysterical laughing, but it was at the wall. The first time she laughed, it was at my mother's face. She cracked up and I couldn't figure out why. After that, it got a lot easier to make her laugh, although she still had a very serious face most of the time.

===== ✳ =====

He is so dependent on adults and so trusting. If he walks in the middle of the street, he assumes that everybody is going to come to a screeching halt. He assumes that no one rips you off; that everybody is nice; and that the teacher or Mom will know where to go, so he doesn't have to worry about directions. So if I say, "Paul, you tell me where to go and that's where I'll go," he doesn't. He doesn't tell you ahead of time, "Well, you are going to have to turn." Maybe a block later he'll turn around and say something like, "Aren't you going home?"

Our son lives in a large family—three brothers and sisters close to him in age—and in a neighborhood with a lot of kids. He also knows and likes the kids in his class. As a result, I think, his social skills are quite good. He is quite natural in how he socializes and relates to friends. He naturally fits in, plays along, and gets along. He may not be as sophisticated as other kids his age, but his social skills fulfill him.

Your Child's Play Skills

Children with mental retardation are, of course, just as interested in play activities as other children are. But what they are interested in playing and how they play may differ. This is because a child's play skills ordinarily reflect her cognitive and social maturity. Your child may have greater difficulty understanding the rules of games because of cognitive or language problems. Because of social skills delays, she may not be interested in playing interactively with other children as early as she would be otherwise. She

may also be more dependent on others to suggest play activities, keep the play going, or introduce new ideas. For example, she might not think about pushing the car under a chair instead of just across the floor unless someone else shows her how. And because many children with mental retardation prefer routine and repetition, your child may want to play the same game over and over, rather than moving on to newer, more challenging games.

All these differences in how your child plays will affect what she learns. This is because play is an important vehicle for learning and practicing cognitive, social, and language skills. Checkers, for example, gives children practice in cause-effect relationships (if I move this checker here, then my opponent can jump me). Go Fish teaches children about colors, while simultaneously giving them practice in asking questions (using language) in socially appropriate ways. Because children with mental retardation do not play such games as early or as well as other children, there are some differences in what they get from play. Although children with mental retardation benefit from play in the same way as other children do and receive the same type of benefits, they just receive less of that benefit than other children receive.

Most children with mild to moderate mental retardation pick up appropriate play skills and get needed practice, but this requires parental and teacher effort. Children with mental retardation do not always choose to use the ability they have to their fullest advantage. Consequently, they may prefer to play the same game or with the same toy repeatedly to the exclusion of other good play opportunities. Parents and teachers need to coax them into a broad range of play activities so they can develop a wide range of play skills. In the end, although there will be noticable differences in their play skills compared to other children's, they will learn play skills that are challenging and fulfilling to them.

The play skills that children with mental retardation learn are the foundation for good leisure and recreational skills. Children and adults with mental retardation can derive tremendous enjoyment and personal growth from leisure and recreational activities, but this does require work. They need education and practice in making decisions about leisure time. For example, they need to learn to seek a balanced range of leisure activities rather than to repeat familiar activities over and over. Learning leisure skills is usually a joint home and school effort. With practice, children and adults with mental retardation can enjoy a broad range of activities like everyone else.

As a result of computer games, he's understanding baseball a lot more. He's got this game where you control the players on the team, you control the types of pitches, the types of swings. Now he can sit and watch a game on television and understand it. He asks questions and comprehends what is going on, which he couldn't do until this year. He's a lot more interested in it from that perspective. But he is still not anxious to go out there and just play and throw.

Ricky plays so much like other kids—he runs, jumps, throws, shoots a basketball, and catches like other kids. Someone who didn't know that he had mental retardation might not be able to see any differences in how he plays.

Although Kimberly's heart is so much in what she does, her skills are just not as polished, fluid, or sophisticated as her playmates'. It is those little differences that strangers might overlook, but which are obvious to me, that remind me of her mental retardation and its many obvious and subtle consequences.

Your Child's Future Development

The preceding sections have pointed out in a general way how development is affected in children with mental retardation. But you probably still have questions about *your* child's development that you would like very specific answers to. Undoubtedly, you would like to know what to expect of your child's behavior and development over the short term as well as the long term. Will she walk and talk? Will she learn to read and do math? Will she graduate from high school? Will she live on her own and contribute to society? Will she marry and have children?

As discussed above, it is impossible to predict precisely *any* child's eventual potential at an early age. So you may not find anyone who is willing to hazard an answer to these types of questions. Instead, it may be more useful to concentrate on what your child is able to do at this time, and work from there. Try asking for a range of possibilities of what to expect a year from now, rather than too far into the future. As Chapter 4 explains, the best beginning point is often a comprehensive developmental assessment—an evaluation by a group of professionals to determine your child's capabilities and problems in all developmental areas. This assessment will help education professionals plan the best ways to help your child maximize her potential.

Whatever the results of your child's assessment, it is important to remember that development is a lifelong process. Even though she has mental retardation, your child can continue to learn new skills and improve on old ones all her life. And because of steadily improving options for job training and living arrangements, you can expect her to grow into the most independent adulthood possible. Today many adults with mild mental retardation live in apartment settings with only minimal supervision. They may need help with budgeting, balancing a bank account, or figuring out the public transportation system. But they can often help support themselves through skilled or semi-skilled jobs such as gardener, maintenance worker, office clerk, child-care worker, or short-order cook, to name just a few. Although adults with moderate mental retardation usually require more supervision in living and vocational settings, they too can move out of their parents' home and find challenging, fulfilling jobs. Their jobs might include performing repetitive tasks such as counting, sorting, preparing mailings, or assembling products. As the next section explains, *now* is the time to begin to lay the foundation for your child's future.

There are a lot of things Nina can do. It's just that we will have to find a slot that matches her skills. I don't think she should do a repetitive job that doesn't let her use her skills. It's going to be a matter of finding somebody who believes in her and who can deal with her missing skills.

I would sell my soul to the devil to know today how our son will turn out in the future <u>and</u> to know what to do now to make sure he turns out OK.

We know where Sandy's going to be. We have her niche all picked out for her. We're a "Joe Catholic" family, so we figure it would be nice if she could clean house or cook or clean dishes in a convent or rectory or something like that. It would be close to home, she could earn a few bucks. . . . Granted, her capabilities might turn out to be a little less or a little more, but we have an idea of what we want for her.

Almost everything I do or think about is aimed at Ricky's future—making sure that what he does today builds toward a future in which he is capable and functional. Ricky, on the other hand, lives entirely in the present—he lives for the moment. These two life-views often conflict. You can't make Ricky care about the distant future (or even the near future). If you want to teach him skills that he will need for the future, you have to make learning those skills enjoyable to him in the present.

Helping Your Child Develop

As explained earlier, two major factors influence a child's development: her biological capacity to develop, and the experiences that help mold her development. Although you cannot alter your child's biological make-up, you *can* make sure she receives the stimulation and teaching that will help her maximize her potential.

Experts believe that the sooner children with mental retardation begin to receive assistance aimed at helping them learn, the more likely they are to reach the outer limits of their developmental potential. This is because later development builds upon early development. If early skills such as spoken language are mastered, there is a better chance that related later skills such as reading will also be maximized.

Today, the primary way of maximizing early development is through early intervention and preschool programs. As Chapter 5 explains, these are educational and therapeutic programs that tailor-make plans to address your child's unique learning needs and strengths. They are aimed at helping children aged birth through five overcome delays in development as soon as possible so they can learn as much as possible, as quickly as possible. This intervention is then continued through your public school's special education program.

In many communities, services for qualified children under three are provided free of charge, under the terms of a federal law known as Public Law 99-457. In other areas, you might need to pay for the services of private teachers and therapists. Sometimes their services are covered by medical insurance. Other parents, as well as ARCs and local advocacy groups, are excellent sources of information on the services available in your area. Once your child reaches the age of three, Public Law 94-142 (new number, Public Law 101-476) ensures that she will receive the individualized special education services she needs without charge. Chapter 8 explains exactly what your child is entitled to under federal laws.

As your child becomes involved in early intervention and special education programs, you will discover that parent involvement is usually considered crucial. This is because children with mental retardation need a great deal of practice both at home and school to master skills. In addition, your assistance is needed to help your child learn to apply skills learned in school or early intervention to home and community settings. Chapter 5 reviews ways of becoming involved in your child's early intervention or special education program; Chapter 6 describes ways to teach your child at home.

Conclusion

One of the sweetest rewards of parenthood is watching your child grow from a tiny, squalling newborn to a unique individual with talents, interests, and a personality all her own. As the parent of a child with mental retardation, you will not be deprived of this pleasure. Although your child may not be able to achieve as much as other children, she can still learn an amazing array of skills and make enormous progress toward independence.

It's true that as your child makes her way along the road to adulthood, you may have to modify some of your hopes and dreams for her. She may never be able to read a comic strip or a lengthy novel, she may not drive a car or be the fastest runner in school. For now, though, try not to set limits on what your child might eventually achieve. Focus on what your child can do today and little by little help her develop the skills she will need tomorrow.

Three

Getting the Diagnosis

Maria P. Dudish*

For the first two blissful weeks of her life, our daughter was a healthy, thriving baby. Then the fabric of our family life slowly began to unravel. First Tara developed a heart murmur; then one of her feet started to turn in. On our monthly visits to the pediatrician, the doctor began pointing out subtle differences in Tara: her eyes were far apart, her ears were high, some of her movements were strange. When Tara was ten months old, the doctor referred her to our hospital's genetics and neurology departments for evaluations. Although they found nothing specifically wrong, they recommended that we enroll Tara in an infant stimulation program.

The doctors' concerns were nothing compared to ours. My husband, Dave, and I didn't have to hear their carefully couched opinions that Tara was "slow" or "delayed" to know that she was not progressing as she should. We had only to look around at other children to see how different she was. When Tara was ten months old, for example, we started taking her to Gymboree, an exercise class for young children. Unlike the other children, Tara couldn't crawl or sit up from a lying position. Instead, she just lay there, often crying. It was so obvious that she was physically and developmentally behind the other children. I remember asking the other moms how they taught their kids to roll over. I felt very alone and my throat

* Maria Dudish is the family coordinator of the Montgomery Primary Achievement Center, a preschool for children with developmental delays in Silver Spring, Maryland. She holds a B.A. in social work from West Chester State University in Pennsylvania and is presently doing graduate work in family studies at the University of Maryland.

burned as I held back the tears. Although the instructor encouraged me to keep working with Tara, I felt that Tara did not belong in the class. Worse, I didn't know where she *did* belong.

During the year Tara was in Gymboree, Dave and I struggled with inconsistent and fragmented information about our daughter's problems. At one point, our pediatrician told us that Tara's gross motor skills were delayed. I specifically asked him if Tara had mental retardation. My eldest sister had profound mental retardation, and my parents had known since her birth. If Tara had mental retardation, I wanted to *know*. But the doctor said no, Tara was just a little delayed.

Because none of the medical or educational professionals ever gave us any reason to believe otherwise, we kept clinging to the hope that Tara would one day "catch up" with other children. Friends, neighbors, and relatives knew we were beside ourselves with grief and frustration, and constantly encouraged us to believe that Tara would outgrow her problems. It was not that Dave and I were denying the problem. We were misguided, and deep down we knew it.

Finally, when Tara was making the transition from one pre-school to another, she was given a psychological evaluation. Not once during that year were the results ever discussed with me. And yet, the school personnel had every opportunity to let me know that something was amiss. I was in constant contact with the teachers and therapists. I observed her class and therapies, and school personnel visited my home regularly throughout the year. At the end of the school year, when Tara was four, I received the psychological report stating that she fell into the moderate/severe range of mental retardation. *That is how we found out.*

Before *your* child was born, you undoubtedly had your own special potpourri of dreams and expectations for him. By reading books and magazines, attending classes, watching TV, or talking with friends, you had likely developed a mental snapshot of what life "should" be like once your baby joined the family. And although you may have felt an occasional twinge of worry, the idea that something could go seriously wrong was probably far from your mind. The possibility of having a less-than-perfect child was un-thinkable.

Most parents eventually have to part with some of their more unrealistic expectations for their child. Not every child can grow up to be president. But when your child has mental retardation, the process is painfully speeded up. You come face to face with reality much too abruptly and must deal with emotions that can be excrutiatingly intense. These feelings are equally painful whether your child is diagnosed when he is several hours, months, or years old.

If your child was born with a genetic condition such as Down syndrome or Williams syndrome, or was born prematurely or after complications, you may have received the diagnosis almost immediately. At the very least, you were probably told of the possibility of developmental delays. Getting the news so quickly can be doubly overwhelming. You expected the hospital stay to be a time of rest and recovery; a time when Mom and Dad could spend special moments with each other and the new baby. Instead, if your child has a health problem, mother and child may be separated. You may not be able to hold your child, and there may even be talk of surgery.

While all this is happening, you must also deal with your emotions and those unanswered questions you may not even be able to verbalize. What is happening to our child? Will he live? Can we take care of our child? What did we do wrong? If your doctor is not open, sensitive, and honest or does not explain information so you can understand it, your sadness, disbelief, and confusion grow.

Typically, both parents feel as if their world is shattered, the walls have caved in, and their minds are in a whirlwind. During the initial stages, the father may bear the additional burden of thinking that he is expected to be strong and take care of his wife and child (or children). He may have to explain to others that "things didn't go quite the way we expected," "the baby is sick," or "there are a few problems." He may feel sad, confused, and left out, but many times his feelings are ignored. Perhaps he has a hard time expressing these feelings, or wonders if he has a right to express them.

The first few days are just as confusing and devastating for the mother. Perhaps the baby was whisked away for tests or intensive medical care right after birth. The mother might be given only the sketchiest explanations of what is wrong, so that she is left to agonize over her baby's chances of survival. If the possibility of mental retardation is mentioned, she may be stunned by the number and magnitude of new worries that she faces. Whereas her biggest worries before may have been about learning to breastfeed or about giving the baby a bath, she may now feel as if her baby's whole future is in jeopardy. She may resist bonding with the baby because she is having a hard time accepting the whole situation or is afraid it may not live. Or she may become so obsessed with taking care of the baby that she won't even let anyone else hold it. On top of everything else, the mother's coping skills are often undermined by going through the physical ordeal of giving birth. Both parents feel cheated of shouting out the good news of their baby's birth.

When parents do not get the news until months or years after their child leaves the hospital, the emotional turmoil is just as great, but for different reasons. If you suspect that something is wrong with your child's development, you are trapped in the sad beginning stages of your own healing process. Because you don't get a diagnosis or straight answers, you are caught between trying not to be too pessimistic and trying to be realistic. You may vacillate between not wanting to know the awful truth and not wanting to lose valuable time. You may even hesitate to discuss your concerns with your spouse for fear he or she may be thinking the same thing. There is a constant ache as you grope for answers—any explanation as to why your child is the way he is. You may go from doctor to doctor, have test after test, in an effort to reach some substantial conclusions. Adding to your confusion and frustration are the mixed signals you receive from others: "He will outgrow it"; "He seems to be catching up." You may get the impression that you can "fix" the problem by reading books, buying educational toys, delving into hours and hours of physical, occupational, or speech and language therapy. Your life is consumed with your child, and it is exhausting. On top of everything else are the feelings of guilt, inadequacy, helplessness, and "why me?"

Unfortunately, there is no magic prescription that can help you feel better about your child's mental retardation. But many parents have an easier time coping with their emotions once they learn to understand and work through their feelings. It can be a slow process with many setbacks, but most parents are eventually able to sort out their emotions and take charge of their life again. This chapter is designed to ease the adjustment process for you so you can then turn your attention to helping your child and your family.

Our son had an Apgar score of 9 when he was born, so we had no clue whatsoever. And the doctors didn't either, obviously. It was kind of a gradual depression that whole first year. Two of my girlfriends also had babies. We would get together for these luncheons and we would take our kids, and my son wasn't doing anything that the other two were doing.

He did what he called genetic studies. He didn't tell us why he was doing these, but he was doing them for two reasons: to test for Down syndrome and to ensure that her sex was female. But he didn't tell us that. We figured it out after the fact. Jenny had some swollen genitalia.

The doctor started to pick her up and do those floppy tests where he would see how her legs went and how her head went up if she was sort of thrown up or whatever. He then said, "Well, I'm probably being overly cautious, but maybe we ought to see a neurologist."

After he tested her in the hospital, we had to wait about a month for certain tests to come back because some were sent to California. I hit the books. I decided on my own what she had. I called him back once to say that I thought she had Down syndrome because she had the epicanthal fold. He was obviously annoyed that I was doing some diagnosing. He said, "Where are you getting those books?" When I said that my husband had a lot of books around, the doctor said to stay away from those, that they were dangerous.

The doctor was very uncomfortable with the whole issue of what to do with the parents.

I was a wreck.

My doctor called me back and asked, "Do you still have some questions?" I said, "I really think you should see my baby now. Why do you want to wait until next month?" I think he made some comment like "Nothing will change, but if you feel more comfortable, then okay."

I didn't become hysterical in the doctor's office because I knew already. I had decided when she was maybe fifteen months old that she was not just motorically involved, but that she was obviously going to have lots of problems.

We heard "mental retardation" thrown around, but nobody was going to take a stand on what she had.

There was no diagnosis; they didn't know.

I remember when people actually wanted me to go to this infant stimulation center, and I would say, "Are you telling me that my child's retarded?" And they would say, "No, I'm not saying that; I just think he might have some gross motor delays." This was back when he hadn't hit a year yet.

Half of the people would say, "She will outgrow it." She was not crawling yet, and they'd say, "She's just lazy; get her moving." Some of my friends would do that.

Coping with Your Feelings

The first feelings you had about your child's diagnosis were probably feelings that focused on yourself. You felt bad for yourself and for your child. You may have felt as if your life had been turned upside down and that it was impossible to see anything but the negatives. This is a hard stage to get past, but one you can get over if you begin shifting your thinking off of yourself and onto your child.

As parents, we have a tendency to want to "fix" things that are wrong where our children are concerned. When we find out that our child has mental retardation, we want to fix that too. Why? Because he will never have the life we dreamed of. By concentrating on these shattered dreams—what *you* would have wished for your child—you can make yourself miserable. But if you allow yourself to get to know your child, then readjust and refocus your dreams to fit his interests and capabilities, you can begin to make strides toward acceptance.

There's no denying that it takes time to refocus your dreams. I began learning how even before I knew Tara had mental retardation. When she was two, I remember taking her to a popular kids' restaurant with two friends who had children the same age as Tara. The other two children ran around chasing one another and giggling. But Tara, who was still unable to walk, just sat and watched. After lunch was over, I cried in my car all the way home. I envisioned Tara feeling very inadequate and isolated because she couldn't keep up with the others. I pictured her yelling, "Hey, guys, wait for me!"

When I got home, I called my mother and told her all about the lunch. Instead of commiserating with me about Tara's differences, my mother said something very important. "Did Tara seem upset?" she asked. "No," I said. "Well, maybe she was content watching them run around. Are you feeling bad for Tara or bad for yourself?"

I had to admit I was feeling bad for myself. I knew Tara had enjoyed herself at the restaurant, laughing and crawling around her friends at her own pace. This realization took me one step closer to accepting Tara for who she was, rather than who I wanted her to be. Of course, it didn't begin to prepare me for the emotions I would have when Tara was actually diagnosed with mental retardation, but it was a positive step all the same.

Some of the common emotions parents feel when they learn or suspect that their child has mental retardation have already been mentioned—grief, disbelief or denial, confusion, guilt, inadequacy, helplessness, frustration. But there are also a host of other emotions that it is natural for parents to feel. In fact, parents are sometimes engulfed in so many emotions at once that they aren't quite sure *how* they feel. To make matters worse, they may feel they need to bottle these feelings up because they are "bad" or "shameful." To help reassure you that your feelings, no matter how extreme, are normal, the following sections explore some common reactions.

Confusion

If your child's mental retardation was not diagnosed for months or years, confusion is probably one of the earliest and strongest emotions you felt. Everywhere you turned, it seemed, you got mixed signals. On the one hand, your child visibly lagged behind other children in many areas. But on the other hand, most people gave your child the benefit of the doubt. Family, friends, and even medical professionals constantly deflected your worries with statements such as "He'll catch up" or "Every child is different," or "My baby didn't do this until she was _____." Should you be worried or shouldn't you? Should you trust your gut instincts or what the "experts" are saying? What should you *do?*

After you get a diagnosis, you may be confused for different reasons. You have this enormous responsibility of raising a child who doesn't fit into Dr. Spock's profile of the typical child. You have so many questions, but who do you ask? Not your mother, who raised two "normal" children; not your friends, who may feel just as clueless and helpless. Eventually, you start to find others who can answer your questions. For example, you may join a support group and swap information with other parents who have children with mental retardation. Or your child begins an early intervention program and you meet therapists and teachers with experience in teaching children like yours. Once you start to get answers, though, you still have to figure out which information actually applies to your child. Which of the many kinds of therapy available would help my child? Would he learn better in a mainstreamed or non-mainstreamed school setting?

Coping styles vary, but in general, there are two ways you can cope with confusion. First, you can seek even more information if you are not satisfied with what you already have. Talk to other parents about their experiences and ask them to recommend therapists, teachers, doctors, and other professionals who would be willing to discuss your concerns with you. Second, if you have reached a saturation point and feel you cannot take in another word, stop and take a look at the information you have. Try to at least weed out the information you don't need. Again, ask other parents and professionals for help.

Over time, you will learn what information is and is not important to your child and your family. You will learn to screen information before you accept any of it. And you will realize that it is your family's prerogative to take the time you need to collect information, review options, and make choices based on your family's priorities.

===== ❋ =====

Well, he didn't walk on time, but we didn't necessarily think anything about that. We just thought he was being lazy. He stumbled a lot when he first started walking, but we didn't really think anything about that either. It could have been his inner ears, or that he didn't have that much experience walking—that kind of thing. There were a lot of things that we could have caught onto had we known there was a problem to begin with. In looking back, you can see that you should have caught these things, but you didn't know.

===== ❋ =====

At about three and a half months, I was thinking that my baby was not holding her head up and that she was real floppy and real mushy. Her legs and arms were almost as if they were filled with fluid. Of course they weren't; they were just real mushy.

===== ❋ =====

The doctor would say, "You know, his movements—something just doesn't seem right." I would say, "What do you mean?" and he would be apologetic because he would sense how defensive I was. This was the

beginning of calling Stewart a puzzle. "This is the most puzzling child I
ever saw."

===== ✳ =====

I walked at eighteen months. My mother said she took me to the doctor's
about it. Of course, my mother came up with all those stories, and so did
everybody else. There was Einstein, who didn't talk until he was three,
and then there was somebody else who was brilliant. We have a very
supportive family. I think they were worried. But what could they say?

Helplessness

Helplessness is an emotion that can swamp you both before and
after your child is diagnosed with mental retardation. In the beginning, you feel helpless because you sense that something is wrong,
but no matter what you do, you can't "fix" your child. You may go
overboard reading books on parenting techniques, reading to your
child, signing him up for extra therapy, doing anything you can to
help him catch up. You may turn to family, friends, and professionals
for advice, but nothing they say really helps. You know you should
keep on trying, but sometimes it just seems pointless to even make
an effort.

After the diagnosis, you may feel helpless due to feelings of
inadequacy. You may ask yourself, "How can I help my child when
I don't know where I'm going or what I'm doing?" All of a sudden,
you expect yourself to be an expert for your child . . . and yet you
haven't taken any courses. Your helplessness could surface every
time your child cries and you don't know why. Is he sick or in pain?
No, you find out later that he has tactile defensiveness. (Try explaining *that* to your friends.)

Over the years, I've often felt helpless when confronted with
some new, puzzling behavior. For example, Tara went through
phases of scratching me in the face whenever I tried to get close to
her. Then we dealt with head banging. I tried desperately to learn
why she acted the way she did. I wanted to know what I could do
to stop her from scratching and head banging. Seeing my daughter
in distress and not knowing how I could help her kept my feelings
of helplessness alive for a long time. Finally, I had to admit several
things and add two important phrases to my vocabulary. Number

one was "I don't know." And number two was "Yes, I could use help."

I started getting over my feelings of helplessness when the information I had gathered over the months and years started making sense. Even though I could not cure Tara's disability, I began to see that there was so much I *could do* for and with Tara. More and more I came to understand that, with some adaptations, Tara could enjoy and experience life much the same as any other child. Over time, you too will learn ways to help your child get the most out of life. Professionals and other parents will give you guidance, and, as you get to know your child better, you will devise your own ways of working with her. Do not underestimate your good sense about your child. Most times your instincts are right.

Those tests all came in negative. I wanted an answer: what do we do now?

I wanted them to tell me what to do and when to do it.

She seemed to be making gains, but they were so slow and I was impatient—we were both impatient—thinking "Gee, I'm going to be dragging this child around for a long time and God knows what else is wrong."

Denial

Profound feelings of helplessness can sometimes lead to denial. If parents think there is nothing they can do to make the situation any better, they may stop making that extra effort. Instead, they may simply pretend that there isn't a problem to solve. If they keep up the pretense long enough, the pretense can turn into a reality for them. Rarely, parents may be so unwilling to accept the truth that it is difficult for educational and medical professionals to convince them that their child has mental retardation.

Sometimes one parent accepts the reality of mental retardation while the other denies it. One may become very involved in working with teachers and therapists to help their child, while the other may use work as an excuse to avoid dealing with their child's disability. The parent who accepts their child's mental retardation may come to feel torn between what she believes is true and her spouse's denial.

Although denial is a normal reaction, this emotion can jeopardize your child's future if it continues too long. Unless you can see your child and his special needs for what they are, you will never be able to give him the help he needs to reach his potential. In many cases, taking the time to truly get to know your child can help denial subside. For persistent feelings of denial, talking with other parents in support groups or getting professional counseling as described later in the chapter are perhaps the best remedy.

I called to get an appointment with the geneticist, and they said it would take two months to get an appointment. That was my perfect excuse to say, "Well, forget it."

One thing you get caught up in a little bit is looking for "miracle cures" or people who know somebody who had a kid just like yours who went away to Mexico for a weekend and came back cured. . . .

I thought the mental retardation would go away. Finally I saw someone who set me straight in a minute.

Guilt

Complicating your other emotions may be tremendous feelings of guilt. You may amaze yourself by how many things you can find to feel guilty about. Most parents blame themselves for their child's mental retardation. Mothers automatically go back and examine their pregnancy, labor, and delivery, searching for something—*any-thing*—they might have done to cause this. Parents think, "These things just don't happen; it must have been something I did or didn't do." They forget that unfortunate things—even bad things—do just happen. Unless they were heavy drinkers or drug addicts, parents are no more the cause of their children's mental retardation than they are the cause of plane crashes, earthquakes, or volcanoes. But in the effort to answer the question, "How did this happen?" parents too often find some way to imagine blame. However painful this guilt might be, you should know that it is natural for parents. Parents can also feel guilty about countless other thoughts, feelings, and statements. Maybe you laughed at or teased a child with mental retardation when you were a child. Maybe you looked at another family with a child with a disability and said to yourself, "Phew! Better them than me." Maybe, after finding out that your child has mental retardation, you screamed at your child's doctor or teacher. Maybe you blamed your spouse for your child's condition.

The sources of guilt—real or imagined—are endless. Some say guilt is a useful tool; that it keeps us from doing or saying bad things. But guilt over your child helps no one. You may not be able to avoid it, but if you let it persist for too long, it will prevent you from dealing with life as you now face it. Guilt can become a vicious circle—first you feel guilt, then you feel guilty about feeling guilt, and on and on. Unfortunately, there are no shortcuts to resolving guilt. But eventually, time will soften the edge of your guilt. In time you will recognize that the blame you placed on yourself belongs elsewhere—or nowhere. And as you start to take action and resume your life, you will have less time to focus on guilt.

I felt guilty because I didn't take Paul to the therapist when he was so little. I felt that Paul missed out because he didn't go to her at three months and start a regimen.

I would get myself into a real depression when I would compare her with other kids, because then I felt that maybe it was something that I missed. I still had a lot of that guilt.

I thought there might have been something that went on in the delivery room and everything—that whole thing.

I think I have gotten over the guilt about not being able to be her therapist as much as when she was little. Still, I would love to do more cooking

with her; I should be taking the bus with her and teaching her how to take the bus down to the mall or something; I should teach her more about money.

=== ※ ===

I went in to work two days a week, but once I finished what I needed to at work, I just quit. I felt like my son really needed to be spending more time doing therapy. Then our second child was born and that put things into a nicer perspective, although I was still very rigid about my therapy schedule with our first son.

Uncertainty

If the cause of your child's mental retardation is unknown, this uncertainty can add another dimension to your feelings of guilt. If you knew the reason behind your child's mental retardation, would you somehow be able to make it "better"? Why, out of all children, did *your* child have to be born with mental retardation? Did you or didn't you do something that caused your child's mental retardation? Could you have done something to prevent it? These questions can gnaw at you forever if you let them.

The fact is, the majority of parents never find out the reason behind their child's mental retardation. That is small consolation if you are thinking of having other children and want to know whether your other children may also have mental retardation. But if geneticists and physicians have ruled out the major known causes of mental retardation, they usually think it's unlikely that it will happen again. You may just have to accept, as I did, that you were an innocent bystander. There are so many things that can go wrong during pregnancy and childbirth and many of them are out of our control.

Rather than torture yourself by continually asking WHY, try asking questions for which there are definite answers. How can I help my child learn to communicate better? Where can I find out more about mental retardation? When can my child start early intervention? Although you may always wonder why your child has mental retardation, if you can start to get answers to your other questions, the uncertainty may trouble you less.

=== ※ ===

They did all kinds of difficult studies. She was so tiny and they were putting holes in her, just testing which size needle to use. It was real difficult . . . and then they came up with nothing. I thought I was going to have an answer.

==== ✳ ====

Really, it's a little easier in some ways to have a child with Down syndrome. It is one of the major causes of mental retardation, so you have this big group you can get together with.

Resentment

Parents of children with mental retardation live in a world just ripe for resentment. You are surrounded by "normal" children and "normal" families. It is not hard to resent what you see as their "easy street." It doesn't help you to hear parents of "normal" children complain about what seem to you to be ludicrously minor problems or setbacks.

I know a father who was driven almost to the point of screaming by a friend who fretted and cried endlessly over her newborn daughter's slightly deformed ear. This father thought his friend was totally insensitive to his life. He thought, "Get real; try my problems on for size for one minute and you'll really have something to fret about." Mostly he remembers thinking that a good hair style would solve her "problem," but what would solve his? He resented her and parents like her tremendously. It was part of longing for the world he belonged to before his child's diagnosis.

I, too, was almost overpowered by resentment at times. Whenever I got together with friends for coffee or lunch, I remember feeling enraged at their so-called problems with their children. I'm sure they were not even aware of how I felt, but, I was very careful to cover up my heartache and wear a smile. I didn't want anyone to know that I felt sad or disappointed about Tara. So, I kept it in—but with every meeting with friends, I felt these feelings grow into resentment. I found myself judging them: "I'd like to see how *you* would handle my situation."

Resentment is a difficult emotion to leave behind you. Because your child is always "different," there is ample opportunity to resent other parents. Over the years, there are countless times each day you can see differences between your child and "normal" children.

It is a short—and natural—step to feeling resentful. But as your acceptance of your child grows, the differences between him and other children become less important and, in time, less noticeable to you. You may also find, as I did, that eventually you can share with friends how you truly feel about things in your life. It can be a great relief to know you can be honest without feeling guilty. Hard as it may be to imagine now, your resentment *will* fade.

When Ricky was born, I resented the way my parents and siblings looked to me to reassure them—as if I was responsible for making them feel better. I resented and still resent that it never crossed their minds and still doesn't that I grieved for my son's condition.

My cure for resentment is just to focus on my kid and to ignore other people. Because doing the right thing by my kid has nothing to do with what other people think, say, or do. I may find people petty, self-absorbed, and shallow, but obsessing on this does not help my kid. Plus, my child never notices this, anyway.

I think you have to give people a break. After all, any parent would be upset about any problem their child had, regardless of how it compares to other problems. People focus on their problems—it's their lives. They don't have (and are not obligated because of me) to have a broader perspective on life and disabilities. People are not obligated to feel lucky when I feel unlucky.

Shock

No matter how strongly you may have suspected that something was "wrong" with your child, the news that he has mental retardation still comes as a shock. The day I read Tara's diagnosis in the psychological report, I felt totally numb. My heart was beating so fast. I was sure I had misread the information. I kept reading it over and over, thinking it couldn't be right. I read the report out loud to my husband. I kept asking, "Why didn't anyone tell us?"

In fact, shock is a normal reaction to a traumatic situation. To keep you from becoming too overwhelmed, your mind instinctively shuts down until it is ready to come to terms with reality.

===== ※ =====

When our son got into a preschool program, that's when we really found out that he tested in the mentally retarded range. That was the first time that we really knew. It wasn't so much that it was surprising, it was just hard hearing it. I can remember leaving the psychologist's office and crying all the way home. I didn't hear the rest of the hour conversation that we had. I mean, I know that he told me all of these wonderful things about Matthew, but I just couldn't hear that. All I kept hearing was "mentally retarded." I tried to call my neighbor and she wasn't home. Then I called my mother and told her, and the first thing out of her mouth was, "So what? Does that change Matthew?" I just kind of sat down for a minute and said, "She's right."

Anger

People get angriest about things they cannot control. And receiving a diagnosis of mental retardation is definitely a situation you cannot control. You may be justifiably angry. You may be angry at your child's doctor for not telling you sooner or for telling you before you were ready. You may be angry at someone or something for causing your child's mental retardation. You may be angry at your spouse or family for failing to support you when you needed it most. You may be angry at yourself for feeling so helpless. Or you may simply be angry at the cold, hard, unalterable fact that your child has mental retardation.

One way to overcome anger is to confront it head-on. Many times, this means confronting someone face to face and telling them why you are angry, how their actions or words made you feel, and how else they could have acted that would have been more effective. Properly channeled, this very specific anger can be used to win positive changes in your child's life. For example, anger that your child has not been placed in the most appropriate educational setting might motivate you to fight for a better placement. Or anger at the lack of appropriate job-training opportunities in your community may inspire you to join with other parents in pressing your legislators for increased funding.

Anger is only a positive force if you know why you are angry and can think through a plan of action to produce change. When you cannot pinpoint your anger, it can consume your life and keep you from dealing effectively with the situation. You may find yourself just feeling lousy. Or you might feel like crying or throwing things for no special reason. In the beginning, I had periods where I would walk around like a zombie, aware of my pain, but not strong enough to act on my anger.

Sometimes you can take the edge off of this kind of generalized anger if you talk to someone—a friend, a neighbor, a relative, a doctor, a teacher. If talking to one of these people doesn't make you feel better, or if you don't know anyone you feel comfortable talking to, someone in your child's education program may be able to help. A school counselor or therapist trained in the field of disabilities within the family may be able to help you work through your anger. Don't feel ashamed and don't feel like a failure if you need to ask for help. It takes great courage and awareness to seek the help you need.

At the parent-infant program, mine was the kid who screamed during physical therapy and hated it. I used to get mad because she would seem to be making less progress than a lot of the kids. A lot of the kids had Down syndrome and seemed to be doing really well as babies. I was depressed that my child didn't seem to be making as much progress as they were. I was angry at the staff, angry at those other kids who were doing better than mine.

The doctor delayed in confirming his strong belief that my son had Down syndrome. So, for a week we sat waiting for news that we knew would come, all the time asking the doctor to just tell us. It wasn't until a nurse casually mentioned it to us that it really hit home. I have been angry at that doctor ever since for being more concerned about covering his ass than in reaching out to us.

Sometimes I get angry at my son for his mental retardation. I think I start by being frustrated by some limitation or problem his mental retardation creates, and then transfer the anger to him.

═══ ※ ═══

I don't think my anger is a positive force. Being angry at some unfair situation doesn't really motivate me to do things for my daughter. I get the most accomplished for my kid when I am excited about something positive that I may be able to make happen.

Relief

You may actually be relieved when you are told your child has mental retardation. This is particularly true if you have been struggling for months or years to understand why your child cannot keep up with other children. Relief may strike you as an inappropriate reaction to getting such devastating news. But it is actually quite a helpful response. Your relief comes because you realize that at long last you can give your child the help he needs, rather than wasting time going down dead ends. You can now start concentrating on daily issues, rather than pinning your hopes on some vague future event that might change your child and your life. And you can take some of the pressure off yourself to "fix" your child's problems.

In my case, relief came after I spoke to a developmental pediatrician who confirmed that Tara had mental retardation. After doing several initial tests and studying her whole file, the doctor sat down and talked with me for an hour. Simply and clearly, she answered all my questions: What was mental retardation? What did the different levels of functioning mean? What would Tara's overall prognosis be? That conversation opened my eyes. Now I could focus on Tara and what her real needs were. I had gone the full circle and saw Tara in a better light. Now I knew there was a reason for her slow development, and that there were things I could do to help her learn. Yes, my daughter had mental retardation, and I walked out feeling a little sad. But I also felt so much lighter. I had found my answer; I finally had a starting point.

======= ⁕ =======

One reason people want a diagnosis is that they need it; they just have to hear it. And yet I'm afraid that I would have put limitations on her if I had gotten the diagnosis earlier.

======= ⁕ =======

From the moment that the doctor told me, I thought, "OK, so he tested within that range." It was no big deal because I already knew my son.

======= ⁕ =======

I sort of knew something was wrong, so when they said something was wrong I think I accepted it then. That's not to say I didn't cry and that's not to say I wasn't mad, but I knew something was wrong.

Grief

When you have a child with mental retardation, grief may seem to be your constant companion. This is not a stage that you move through in the early days, and then blithely get on with your life. Often, as your child grows and changes, so does your grief. In the beginning, for example, you may mourn the loss of the normal, perfect child you dreamed of, and the loss of normal family life. Later, you may grieve that your child can't keep up with what the neighborhood children are learning and doing. And all your life you may grieve to think that for all your love and support, you can never make your child's mental retardation go away.

If you suspected that something was "wrong" with your child for months or years before he was diagnosed, you are probably no stranger to grief. Even before I had a label for Tara's delays, I was often consumed by sadness when I compared my daughter's achievements with other children's. These feelings were especially acute when I visited a friend who had a child six weeks younger than Tara. As time went on, it became very hard for me to visit without becoming sad and depressed. While I was still carrying my two-year-old who couldn't walk or utter a sound, I had to listen to my friend complain about concerns I would have given anything to have: "She gets into everything"; "She talks my ear off." Another time, Tara and I were at church where the second graders were receiving First Holy Communion. One of the children receiving communion was a little boy with cerebral palsy who had been in Tara's early intervention program. I felt so proud of that little boy, but also very sad that Tara wasn't yet ready to receive communion.

My grief finally became more manageable when I was able to look at my daughter for who she was. As I began to take pride in her achievements, no matter how small, comparisons shrank in importance. True, I still felt twinges of grief every now and then when something happened to remind me of how far behind her peers Tara was. But I gradually came to see that what mattered was not what Johnny-down-the-street could do, but what Tara could (and couldn't) do with our encouragement. When Tara took her first steps independently, my husband and I were overjoyed. Our daughter was making slow, but steady progress; she was doing the best she could and deserved to have her accomplishments appreciated.

We both felt that we were never going to be happy again, that this was not a normal life and that everybody else was leading a normal life but us, and that we were not going to. We were even thinking of going on vacation once but decided not to because we thought we would just be miserable there too.

I would take her to K-Mart or Sears for a picture and they couldn't make her laugh. I was getting really sad about doing that. I just remember how I hated to take her, but I felt like I had to. I remember going with a friend whose daughter was about three months older. Of course, I could always say that her kid was more advanced because she was three months older, but then I would look back at three months ago when we had gone for pictures previously, and her daughter really was doing better than mine.

I recall rocking him once, crying, thinking "But I want you to be able to be married and be happy. I don't want people to look at you."

═══ ✷ ═══

When I was in the infant program and the class for two-year-olds with her, some of the parents looked like they were real put-together. They were laughing and having a good time together, and I thought, "God, that's really weird. How can they do that?" I really did not think that I would ever be happy.

Betrayal

After the news of my daughter's mental retardation sank in, the deepest emotion I felt was betrayal. Why hadn't anyone at school told me that Tara had mental retardation? I had always trusted her teachers and her doctors, and yet they let me learn my daughter's diagnosis second-hand. How could they be so indifferent to our needs and concerns?

Frequently medical and educational professionals hesitate to tell parents that their child may have mental retardation. Although teachers and therapists may suspect that a child has mental retardation, they may delay telling the parents for several reasons. First, as discussed in Chapter 4, some professionals claim that you cannot be sure of a true diagnosis of mental retardation until a child is five. As a result, there may be a policy at the school or program that teachers and therapists are not allowed to suggest to a parent that their child may have mental retardation. The school may fear lawsuits if a child is incorrectly labeled. Second, if a child does not have a diagnosis, education professionals may not want to create a conflict with the child's pediatrician. Finally, both education and medical professionals may hesitate to offer a diagnosis simply because they don't want to be the bearer of bad news. It is hard, hurtful information to give, and no one wants to be the bad guy. Many teachers and doctors just feel unequipped to deal with parents' initial reactions and therefore wait for someone else to do the dirty work.

Of course, none of this excuses the experts' behavior. Professionals *ought* to be upfront with parents and not withhold information that can be used to help your child. Chances are, you have a right to feel betrayed. But the worst thing you can do is to let these feelings turn you and the professionals into adversaries. The only way to ensure that your child receives the best possible medical care and education is to work as a team with your child's doctors, teachers, and therapists. Now that your child has a diagnosis, you and the professionals must share information about your child openly and frequently so that everyone has a clear understanding of his needs. So, even if you think you can never find it in your heart to forgive these professionals completely, for your child's sake, you must put aside your feelings.

We don't care what kind of news we hear as long as it's the truth. The problem with the teacher was that she led us astray all year long. We were led to believe all year long that "she's doing good, she's doing good." And then at the end of the year, the teacher said that she's at the bottom of her class, she's doing terrible. That was a slap in my face and I'll never forget it.

Everybody's afraid of lawsuits. I guess people are all in a position where they don't have the authority to say what they probably would really like to say or what they know to be true.

When our daughter's first infant program referred us to another program, I asked, "Why are you referring her somewhere else?" And they said, "I think it would just be better for her." I said, "But why would it be better?" They said, "She needs the structure." I asked, "Why, what is this all leading to?" The answer was, "Well, she's still pretty young. . . . We can't label her." They're in the teaching profession, but they cannot say somebody is retarded even though they are retarded. I have a problem with that because mental retardation is not the flu; it doesn't go away. You either have it or you don't.

"Off the cuff, just tell me." "Off the cuff"—I don't know how many times we said that phrase—"just tell us." I'd say, "I won't sue you, I promise.

I'll sign something that says I won't sue you . . . just tell me what's wrong." They still wouldn't tell us what they thought.

===== ❋ =====

When Jenny was eighteen months and we had a lot of "if" questions, one doctor said that she was probably going to be physically delayed, but not mentally or socially delayed. That same person then turned around as if she didn't remember saying that, and then plunged into a label of mental retardation. She said, "I told you she was going to be like this. Of course you know she's retarded."

Shame

Although public attitudes toward people with disabilities are slowly improving, the words "mental retardation" still have a certain stigma attached to them. Sadly, pockets of our society still view mental retardation as something to be ashamed of. And there are still people who use words such as "retard" or "retarded" as the ultimate insult. Others may use "retarded" to mean ignorant, foolish, or ridiculous; nevertheless, the word wounds *you*.

As a member of this society, you have probably encountered prejudice against people with mental retardation. And now that your own child has been diagnosed with mental retardation, you may find it hard to shake off those old perceptions. Even though you know in your heart that your child's mental retardation is nothing to be ashamed of, at times you may still feel embarrassed by her condition or her behavior. For my part, I often felt ashamed when Tara was with normally developing children whose parents were unfamiliar with the world of special needs. Many times I found myself making excuses or apologizing for Tara—especially when her behavior left something to be desired. Not only did Tara's crying, head banging, pinching, and scratching embarrass me for her sake, but it also embarrassed me to think that others would view me as an "inadequate" parent.

Getting acquainted with other families of children with special needs can help you learn to cope with your embarrassment. Not only can they let you in on some practical tips for handling behavior problems, but they can also help you see that your child and her behavior are not as out of the ordinary as you may think. A good sense of humor helps, too. Take pride in what your child can do.

Coping Strategies

Take Your Time

After your child receives a diagnosis, you may feel pressure to make immediate decisions about therapies or other services. But when your emotions are still in a turmoil, you probably cannot make the wisest choices about your child's future. Even if you *feel* in control of your emotions, you still lack information about mental retardation and ways of minimizing its effects. Rather than rushing into anything, it is better to wait until you have mustered the facts and the frame of mind to make the best decision.

Eventually you will be able to face the future and resume a more normal way of life. But in the beginning, don't hurry things. Take your time wrestling with your emotions. Everyone has their own rate and style of coping, and your way will likely be different than anyone else's. Take your time, too, in gathering the information you need to help you understand mental retardation and how you can best help your child. And take your time getting back into the swing of things—your job, your household responsibilities, your social life. If you don't feel up to working on that promotion, mowing the lawn, or accepting a dinner invitation, let it slide. Others will understand that you need time to adjust to the tremendous changes in your life; you should, too.

There's a point where you just have to take things a day at a time. You just have to wait and see what the situation is. Certain things in the future you just can't worry about too much. I try to take it a day at a time, but I have a tendency to worry more about Jenny than the other two because most probably Mandy and Melissa will get married and have families of their own. But with Jenny that won't be true.

I went to the National Down Syndrome Convention when he was about a year old. I enjoyed everything until after the banquet when the teenagers were going to dance. Then I was uncomfortable. To see someone who was more obviously retarded . . . I knew they were having a good time, but it made me uncomfortable. I didn't want to deal with

that yet. **As far as I'm concerned, every little child with Down syndrome is gorgeous. But then they become a little bit less cute, a little bit. . . .**

Share Your Feelings

Some parents have an easier time opening up about their emotions than others. For my husband and me, Tara was always the main topic of conversation after her diagnosis. We discussed all our fears and frustrations, and we were constantly on the phone with our parents and siblings. Many parents, though, may not feel up to talking about their child's mental retardation with anyone. For example, you might feel you need to "protect" loved ones from the news. But you will discover that sharing your feelings—with your spouse, if nobody else—is key to your emotional and physical survival. If you vent your feelings, you will often find that your spouse is going through the same emotions. And if you express your worst fears, you may together be able to devise a way to get them under control.

Like you, your spouse may feel that his emotions are abnormal or too extreme. Consequently, the two of you should try to be non-judgmental when sharing your feelings. Try to foster an open, accepting atmosphere in which you both feel it is "safe" to express yourself honestly.

Creating the right atmosphere for sharing feelings can be tricky. Every relationship is unique, so there is no one right formula for successful communication. But here are a few suggestions that *may* help:

1. Just say it. Sometimes just coming out with what is on your mind can get a discussion started. Don't try to plan out what you want to say. Just say what you feel. At the least, it may be enough to get your spouse's attention.
2. Don't judge. Nothing kills communication deader than criticizing someone's feelings. Let your spouse say whatever he or she wants without comment, rebuttal, or critique. Even if you blame your spouse for your child's mental retardation or feel some other emotion you think would upset your spouse to hear, it is important to share your feelings. Otherwise, these feelings are bound to come between you and affect your abilities to work with your spouse as a team. Also, try not to over-analyze what is said. Remember that feelings

are usually straightforward. Fear, shame, guilt, and anger are not complicated.

3. Find a comfortable place to talk—someplace where you won't have to yell to be heard above the TV or a noisy dishwasher and where you can both feel relaxed. Some of our best talks were at the kitchen table or in bed before falling asleep. If you can't seem to talk about important things at home, try to get out of the house. Sometimes a new environment relaxes you so you can just talk. Sometimes getting away from the environment where the stress exists helps put things into perspective.

4. Keep trying. Don't pester your spouse to share feelings, but don't let too much time go by. If something you tried worked once, try it again.

When discussing feelings, bear in mind that both of you need to come to terms with your emotions in your own way, and in your own time. You may choose to cope by reading everything on mental retardation you can put your hands on, while your spouse might want to sleep all day. You may worry more about what you should be doing with your child now, while your spouse may agonize about what your child will do when you are no longer around to care for him. As my husband and I did, you may find yourselves more or less taking turns feeling depressed or frustrated. When one of you is down, the other may be feeling strong enough to rally both your spirits. Or you may wind up on completely different emotional schedules. Do not try to rush your spouse if he or she seems to spend more time in one stage than you do. If you keep the lines of communication open, eventually you will be able to help one another adjust.

But what if one or both of you simply cannot or will not articulate your feelings? This is often a problem for men who grew up with the idea that "real men" don't say things like: "I'm scared," "I need help with this," or "What can I do?" Men may also have problems expressing their feelings if they feel as if their role is to be the pillar of strength, the one in control. Women, too, may feel as if they have to be strong, or as if their emotions are too painful to share. If you find yourself in this predicament, you may just need to be left alone for a while. If you begin to feel too isolated, though, it may help to seek support through one of the avenues described below. It may also be worth your while to consult a mental health professional.

═══ ❈ ═══

We were pretty together on things.

═══ ❈ ═══

The only thing I can say is that I resented my husband, when our daughter was under a year old, because I felt like he could go away to work and I couldn't. I couldn't deal with the baby at the grocery store, so I would go late at night.

═══ ❈ ═══

We both felt the same way. We both felt like we were in mourning over our child.

═══ ❈ ═══

People reach a different point at different times. I felt like I needed more action and less discussion.

═══ ❈ ═══

I think my wife was the optimist and I might have been the realist, and I think that's the best way to say it.

Get Support

When your child is first diagnosed, you may feel tremendously isolated. You may think that you are the only person in the world struggling under such an emotional burden, and that no one else could possibly lighten your load or understand how you feel. You may feel that no one shared your particular dreams that have been destroyed, and, therefore, can't begin to understand your sadness and pain. You can feel so cut off that you really start to doubt the importance of friends and family. But the fact is, thousands of people have stood in your shoes. Many of them are willing to help you adjust—if you give them the chance.

If your child is enrolled in an educational program that requires or encourages your participation, you may meet other parents of children with mental retardation. You will be naturally drawn to one another because you have children with common needs. Finally, you are talking to someone who knows how it really feels. You don't have to hold any of your thoughts or feelings back. Together you can unload frustrations and develop some concrete solutions, or at least promising suggestions, to difficult issues. You can also share information about doctors, therapists, child care providers, and ways of handling particular problem situations or behaviors. Best of all, you may form some lasting friendships.

If you have trouble meeting other parents informally, there are a variety of parent support groups you can contact. In your area, there may be groups of parents whose children have a variety of disabilities, as well as groups sponsored by local chapters of the ARC or other organizations that deal specifically with mental retardation. In the past, these support groups were often geared more toward mothers' needs, if only because they met in the daytime when working fathers could not attend meetings. Recently, however, professionals have begun to realize that fathers, too, have important emotional needs. Now many hospitals, school programs, and other agencies are beginning to offer support groups specifically for fathers. The Resource Guide at the back of the book explains how to locate support groups in your state.

Don't worry if you don't feel ready to share your feelings with a group of strangers. Nobody in a parents' group will force you to talk. Listening to other parents' stories; learning that you are not alone may be all the support you need right now.

I, for one, had a hard time opening up to other parents and professionals about my daughter. But as I began to talk about Tara to people who knew her, conversations began to come more easily. One of my most gratifying discoveries was that I could talk naturally about Tara without anxiety, fear of rejection, or worries about what others were thinking. And the people I spoke with responded just as naturally. I could answer their questions without getting defensive, and I could really appreciate their concern, interest, and sincerity. In the end, their emotional support was well worth the initial awkwardness I felt about sharing my feelings.

═══ ※ ═══

I found out, in meeting other parents, that they all felt the same way. The greatest support was meeting other parents.

Wife: There was a parent group we went to at night through the ARC. My husband doesn't like that kind of stuff; he doesn't like the touchy-feely sessions. It really wasn't like that, though. It was a support group and people did talk about their feelings.

Husband: But it really wasn't a support group because everybody had their own individual problems and everybody wanted them solved. I didn't think it was of much help. It wasn't much help in coping with the problems you had. I mean, to know there were four other people who had big problems was no consolation.

Wife: But it was helpful to me to meet other parents.

We got into the parents' support group and they really helped me.

Finally I was able to talk to other people who knew where I was coming from.

I was really not feeling great about the parents' group. I felt that I could have done without all the talking we did. I wanted something more. I was always very anxious for more action.

There are people in our group who are still hurting. One mother is involved in the group and everything, but isn't ready to attend the Down Syndrome National Convention yet. Several of us have said that she just isn't facing facts yet, but it's not up to me to say where she is in her route.

I found there were good listeners even just around the neighborhood. I'd take the kids to the pool and talk to some of the other mothers there. They didn't have kids with special needs, but one had lost a child with Tay-Sachs disease, although I didn't know that at the time. But she was real anxious to listen to me talk about day-to-day things and also about all my worries—like where Paul would go to school next and whether to

send him to a special education camp for the summer or just let him have some fun for a while.

═══ ❋ ═══

I feel it is good to share some things, like information and energy. I feel that when you're down or someone else is down, you boost each other. You think the same way, you have a lot of things in common. To me, it's very, very helpful to be in a support group, but everybody doesn't feel that way.

Get Information

There is nothing more frustrating than hearing terms and labels such as "developmental delay," "learning disability," or "sensory integration dysfunction," and not knowing what they mean; and nothing more frightening than being referred to geneticists, neurologists, or other specialists and not knowing why. Unfortunately, this happens to too many families.

Ideally, a psychologist or other knowledgeable professional will give you the basic information you need to understand your child's diagnosis and potential. Your doctor should also explain why your child is being referred to specialists and help you interpret the information you receive from them. If the doctor does not volunteer the information you want to know, *ask*. Initially, you may find this hard if doctors intimidate you because you think they know everything. I know I was very naive at first and was afraid to ask questions or even question their suggestions. But as time went on, my husband and I both realized that we had to make decisions about Tara's future on our own. I learned that I could ask doctors—and teachers, too—anything I wanted, as many times as it took for me to understand what they were saying.

If your doctor will not or cannot answer your questions satisfactorily, confront him or her. Write down all your questions beforehand so you don't forget any of them, then bring them up one by one. If you still do not get satisfaction, consider finding another doctor who specializes in children with special needs. Ask other parents, people at the ARC, or your child's teachers or therapists for recommendations. Also see Chapter 9 for tips on building good working relationships with medical professionals. There is no substitute for open and honest communication between parents and professionals.

In the beginning, you may be easily overwhelmed by information about mental retardation and may need to absorb it in small doses. But sooner or later, you will probably be hungry for additional information about how you can help your child. The Reading List at the back of this book can direct you to many helpful publications. Your local chapter of the ARC can also recommend reading material and may operate a lending library. Many preschool programs, too, have libraries of their own with useful books and magazines. In addition, through inter-library loan, your local public library system can obtain books and other materials for you from libraries all over the country.

We were young and dumb. If the doctor had told me to paint her face purple, I would have done it. Now I would say, "You tell me why and then I'll tell you whether or not you can do it."

In the beginning, I was so uneducated about genetics. I said, "You mean you're just trying to see if her children will have the same funny toes?" And he said yes. He really didn't want to deal with the issue.

I guess the point is to question some things—not to be irate about things, but to question why. Why are we being asked to get these tests done? and so forth.

Don't Give In to Discouragement

Life with a child with mental retardation is constant trial and error. Every day you must make adaptations and changes so your child can participate in daily activities. This can make day-to-day management exhausting. The upshot is that it may not be the actual diagnosis of mental retardation that has the biggest impact on your life, but all the other issues that come with it. For example, you may plan an activity for your child that you think he will love, but he reacts with anxiety. Or your child may behave so inappropriately during a simple trip to the shoe store that you end up wondering if it was worth the hassle. Or your child may have so much trouble making transitions that you feel as if you have to fight World War III every night at bedtime.

There is no denying that it can be discouraging to deal with these situations on a daily basis. But it is also true that parents sometimes set themselves up for discouragement. Although some discouragement is probably inevitable, there are some ways of thinking about and doing things with your child that can help you look at the situation in a more positive light.

1. As you get to know your child, you will find things that he enjoys. At first, just stick to the things that work. And don't feel guilty about sometimes excluding your child from activities that the rest of the family enjoys if they don't go well for him.

2. If you know there is a particular time when you feel overwhelmed and bogged down, try to arrange support for those times. For instance, if you have trouble handling all your children at the park, try to go with a friend or bring a babysitter along to help out. Together you may laugh over things that would be upsetting if you were alone.

3. Have realistic expectations for your child. For example, if your child has a hard time with new surroundings and overstimulation, don't try to spend two hours at the mall with him. Instead, try ten minutes the first time and gradually increase the time.

4. Don't feel as if your child has to like every activity or be successful in everything. All children have unique sets of likes and dislikes, strengths and weaknesses. There are many programs and activities for children with mental retardation and your child is bound to find at least a few that suit him.

5. Spend some time with older children with mental retardation and their families. Nothing helps banish discouragement quite so much as seeing other children succeed at various activities. Nothing helps strengthen your resolve so much as seeing other families who didn't quit, but took risks that paid off.

==== ※ ====

I'm not saying that people should have false hope. I am saying that we did not put a lot of limitations on her. I was sure that if we worked hard enough, she would make the kind of progress she already had made. So we kept going for it.

===== ✳ =====

The sooner that parents can see their kid's mental retardation and let it sink into their head that it's not that bad, the better off it probably will be for them.

Your Family and Friends

This may seem like one of the loneliest times of your life. Perhaps you have been keeping the news from your family and friends for fear of their reaction. Or perhaps your life is consumed with meetings, testing, doctor appointments, therapy sessions, and other children, and you feel you don't have time for relationships. You may think family and friends couldn't begin to understand what you are going through and so see no point in trying to explain. Then again, you may think that your family may need more support than you could give them right now.

Don't tell friends and loved ones the diagnosis before you are ready to. Take your time; you control who gets told what in the period following your child's diagnosis. But remember: if you withdraw from family and friends indefinitely, you will shortchange both your child's life and your own. True, the diagnosis of mental retardation is almost as shocking for family and close friends as it is for parents. Telling them about your child can be a difficult task, and you can never predict how someone may react to the news. But once your friends and family adjust to the diagnosis, they can give you immeasurable support. They can help with baby sitting, go along to doctor appointments and meetings with educational professionals, pitch in with household chores, and, most importantly, offer a listening ear. They can be a vital part of your child's team if you let them.

Grandparents

Just as parents do, grandparents of children with mental retardation go through a period of sadness and confusion. They may be angry and resentful for all the same reasons that you are, and may search for someone or something to blame for your child's disability. They, too, need time to digest the news and sort out their own feelings. You can help them with this adjustment process by answering all their questions and encouraging them to share their feelings with you. More importantly, you can help them get to know their grandchild. Let them accompany you to doctor appointments, therapy sessions, and school programs. The more involved they become, the more likely it is that their relationship with their grandchild will blossom into a very loving and "normal" one. Once they know their grandchild's likes and dislikes and how to handle particular situations, all the things they've always dreamed of doing with their grandchild may become a reality.

Sometimes grandparents, like parents, have difficulty accepting that their grandchild does indeed have mental retardation. They may continue to deny the disability long after the parents have accepted it and have begun to get on with their life. They may continually question education and treatment decisions so that parents must endlessly defend and explain the course they have chosen for their family. When this happens, you have to recognize that there is only so much you can do. You can give grandparents the opportunity to be involved in your child's life as much as possible and to talk with you about your child's abilities and disabilities. But in the end, you *cannot be responsible* for their feelings about your child and his mental retardation.

In our case, both sets of Tara's grandparents were very supportive even before we got the diagnosis. While we searched for the reason for her delays, they helped us look on the brighter side. From the beginning, they focused on Tara's best qualities, not her weaknesses. Because Tara was the first grandchild on either side of the family, all they saw when she was born was their beautiful grandchild. Even after Tara's delays became obvious, they still reveled in her beautiful smiles. Our conversation during visits capitalized on the good things. ("She loved her bath; she took a good nap; she ate so well.") They weren't hung up on her developmental status. They enjoyed the present moments—the beauty that the here and now brought.

Of course, Tara's grandparents had their sad moments, but they never "brought me down." Although they don't live nearby, we were able to keep them up-to-date over the phone, so that when they actually learned the diagnosis, it was not such a shock. The reaction was something they gradually grew into, so it wasn't as hard as it might otherwise have been. Today they treat Tara like their other grandchildren and try to follow whatever we recommend if they are unfamiliar with a particular issue. *But,* many times their own way of handling problems works better than my way. For example, my mother showed me a way to make Tara's bed by adding a layer of plastic and a flat sheet around the diaper area. When Tara wet the bed, I could then simply pull off the extra layer and have a dry bed without having to change the whole bed. Both Tara's grandmothers taught me that I didn't have to do everything perfectly—the way a childcare book or a teacher said to. They taught me to be more realistic and give myself a break now and then.

My parents have supported us in everything we have tried to do with our daughter. Being from an older generation with radically outdated notions of mental retardation, they are remarkably accepting of our child. I always hear that it is important to accept your child for who he or she is; I think you have to accept your child's grandparents for who they are, too—outdated ideas and all.

My wife's parents have that wonderful stoic attitude about our son. They say, "Of course, we will do the best we can for him. What other choice is there?" And with that, they move on. Well, it isn't that simple for

parents. It's easy to be stoic when you're not the one who has to deal with problems every day.

═══ ❋ ═══

Having a kid with a disability has made me think about what I should do when I have grandkids. When my kids are grown up, I need to make sure that I let them know that I know being a parent is hard work. Encouragement is good, but sympathy is great.

═══ ❋ ═══

I didn't share a lot of what I really felt with anybody. I guess our family didn't know the half of what we were really going through. They were far away, and I'm not the person to call them up and cry my eyes out. We told them the facts and they were very good about it. They were understanding and they were good support, but we were on our own. . . . We were just left totally out in the wilderness together.

═══ ❋ ═══

My mother still has questions. She said to me one time, "She has only a little bit of Down syndrome, right?" She is working really hard at understanding what Down syndrome and mental retardation mean, but it's hard.

═══ ❋ ═══

I want my parents to be more understanding about Down syndrome and patient with people who are retarded. But I wish the same thing for myself. I mean, even now I can go to the Special Olympics and feel uncomfortable.

═══ ❋ ═══

My mother didn't know what retarded meant. "What is that going to mean?" Of course, as she has seen him and visited him, she's gotten to feel closer to what we do, and understands that his mental retardation is not going to mean a gigantic thing in the next few years.

Friends

After your child's mental retardation is diagnosed, you may drift apart from friends for a variety of reasons. Some well-meaning friends may think you are too overwhelmed to talk, so they don't call. Others may not know what to say, so they don't say anything.

Still others may feel as if they have reached out to you and you have rejected their help. Then again, you may unconsciously push friends away. Perhaps you think they couldn't possibly understand your new life, or you resent what you perceive as their pity, or you can't bear to hear them talk about their "normal" children.

Looking back, I can see that I was the one who isolated myself from my friends. My friends were deeply concerned, and I know they made many attempts to make me feel better. They offered to babysit and to accompany me to doctor appointments. At first, I couldn't accept their offers because I didn't think they were really sincere. Besides, I wanted to do everything myself. I wanted to show others that I was strong enough to meet this challenge on my own. Accepting help was a sign of defeat and weakness—an admission that I couldn't adequately take care of my own child.

As time went on, I began to realize that yes, I had a hard job, and I did indeed need help. Verbalizing the phrase, "I need help," and being able to accept help from my friends was a milestone that brought me closer to acceptance of my new life.

Whatever *your* situation may be, give your old friends a chance. Do not try to second guess their feelings about you and your child. Although they may not feel the same emotions to the same degree as you do, they may very well understand more than you think they do. Talk to them and find out what they want to know. Then you and your child can be their teachers. Offer them books and pamphlets about mental retardation to read, and answer their questions. Talk about your child and what your day is really like, but don't overdramatize or play the martyr. Like you, your friends will not adjust overnight, but if you give them time, they most likely will offer you abundant understanding and support.

I think my friends who had babies Karen's age really didn't know what to say. They saw it coming. I've asked them, "Did you really notice back then that there was something wrong with Karen from the way she looked?" And they said, "Yeah, but I really couldn't tell you then." I guess they saw worry in my face and they couldn't . . . they probably felt guilty because they had a happy and normally developing child and I didn't.

One of the people who noticed something different about her was a babysitter I used to take her to who had seven kids of her own. She was real clear on what an infant's development was like. She was very concerned. I remember when I said I was going to a neurologist, she said, "Oh, I'm glad you are, because I was going to talk to you about that."

When I first learned of my child's mental retardation, I didn't have the perfect, canned reaction at the ready. I floundered around, trying to figure out how to deal with it . . . what to say. You have to expect your friends to have the same problem. When you tell them something as important and startling as this, it isn't fair to expect them to say just the perfect thing in response. Give your friends time to grapple with it. It's not their immediate reaction that matters, but whether they will be there for you for the long haul.

These days we all live such insular lives. We continually project that we are masters of our fates and fully in control of our lives, no matter what hurdles appear in our way.

It's no wonder that comforting people has become a lost skill. Friends often want to help, but don't know how to approach you.

Your Other Children

Unless your other children are much older than their brother or sister with mental retardation, there probably won't be a clearly identifiable moment when you break the news of their sibling's disability. Most likely your other children will have noticed many differences about their sibling by the time they are toddlers. They might observe, for instance, that your child has trouble saying certain words or doesn't seem to understand the rules for Hide and Seek. For a time, they will probably accept that these differences are simply a part of their brother or sister. Tara's younger brother and sister, for example, think that Tara is just Tara, not their sister with mental retardation.

I have found that the best way to explain mental retardation to siblings is to answer questions as they arise. I try to make my answers as simple as I can. If I go into a long explanation, my children usually tune me out because I am giving them information they are not interested in at the time.

I try never to brush them off or withhold information because their questions make me uncomfortable. Usually the things that

bother Tara's siblings bother me, too, and I share that—but with a touch of encouragement. For example, one of my children might ask, "Why does Tara scream, Mom? I hate when she does that." And I might answer, "I don't like it either. But Tara has a hard time with her words, so when she is frustrated or excited she screams instead. She won't scream as much when she knows more words." Because I always try to give honest answers, sometimes the best answer I can give is "I don't know."

As your other children grow older, you can expect that they will go through many of the same emotions you have to cope with. At times your child's mental retardation will make them feel angry, resentful, sad, helpless, frustrated. I know this from experience, having grown up with a sister with mental retardation. What made it easier for me to cope was: 1) being able to talk to my parents about my questions and feelings; and 2) not feeling the burden of responsibility for my sister—not being given the message that my parents *"depended on me."*

Chapter 7 discusses long-term sibling relationships in more detail, but at this point, it may be helpful for you to know that there are support groups for siblings, too. If your other children are having trouble coping, your local ARC may be able to refer you to the nearest sibling group. You will also find a sibling support organization listed in the Resource Guide.

===== ✳ =====

I don't know that my son had any reason to think there was anything wrong about the way his older sister was. He was three, four, five, and what did he know? Anybody bigger than you should be able to do more than you. We probably initiated more than he asked—we would say Jenny had problems and that was why we were doing this or that.

===== ✳ =====

Our daughter will ask, "Why is Philip screaming?" or "Why can't Philip ride the bicycle?" It's not real deep questions. He'll mouth one of her books, and she'll say, "Philip's biting my book." And I'll say, "Jennifer, you know that he doesn't really mean to do it, but in a way he can't help it."

Give Yourself a Break

Your child probably needs a good bit of care and attention, but don't let his needs rule your life. You cannot restrict your reading to publications about disabilities or let your social life revolve solely around doctor appointments, support groups, and conferences. You need time off from the constant demands of child care to recharge your batteries, cultivate your own interests and activities, and work on your marriage and other relationships. You need to look after your own health and spend time alone with your spouse—if only to take a walk in the park or go to a movie together.

Right now, you may feel guilty at the thought of leaving your child with someone else for even a couple of hours. But finding a babysitter is crucial not only for your own physical and emotional well-being, but also for your child's. All children deserve the opportunity to be exposed to new and exciting experiences. They need to meet other people so they can broaden their social skills. For your part, you need to "let go" slowly so that your child can gain independence and grow. Although you may feel you are taking a risk by leaving your child, it's a risk all parents must take.

If your child's grandparents live nearby, they can make excellent first babysitters for your child. You will gain peace of mind knowing that your child is in good hands, while the grandparents will have a chance to get to know your child better. If calling on grandparents is not an option, you can often find competent, caring babysitters through your local ARC. Students majoring in special education or nursing at a nearby college are often eager to get firsthand experience caring for children with disabilities, and special education teachers at area schools may be available as well. A more practical alternative is to trade off with another couple with a child with mental retardation. This works especially well if each couple goes out on a regular basis, rather than just when they have an invitation. It is also a nice arrangement if the "girls" or the "boys" want a night out with each other.

I really felt like "Well, maybe now's the time to hire somebody to help me out." She was wonderful. She only came once a week and I didn't feel that that was enough, but I felt like she got me started.

Conclusion

Right now, the fact of your child's mental retardation may cast a shadow over everything you do. You may feel as if the condition that has robbed your child of part of his intellect has also drained all hope and joy from your life. It may take every drop of strength you have to get through each day, and the future may be impossible for you to contemplate.

Incredible as it may seem, the sun will come out again. You will laugh about yourself and your child. You will laugh with your spouse and friends. And you will laugh with your child. Once you are no longer overwhelmed by your own hurt, confusion, and despair, you will find yourself making joyous discoveries about your child and his abilities. You will be able to see beyond the label of "mental retardation" and glimpse the child beneath it. You will see that mental retardation only affects how and at what rate your child learns and reacts to the environment, not his essential humanity. You will see that mental retardation in itself does not predict your child's future or ultimate accomplishments. And you will recognize that your child is a unique human being with many of the same desires, emotions, and abilities as other children.

For my part, I have gradually come to realize just how many needs, characteristics, behaviors, and likes and dislikes my child with mental retardation shares with her siblings. For example, when my other two children were young and wanted to get a cookie after I'd already said "no," they would whine or cry. Even when Tara was nonverbal, she would use similar tactics—screaming or yelling—to wear me down. Just as my other children did, Tara knew what she wanted and used any resources available to express her desires.

Above all, I've learned that parents should not give up on dreams for their child just because he happens to have mental retardation. Your child, like every child, has special qualities and the capacity to develop those qualities. It may take a little more digging for you to uncover those qualities, and your child may need more help to achieve his potential, yet his possibilities for growth and fulfillment are still endless.

It would be impossible to even begin to list all of the ways that Tara has surpassed our early expectations for her. She learned to walk by herself, and then to walk our dog on a leash. She learned to use words, and then to spell her name. She is thriving in an integrated educational setting, and her IEP now includes reading goals. Along the way, Tara has become a cherished, integral part of our family. She is the "spice" of our lives. Our family is . . . because of her.

There is, of course, no denying that life is a challenge when you have a child with mental retardation. But it is just as undeniable that it is a challenge well worth rising to. You can help your child create and shape his own destiny. You can help him achieve his promise. And to begin, you have only to open your eyes to everything your child has to offer.

Four

=== ❊ ===

The Multidisciplinary Evaluation Process

Clyde L. Robinette, Psy.D.*

When your child is developing normally, you can pretty much just stand back and watch, from time to time bragging to friends and relatives about her latest feats. But when your child does not learn as well or as quickly as others, she needs special, individualized assistance to help her make progress.

To determine the best and most effective ways of helping your child develop, it is important to answer several key questions. First, what are her abilities in each of the developmental areas (cognitive, speech and language, social-emotional, fine and gross motor, self-help)? Second, how do her abilities compare to those of most other children her age? Third, in those areas where her abilities are significantly below average, what are the best ways to optimize her development and monitor her progress? Arriving at answers to these questions is the primary purpose of a developmental evaluation. Evaluations are also periodically completed to determine whether your child is making the expected progress, and to develop new ways of helping her learn if current strategies are not effective.

Because the evaluation process can be very confusing for parents, this chapter will attempt to make sense of it for you. It

* Dr. Robinette is a Licensed Psychologist and Certified School Psychologist who has worked with young children and their families for the past fifteen years. He is the team leader for the Early Childhood School Psychologists in the Howard County (Maryland) Public School System. He also maintains a private practice in Bethesda, Maryland. Dr. Robinette recently received an award for Outstanding Practice by the Maryland School Psychologists' Association for his work with the Infant and Toddler and Preschool Programs.

describes the types of evaluations your child will encounter, the professionals involved and the evaluation techniques they use, and how the information gathered is used. With this background, it will be easier for you to get beyond the jargon and "alphabet soup" of the professionals and understand the information they can provide you about your child and her special needs.

The Evaluation Process

Over the years, your child will be given a variety of different types of evaluations, by a variety of professionals for a variety of reasons. Before taking an in-depth look at the different types of professionals and evaluation techniques, a brief overview of how the evaluation process works should help you get your bearings.

The evaluation process can be set in motion in three ways. When it is first suspected that your child may have special needs, you may be sent to a group of specialists for a diagnosis. Or, once your child has been diagnosed, she may need additional evaluations in order to enter or continue in an early intervention or special education program. Lastly, you may request an evaluation at any time, but especially if you disagree with the results of an earlier evaluation.

If your child's intervention or education program requests the evaluation, they will make all the arrangements for you. They will schedule your child for all the appointments she needs and tell you where to bring her for the evaluation. Usually, evaluations are given in a hospital, a private clinic, or a multidisciplinary evaluation center run by your local public school system. The evaluation will be completed at no charge to you through a federal program known as Child Find. (Note: if *you* are the one requesting the evaluation, rather than the special education or early intervention program, you may have to pay for it. See the section on "Seeking Private Evaluations.")

During your child's evaluation, specialists from various fields will evaluate your child in their area of expertise. They will look at the nature and extent of your child's special needs and then use that information to design learning strategies tailored to those needs. Types of specialists who may assess your child include psychologists, special education teachers, speech/language pathologists (therapists), occupational therapists, physical therapists, physicians, nurses, and social workers. The training and techniques of each of these specialists is discussed later in the chapter.

To evaluate your child's abilities, most specialists use *standardized tests*. During a standardized test, your child is given a series of tasks in exactly the same way they were previously given to a large number of children of various ages. For example, she may be asked to label pictures or remember where particular objects were hidden. Your child's performance is then compared to the average score achieved by children her age. To determine how far above or below average your child's abilities are, the professional uses a technique similar to the method of "grading on a curve" you may remember teachers using in school. Just as most scores on a math or history test tend to cluster together, defining the average range, so do scores on tests of developmental skills. Some people do a little better or a little worse than average, and only a very small minority score significantly above or below average.

Your child's scores on standardized tests may be expressed in several ways. First, they may be expressed as *standard scores*. As Chapter 1 explains, this is how IQ scores are given. Using this system, a score of 100 is usually considered exactly average. That is, exactly as many people taking the test will score above 100 as will score below it. People who score within 15 points above or 15 points below 100 are generally considered to be in the average range. About 68 percent of all scores fall into this range.

Another way a score on a standardized test may be expressed is as a *percentile*. A percentile is a description of what percentage of children the same age would have scored lower on that test. For example, if a four-year-old's score is at the 20th percentile, that means that 20 percent of children her age would receive a lower score on the test, while 80 percent would receive a higher score. Most children with mental retardation have percentile scores of 2, 1, or less than 1 on most standardized tests.

A third type of score that you may see is an *age equivalent*. This is simply the age at which the average child gets the same number of items correct as your child gets correct. For example, if your child got 34 items correct on a test of expressive vocabulary and the average score for children 28 months of age is 34 items correct, then your child would be said to have an age equivalent of 28 months in this developmental area. There is a particular type of age equivalent that is often used in psychological tests, the *mental age*. That is the age at which the average number of items correct is the same as the number of items your child got correct on a standardized test of intelligence.

Many tests give scores only in age equivalents, but there are a number of problems with this type of score. First, it only tells you that your child had the same number of items correct as the average child of a particular age group. It does not tell you which items were correct or how her responses may have differed. For example, in response to "Tell me about a rabbit," several answers might be counted as correct, ranging from "long ears . . . hop," to "It's a furry animal with long ears that hops and has a bunny tail." A second problem with an age equivalent is that it does not tell you the significance of the difference between your child's chronological age and her age equivalent. A twelve-month delay in a developmental area is much more significant in a two-year-old than in an eight-year-old. A third problem is that the difference between chronological age and age equivalents grows larger for children with mental retardation as they get older. While the age equivalents will continue to go up, you will not know if she is continuing to develop at a rate you would expect.

Using standard scores eliminates many of the limitations of using age equivalent scores. It is possible to compare two different tests to see if she performed better on one test than another, allowing you to look for patterns of strengths and needs. Standard scores also allow you to look at her performance in the same areas over time. For example, your child may be given a test of visual-motor integration, in which she is asked to copy designs such as straight lines, circles, and squares, and later more complex designs. She can be given the same test at 3, 6, and 9 years of age, and her standard scores can be compared over those three test sessions. Is she continuing to progress at a rate we would expect in a given developmental area?

By collecting your child's standardized scores in every developmental area, professionals can begin to develop a profile of her unique strengths and needs. But standardized tests cannot be the only source of information on your child. A standardized test can measure your child's abilities on only a small sample of the skills she needs to learn. Consequently, members of the evaluation team will also observe your child in a variety of settings to get an overall idea of how she uses her abilities. For example, to assess your child's fine motor skills, an occupational therapist might observe how she plays with small toys in the waiting room. Or a psychologist may observe your child in her classroom to see how well she follows routines, expresses her wants and needs, and interacts with other children.

A third important source of information comes from you, the parent. Your observations about what your child can do at home and in the community are invaluable. This is because the evaluators cannot observe everything themselves and because your child may not be willing to do everything she is capable of when she is in a test situation. To get your input about your child's development, members of the assessment team may interview you or give you a checklist to complete.

Once all the standardized tests, observations, and interviews are completed, the professionals involved in the evaluation will confer among themselves, sharing their findings, and discussing ways to help your child's development. Later they will meet with you to discuss the test results and their recommendations. They will give you copies of all reports and invite you to ask questions. Only after you are satisfied that your questions are answered and that you understand the recommendations, will you need to make any decisions about treatment recommendations and your child's educational placement.

Types of Evaluations

There are two types of evaluations that all children in special education receive. The first type, the *initial* or *triennial evaluation*, involves the most comprehensive, standardized testing of your child's abilities. The team that conducts it usually includes some professionals such as a psychologist, pediatrician, or social worker who may not work directly with your child in an ongoing special education program. Your child will receive one of these evaluations at least every three years, starting from the date of her first evaluation. The first time she receives it, the evaluation is called the initial evaluation; after that, it is called the triennial evaluation.

The second required type of evaluation is the *annual review*. As the name implies, it occurs once a year (sometimes more often, if your child is very young). It is usually less formal than the initial or triennial evaluation. The review is completed by the professionals who are working directly with your child in her education program and focuses on your child's progress in achieving specific goals that have been set for her.

Occasionally your child may need an evaluation before her next annual review is scheduled. For example, her teachers may be considering a major change in her education program, or a sudden change in health may be interfering with her learning. Or you may feel she is making rapid progress in one area, but little progress in another. You may want to have some of the tests repeated to see if she will qualify for services in the area in which she is now making slower progress. In situations like these, either professionals or parents may request that evaluations be updated.

To help you better understand why these evaluations are necessary, the next sections explore their purposes in more detail.

Initial and Triennial Evaluations

One of the main purposes of the initial and triennial evaluations is to identify your child's unique pattern of strengths and needs. This is accomplished by giving her a series of standardized tests and then comparing her level of ability in all developmental areas (language skills, motor skills, socialization, and cognition). Everyone has some areas of learning that are stronger than others. For example, you may be able to understand complex mathematical equations with ease, but may be "all thumbs" when you try to follow the instructions for assembling a bicycle.

Recognizing your child's strengths and needs is vital to developing strategies that will help her learn. Knowledge of her areas of need helps educators know where to concentrate their efforts. And knowledge of her strengths tells them what areas can be used to compensate for or "teach around" her areas of weakness. For example, your child might be weak in expressive language skills—that is, she has trouble coming up with the words to express her thoughts. But she might have strong fine motor skills and a good visual memory. To help her learn how to communicate her thoughts to another person, teachers might therefore use sign language and pictures on a language board.

The second major purpose of these evaluations is to determine your child's rate of learning. During the initial evaluation, this is estimated by comparing the progress she has made in developmental areas since birth with the progress made by other children her age. If her rate of progress up to now is significantly below average, she is given the diagnosis of mental retardation. On subsequent triennial evaluations, her progress is once again compared with other children's her age to determine whether the level of mental retardation remains the same.

A third purpose of the initial and triennial evaluations is to assess your child's progress in each of the developmental areas. For example, what kind of improvement is your child making in speech and language skills? Has she developed the fine motor skills to tie her own shoes? As with all children, your child's rate of progress in each area may vary over time. At times her progress may appear to level off, or reach a *plateau;* other times, she may make rapid progress, or have a *growth spurt.*

Growth spurts and plateaus may result from normal cognitive, physical, or environmental changes which demand more energy from your child in one area at the expense of growth in another area. For example, a child with gross motor delays who is learning to walk often has a plateau or leveling off in her expressive language skills. You only need to see the determination in her face as she tries to get across the room to know where her energies are directed. Another common situation that may trigger a growth spurt followed by a plateau is the development of a basic ability that affects a number of areas at once. For example, when your child learns to imitate others, it opens up the possibility of growth in many areas. As your child first begins to imitate your speech, behavior, and actions, you may see rapid skill development in language, social, and cognitive skills for a period of time.

Like growth spurts, plateaus are a normal developmental experience for all children. Following a growth spurt, a child's progress slows as she consolidates her skills and abilities at that developmental level. The reason it is important for you to understand the phenomena of spurts and plateaus is that parents and teachers of children with mental retardation are so attentive to developmental changes that these normal fluctuations can become a roller coaster ride of emotions. The changes occur more slowly, the plateaus seem interminable, and parents and teachers can become very discouraged at the child's lack of progress for a period of time. If you know that this is a normal developmental fluctuation and that there will be another growth spurt in the future, the plateaus seem more tolerable.

Annual reviews are often more sensitive to growth spurts and plateaus. As a result, a very favorable annual review one year showing significant gains in several areas of your child's individualized education plan (IEP) may be followed by an annual review in which very few IEP goals were met. The initial and triennial evaluations can provide a better overview of the effects of these changes over a longer period of time and across more areas.

The final purpose of the initial and triennial evaluations is to look at physical or medical changes that may be affecting your child's development. For example, extended illnesses, chronic conditions such as seizures, or a new hearing aid can all have an impact on the quality and rate of your child's development. How much these changes affect each developmental area can vary. For example, if your child develops a serious seizure disorder, the changes in her brain that are causing the seizures might affect learning in most areas. But her development of cognitive and language skills might be more affected than her development of motor skills. By comparing your child's performance on standardized tests before the seizures began with her performance after they began, members of the evaluation team gain a better understanding of how the changes in her brain affect her development. With this knowledge, they can set more realistic goals for her IEP, or they may change their strategy for reaching a particular goal. They can also let medical professionals know if the treatment being used is having an adverse effect on a particular ability, such as short-term memory or attention. Based on this information, different treatments may be considered.

The theory of plateauing has always gotten to me. Nobody plateaus out across the board. Even if your child has reached her level of comprehension in reading, for example, that doesn't mean she will stop gaining new

information from reading. She can also continue with reading as a leisure skill. You shouldn't say, "Well, she's reached her plateau, so we just won't work on it anymore."

Annual Reviews

Like the initial and triennial evaluations, your child's annual reviews will concentrate on her areas of strength and need, rate of learning, and pattern of development, as well as the effects of physical or medical changes on her development. The main difference is that the annual review focuses on how your child is progressing on the goals you have set for her, rather than on how she compares to other children her age. For example, if your child has a language goal of using more two-word phrases, the professionals assessing your child would look at her progress in meeting that goal, instead of whether her language skills are appropriate for her age.

As mentioned earlier, annual reviews are more informal because you are meeting with the professionals you see and communicate with on a regular basis. An annual review may or may not involve formal, standardized testing. If it does, the professionals will often use tests that give approximate age levels for each skill area rather than standard scores. If tests are not used, the teacher will review your child's progress on each goal based on her observations in the classroom. You may hear, for example, that your child is consistently identifying circles and squares but not triangles. The professionals' evaluation of your child will be based on their experience with your child over the past year and her progress on educational goals.

Because the professionals involved in the annual review know your child well, they are usually more sensitive to her growth spurts and plateaus. At an annual review, you may therefore feel great elation at your child's progress in one area and frustration at slow progress in another. Identifying those spurts and plateaus is then helpful in setting IEP goals for the next year that can capitalize on areas in which your child is making rapid progress and focus on areas that may need more attention over the coming year. This type of fine tuning of her program will keep her moving in all developmental areas.

At the annual review, you or one of the professionals treating your child may recommend that she have another triennial evaluation sooner than is scheduled. This might be necessary if your child is developing much slower or faster than expected, if significant changes in physical or medical conditions could affect her overall development, or if a change to a different educational program is under consideration.

Seeking Private Evaluations

Up to this point, the chapter has focused on the evaluation process that is offered through the public school system and is available to parents free of charge. There are also times when parents seek private evaluations, independent of the public school programs. One reason parents seek a private evaluation is that they think their child may benefit from more therapy time than the school is providing. Remember, schools are required only to offer a free and *appropriate* educational program. Because of budgetary constraints or school system policies, a school may offer less therapy time than parents feel would be *optimal* for their child. So, for example, if parents want their child to receive additional speech/language therapy, they may ask a speech/language therapist in private practice to evaluate the usefulness of additional therapy time.

A second reason parents may seek a private evaluation is that they think another group of professionals may be able to evaluate their child's strengths and weaknesses more accurately than the public school evaluation team. This is most often the case when a child has a syndrome or specialized disability and there is a nearby clinic or specialist with expertise in that area. For example, if your child has fragile X syndrome, a local teaching or research hospital may have a group of professionals who have considerable experience working with children who have that diagnosis. You may prefer to have that team complete the evaluations and submit them to the school for review. This is most appropriate if you plan to have that group follow your child as she grows up.

Yet another reason for seeking private evaluations is that you disagree with the findings of an evaluation conducted by a member of the school's evaluation team or you lack confidence in the results. In this situation, you may appeal to the school system for payment of a second-opinion evaluation, but there is no guarantee that they will agree to pay. Any other time you request an evaluation on your own, it is your responsibility to pay for it. (Insurance may cover some costs, depending on your policy.) It is also your responsibility to contact the professionals and schedule the appointments, usually at the professionals' offices. In addition, you will probably have to organize and make sense of the various recommendations and results. Most often, the professionals will not share information with one another or present their findings as a team.

Professionals on the Evaluation Team

The specialists on your child's public school evaluation team will probably be part of a *multidisciplinary team*. That is, they will each have different areas of expertise. Each will look at the area of development that he is specifically trained to evaluate and treat and will bring his perspective to understanding your child's unique needs. The advantage of having a multidisciplinary team is that the members work together to understand your child's developmental strengths and needs. They share information they have gathered among themselves, and together arrive at an overall picture of your child and her needs. They then discuss their findings with you and make joint recommendations for her treatment and education. You do *not* have to take information collected by many individual specialists working alone and try to make sense out of it yourself. (The only exception, as explained above, is if you seek a private evaluation.)

To help you understand each specialist's role in the evaluation process, the following sections describe what different professionals evaluate and how that information is used. All of the professionals discussed below will generally take part in your child's initial and triennial evaluations; some, but not all, will take part in annual reviews as well.

Psychologist

The psychologist is a professional trained in the science of human behavior and learning. She has expertise in the areas of cognitive, behavioral, social, and emotional development. The psychologist who sees your child will have a background in evaluating and treating both normal and abnormal child development. Her knowledge of cognitive development, or how children learn and

how that learning process changes with age, will be particularly important in evaluating your child.

To assess your child's cognitive development, the psychologist looks at how your child goes about solving problems, both on tasks that are familiar to her and on unfamiliar or novel tasks. An example of a familiar task would be labeling or pointing to pictures of common objects, which is something parents often do with their children. An unfamiliar task would be to have her quickly place different-colored pegs with different pictures of animals to match a model at the top of the page.

As part of the cognitive assessment, the psychologist will ask your child to solve a series of problems of increasing difficulty. Each series of tasks or problems is organized into a small test or subtest. A series of subtests that sample problem-solving skills in a number of developmental areas is grouped together to form a standardized *intelligence test* or *IQ test*. These tests are organized around different skill areas, including language skills, memory skills, attentional skills, and visual-spatial problem-solving skills. Giving your child an intelligence test enables the psychologist to compare your child's scores on different developmental areas, giving her an overview of your child's pattern of learning strengths and needs. It also enables the psychologist to compare your child's performance with that of other children her age.

Many of the tasks the psychologist will ask your child to do are similar to those evaluated by other professionals on the team. For example, the language tasks on an intelligence test often overlap with areas evaluated by the speech/language therapist, and the fine motor tasks overlap with the testing by the occupational therapist.

The psychologist, however, focuses more on how your child *processes* different types of information than on her language or motor skills. As Chapter 1 explains, an intelligence test yields a specific standard score, or *IQ score,* that indicates how your child's overall cognitive functioning compares with that of other children her age. However, the psychologist is looking for information beyond the IQ score to better understand your child and to help plan educational interventions. Specific information she is looking for in doing an intelligence test includes:

- Overall cognitive developmental level, or how well your child is able to understand, organize, and make sense of her world. For example, does she understand that different objects can have similar properties and be grouped together? A cow can be a farm animal, a brown thing, or a toy.

- Learning *modalities,* or through which senses she learns information best. For example, does your child learn better when you show her how to do something or when she is told about something?

- The conditions under which your child learns best. For example, does imitating others help her learn a skill more quickly? Does she need to have someone physically prompt or guide her through a task the first few times? Do auditory cues such as "look at me" help focus her attention? In other words, what can a teacher do to make her more available for learning?

- Memory. Your child's ability to remember information she has seen or heard (visual or auditory memory) on a short-term and long-term basis.

- Attention, concentration, and independent work skills. How well can she attend to, respond, and follow through on a task to completion? Can she correct her answer if she has made a mistake?

One problem in assessing preschool-aged children is that there is no one intelligence test that works well for children with mild to moderate mental retardation. Often, a psychologist will use two intelligence tests or will use parts of two or three tests to fully evaluate intellectual ability. The most commonly used intelligence test for preschool-aged children is the Wechsler Preschool and Primary Scale of Intelligence—Revised (WPPSI-R). It provides separate IQ scores for verbal and non-verbal reasoning, as well as overall IQ scores based on an average of those two scores. An example of a verbal reasoning task would be to ask your child to finish a sentence that asks for another example of a class of objects. ("One color is red, another color is . . . what?") A non-verbal reasoning task (also called a performance task) would be to ask her to arrange three colored blocks in a row in the same order as a model. A list of common intelligence tests used for young children is included in the back of the book.

In addition to looking at these areas of cognitive development, the psychologist will look at your child's emotional and behavioral development. She will observe your child in a variety of situations, noting how she behaves during the intelligence testing, and how she acts with you, with other professionals working with her, and with other children in her educational program. The psychologist will also ask you about your child's behavior at home and in community settings such as the grocery store or a neighbor's house. She will look at how your child handles both new and familiar situations, and how she handles transitions from one situation to another. For example, does she leave the toys in the waiting room easily to accompany you to the testing room, or does she need much preparation and cajoling to leave? Other aspects of your child's behavior the psychologist will look at include: How does she handle frustration with a difficult task? How does she communicate her wants and needs to an adult? How does she relate to others in her environment? For example, does she talk easily with new people, shy away, or ignore them?

If there are specific concerns about your child's emotional or behavioral development, the psychologist may ask you to complete a child behavior checklist. This is a list of common behavior concerns for children her age with spaces for you to indicate which concerns are characteristic of your child. The Achenbach Child Behavior Checklist is one of the commonly used checklists. It asks you to rate your child's behavior over the past two months on a variety of concerns, such as "Disturbed by changes in routine" and "Clings to adults or too dependent." Your ratings of your child's behavior can be compared with other children's to see if there are more than the usual concerns in any area. The psychologist can then identify areas that may need to be addressed in your child's IEP or through consultation.

A third and related area the psychologist will assess is your child's adaptive behavior, or how independently she gets along at home, school, and in the community. For example, how independent is she with bathing or toileting? What parts of dressing and undressing is she able to do herself? For this part of the evaluation, the psychologist will give you or your child's classroom teacher a standardized checklist or *adaptive behavior scale* to fill out. The psychologist will likely go over this scale with you in an interview and ask you about your child's communication, self-help, socialization, and motor skills at home. This provides information on how your child uses her cognitive skills to solve everyday problems in a familiar environment. The adaptive behavior scale yields a standard score that is similar to the IQ score and can be compared to the IQ score.

Once she has finished gathering information about your child's strengths and needs, the psychologist will have an idea of what areas your child needs to work on now, and how best to help her learn. By comparing your child's cognitive and adaptive abilities with those of other children the same age, she also will be able to assess the degree of your child's mental retardation—mild, moderate, severe, or profound. (As Chapters 1 and 2 explain, the degree is determined by how significantly your child's abilities differ from the average range for children her age.) Based on your child's level of mental retardation, the psychologist will predict the range of skills your child can be expected to learn over the next few years. This prediction will help to determine the most appropriate educational program and goals for your child.

The psychologist tested our son and asked a lot of questions, but she was very careful not to say certain things in front of our son. Then she went over every single bit of information I had collected about him. She sat down and the first thing she said was, "Let me tell you what a learning disability is," and she told me. Then she said, "Now let me tell you what mentally retarded is." She drew me a chart and she told me that he is

moderately mentally retarded, not severely retarded. He is working at half of his age level. "Did anyone ever tell you what he is going to do when he's 18?" she asked. I said, "Nobody has ever said to me what he's going to do tomorrow." She said, "Well, let me tell you. The least you can expect from him. . . ." And I wrote this all down. I walked out of there and I had a head full of information. She explained everything to me in language that I could understand and I felt so much better. Now I knew what we needed to do. I got the answers that I needed and that I had waited all these years to find. I went home feeling like I had lifted this huge weight off my shoulders.

If you ask me what the cognitive scores are, I don't even know and I don't care. I do read them, though. I mean I read them once and then file them. I don't follow every little sentence.

Special Education Teacher

The special education teacher is trained in developing and using special instructional programs designed to meet your child's unique needs. He has a background in teaching academic skills such as basic reading and math skills, as well as pre-academic skills such as recognizing differences and similarities in pictures and sounds. He also has training in the assessment of special learning needs.

In evaluating your child, the special education teacher focuses on determining what academic and pre-academic skills your child has learned and in what areas she needs specialized instruction. If your child is a preschooler, he will not give her tests of reading, spelling, math, or other academic skills. Rather, he will look at pre-academic, or academic readiness skills—the skills your child needs to have to be able to learn basic academic skills later. For example, before your child learns the different letters, she must be able to distinguish between similar and different shapes. Here are some of the areas the special education teacher will assess:

- knowledge of concepts, or being able to generalize about qualities or characteristics of things—for example, colors, shapes, sizes.
- knowledge of relational terms—words such as bigger, taller, and longest which express a relationship between one object and another.

- ability to match visual patterns, showing an understanding of the concepts of same and different.
- rote counting abilities; knowledge of one-to-one correspondence. In other words, can your child count a number of objects by saying one number for each object she touches?
- ability to recognize and name letters

Scores on tests of these skills are frequently given as age levels or *age equivalents*, rather than as standard scores. For example, your child might receive an age equivalent of twenty-eight months on a task involving matching similar shapes. If her chronological age is forty-two months, this means her score is the same as the average twenty-eight-month-old child's and that she has a fourteen-month delay. By comparing your child's age equivalents in all areas assessed, the special education teacher can identify specific learning needs. He can then develop an educational plan that includes the types and amounts of instruction that will best help your child learn.

Besides me, the person who knows Janeen best is her teacher. I count what she says more than any other evaluator because, next to me, she spends the most time with my daughter. She knows best how Janeen learns, what works and doesn't work, and what interests her.

We've learned a lot about how our son learns best from the special eduation teacher. He is such a strong visual learner, that it helps if the teacher signs some as she goes along. If he sits back and watches the other children, he'll realize, "Oh, I'm supposed to be up and over there." But he doesn't pick it up when she says, "Let's go play now."

Speech/Language Pathologist (Therapist)

The speech/language pathologist (SLP) is a therapist with expertise in the development of communication skills. She has knowledge about normal and abnormal development of communication skills, including the sensory and motor skills needed to articulate words so others can understand, the development of word meanings, the development of the structure of language, and the development of its use in daily living. She evaluates:

- *oral sensory-motor development*, or how well your child is able to perceive sensations such as touch, temperature, and texture in and around her mouth.
- *oral motor development*, or how your child develops the muscle control to eat, drink, and produce speech sounds.
- your child's understanding of the meaning of language (*semantics*), including her understanding and use of vocabulary, her understanding of concept labels, her ability to listen to and follow directions, how well she understands and makes statements that provide information, and her understanding and use of categories.
- her understanding and use of grammar or the underlying structure of language (*syntax*). This includes the rules of language we all know about how we join words together to communicate. It also includes the small changes we make in words to change their meaning (for example, adding "s" to the end of a noun to make it plural).
- *pragmatics*, or how your child uses language socially.

The SLP evaluates all of these areas through a combination of observation, language sampling, structured tasks, and standardized tests. During an observation, she may play with your child in the waiting area, watch her eating a snack, and observe her with other children, if possible. For a language sample, she will set up structured play situations with your child and listen to her conversation during play. Structured tasks may include having your child imitate oral movements and sounds, name pictures, or play games that will require your child to use certain words or sentence structures. And standardized tests will involve tasks similar to those asked by the psychologist, but focusing on her communication skills. For example, your child may be asked to identify pictures when given a word, sentence, or concept; answer questions; or define words.

One of the specific areas the SLP evaluates is your child's speech. During this part of the evaluation, the SLP will look at your child's ability to articulate speech sounds. She will listen to how your child says specific sounds in words during the language sample. She will also ask your child to imitate sounds and words. The SLP will look at the specific sounds that give your child trouble and decide whether those errors are expected for her developmental level, or whether she should have therapy to work on those sounds.

The SLP will also complete an oral sensory and motor evaluation to determine how well your child is able to use her tongue, lips, palate, and jaw to produce speech. The SLP will assess muscle tone around your child's face and mouth by observing her ability to move the articulators (parts of her face and mouth) smoothly and rapidly enough, given her developmental age. She will also evaluate control of saliva, posture of jaw, lips, and tongue at rest and during speech, eating, and fine motor activities. In addition, she may give your child foods of different textures and temperatures or ask about your child's preferences and sensitivities. This enables her to detect any over- or under-sensitivities that may indicate problems with sensory feedback from the face and mouth. If part of the evaluation involves observing your child eat a snack, an Occupational Therapist (OT) may join the SLP for this part, as there is significant overlap in the area they are assessing (more on this in the next section).

To evaluate your child's understanding of language meaning or semantics, the SLP will use observations, a language sample, and standardized tests. The SLP will give your child a series of tasks designed to indicate her vocabulary, understanding and use of concepts and categories, and ability to make statements that provide information. For example, to assess your child's understanding of concepts, the SLP may show her three balls and say, "Give me the big one" or "Give me the red one." To evaluate her knowledge of categories, she may be shown a horse, a ball, a pencil, and a flower, and asked "Give me the animal." And to assess her understanding and use of statements, she may be asked to tell about a cat: "What is a cat? Tell me about a cat."

The SLP also evaluates your child's understanding of the underlying structure of language (syntax)—how we join words together to communicate. For example, the first grammatical forms young children master are often action-object ("Gimme cookie") or subject-action ("Erica want"). As part of the language sample, the SLP will observe what grammatical forms your child uses to express

her ideas. The SLP will also assess your child's understanding of morphology, or the small changes we make in words to change the meaning. For example, she may ask your child to "put the block*s* in the box," as opposed to "put the block in the box" to see if she understands the difference.

An additional area the SLP assesses is *pragmatics*, or the way your child uses language socially. Pragmatics includes social niceties such as "please" and "thank you," "sorry," "excuse me," etc. It also includes knowledge of rules of conversation: For example, that "Why?" questions should have responses like "Because..." or even "I don't know." Through a language sample and standardized testing, the SLP will determine how your child's pragmatics stack up developmentally with other children's.

Finally, the SLP will use the information she gathers on your child's communication strengths and needs to determine if your child needs to use some other means in addition to speech to communicate. If your child is able to understand significantly more language than she can express, she may be a candidate for an augmentative communication system. Augmentative communication refers to using various non-verbal methods of communicating. This may include teaching your child to use manual signs and gestures, pictures, or electronic devices to communicate. Chapter 5 covers these approaches in more detail.

As a parent, I see my kid every day. Consequently, it's hard to see the gradual progress he makes in areas like speech and language. That's why the annual evaluations from his speech therapist are so helpful. She can

quantify his progress from one year to the next. This lets me see how far he has come, and appreciate his growth.

Occupational Therapist

The occupational therapist (OT) specializes in evaluating and teaching the gross and fine motor skills needed to function in daily life. These skills include those used for eating, dressing, grooming, cutting, drawing, and writing. The OT is knowledgeable about the way small muscles are used to make precise skilled movements and in the coordination of small and large muscles to perform daily living activities.

The OT may also have special training in *sensory integration* (S.I.), or in how your child perceives and interprets information from her senses, and then combines and organizes everything to make sense of the entire situation. Types of sensations that are integrated include not only the well-known sensations of sight, sound, touch, taste, and smell, but also those relayed by the *kinesthetic/proprioceptive* (muscle movement) and *vestibular* systems. The vestibular system (or sense of balance and posture) processes information about movement and gravitational pull. The vestibular system is what enables you to know, for example, where your hands are in relation to the rest of your body even when your eyes are closed.

Obviously, the ability to process just one sensation in one part of the body can profoundly affect development in many areas. For example, a major part of learning to speak is remembering what parts of the mouth, tongue, hard palate, etc., need to touch or come close together in order to make a particular sound. Children need to learn to feel how the parts touch, how long they touch, and how to get into position from wherever the parts were for a previous sound. Generally, the abilities to integrate *all* types of sensory information improve as children grow older.

It is the OT's job to look at how your child processes input from her various senses to her brain, plans what she wants her muscles to do to accomplish a task, and then coordinates her muscles to perform the task. To jump up and reach a game off a high shelf, for example, your child must first calculate how much higher the shelf is than she can reach. Then she must plan the jumping movements she will need to do with her legs, and the reaching movements she will need to do with her arms and fingers.

Specific areas that the OT looks at in evaluating your child include:

- Neurological function: whether your child has the neurological development necessary to perform fine motor skills and whether any neurological problems interfere with her ability to perform them.
- Muscle tone, strength, and range of motion (the degree of movement capable by a joint). Does your child have low muscle tone, so that it takes more effort to use her muscles? Are movements difficult to control because her joints have more than the usual amount of range of motion?
- Gross and fine motor development: how well your child is able to use large and small groups of muscles.
- Sensory processing and integration: as Chapter 2 explains, your child may be overly sensitive to certain kinds of sensory information, or under-sensitive to it. For example, she may not be able to tolerate certain kinds of movement, or may dislike being touched.
- Visual perception and visual-motor integration (eye-hand coordination): the skills that allow your child to make sense of what she sees and apply that information to a purposeful motor activity, such as drawing. Parts of visual perception assessed include visual memory (what your child remembers about what she sees) and visual figure ground (picking out an object without the background interfering).
- Activities of daily living such as feeding, grooming, dressing, and toileting.

To evaluate your child's abilities in these areas, the OT may give a standardized test, use checklists to guide his observations of your child's fine motor movements, and ask her to do a number of activities in a playroom with specialized equipment. As with the other professionals who evaluate your child, the OT will work with your child in a play-like situation. He will ask your child to do things with her hands (build with blocks, complete a puzzle) to see how well she manipulates small items. He will also ask your child to do some preschool-type tasks such as copying lines, tracing within lines, and cutting out shapes with scissors. And to evaluate your child's response to gravity and movement, the OT will have your child attempt specific movements on play equipment. Play equipment might include climbing bars, various types of swings, large balls, etc. Often, the OT and a physical therapist will evaluate your child together in the playroom, as there is significant overlap in the types of motor coordination skills they assess. Finally, the OT will ask you about the things your child does independently at home, such as using a spoon or fork, dressing, toileting, and opening containers or doors.

Sometimes my kid's OT can solve mysteries about problems he is having. Often she can explain why he is having trouble doing something that his teacher or doctor can't explain. This is because OTs look at the very basic elements of movement that underlie so many skills.

Physical Therapist

The physical therapist (PT) specializes in identifying and treating problems with movement and *posture*, or body position. She has expertise in the way the muscles of the body work together to coordinate large muscle (gross motor) movements and to stabilize the body so that fine motor movements can be accomplished. In contrast to the OT, who focuses primarily on fine motor skills, the PT concentrates mainly on the development of the gross motor skills involved in sitting, standing, crawling, and walking.

Much of what the PT evaluates overlaps with what the OT evaluates, so these two professionals may assess your child at the same time. They each might observe your child doing the same activity, but for different reasons. For example, the PT might watch as your child gets into a chair to play with blocks at a table, how well she maintains her posture while sitting, and how she gets out of the chair and walks to the shelf to put the blocks away. The OT, on the other hand, might focus on how she manipulates the blocks.

The areas the PT will assess include:

- Muscle strength, tone, and endurance, especially of the large skeletal muscles of the neck, shoulder, trunk, pelvis, and legs.
- Balance and coordination of these muscles. How well is your child able to make transitional movements between positions—for example, in going from a lying to a sitting position, or from standing to walking? Children with Down syndrome and fragile X syndrome are especially likely to have a hard time developing balance and the ability to shift their weight in different positions (sitting, standing, walking).
- Mobility and flexibility of joints. To accomplish gross motor movements, your child's joints need to be able to move within a certain range and also have the right amount of flexibility, neither too rigid nor too loose.
- *Primitive movement patterns.* Does your child continue to use ways of moving that were appropriate when she was younger, but that she should have outgrown by now?
- Response to touch. Is your child over-sensitive (*hypersensitive*) or under-sensitive (*hyposensitive*) to touch?
- Positional stability and posture. How well does your child maintain her posture when her equilibrium is disrupted?

To evaluate your child's abilities in these areas, the PT may use standardized measures such as the Gross Motor Scale of the Bayley Scales of Infant Development or developmental checklists such as the Learning Accomplishment Profile (LAP). Or she may use her own system of formal observations based on her experience and knowledge of normal gross motor development.

In the course of evaluating your child, the PT will observe your child make movements such as lying on her back and on her stomach, rolling over, sitting up, standing, using stairs, riding a trike, and using a slide or other play equipment. The assessment questions in her mind as she watches these movements include: Does your child's muscle tone change as it should? Is the movement fluid and of good quality? Is your child using the sequence of movements expected for her age? Which part of your child's body stabilizes so that the rest of it can move? Are there any asymmetries in your child's body (does she use one side of her body more capably than the other)?

Medical Professionals

A variety of medical professionals may take part in your child's initial and triennial evaluations. Their role is generally to identify any medical problems that may be affecting your child's development and recommend and evaluate treatments.

Registered Nurse. The medical professional most commonly involved in evaluations is the registered nurse (RN). She is experienced in working with children with special needs and familiar with the medical concerns that often accompany those needs. At your child's initial evaluation, she will interview you about your child's health and may conduct a routine medical screening, including height, weight, hearing, vision, and general physical appearance. Some of the areas she will question you about include:

• Your family's medical history, including whether anyone in your family had mental retardation, a seizure disorder, learning problems, or behavioral problems.

• Your child's birth history, such as length of pregnancy, complications with pregnancy, time in labor, type of delivery, complications with delivery (emergency C-section, cord around neck), and post-delivery complications (lack of oxygen, extreme jaundice).

• Childhood illnesses and significant medical concerns.

• Developmental milestones, such as when your child was able to walk, say her first words, and eat solid foods.

If necessary, the nurse will recommend further medical evaluations by various specialists.

Developmental Pediatrician. One of the specialists your child might be referred to is a developmental pediatrician. This professional is a medical doctor (M.D.) who specializes in working with children with developmental disabilities such as mental retardation, autism, and cerebral palsy. The developmental pediatrician is aware of the way a child's special needs can affect her education and family, as well as her health. Your child's developmental pediatrician might be willing to serve as your child's *case manager*—that is, to coordinate the medical evaluations and ongoing medical management she receives from a variety of professionals, as well as to help your family review educational records and programs.

Psychiatrist. Your child might also see a psychiatrist, a medical doctor (M.D.) who diagnoses and treats emotional and behavioral problems that may have an underlying physical cause. The psychiatrist can prescribe medications for emotional and behavioral problems such as hyperactivity, sleep problems, or serious aggressive behaviors. (While psychologists also treat emotional and behavioral problems, they do not prescribe medications because they are not medical doctors.) The psychiatrist will interview you, interact with your child in his office, and consult with her teachers and therapists to diagnose any emotional or behavioral disorders that might respond to medical treatment.

Neurologist. A neurologist is a medical doctor who specializes in diagnosing and treating disorders caused by physical problems in the brain and spinal cord. Your child will likely see a neurologist if she is suspected of having seizures or has shown a loss of skills that may be caused by physical changes in her brain or spinal cord. The neurologist will evaluate your child through an examination performed in a doctor's office or developmental clinic. She will check your child's reflexes and judge her muscle tone, motor skills, and coordination. She will also do a brief exam of vision and hearing, and may observe your child's speech, social behavior, and behavior control. Finally, the neurologist may prescribe a number of test procedures, including the EEG, CT Scan, and MRI. Chapter 1 discusses these tests in detail.

Geneticist. If your child is known or suspected to have Down syndrome, fragile X syndrome, Williams syndrome, or any other genetic condition, you may wish to consult a geneticist. A geneticist is a medical doctor who specializes in identifying disorders that may have a genetic component—that is, conditions caused by an alteration in the normal make-up of the genes or chromosomes. If your child is suspected of having a genetic condition, a blood sample may be taken and a chromosomal study completed to see if the diagnosis is confirmed. If your child has already been determined to have a known syndrome, then the geneticist or genetics counselor can give you information on a variety of issues, including the risk of the genetic abnormality occurring again in your family and how your child's condition may affect his development. Although a geneticist is seldom part of a school's multidisciplinary team, you may find it worthwhile to consult one on your own. See Chapter 1 for more information on geneticists.

Other specialists your child might be referred to include an audiologist, or specialist in the diagnosis and treatment of hearing loss, or an ophthalmologist, a medical doctor with expertise in diagnosing and treating vision problems. Chapter 9 explains the evaluation procedures used by these professionals.

Sometimes medical professionals are part of the multidisciplinary evaluation team, especially in the multidisciplinary evaluation centers in public schools. The medical professional most often included on the team is a registered nurse who has experience with children with disabilities, as well as with the medical concerns that may be related to these disabilities. Sometimes a developmental pediatrician, neurologist, or psychiatrist may be available on a consulting basis. Often, however, children with possible medical problems are referred to private specialists for further evaluation. These outside evaluations may be covered by your private medical insurance. Be sure to ask your insurance company what procedures you need to follow to assure your child's evaluations will be covered.

They told us she's a puzzle. But when we talked to the developmental pediatrician, that's when the puzzle ended. She said our daughter is not a puzzle.

Family Coordinator or Social Worker

Some evaluation teams include a mental health professional who assesses your family's social and emotional needs related to having a child with mental retardation. This person may be a social worker, psychologist, or special educator with counseling training.

The family coordinator will talk with you about your family, rather than your child. She will look at the resources your family has to deal with your child's special needs. These resources might include your financial resources, health insurance coverage, family/neighborhood support system, childcare arrangements, the strength of your marriage, and each parent's emotional status. Then she will discuss with you the areas in which you may need support. For example, if you and your spouse are having difficulty finding time to spend together, she may refer you to a program where your child can be left with trained, competent child-care providers. Or if one or both parents feels isolated, she may help them find an appropriate support group. And parents who disagree on discipline may be referred to a parenting skills course for parents of children with special needs.

The family coordinator may ask you and your spouse about the following areas:

- Your family's emotional reaction to having a child with mental retardation;
- Discipline and management problems with your child with mental retardation;
- Reactions of brothers and sisters to having a sibling with mental retardation;
- Financial and other family resources, including insurance; child care costs, arrangements, and availability; medical expenses.

Although the coordinator's interview may seem like an invasion of your privacy, bear in mind that she is well aware of the impact a child with mental retardation can have on family life. She is there to give you support and information, not just to assess your family's needs. The types of questions asked are usually open-ended and fairly non-intrusive. In addition, it is very much up to the parents to decide how much information they are comfortable providing. The information you provide is confidential. When a family coordinator or social worker is part of the center's or school's team, the information she gathers is treated as much a part of the record as the psychological evaluation or health information. Others will make use of the information only if it is relevant to your child's special education. For example, if you have trouble setting limits for your child's aggressiveness, the psychologist may want to consult with you and your child's teachers on ways to encourage more appropriate behavior at home and in class.

Your Role in the Evaluation Process

As a parent, you are also an important member of the evaluation team. At times, the professionals on the team may ask you to participate directly in the evaluation process. For example, if your child is younger than three and is receiving her initial assessment, you may help each specialist give the tests and interpret your child's responses.

When your child is older, you will probably not be in the room while your child is being evaluated. This is for two reasons. First, educational programs for children older than three are usually in classroom settings directed by a teacher, so it is important to evaluate your child's ability to solve problems independently. Second, tests for older children are usually standardized tests meant to be given with one child and one evaluator in the room. Often, however, you can still observe your child and let the professionals know later how her performance compared to the abilities she shows at home. For example, your child may talk fairly fluently at home, but not say anything during a test if she is very shy in new situations. Or your child may complete nine-piece puzzles at home, but not be able to complete a three-piece puzzle during her evaluation, perhaps because she is used to puzzles with cardboard backings, rather than loose pieces and no backing. And, as discussed above, the professionals will ask you many questions about what your child can and cannot do at home.

Besides participating in the ways requested by your child's evaluation team, you can also take part in other ways. Most importantly, you can take steps to ease the evaluation process for yourself and your child.

One of the best ways you can prepare yourself for the initial and triennial evaluations is to keep all your child's records organized and in one place, so you can retrieve the information quickly. For the initial evaluation, when you will be questioned about birth history and developmental milestones, take along any records you may have from the hospital or pediatrician. Also bring your child's baby book if you filled in dates on the various milestones.

To keep medical and educational records organized, you may want to get a three-ring notebook, subject dividers, and a three-hole punch. Some subject headings you might want to use in setting up a notebook include:

• IFSP or IEP—your child's educational plan for the coming year.

• Therapy progress notes—any reports you may receive from the therapists working with your child. If you have private therapies in addition to school-based therapies, you may wish to keep these in a separate section.

• Evaluation reports—the written reports from each professional described in this chapter.

• Medical reports—any reports from your own pediatrician or other medical professionals outside of the educational program, especially if the information is related to your child's developmental progress (for example, a neurological exam that found significant problems).

• Correspondence—copies of informed consent forms you signed to give permission for the various evaluations; notifications of meetings or appointments; other correspondence with medical and educational professionals; and release of information forms, giving permission for your child's records to be released to other parties (such as from the school to your medical specialist or vice versa).

Although this is not an exhaustive list of categories, it should help you start organizing all of the paperwork you will receive as you and your child proceed through the special education process. That way, when you are asked a question about medical history, you can answer as best you can and offer to let them read the physician's report for further information.

Preparing your child for her evaluation is somewhat trickier. The professionals involved are all experienced in working with young children and strive to make the waiting areas and testing areas as "child-friendly" as possible. They are experienced with helping children warm up and feel more comfortable in a new setting. Unfortunately, initial evaluations are almost always given in settings that are not familiar to you or your child, and sometimes the centers may be located in a hospital or look like a medical center, with a waiting room and a long hallway with "examination rooms."

To help your child adjust to the unfamiliar people, places, and procedures she will encounter, there are several steps you can take. First, if possible, visit the center prior to the evaluation date to see the setting and to find out who will see your child and what evaluations will be completed. Having your child visit the center before the evaluation date may be risky, as there may be a child in the waiting room who is having difficulty with the testing situation. It is better if you can talk to her about what she will encounter when she arrives. The day before the testing, you may wish to tell her that you have been talking to some new friends about all the neat things she can do, and they want to meet her too. Their names are Miss ... and Mr. ... and you are going to see them tomorrow and play some games with them. You may ask her to help you pick out what she wants to wear, if she likes to choose, and what toy or stuffed animal she may want to take to show to them. Then be sure she gets a good night's sleep.

On the morning of the evaluation, there may be some question as to who is more nervous, you or your child. As much as possible, keep the morning light and allow plenty of time to eat a good breakfast, dress, and drive to the center. Look for ways to keep your child (and yourself) occupied with fun activities until your appointment time arrives. If your child usually has a snack in the morning, bring along a favorite snack she can enjoy during a break in the testing. If your child begins to react as she would if she were in a physician's office, or if she hears someone referred to as "Doctor" and gets nervous, reassure her that it is not that kind of doctor. It will be all talking and games and no needles.

As mentioned above, you may or may not be asked to accompany your child to the testing area. If you and your child must be separated, it can be difficult. Remember, though: the professionals doing the evaluations work with young children every day. Work with them to let them know how your child is reacting and what you think will help them make the transition. Most children are able to handle the separation, calm down if upset, and do well on the evaluations. But if your child has a difficult time throughout the evaluation, that will be considered when interpreting any test results. The items your child was able to pass will be considered a minimal estimate of her abilities, and additional information from you will be important.

If your child does not have a good experience at one evaluation, the next evaluation may be more difficult. You may wish to ask if your child can visit the professional involved in his evaluation room so she can become more relaxed with him before the next evaluation. The real keys are for you to know your child and stay in control of your own emotions in order to make the evaluation process work for her.

I hate standardized tests. First of all, our daughter doesn't test well. Her attention span does not put up with what she needs to do for the test. And she might not necessarily do what she would do for us at home. So she comes out looking like she doesn't have abilities that we see her using on a day-to-day basis.

I know this sounds weird, but Cindy has given me the most fascinating education of my life. I find all the information about how mental retardation affects her life, how her brain works, and how she learns tremendously fascinating. I actually look forward to tests and evaluations because I can quiz the teacher, therapist, or psychologist about mental retardation and special education.

Interpretation and Use of Evaluation Results

As a parent, you will probably be anxious to hear the results of your child's evaluation immediately. But before the specialists share their findings with you, they need to share what they have learned with one another. Although the wait may be frustrating for you, the quality and accuracy of the information you are eventually given will be better if the multidisciplinary team has first discussed it alone.

After all the members of the team have completed and scored their respective tests, they will meet to compare their results and observations. Each member will share his observations about your child's performance in his particular area of expertise. The team will come to a conclusion about your child's strengths and needs, rate of learning, pattern of development, and effects of physical or medical difficulties. They will then schedule a meeting to give you the results of the evaluations and their recommendations for your child's educational program based on these results. This meeting must be held within thirty calendar days after the evaluation is completed.

At the meeting, you will be given copies of the reports written by each professional, which will include test scores, interpretation of those score, and recommendations for her educational program. Often, all or most of the professionals who evaluated your child will be present at the meeting to review the results of their particular evaluations. Frequently, however, the team presenting the results will not include all of the professionals involved, especially if medical specialists who served as consultants were involved. If any team members are not present, another team member familiar with their results will review their report and answer your questions.

You will be given a lot of information verbally, so come prepared to take notes and ask questions. Do not feel that you have to understand everything that is written in the reports or make any decisions. Instead, try to concentrate on the general ideas that are being discussed and the type of program that is being recommended. You can go back over the reports in detail when you have more time. You do not have to agree to anything until you have had time to think everything over.

As the professionals should explain, the evaluation results discussed at this meeting have two primary uses, both related to your child's education. They are used to determine the most appropriate handicapping condition and the most appropriate educational program. Both of these are discussed below.

——— ✳ ———

It is not so much what the psychologists or teachers say about our son as how they say it. I mean, do they remember that this is <u>your child</u> they're talking about, or just another set of test scores?

Your Child's Handicapping Condition

Because of their special needs, some children must receive individual attention from educational specialists to make appropriate educational progress. Because schools cannot afford to give all children this kind of intensive help, there are strict laws governing who is eligible to receive it. In almost all states, only children who have been found to have a "handicapping condition" qualify for special education services. A handicapping condition is a disorder or disability that results in educational needs that can be met only through an intensive, individualized educational program. Having your child "labelled" as having a handicapping condition is the key that opens the door to special education services.

As Chapter 8 explains, federal law has identified a number of handicapping conditions that qualify children for special educational help. Each state can also single out additional conditions that they feel warrant special educational services.

Examples of handicapping conditions include mental retardation, learning disability, speech/language impairment, hearing impairment, and emotional impairment. It is also possible for a child to have "multiple impairments"—that is, to have more than one handicapping condition. For example, if your child has a hearing impairment in addition to mental retardation, she may be considered multiply impaired.

For each handicapping condition, there are specific *diagnostic criteria*, or certain characteristics your child must have to be diagnosed. Chapter 1 explains the diagnostic criteria for mental retardation in detail, but they include cognitive abilities and adaptive behavior that are significantly below average. In most states, your child's abilities are considered to be "significantly below average" if she has standard scores lower than 70 on tests of intelligence and adaptive behavior. If you have any question about the cut-off score for your state, you may contact the special education department at the state department of education.

For educational purposes, only a "qualified examiner" can determine whether your child satisfies the diagnostic criteria for a particular handicapping condition. The qualified examiner is the professional whose area of expertise is most vital to diagnosing the condition. In the case of mental retardation, the psychologist is the qualified examiner. This is because mental retardation is diagnosed primarily on the basis of your child's scores on the tests of intelligence and adaptive behavior given by the psychologist.

Although these cut-off scores may sound very specific, they are only guidelines that the psychologist will use to determine whether your child has mental retardation. The psychologist will also take into account any cultural or language differences that may have led to lowered scores, rule out an emotional basis for poor test performance, and take into account your child's scores from Speech/Language, OT, and other evaluations.

For your purposes, it is important to remember that the qualified examiner is the professional who should know the most about educational options and the long-term prognosis for your child. Don't hesitate to ask the psychologist any questions you may have about your child's "handicapping condition" and how it may affect her.

The psychologist told us that our son was mentally retarded. I didn't like that too much because I felt that what he really had was some kind of motor delay. I was rationalizing. A lot of what the kids are tested on at that age has a motor component, so I decided that the psychologist was going to be wrong. So we went about trying to ignore the diagnosis. I didn't want to put any limitations on our son or have any experts do it either.

═══ ⁂ ═══

Every time my son gets an evaluation, and every time it comes back showing mental retardation, I go through a brief depression because it reminds me of the first time I was told about his mental retardation.

═══ ⁂ ═══

After we got the diagnosis, we had a direction to go in. We kind of knew what we needed to be working toward. We had a definition. We had information that no one was able to give us before.

Appropriate Educational Program

In most states, schools do not use a child's handicapping condition to determine where she receives educational services until after the preschool years. Young children with all different handicapping conditions usually attend class together in "non-categorical" programs—that is, in programs that do *not* group children with similar handicaps together. Thus, in your child's early intervention or preschool program, there may be children with hearing impairments, vision impairments, cerebral palsy, or other conditions.

Once your child reaches elementary school, however, her handicapping condition may affect her class placement. In many states, schools group children into classes based on handicapping condition alone. A school system may have separate classes for children with mild mental retardation, children with language impairment, and children with learning disabilities. The reasoning is that different teaching techniques are needed to help children with different handicapping conditions learn.

In some areas, there is a trend away from this kind of "categorical" classroom. Many parents and professionals insist that the similarities in programs and techniques used for children with different handicapping conditions outweigh the differences. Thus, some schools place children with many different handicaps in the same classroom.

In still other areas, children with mental retardation may be "mainstreamed" or "integrated." That is, they may be placed in regular education classes with non-handicapped classmates and receive special educational support within the classroom. Many school systems, however, have been hard pressed to find the funds to provide the extra support children with mental retardation need in a regular elementary classroom.

Wherever your child receives her education, her educational program will be based on her needs as identified in her assessment. If your child is under three, a comprehensive intervention plan known as the Individualized Family Service Plan (IFSP) will be drawn up for her, and if she is older than three, she will have an educational plan known as the Individualized Educational Program (IEP).

Chapter 8 discusses the laws that require these educational plans, as well as the specific elements they must contain. In general, however, you should know that your child's IEP or IFSP will address the areas of strength and need identified during the evaluation process. Her plan will include strategies for meeting overall areas of need, as well as more specific needs within those broad areas. For example, if your child's speech/language evaluation found that she has especially weak expressive language skills, a global area of focus will be on increasing her expressive language skills. To help her meet that overall goal, smaller, specific goals will be set. Specific goals might include, for instance, increasing the number of words your child uses regularly and increasing the average length of her sentences to three words. Results from other areas of your child's assessment might suggest techniques for helping your child achieve her speech/language goals. For example, the psychological evaluation may have found that your child does not recognize that a picture can represent an object. If so, she may need to hold or look at real objects or toys when she is learning language, because pictures may not be as meaningful to her.

Global areas of need and specific goals will be identified in all areas in which your child needs special help. As a parent, you are required by federal law to be allowed to attend your child's IFSP or IEP planning meeting. Do not hesitate to make suggestions about the goals and teaching methods you think would be best for your child. See Chapter 5 for more information on your role in the IFSP and IEP processes.

=== ❄ ===

We did a lot of floundering in trying to figure out how our child would learn best. Does he learn best verbally or visually? What's the best way to teach him reading? When we finally found a psychologist who could give us insight into these questions, things really improved. We could go to teachers and tell them how to solve the puzzle of our child's mental retardation.

Disagreements with Your Child's Evaluation Team

You may not always agree with the conclusions drawn by your child's evaluation team. You may, for example, think that they have chosen the wrong handicapping condition. Perhaps you think that the correct handicapping condition for your child is learning disabled, not mentally retarded. Or perhaps you think that your child has mild retardation, rather than the moderate retardation that the evaluation team says she has. As a result, you may fear that your child will be placed in a class that is not challenging enough for her to make optimal progress.

More often, parents disagree not with the handicapping condition, but with how evaluation results are being used to develop an educational program or decide on a placement. For example, you may feel that the evaluation results show that your child has significant problems in language development and therefore needs intensive speech/language therapy. But the school system may refuse to include speech/language therapy in her educational program. Or you may feel that your child has the cognitive abilities to handle the work in a regular classroom with just a little extra help. The school system, however, may insist that your child would do best in a class with other children with mental retardation.

When disagreements like these arise, you have several courses of action. First, you can seek a second opinion evaluation on your own. As noted earlier, this would be at your own expense. You would then submit the results of the private evaluation to the multidisciplinary team at your school for their review. The school system is required to at least consider the results of private evaluations. If you are not satisfied with the team review of the results, you can appeal to a special education supervisor or director for further review.

Second, if you are certain that the results of the first evaluation were significantly inaccurate, you can request another evaluation at the school's expense. You will need to present a reasonable explanation of why the first evaluation was inaccurate. For example, perhaps you think the examiner used an inappropriate test for your child or omitted a test that would have yielded different results. The school system will not automatically pay for a private evaluation under these circumstances. But it may agree to pay in order to reach an agreement with you. If, after considering the results of the second evaluation, you still disagree about your child's handicapping condition or recommended educational program, there is a third alternative. By federal law, you can use a due process procedure to bring your disagreement to court. Chapter 8 discusses this procedure and explains how to set it in motion.

I make sure that my input is considered in my child's evaluations. Otherwise, the evaluator gets only a partial picture. Ricky has many skills that he may (on a good day) or may not (on a bad day) show during a test.

We used to get bummed out every time we saw test scores. But now we know she can do things even if some score says that she can't do it. You have to question some of the testing.

Conclusion

The multidisciplinary evaluation process can be difficult for parents of children with mental retardation, especially during the initial evaluation. You are afraid something is wrong with your child. You can only watch as she is tested and prodded by numerous professionals whose specialties you may never have heard of before. Getting the diagnosis or results can be devastating.

If all children with disabilities were alike, there would be no need for developmental assessments. Schools and intervention programs could use the exact same set of educational services to help all children with special needs learn. But each child with mental retardation has her own unique combination of developmental strengths and needs. Consequently, the amounts and types of developmental help your child needs can only be uncovered through careful, thorough developmental evaluations. As a parent, you can help make sure that your child's evaluations paint the most accurate picture possible of her abilities. This, in the long run, will assure that your child receives the kinds of help that will best help her grow. Just remember that your child's evaluations do not tell the whole story. Your child is not a score or a point on a bell-shaped curve. These tests only measure what the professionals need to know to plan her educational program. They do not measure the child you have grown to love, her personality, or the way she makes her family's eyes light up when she walks into the room.

I have learned a lot from the tests our son has taken. But I still think that how he functions in his life is much, much more important than how he performs on a test. There are many aspects of his abilities—his motivation, perseverance, and niceness—that are not usually measured on tests but will have almost as big an impact on his life as his IQ.

Five

Early Intervention and Special Education

Helene Berk, M.Ed. *

In the past, children with mental retardation were often shortchanged when it came to education. Because society underestimated their learning abilities, many were given few, if any, opportunities to learn. And because there was no organized system to teach them, they unfortunately didn't learn very much.

Thanks to increased understanding about mental retardation and how it affects development and learning, this cycle has now ended. Today, it is recognized that children with mental retardation can and do learn, and special education professionals are constantly looking for new and better ways to optimize learning. Teachers are better able to challenge children with mental retardation and to help them grow to be as independent and knowledgeable as possible. And children with mental retardation are reaping tremendous benefits from these improvements. Many of them are achieving in "academic" subjects such as math, reading, and spelling, as well as courses in vocational and daily living skills. As a result, they are living increasingly fulfilling and meaningful lives.

How much *your* child will learn depends significantly on the degree of his mental retardation. But it also depends on a variety of other factors, including how well his educational program matches

* Since becoming a special education teacher in 1973, Helene Berk has worked with children with a variety of disabilities, including developmental delay/mental retardation, multiple handicaps, and visual impairments. She is currently the Infant-Toddler Program Coordinator at the Ivymount School in Rockville, Maryland.

his learning style, the skills and proficiency of the individuals who work with him, the encouragement he receives at home, and his own motivation. Obviously, some of these factors are not under your control. But because many of them are, it is essential that you learn about the who, what, where, when, and why of education for children with mental retardation. This chapter is designed to give you some of that information, as well as to help you make an informed decision when selecting an educational program for your child.

Getting Started

Before your child can receive special educational help, he must satisfy one major formality. As Chapter 4 explains, he must be evaluated to determine whether he has learning problems that would make it difficult to learn in a regular education program. If he is determined to have special learning needs, he will be eligible to begin receiving special instruction or therapies at public expense. If your child is older than three, the services he receives will be referred to as "special education" services. If he is younger than three, you may hear these services called either "special education" or "early intervention" services. As the sections below point out, services for older or younger children are the same, no matter what they are called. There may, however, be some differences in how often and where the services are provided.

What Is Special Education?

Special education is instruction that is individually tailored to meet the unique learning needs of a child with disabilities. It is designed to take into account each child's individual learning strengths and weaknesses, rather than following one set curriculum as regular education does. A major goal of special education is to enable children to live the most independent lives possible. Consequently, special education does not just focus on helping children in academic subjects such as reading, math, and history. It also includes special therapeutic and other services designed to help children overcome difficulties in all the areas of development discussed in Chapter 2. For example, special education can help a child improve his social skills or motor abilities.

By law, a child's special education program must include all special services, or "related services," necessary for him to benefit from his educational program. These services are provided by one or more professionals trained in working with children with special needs. For children with mental retardation, related services may include speech/language therapy, occupational therapy, physical therapy, psychological services, or services provided by specialists in educating children with vision or hearing impairments. Special education and related services may be provided within the regular classroom or in a classroom of only children with special needs. Where a child receives services depends on how and where a child learns best, as well as what program options exist in the community.

Special Education Settings

As Chapter 8 discusses, federal law requires that all special education students attend school in the *least restrictive environment*— or in the setting that permits maximum contact with normally developing children. For some children with mental retardation, this might mean having recess, lunch, physical education, and assemblies with children in regular education programs and all other activities in a special education classroom. For other children, it might mean working on some academic subjects in the regular classroom—perhaps with the help of a special teacher or aide—and working on others in a special education classroom. Still other children might not have any contact with students who don't have disabilities during the course of a school day. For example, children who need very intensive instruction to learn, have great difficulty focusing their attention unless distractions are kept to a minimum, or become very excited or aggressive when around other children may need to attend a school just for children with disabilities.

It is impossible to discuss the concept of least restrictive environment without also discussing the concepts of *mainstreaming* or *integration* and *total inclusion*. Mainstreaming (integration) refers to the practice of placing children with disabilities in classes with normally developing children for at least part of the day. Total inclusion means that a child spends all of his time in regular education programming. There are many arguments pro and con.

Some of the arguments *for* mainstreaming are:

1. Children with mental retardation learn social skills by interacting with "normal" peers.
2. Children who are mainstreamed develop the skills needed to learn, cope, and survive in a more "normal" environment.
3. Children without disabilities learn to accept children with differences by interacting with them.

Some of the arguments *against* mainstreaming are:

1. Children with mental retardation may not have the developmental, social, or academic skills needed to succeed in such an environment.
2. Learning social skills from peers fades in importance if a child cannot also learn other skills from peers because the difference in abilities is too great.
3. If other students are academically too far ahead of a child with mental retardation, his self-esteem can suffer.

Unless your child attends a school that is only for students with disabilities, your child will probably be mainstreamed to some extent. In a less mainstreamed setting, he may attend a regular school in a *self-contained classroom.* Here he will receive most of his instruction in a classroom with other children with disabilities, and remain with the same group of children and the same teachers for most of the day. Activities such as lunch, music, physical education, recess, and art may be with nondisabled children. In more mainstreamed settings, your child may receive instruction in one or more academic subjects in the same classroom as students who don't have disabilities. Depending on his needs, a special education teacher or aide may also work with your child on that subject.

Your child's specific learning needs determine the setting in which he receives his education. For example, children with mild mental retardation are usually more likely than those with moderate mental retardation to be socially and academically successful in more integrated settings. A child who needs intensive, one-on-one support to keep his attention focused on his work may learn skills like reading and math best in a self-contained classroom. If he picks up social skills most easily by watching and imitating normally developing children, he might be encouraged to spend recess, lunch, and other free time with nondisabled students. Because each child's needs are unique, designing a completely different program for each child is not realistically feasible. Therefore, school systems look at what programs are available, and then work to match your child's needs to a program. As Chapter 8 explains, federal law requires only that schools provide an *adequate* education. This is not always the *optimal* program for a child.

===== ※ =====

I don't really know what I want for our daughter at 7, 8, 9 years of age. Right now at 3, going on 4, and up to 5 and 6, I think she should be mainstreamed as much as she can. If the kids point and laugh because she can't speak right and she cries, than I wouldn't want her to be in that situation. We may not be able to find the perfect place.

===== ※ =====

To me, it's only fair to give our son a chance to go into his home school kindergarten. I don't know that he can be mainstreamed his whole life long, but I want him to have opportunities that other children have, for many reasons. One reason is that I think it will be best for him. If he is in a situation where certain things are expected of him, he's just that more likely to do them.

===== ※ =====

Our son is certainly not ready for a full-blown regular classroom. He's going to have up to fifteen hours a week with the special resource people. So he'll be out of his regular classroom getting some help with reading and writing, language, speech, and that kind of thing. What we're doing is creating a "buddy system" with regular education students.

===== ※ =====

I really think that most parents would not mind a kid with hearing impairments or spina bifida in their kid's class. But a retarded child, I think, turns many people off or makes them hesitate because they feel that the class is going to be pulled down because the kid is going to be slower.

===== ※ =====

He's mainstreamed in every other aspect of his life. Why not school? Why can't he go to school with the kids that he plays with all the time? We'd just want to make sure his special needs were met as well.

I am not interested in integration for show. I don't need to see my son sitting nicely at a desk in a "regular" classroom to feel good about him. I want him learning, whatever classroom he is in.

"Early Intervention"

Early intervention is special instruction or therapy designed to help infants and toddlers with special needs improve their developmental skills. This intervention is intended to optimize a child's abilities and set a foundation for further learning. The therapeutic and educational services in your child's program will be tailored—with your assistance—to meet his unique learning needs. Frequently, services include infant education; physical, occupational, or speech/language therapy; or counseling services for your family.

Early intervention is important for children with mental retardation because they don't learn as easily as other children. If your child can begin in a program at a young age, he will have more practice and support learning the skills he needs. Through early intervention, he can develop skills that form the foundation for later learning. Skills that are often taught and reinforced include paying attention to people and objects in the environment, communication and imitation skills, self-care abilities, independent play, and ways of exploring the environment that enhance learning.

Early intervention is also designed to benefit families. Parents learn to understand their child's abilities and disabilities, as well as how they can help their child develop. They can also receive support in dealing with emotional issues that may be a result of having a child with special needs.

In the past, early intervention programs used either a child-centered or a family-centered approach. The traditional child-centered program revolved primarily around the child's needs and the skills required to meet those needs. For example, if the child was delayed in learning to roll from his back to his stomach, early intervention therapists would work on that skill. Teachers and therapists usually determined goals for the child. Parents had the legal right to give their input about their child's program, but often were not closely involved in planning it. This changed with the enactment of Public Law 99-457. This law (explained further in Chapter 8) requires early intervention programs to be family-centered. In family-centered programs, the focus is on the needs of the family, not just the child. Parents usually play a primary role in identifying and working on the goals they would like their child to reach. For example, if a child has difficulty feeding himself, teachers and therapists work with the family on how to encourage self feeding without disrupting the family's mealtimes, and simultaneously help the child to learn the necessary skills. In this way, parents, teachers, and therapists work as a team. Research has shown that this approach works best, because the child is treated as one part of the whole family unit.

Another way early intervention programs can differ is according to where your child receives his services. Most programs are either home-based or center-based. A child might also receive early intervention services in a hospital if he needs to be hospitalized for an extended time.

In a home-based program, teachers and therapists work with your child in your home. They may come alone or together, one or more days a week. Program staff may involve family members in determining and working on goals for your child. A benefit to home-based programs is that all learning takes place in a familiar environment and no travel is required. Home-based programs are frequently used with the very youngest children or with children who are ill or medically fragile.

In a center-based program, your child goes to a school, hospital, ARC or UCP office, or other place where teachers and therapists work with him individually or in a group. Depending on your child's needs and the scope of the program, he may visit the center for as little as one hour or as much as five full days a week. Your child's program may serve only children with mental retardation, or it may serve children with a variety of mental and physical disabilities. You may be asked to stay to observe or help with your child, or you may be asked to leave your child with the staff.

Center-based programs are often preferred for older children. One reason is that they give both children and parents the opportunity to socialize with others who have similar needs. The children learn how to be members of a group, as well as how to pay attention and gain skills in a school situation. In addition, a center usually has more instructional materials, games, and therapy equipment on hand than the staff of a family-based program can bring to a child's home. An additional advantage may be that the teachers and therapists involved in a center-based program may find it easier to consult one another on a regular basis.

Depending on the programs available in your community, your choice of services may be limited. As Chapter 8 explains, free early intervention services are available in all states under the terms of Public Law 99-457. This law, however, does not specify how or where children should receive their early intervention services. Consequently, there may be only one type of public (no-cost) early intervention program in your area. If you are dissatisfied with the public early intervention program in your area, you may still have other choices. Some parents pay for services through a private special education school or put together their own team of private therapists. Depending on your personal financial situation or insurance coverage, these may or may not be choices for you.

To obtain information on early intervention programs in your area, call your local public school, pediatrician, or hospital social service department.

Another parent said something like, "Did you know you could have your child in an infant program?" I was beside myself with relief. Up to that point, nobody had told me what to do with my child. It was great just to know there was a place to get help.

Early intervention does not cure mental retardation, but it helps in lots of ways, even if this can't be proved to a "scientific certainty." You can't prove early intervention works scientifically because no parent is willing to be the "control" group—the group that does not receive EI so scientists can judge the difference. But even if you can't prove it works, my opinion is that you have to take the shot.

Early intervention taught Ricky a lot of important foundation skills— paying attention, understanding what school time meant, finishing a task, and responding to requests. On the other hand, it also taught him how to manipulate teachers and therapists by being cute or throwing a tantrum. On balance, though, early intervention was well worth the time and effort.

Too much was expected from us in early intervention. We had a teacher, PT, OT, SLP, and family coordinator working with us, and each of them wanted us to do something else with our daughter. There was more work than we could handle. As a result, I always felt guilty for not doing enough.

Professionals

Because children with mental retardation need special help to learn, the professionals who teach them often have special training. In fact, for each developmental area in which your child has delays, there is an individual with expertise in working with those special needs. For example, the speech/language therapist focuses on disorders in the development of communication and eating skills; the physical therapist, on gross motor problems; the occupational therapist, on fine motor or sensory difficulties; and the special education teacher, on problems with reasoning, building concepts, and other cognitive skills.

Through your child's preschool years, these professionals usually work together as part of a multidisciplinary team. As Chapter 2 explains, this is because development in one area often affects development in others. Your child cannot learn, for example, to call his mother "Mama" until he has the cognitive ability to understand the connection between that word and his mother, and the motor skills to shape the sound. And he cannot master the handwriting skills he needs to do his schoolwork without the necessary motor skills. Consequently, it helps tremendously if each professional involved in your child's special education program works closely with other members of the team to understand all aspects of your child's development. This is true even after your child reaches kindergarten age, the age at which subjects often begin to be taught as separate, rather than as inter-related disciplines. At this stage, parents often choose to act as the informal liaison between their child's teachers and therapists by sharing information. This can help ensure that everyone understands how their child's skills in one area affect his skills in another.

The precise makeup of your child's multidisciplinary team will depend on his individual learning needs. His team will not necessarily include members from each discipline. There are, however, a variety of professionals that many children with mental retardation encounter. Chapter 4 introduced these professionals and explained how they evaluate your child. This section explains how they will work with your child in his early intervention and special education programs.

Special Education Teacher

A special education teacher, or child development specialist, is trained in using specific techniques for teaching children who have difficulty learning in a regular classroom. Her role is to evaluate your child's cognitive strengths and needs. She will look at his learning style, which is how he approaches and interacts with his environment. For example, does he learn a new skill by watching others or by practicing it over and over again? Does he learn better if you sing a song while you are doing an activity? The special education teacher also usually assesses needs in the social and self-care areas.

When your child is in early intervention, one of the primary goals of the special education teacher will be to help him become more receptive to learning. For example, she might "teach" him how to improve his attention span. She may do this by having him do very short activities, and then gradually building up the length of time he is expected to concentrate. If he becomes distracted by noises, she may set up a very quiet place for him to work. If he loves music, she may use songs to keep his interest and help teach new concepts. You may also see the teacher reward your child with praise, hugs, or tangible rewards such as stickers when he stays on task.

During your child's early years, the special education teacher will help your child master important cognitive concepts such as those of cause and effect and object permanence (objects or people don't cease to exist just because you can't see them). She will likely help your child learn the names of objects in his environment and how they are used. She will also help him discover how to use toys and materials such as crayons, paints, and blocks.

As your child reaches preschool age, the special education teacher will continue to help him improve his learning skills. She will keep working on his attention problems, if necessary, and help him learn how to behave in a classroom. When your child is ready, she will teach him more advanced concepts, such as colors, shapes, and numbers. As your child gets older, his teachers will work with him on math, reading, and other academic skills.

Whatever your child's age, the special education teacher will tailor her teaching techniques to your child's individual learning strengths and needs. For example, if your child enjoys music but has difficulty with fine motor activities, he may be allowed to listen to a favorite tape after each short session working on puzzles. Or if your child has trouble sitting in a regular chair for long periods of time, he may be given lessons at the blackboard, while sitting in a rocking chair, or during a motor activity.

In working with your child, the special education teacher will use techniques that are often effective in teaching children with mental retardation in general. For instance, in teaching your child how to do something, she will likely break the task into many little steps, then work with your child on mastering one step at a time. She might have your child begin by putting just the last puzzle piece in, then the last two, and so forth. She will also encourage your child to learn through hands-on activities, such as counting real objects or using real money in a school store. In addition, she will help your child learn to generalize—to apply something he has learned to do in one setting to another. To do so, she may teach a concept in one situation, then have your child practice it in many different ways. For example, if your child waves "bye-bye" to Daddy each morning as he leaves for work, the teacher might encourage him to wave goodbye when Mommy drops him off at school, when the therapist leaves the room, and when your child goes home for the day.

The strength of special education is that the teachers are used to focusing on individual strengths. The first three years, Gary's teacher really did this a lot. If he wasn't learning something a certain way, she was on the phone with me, saying, "Look, he's not catching on to this. See if you can think up a way that we can do this." Then I would come up with something, and she would implement it the next day.

Jenny really respected and liked her first teacher. And the teacher really enjoyed Jenny, although she was strict with her. She could control Jenny's behavior, which is something. It takes someone who is attentive to the children and who genuinely likes them, as well as someone who has enough energy to be stubborn with the kids when necessary.

Our son learns better with some teachers than with others. With some teachers, he just clicks—they are able to present lessons in ways he can absorb and can get excited about. Those teachers are worth their weight in gold—they should be treasured because they can make all the difference in his life.

Physical Therapist

Not all children with mental retardation need physical therapy. But your child may benefit from working with a physical therapist if:

- he has trouble moving from one position to another (for instance, from sitting to standing);
- he is fearful of movement (for example, he will not try to go downstairs without being carried);
- he doesn't like to be touched (perhaps because touch feels irritating to him, or he feels as if he is going to lose his balance);
- he seems "stuck" in his development of certain motor skills (for example, he walks with his hands slightly up and out for balance, and therefore can't carry anything in his hands while he walks);
- he will not (or cannot) bear weight on his legs or use his arms and hands.

In general, you can expect the physical therapist (PT) to work with your child on the development of gross motor skills such as rolling, crawling, sitting, walking, climbing stairs, riding a bike, and using playground equipment. She will give special attention to improving your child's ability to move and to maintain good body posture or position.

Exactly how the PT works with your child will depend on your child's specific gross motor problems. The PT might use *therapeutic handling* to help your child learn to make new movements. That is, she would guide or gently manipulate parts of your child's body to help him learn or become accustomed to a new movement or posture. This technique is often used with children who have high muscle tone due to cerebral palsy.

The PT might also have your child play with toys that will encourage him to meet the movement goals on his IFSP or IEP. For example, to help your child build strength and endurance in his legs, she might have him pedal a riding toy. Or to help him develop independent walking skills, she might have him push a doll stroller or other push toy.

Another way the PT might help is to recommend furniture or ways of arranging furniture that will help your child make progress in gross motor skills. For example, if your child needs to build his strength and endurance for sitting up, she may suggest that he sit on a stool instead of a chair with a back while he watches TV. But when your child needs more support so that he can freely use his hands and mouth to eat or play with toys, a chair with a back may be preferable. Similarly, the PT might suggest that you put your child's toys on a high table if he needs encouragement to stand up.

Finally, the PT can suggest special equipment that can make it easier for your child to move or position his body properly. For example, if your child has low muscle tone, he may stiffen up when he stands or walks because he feels as if his ankles are not very stable. If so, the PT might recommend an *orthotic,* a lightweight device often made of plastic which provides stability. The orthotic would be fitted to your child's foot and help keep the foot and ankle in proper alignment, as well as give extra support. If your child has cerebral palsy in addition to mental retardation, the PT can help you select special equipment for a variety of needs—from special seating for eating, bathing, and transportation to walkers, crutches, and other mobility devices.

Once when both sets of grandparents were visiting, I thought we were going to die. The PT took Jenny into another room and tied her legs close together with a rag to help keep them rotated in the right orientation. Jenny looked like a crab. But eventually it worked.

Occupational Therapist

An occupational therapist (OT) helps children develop the motor skills—fastening buttons and zippers, handling eating utensils, cutting with scissors, brushing teeth—they need to live as independently as possible. One way the OT might help your child develop these skills is to work with him on sensory-motor (sensorimotor) development. That is, the OT will focus on how your child receives input from senses such as vision, hearing, touch, and movement, and then responds to that input in an appropriate way. For example, when tracing a drawing with a crayon, how well can he translate what he sees into movements of his hand? Or in climbing stairs, how well does he visually gauge the distance between steps, keep his balance when changing positions, and so forth?

If your child has trouble carrying out a sequence of movements such as climbing stairs, he may have *dyspraxia*—difficulty planning and executing movements. Children with dyspraxia often have trouble learning new movements such as figuring out what to do with an unfamiliar piece of playground equipment. A preschooler who has dyspraxia might scramble up onto a seesaw facing the wrong way, and then not know how to turn around to face the right way. If your child has dyspraxia, the OT will help him learn new sequences of movements by physically guiding him through the movements involved, by demonstrating, by explaining how to do it, and by relating the movement to something your child already knows how to do. For example, if your child is attempting to get onto a bolster swing, the OT might say, "Get on it just like you get on your bike."

Often the OT will work on your child's sensory motor skills by focusing more on building up your child's automatic responses to specific kinds of sensations than on practicing how to do certain activities. For example, if your child needs help in adjusting to movement through space, the OT may hold him on a huge therapy ball and roll him around, or have him swing on a platform swing. Outside of therapy situations, your child may never again encounter such equipment, but he can use the balance reactions he develops in many situations. Chapter 2 discusses some other sensory problems the OT can help children with mental retardation overcome.

Besides working on sensory motor development, the OT will also help your child develop the muscle strength, coordination, and stability he needs for functional skills such as eating, dressing, using the toilet, combing his hair, and writing. The OT can help your child develop the foundation for these skills in a variety of ways. For example, if your child's wrists and hands are not yet stable enough to allow him to write, the OT might have him do activities that require him to bear weight on his wrists and hands—wheelbarrow walking, propelling a scooterboard (similar to a skateboard) with his hands, or lying over a large therapy ball and supporting himself on one hand while he reaches for toys with the other hand. If your child

is older, the OT might have him play games that require him to use his hands to navigate a marble through a maze or to maneuver other small objects.

Both at home and school, the OT can suggest ways to help your child learn to take care of some of his own daily needs. For example, if your child doesn't yet have the neck stability to push his head through the neck hole of a T-shirt, the OT might suggest you buy large-sized shirts or shirts with v-necks. If your child can't tie a shoelace, the OT may suggest velcro straps or slip-on shoes. Your child's OT will also know about products that can make it easier for your child to use tools and utensils. For instance, there are grips that can be used on pencils and eating utensils to make them easier to hold, and scissors with different kinds of handles.

Check with your OT. He will know what would work best for your child's particular mix of strengths and needs. He can advise you whether tools should be adapted for your child or whether he needs more help and encouragement to learn to hold his pencil, button his shirt, or learn to roller skate.

The OT was very helpful because she helped us learn to notice areas where our son needed work.

Speech/Language Therapist

The speech/language therapist or pathologist (SLP) will focus mainly on your child's communication skills—both his ability to understand spoken language, and his ability to express himself with words and gestures. She will also work on any eating difficulties caused by poor muscle tone and strength, sensory problems such as over- or under-sensitivity to touch, or difficulty planning movements (*dyspraxia*).

What the SLP works on with your child will depend on his skills and his relative strengths and needs in communication skills. Often, though, children with mental retardation have better language comprehension skills than expressive abilities. If this is the case with your child, the therapist will likely encourage you to use longer or more complex sentences at times to stretch your child's receptive skills, and simpler language at other times to provide a model for your child's expressive development. The SLP will also work directly with your child to help boost his ability to use and understand words. For example, she will work with your child on identifying pictures, and later on naming details within them. She will also help your child learn to organize the world into categories—to understand, for example, that balls, puzzles, and dolls are all toys.

Besides helping your child learn to understand and use single words, the SLP will help your child understand and use combinations of words. At school, she will give your child practice in following increasingly complex directions. She will begin with directions your child has heard many times ("Give Mommy some") and gradually work up to more complicated, novel directions ("Go get your bookbag and coat and put them over here on the table"). She will also help your child learn to respond to and use questions. Often, the SLP will suggest activities and games you can do with your child at home to help reinforce what he is learning at school.

While she helps your child to use and understand different types of sentences, the speech/language pathologist will also work with your child on grammar—the rules by which we combine words into sentences. For example, we say "I *am*," but "He *is*;" "I want a cookie," not "Me want cookie." She will also help your child with morphology—the system of grammatical rules by which we change words to modify their meaning. For example, we add "s" to a noun to indicate more than one, and "-ed" to a verb to indicate that something happened in the past. The SLP may use structured play activities, stories, or practice activities to help your child learn rules of grammar. Often, she will look for ways that other staff members can make learning about grammar a part of other classroom activities. For example, at snack time, the special education teacher might talk about having cracker*s* or carton*s* of milk. What is important is that your child hear and notice this added "s" and start to see how it is used.

The SLP will pay special attention to speech sounds that give your child trouble. For example, your child may have little difficulty saying the initial consonants of words, but more difficulty with the final consonants. He may say "beh" to mean both "bed" and "bell." Or he may confuse the "b" and "p" sounds or the "t" and "d" sounds. Whatever your child's difficulties, the SLP will devise games and practice activities to help him learn to produce these sounds correctly.

Sometimes, children with mental retardation have a great deal of difficulty controlling the muscles in their face and mouth. They may be unable to use speech to express themselves and communicate with others, even though they can understand what others are saying. Other children may have difficulty understanding speech, even though they have no hearing impairment. In these situations, the SLP may recommend an augmentative communication sys-

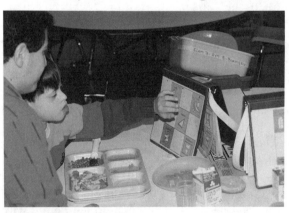

tem—a non-speech system such as signs, gestures, or pictures that supplement his speech abilities. When a child learns to use pictures to communicate, they are usually arranged on a *language board*. Your child's first language board might be set up to provide choices among foods, toys, or activities. Later, the language board is likely to be set up to reflect spoken sentence structure. For example, pictures of the child himself and others might be on the far left of the board, actions might be in the middle, and pictures of things and activities your child might want to ask for might be on the right. In putting together a sentence, your child would therefore use the same subject-verb-object sequence used when you speak.

If an augmentative speech system is recommended for your child, it will likely be used only to *supplement*, not replace, his speech. These systems are used only to help a child communicate while he continues to work on speech skills. In most cases, a child uses an augmentative system for several years, at the most. The SLP will work with your child, your family, and his teachers to determine the most appropriate augmentative system. It is important to select a system that *everyone* can use with your child, wherever he is. Otherwise, it will be difficult for your child to understand why he should use the system if it doesn't help him understand others or get them to understand him.

The therapists who worked with our son in early intervention were really helpful. They were able to focus on specific problems and delays rather than on the big picture. For example, the SLP could focus on his poor oral motor ability and just work on that. This enabled him to make progress in selected areas and enabled us to see progress.

Mental Health or Family Support Professional

Some special education programs have counselors, social workers, family coordinators, or mental health professionals who can help you and your family deal with the special issues you face because you have a child with mental retardation. This professional can help you work through the feelings you have as you learn about your child's disability and confront problems in dealing with his day-to-day needs. She might also help you find community support groups composed of families in similar situations. In addition, she might help you locate or obtain services such as respite care, medical care, or S.S.I. benefits needed by your child or family. Finally, the family support person can suggest ways to help you communicate with the other individuals who work with your child.

What Your Child Learns

The preceding section explained in a general way how special education professionals work with infants and children with mental retardation. But you would probably like to know exactly what they will teach your child. Will your child learn to read? Will he learn to count to 100 and make change for a dollar? Will he be able to use a bus schedule? Will he be allowed to enroll in driver's education? Will he have a job as an adult, and if so, what kind? It is difficult if not impossible to answer questions like these when a child is young. Children have different learning styles, rates of progress, and patterns of development. Just as you cannot walk into a "normal" nursery school and predict who will become a book worm and who will gravitate toward sports, you cannot predict what a young child with mental retardation will eventually be able to do. Yes, many children with mental retardation learn to read, write, count, and do simple arithmetic. Others continue to have great difficulty learning new skills throughout their life. Still others may be totally dependent on their families even as adults. For now, educators will focus on what your child can do at present, and work from there. This is something you can do, too.

Your child's educational program will be based on his unique learning strengths and needs in each area. As Chapter 4 discusses, a picture of those strengths and needs will be developed during the course of your child's initial evaluation. Later evaluations will keep track of how those strengths and needs change over time. As a parent, you will be asked for your input about what your child can and cannot do at home and in the community.

Once the picture of your child's strengths and needs is complete, you and school staff will meet to write an educational plan designed to maximize your child's learning. As Chapter 8 explains, if your child is under three, this plan is called an Individualized Family Service Plan (IFSP). The IFSP will detail long-term and short-term goals ("outcomes") for your child and family, and the specific early intervention and other services needed to meet those goals. For example, a goal for a young child might be to learn to play independently with toys. He may need the services of a special education teacher and physical or occupational therapist to meet that goal. If your child is preschool age or older, the plan is called an Individualized Education Program (IEP). The IEP describes your child's learning goals, lists the services the school must provide for your child, specifies who will provide the services where, and explains the methods that will be used to determine if your child has met his goals. For example, if one of the goals for your child is to learn to count to ten, his IEP might specify that the special education teacher is to teach him this skill within the special education classroom, and that she will test him on a standardized test, as well as through her own observations during class time.

In general, the skills that children with mental retardation learn in special education fall into two basic categories: functional skills and academic skills.

Functional Skills

Functional skills are skills that enable someone to look after his own day-to-day needs so that he can get along as independently as possible in society. Examples include:

1. self-care skills such as feeding, dressing, toileting;
2. housekeeping skills such as bed-making, vacuuming, cooking, shopping;
3. functional reading skills, including the ability to read street signs and labels and to fill out job applications;
4. functional money skills, such as being able to make change or handle a checking account;
5. community living skills, such as crossing the street safely, riding a bus, or holding a job.

Obviously, many of these skills are skills that even children with average intelligence are not expected to master until late adolescence. But whereas "normal" teenagers can usually pick up these skills fairly easily on their own when they need them, children with mental retardation need more time and help to learn them. Consequently, special education programs often emphasize functional skills so that children with mental retardation don't reach the end of their school years without learning them.

The functional skills emphasized in your child's program will depend on what he is already able to do for himself. For example, if he has already learned to brush his teeth and fasten buttons at home, his educational program should stress more advanced goals with enough practice to retain the skills he has already learned. The functional goals set for him will also depend to a certain extent on the level of his mental retardation.

On the next page are samples of functional skills children with mild or moderate mental retardation might be expected to learn over the course of their elementary and high school years. Remember that these are only very general guidelines. Some children with mild or moderate mental retardation will achieve more, and some may achieve less. This list is only meant to give you some idea of goals to shoot for.

We are really excited about our son's community-based program now that we have an idea of what the expectations are for the kids. His class will do some academics, but they will concentrate on functionality of living, how to shop, how to make change. . . . We think the program will serve his needs well.

Our daughter is learning about maps. I don't know that she can read one yet, but she recognizes landmarks. She wants you to show her where a place is on the map. I don't know how much she grasps in terms of understanding distance, but she knows where our street is on the map. She's getting there.

At school he's learned to keep a file of prices of groceries and how to categorize them. It's wonderful. He goes to the store with me, and I'm thinking "Now where is that?" and he finds the thing on his list and knows which aisle to go to.

Academic Skills

Academic skills are subjects such as reading, writing, and arithmetic that most people think of as traditional school subjects. Before children can learn these academic skills, they must have certain "preacademic" skills which form the foundation for learning. Preacademic skills your child's special education program may focus on include:

1. basic skills such as paying attention, sitting and listening, following directions, taking turns;
2. verbal and communication skills such as answering questions, imitating words, and expressing ideas;

Skills Achieved by Children with Mild Mental Retardation

BY THE END OF ELEMENTARY SCHOOL

* Self-care skills such as bathing, grooming, and dressing (but may need help choosing appropriate clothes for weather conditions, etc.)

* Understanding of basic safety rules (such as looking both ways before crossing street), but may still be impulsive at times

* Early meal preparation skills (making self a snack, assisting in cooking, following a picture recipe)

BY THE END OF HIGH SCHOOL

* Basic housekeeping skills, including making bed, vacuuming, washing clothes

* More advanced meal preparation (following recipes involving measuring)

* Financial management (budgeting, balancing checkbook)

* Ability to use public transportation for familiar routes; may be able to qualify for driver's license

* Basic independent job skills (arriving on time, staying on task, interacting appropriately with co-workers)

* Job-specific work skills acquired through on-the-job training (filing, typing, mopping, cooking, lawn care, etc.)

Skills Achieved by Children with Moderate Mental Retardation

BY THE END OF ELEMENTARY SCHOOL

* Many self-care skills such as eating and toileting (but may need supervision of bathing and personal hygiene to ensure done adequately, or help with clothing fasteners)

* Basic knowledge of home safety rules, but some child-proofing may be necessary

* Basic knowledge of neighborhood safety rules (can go down block to friend's house alone), but needs supervision

* Early meal preparation skills, but needs supervision (can make peanut butter and jelly sandwich, but may prepare 5 sandwiches instead of 1, or use half a jar of jelly)

BY THE END OF HIGH SCHOOL

* Housekeeping skills, with supervision or prompted by cue cards

* Meal preparation skills (following picture cards to make a recipe)

* Basic job skills (arriving on time, staying on task, interacting appropriately with co-workers)

* Job-specific work skills acquired through on-the-job training (usually involving a lot of repetition)

* Ability to use public transportation with some supervision

3. identification skills, including learning the names of body parts, colors, shapes;
4. pre-writing skills, such as learning to hold a crayon;
5. pre-reading skills, such as looking at and describing pictures.

Some children with mental retardation master these pre-academic skills in the preschool or early elementary school years. Others need to work on them longer. Again, how quickly your child will learn pre-academic skills often depends on the level of his mental retardation and his individual abilities.

The chart on the next page summarizes the academic skills children with mild or moderate mental retardation often achieve in elementary school and high school. Again, remember that these are only general guidelines. Your child may achieve more or he may achieve less.

One day I asked the teacher why my son wasn't further along with this particular little group of words he was supposed to be learning to read. She said something like, "Well, Mrs. L., hasn't anyone ever told you your son's retarded?" As if that was an answer to anything. I just about cracked up.

═══ ※ ═══

Abstract academics do not work for Ricky. Motivation and attention are everything in his education, and he doesn't care about learning abstract numbers that do not relate to things in his life. He doesn't care about reading a story about butterflies or outer space. But he does care about learning to read a fast food menu

Skills Achieved by Children with Mild Mental Retardation

BY THE END OF ELEMENTARY SCHOOL

- Core sight-word vocabulary, with some ability to sound unfamiliar words out
- Reading skills at about first-grade to early third-grade level
- Literal reading comprehension (can understand surface meaning of sentences, but can't make inferences about what character is feeling, what might happen next, etc.)
- Ability to identify main idea in simple paragraph
- Ability to spell simple 3-4 letter words
- Can write short sentences with help
- Simple addition and subtraction using a calculator or objects
- Can tell time on the hour and half-hour and understand time-related words such as "month," "tomorrow," "night"

BY THE END OF HIGH SCHOOL

- Reading skills at around fourth- or fifth-grade level
- Can follow written directions to complete a three- or four-step task
- Literal comprehension of stories written at reading level; perhaps also some ability to make inferences
- Can write simple letter, write out lists (of groceries, things to do); may be able to complete forms such as job applications
- Can use calculator in functional ways (to plan budget, balance checkbook)
- Simple multiplication and division

Skills Achieved by Children with Moderate Mental Retardation

BY THE END OF ELEMENTARY SCHOOL

- At least limited sight-word vocabulary of "survival words" (restroom, exit signs; restaurant logos)
- Interest in looking through books independently and in being read to
- Pre-writing skills such as copying designs, circling choices
- Can write own name
- Addition and subtraction using objects
- Can count to at least 10 or 20
- Basic understanding of money (which denominations are worth more)

BY THE END OF HIGH SCHOOL

- Expanded reading vocabulary (sight-word reading)
- Can follow directions on picture cards
- Can write name in cursive; may be able to write other personal information such as address
- Can copy written information (for example, copy own address from a card onto a job application form)
- Can understand that a written number represents a specific quantity (for example, can get 5 bowls from cabinet)
- Can match time on clock face (recognize what 9:00 looks like and correlate it with time school begins)

and to add the prices on it. If that's the kind of reading and math he wants to do, that's fine with me.

I used to hope that June would learn to read and would share my joy of reading for its own sake. But that has not happened. After eight years of getting to know June, I will now happily settle for her being a capable functional reader. She does not have to meet my educational goals—I want her to meet hers.

Balancing Functional and Academic Skills

The goals of your child's education program should be the same as those of any other child: to help your child learn as much as he is capable of, and to help him fit into society. *Everyone* needs to learn both functional and academic skills to accomplish these goals. But what if you think your child's program is stressing one or the other type of skill too much?

Many programs for children with mental retardation place a great deal of emphasis on functional skills. The goals are directed toward helping children with mental retardation learn to live independently, develop good work skills, take care of themselves, and learn recreational and social skills. Other programs emphasize academics, with reading, writing, and math as the main focus. In teaching these academics, these programs use special education methods tailored to the child's particular learning style. For example, rather than teach reading solely by phonics, it might teach sight-word reading. Many programs mix both functional skills and academics. For example, these programs teach "functional" reading, using words that are common in the child's world, like "hamburger," "car," "toothbrush," and "school."

The decision about where your child's curriculum should fall on the academic-functional spectrum can be quite difficult. Do not let the academic focus of the program be the only factor you consider in choosing a program. Evaluate each program apart from where its academic-functional focus is. Evaluate the school setting, the teachers and therapists, and the school day schedule. Perhaps you might choose a nonacademic program because the teachers are better or because they are more willing to accommodate your child's particular needs. The opposite may also be true. There are additional suggestions about what to look for in an educational program later in this chapter.

Remember that you are in charge of your child's education. When designing the IEP, request a program that provides the mix of academics and functional skills that you want for your child. After the IEP is written, if you think his program's curriculum is unbalanced in some way, speak up. Tell his teacher and, if necessary, the school district. IEPs are not set in stone, and may be altered during the school year as needed.

Functionally-based curriculums—curriculums that teach academic skills in functional settings—work best for our son. The labels put me off in the beginning—I always imagined my son learning academics—but he really does learn best in a functional setting.

Your kid can still learn academics in a functional classroom. A functional approach just chooses the context in which the same skills are learned and applied.

Working with Education Professionals

Most special education professionals realize that parental input is essential in helping children with disabilities reach their potential. Indeed, as Chapter 8 discusses, federal law *requires* that parents be involved in developing their child's IEP and that they be consulted before any changes are made in his educational program. You also have the right and responsibility to ask questions, request information, observe your child's class, and provide information about your child.

As a parent, one of the most useful things you can do for your child is to offer his teachers a different perspective on his abilities and disabilities. Teachers and therapists only see your child for a limited number of hours in one setting: the classroom. You have a much broader view. You have seen how your child handles himself in many different situations: at home, at school, in individual therapy sessions, in the community. Probably better than anyone else, you know what he likes and dislikes: what his favorite food is, how he likes to entertain himself, what situations make him throw a tantrum, and so forth. By sharing what you know about your child with teachers and therapists, you can help ensure that his educational program will meet his needs.

Sometimes you may disagree with education professionals about your child's capabilities. You might feel, for example, that the goals school staff are setting for your child are too low or too high, or that the setting they are recommending is not integrated enough. These disagreements can arise due to errors on both sides. For example, a teacher or therapist may only be taking into account what your child can do in the classroom, and may not realize that his behavior is different at home. She may not know that even though he won't complete the puzzle she tests him with, he has mastered numerous other puzzles at home. The teacher may hesitate to credit your child with having achieved a particular skill you have reported, thinking that you are exaggerating what he can do. For example, at home your child may consistently respond correctly when you say, "Play pat-a-cake," but the teacher or therapist may think he is responding more to your gestures or intonation than to your words. Or a teacher might think you're "reading into" your child's response—hearing or seeing more than the teacher actually thinks your child is responding.

It is also possible for parents to misjudge their child or let their feelings cloud their objectivity. For example, you may not want to believe teachers and therapists when they give you disappointing news about your child. You may reject what they're saying if they tell you that your child is not making the progress everyone hoped for, or if they tell you something else that you don't want to hear.

When you disagree with something a teacher or therapist says about your child, you should make your objections known. Teachers and therapists make mistakes, but they generally want to know so they can do what's best for your child. If you explain why you disagree, you can often help them understand your child better.

You may want to plan how and when you voice your concerns. If you try to talk while you are very angry or disappointed, you can put your child's teachers or therapists on the defensive and have difficulty listening yourself. This, in turn, makes it difficult to talk things through and come to an agreement. If you are feeling very upset or confrontational, it may help to set an appointment with school staff for another time, or ask a spouse or friend to help mediate. (The same holds true if you feel the staff is being confrontational, refusing to budge from their opinion.)

Be open to listening to the educators' opinions, too. If you find that many people working with your child view him similarly, it is worth considering their observations carefully. Teachers and therapists can often look at your child's development more objectively. They can look at your child's skills in light of what they see other children do in the same situation. The information they share may be difficult to hear, but it can help you understand your child's special needs and how they may affect his development of skills.

It is neither uncommon nor wrong for parents and teachers to look at children's abilities and disabilities differently. It happens in special education, and in non-special education programs. The goal is to work toward open communication so you and the teachers and therapists can jointly decide what is best for your child.

But what if your child's teachers or therapists don't seem to listen to you? You may find teachers or therapists who have little training in communication techniques and may therefore have difficulty collaborating with you. They may act defensive or seem to avoid your questions. Perhaps they feel that you expect them to "fix" your child, and they don't want to tell you that they cannot. Perhaps they are disappointed themselves that your child is not making more progress. Or perhaps they are afraid of how you might react to "bad" news, so they do not share information with you until IEP planning time rolls around.

In cases where you think your input is being slighted, the first solution is often to directly question the teacher or therapist about the behavior that bothers you. For instance, you might say, "I'm confused about why you have been saying he's doing well, when he hasn't made any progress on his IEP." The teacher might respond by telling you that she didn't want to worry you. Or then again, she may tell you that she's seen improvements that are not reflected in your child's IEP goals, but that he has made other progress. Perhaps his ability to participate in class has improved, or he has mastered skills that weren't on his IEP. If so, it's just a simple case of misunderstanding—the teacher has not been ignoring you as a member of the team. But if she *has* been withholding bad news, it is important to let her know how that makes you feel. You might say, for instance, "It disturbs me that I have believed all along that he was doing well. It's more helpful to me to know that things are not progressing well so that we can look at the situation together and see if there are things we can change."

Fortunately, more and more special educators are incorporating the insight parents have to offer into their child's education program. Most teachers and therapists you encounter will not only welcome your comments and questions, but also actively solicit your help. Here are some methods you can use to make sure you stay in touch: 1) Ask the teacher to keep a notebook describing your child's problems and progress, as well as things you can do to help, and have her send it home periodically with your child. 2) Regularly schedule phone calls to the teacher, meetings, or classroom observations. 3) If you drop your child off or pick him up at his school, ask briefly about your child's current behavior, activities, or anything else you may be wondering about.

Remember these principles of effective communication:

- Be honest and open in your concerns.
- Don't be afraid to ask questions or to have terminology explained, so that you're sure you understand what's being said about your child.
- Don't be intimidated.
- Share what you know about your child, but be open to different perspectives or opinions.
- Don't be afraid to disagree or to have others disagree with you.

Developing a good relationship with your child's teachers and therapists is essential to maximizing your child's development. The education professionals can help you understand your child's current skills and how he has progressed, as well as any factors hampering his development. They bring their knowledge of learning and development to you. You, on the other hand, bring knowledge of your child—his unique skills, interests, personality, and needs—to them. By collaborating as equals, you can develop an accurate picture of your child. When everyone's goal is to establish an effective working partnership between parents, teachers, and therapists, your child benefits from a program that can better meet his needs.

I've been asking the teacher to help her participate in class more, not just accept her. I don't want to tell people, "Yes, our daughter is mainstreamed," when in reality she's just being babysat. I don't want them to let her get away with things because they think she can't understand.

I think maybe I was too hard on my son's teacher in the beginning. I was very polite and pleasant, but inside I was worried that the school wasn't going to give him a chance to succeed in that classroom. I'm sure she knew I was watching her with an eagle eye. Things were pretty tense for a while.

The thing that has made the biggest difference in Ricky's education has been the interest and involvement in it that I have had. I would strongly encourage parents to make their positive presence known—not to be a supervisor or enforcer, but to be a partner with your kid's teachers. For example, sometimes Ricky's teachers run into the same type of obstacles that my wife and I encounter. They need help overcoming them, and often I have been able to help the teachers do that.

One thing that really helps is to tell teachers what you see as the ultimate long-term goals. I try to explain to June's teachers where I see her education leading. She's nine now, but it helps to say what I see for her when she is older. It helps teachers and me form the short-term goals. If you know where you want to go in the future, you can plan the short-term goals that will get you there.

Finding the Right Program

Special education programs available to children with mental retardation vary widely from community to community. In some communities, children with mental retardation in a certain age range may be served in only one school, or in only one classroom within that school. Other communities offer more options. Before agreeing to a particular placement for your child, you should first find out what all your choices are. Talk to professionals, advocacy groups, and other parents to find out what programs are available in your area. And if you do have a choice, plan to visit each program that *may* be appropriate for your child to determine which one actually *is* appropriate. Try to do this before your child's IEP meeting.

Here are some factors to consider when observing programs:

1. Size of classroom (number of students in the class). If your child is distractible or has difficulty paying attention, a classroom with relatively few students is more likely to give him the quiet environment he needs to learn. But if your child is very sociable and learns well by imitating others, a class with more students might be more appropriate.

2. Staff/student ratios. The more staff members there are per child, the more individualized attention each child receives. Some children with mental retardation need a 1:1 teacher to child ratio to learn; others can pay attention and learn in a small group. Most children need some time when they aren't being directly supervised so that they can have opportunities to direct their own development—to choose for themselves what they are going to do and who they are going to do it with. Your child's need for individualized attention may change as his skills, needs, and abilities change.

3. Professionals on staff. There are several things you need to find out about the teachers and therapists who would be working with your child. First, and perhaps most importantly, what is their general attitude? Do they treat parents and children with respect and interest and listen to what they have to say? Second, do they have training and experience in working with children with mental retardation? Third, how will each staff member interact with your child, and will that satisfy his needs? For example, the speech/language therapist may work with children in a small group, rather than individually; the occupational therapist may work with children in the classroom, rather than in a separate room.

4. Flexibility/structure of daily schedule. Having a routine to follow sets boundaries for all children, letting them know

what to expect and what is expected of them. Routines are especially important for children with mental retardation, who learn best by repetition, and often have trouble getting organized, keeping on task, and understanding new situations. Consequently, it is important that a certain amount of predictability be built into your child's school day. For example, snack time may always come after circle time, or occupational therapy may always come after lunch. But it is also important for routines to occasionally be altered—your child needs to learn to adjust to change and to use skills learned in one situation in another.

5. Teaching materials used. Because they often have difficulty with abstract thinking, children with mental retardation learn best if concrete teaching materials are used. That is, if they are learning to make change, they learn more easily if they can handle real coins, or if they are learning about animals, it helps if they can see pets or go to the zoo. It is also important that teaching materials be age-appropriate. They should be sufficiently interesting to your child to hold his attention, but not too complicated or confusing. For example, although your fourth grader may read at a first-grade level, he may not enjoy books for the typical first grader, as characters in these books may not engage in activities that interest him.

6. Academic vs. functional emphasis. The emphasis in your child's program should depend on the goals that you and his teachers have jointly set in his IEP. Theoretically, every child in a given classroom might be given a different mix of academic and functional instruction. As you observe classrooms, notice whether there does seem to be a distinction in types of skills each child is learning, or whether each child seems to be learning basically the same lessons.

7. Amount of family involvement. Programs vary widely in their expectations for family involvement. Some programs, particularly for young children, expect parents to take an active role in reinforcing skills at home—for example, practicing counting toys or spoons. Others do not routinely ask parents to teach skills unless they ask to be involved. Most family-oriented programs will let you tell them how and to

what extent you want to be involved. At a minimum, however, your child's program should have procedures for letting you know on a regular basis how your child is doing.

8. Mainstreaming. There are no clear-cut answers as to the degree of integration that is right for any one child. It is not always easy to predict how a child will do in a more or less integrated classroom. In good programs, everyone tries to make these decisions based on what they know about your child, and their experience with children with similar learning styles in different situations. If in doubt, you may need to just try a particular placement and see how it goes. You can always ask that your child be moved to a more or less integrated classroom if he is not learning up to his potential in his first classroom.

9. Behavior management. There are many different techniques for teaching appropriate behavior and for eliminating inappropriate behavior. You should be comfortable with how your child's behavior will be handled in school. Discuss any behavior problems your child might have and ask the teachers in the program how they would respond.

In the end, you need to remember that there is no one right program for all children with mental retardation. You need to make your decision based on what you have learned about your child from observation and from the teachers and therapists who work with your child. Sometimes your choices are more clear-cut than other times. Your child might more obviously "fit" in one program better than in another. Frequently, there are trade-offs. For example, one program might offer a "good" teacher, but an environment that seems too busy for your child. Another might have a good teacher-to-child ratio, but the therapists might travel from school to school and rarely communicate with the teacher. What you can do is gather information and sort it out, ask teachers and therapists for their opinions, and then choose the placement that best matches your child's needs.

Jimmy's current program really fits his needs. He fit into it just like a hand in a glove. They stopped a lot of his negative behaviors or brought them

under control. A prime example occurred about three months after school started. He was having sleeping problems. The school staff came here one night and probably stayed until 9:30 p.m., setting up a bedtime program for us. They didn't play any games; they did what they had to.

===== ❋ =====

Sometimes it can be real difficult to find something that's going to fit your child. Sometimes you have to create something to fit your child.

===== ❋ =====

We got help choosing a program. We went to the director of the preschool she was in and said, "What do you think? What is her biggest problem now?" We were thinking our daughter needed a program with a lot of emphasis on learning language, and the director confirmed that.

===== ❋ =====

The first time we saw our daughter's school, they took us into a classroom where there was a window knocked out at the bottom and you could feel this draft coming in the window. I was also kind of shocked to see a teacher walking down the hall in jeans. <u>Now</u> I realize that things like how a teacher dresses don't make a big difference. The things those teachers go through during the day, they probably have to wear jeans. I love this school; I love everything about it.

Conclusion

Education can open many doors for children with mental retardation—to new skills, friendships, feelings of self-esteem, and perhaps, most importantly, to future independence. Your participation in your child's special education program is the key that can unlock these doors to opportunity. Your child will have many different teachers and therapists during the years he spends in school. But *you* are the constant in your child's life. As a parent, you can ensure that your child's program not only meets his needs today, but that it continues to do so tomorrow. Your reward is the happiness and self-esteem of your child as he takes his place in his family and community.

Six

❈

Daily Living

Marya T. Pecukonis, M.S.*

Parenthood is never a 9 to 5 job. Especially if parents have young children, they must be ready to care for their children's needs around the clock. Everyday, without fail, they must see that their children are safe, warm, fed, clothed, clean, and healthy. Most important, parents need to spend time just playing with their children and helping them learn about their world.

When you have a child with mental retardation, many aspects of child care are the same as they are for other parents. For example, your child may love bathtime or hate it. She may be a picky eater or love everything she tastes. She may wear holes in her clothes the first day she puts them on, or put so little wear on clothes that you can pass them on to younger siblings. In short, many of the characteristics that affect how easy she is to care for depend on the temperament she was born with, which has little or nothing to do with her mental retardation.

Of course, your child's mental retardation *will* affect your daily care routine in some ways. First, because of her mental retardation, your child will learn the skills needed to be independent at a slower pace, and will often be less skillful at them. Second, you will have to specifically teach your child skills that other children seem to pick up instinctively. Whereas you may have found your other child taking off and putting on every shirt in her drawer one day when

---

* Marya T. Pecukonis holds an M.S. in communicative disorders from Johns Hopkins University and is currently working on a doctorate in education. She has experience teaching children with mental retardation, learning disabilities, and emotional impairments in both public schools and private practice, and has taught college-level courses on early childhood and children with special needs.

she was two years old, you may have to consciously teach your child with mental retardation every step involved in dressing. Third, your child will probably need a great deal of repetition and routine to learn the rules and skills that make everyday life go smoothly. For example, you may repeatedly tell your child, "We don't rip books," but she still reduces a beautiful book to a heap of cardboard and paper in no time.

Because mental retardation affects how quickly and easily your child learns, you will probably have to be actively involved in her daily care for longer than usual. There may even be stages in your child's development when you feel overwhelmed by the responsibilities that go with caring for her. But even though mental retardation may complicate your daily care routine for a while, it *will* get easier with time. Your routine will also change as your child's needs and priorities shift. Like all parents, you can learn more efficient, effective child care techniques. And with proper guidance, your child, too, can learn to take care of her own needs and to work toward independence. Granted, your child may not master self-help skills as rapidly or as thoroughly as other children do, but—whatever the degree of her mental retardation—she *can* make giant strides toward independence.

Teachers and therapists who work with your child can give you individualized guidance in solving special problems that make daily care of your child more challenging. This chapter describes more general methods for handling some of the daily challenges that confront most parents of children with mental retardation. You may not get instantaneous results with these strategies, but if you are persistent and patient, your work should pay off. Through trial and error, you will develop a personal style of setting limits, guiding, and teaching that works best for your child. Make a plan for yourself, then put it into action, remembering that you can always try a new strategy if the one you're using doesn't work. Your child's—and your family's—daily routine *can* become more manageable.

Daily Care Routines

Many children with mental retardation can eventually take care of many or most of their own daily living needs. But while your child is young, you may need to play a more "hands-on" role in caring for her than you would if she had normal intelligence. To help make your daily care routine more manageable, the sections below provide suggestions about some potential difficulties.

Mealtimes

When you have a child with mental retardation, mealtimes can be a challenge. But if you do not allow your child to monopolize mealtimes, many problems can be reduced or eliminated. Remember, you are a family and your child should not always be the center of attention.

One factor that will likely complicate mealtimes at first is your child's delay in learning independent feeding skills. If your child cannot feed herself, you will naturally have to spend more time helping her than you would otherwise. Take care, though, to allow her to try as soon as she seems ready. You don't want to inadvertently discourage your child from learning by giving her too much help.

If you do not want your child to eat with her fingers at a restaurant when she is four or five years old, you must start encouraging independence early. Don't forget, you can speed learning by rewarding your child for each step in the right direc-

tion. For example, eating applesauce with a spoon or drinking from a cup without a top are great accomplishments for a young child and deserve to be praised or otherwise rewarded.

Although your child may seem to have more than her share of spills, remember that *all* young children often seem to have more food *on* them than *in* them. It is far better to endure a little disarray when your child is young than to allow her to grow up without learning basic feeding skills. An old shower curtain or drop cloth under the table can make cleaning easier, as can a bib. If your child spills food at the table, you can also use the opportunity to teach her that sweeping the floor or wiping off the table is part of the mealtime routine.

If your child has trouble handling utensils because of fine motor problems, you can buy special equipment to make feeding easier. For example, there are utensils with molded, built-up handles that are easier to grasp, and non-slip place mats that can help to anchor your child's dishes to the table. Cups with plastic tops or built-in straws to minimize spills may also be helpful. You can find much of this equipment in baby- or child-care stores. An occupational therapist can also provide you with specialized equipment or modify equipment to fit your child's special needs.

Whether or not your child needs special utensils, the best way to teach her to handle utensils is hand over hand. With your hand over your child's, guide her through the motions of scooping with a spoon or spearing with a fork and then bringing the food to her mouth. Using a knife takes some practice, but you can teach this skill later on by first letting your child cut through soft foods such as a baked potato or fried egg. For safety, use a toy knife made of soft plastic—not a brittle plastic knife that could easily break.

Aside from problems with independent feeding, your child may also have some behaviors that make mealtimes more difficult. For example, some children with mental retardation cannot sit still in a chair long enough to eat their meals. Constant reminders to sit down are generally useless. Not only are they easy for your child to ignore, but you can also wind up with a cold plate of food if you are continually nagging your child to eat or sit. If your child is not behaving as you'd like, you must give her an alternate behavior to try. Place your child in her chair and immediately give her something she likes to eat. Remove her food if she gets out of the chair. Eventually, she will learn that you mean business, and that if she wants to eat, she will have to sit. Don't let her get into the habit of eating as she walks around. Not only is this potentially dangerous, but later on it will be hard to change the rules.

Like most children, your child will probably also go through a phase in which she experiments with dropping food on the floor to see what happens to it. When she finds that an adult will generally pick the food up, it can become quite a game. Since children with mental retardation spend more time at each developmental stage, this behavior can seem to go on and on. The only solution is to let your child know that dropping or throwing food is not tolerated. If a simple "no" is not enough to stop the behavior, take the food away and substitute another food that cannot be so easily dropped. For example, provide a spoon food like applesauce in place of green beans. If this doesn't work, try distracting your child by singing or talking to her. If she still continues to throw food, stop the meal. Try feeding her again in about thirty minutes—not too soon, or this may become part of the "game" in her mind.

Another problem may be crying, yelling, or grabbing other people or their food when your child wants more attention, more food, or someone else's food. Once again, try distracting her. If this doesn't quiet her down, warn her once or twice that if she can't behave as you ask, she'll have to leave the table. Be consistent in giving directions. And if she doesn't do as you request, have her leave the table.

If your child has tactile defensiveness, mealtimes can be especially trying for everyone. It is important to realize, however, that your child is not purposely being hard to get along with. She truly is bothered or frightened by the way certain food textures or temperatures or utensils feel inside her mouth. Your child may even gag if her body decides that something is not in a form to be swallowed. Sometimes, too, children who have learned to control their gag reflex may gag on purpose to resist foods they think will be frightening or will taste bad. If tactile defensiveness is a problem, an occupational therapist or speech/language pathologist can show you ways to help your child with eating. For instance, a therapist can show you how to introduce new foods gradually, use favorite foods as rewards for trying new foods, or mix familiar foods with new foods. Be prepared, though: sometimes young children choose to go without eating for a while rather than change old habits. But if you don't want your child to eat only a few foods at the age of five or still eat only pureed foods at the age of three, you have to choose a plan and stay with it.

Finally, remember that you do not have to be teaching every minute of every mealtime. You need not—and should not—harp on every lapse in your children's manners or on every morsel dropped on the floor. You can indirectly reward negative behavior so that your child learns to expect a comment when she misbehaves. What you can and *should* reinforce are the moments when she is behaving well.

Although teaching daily living skills *is* important, you should also allow your family a chance to relax and enjoy their meal. Sometimes parents find that the best way to have a quiet, relaxed meal is to feed their child with mental retardation (or all their children) first and eat later themselves. If you try this, your child can snack or play in her chair, or elsewhere, while the rest of the family eats.

There for a while mealtimes were pretty tough. It didn't bother me if our daughter was yelling and complaining. I'd just try to get some pieces in her mouth and tell her to chew just three more, but my wife couldn't eat. She would get a knot in her stomach, so I think we backed off a little. I've shoved stuff back in our daughter's mouth many a time, but my wife usually won't, especially if it's our mealtime, too.

I think the truth is that I'm not pushing him to learn to eat table food. Part of it is that I think, "Oh, it's not going to kill him to eat baby food," part of it is that I'm very busy, and part of it is my age, which I hate to admit. I say to myself that if I was twenty-three and had a three-year-old, I would be a lot more uptight. Having two children who have grown up and are alive and well, I realize that a lot of things you may think are terrible aren't that terrible.

When she was little, she would only eat bananas and Life cereal. Those were her staples, just about. This is the hypersensitivity issue.

The only two things I get depressed about are his eating and his speech. Not all the time, but every once in a while it hits home and I think, "Gosh, if somebody asks me how old he is . . . he's going to be four soon and he doesn't eat anything."

Toilet Training

It will likely take longer than usual to toilet train your child. How long it takes will depend on the level of her mental retardation and her awareness of her body and sensations, but the usual age for children with mild to moderate mental retardation is three to five years. Training essentially takes the same form as it does for any other child, and involves teaching about the potty and what it's for. Your child's teacher will have experience with toilet training children and can give you advice on what to do and when, what kind of potty seat might be best, and the like.

You can begin pre-training your child as early as two years of age. To introduce her to the idea of toilet training, you can buy her "big girl pants" and explain to her that big girls keep their pants dry. (You may, of course, first have to teach the concept of "dry.") You can also purchase a potty chair, and encourage her to sit on it—with her diaper off—at times tied into her daily routine. For instance, you can have her sit on it when she first wakes up, right after a meal, or before she goes to bed. In addition, you can begin reading children's books on toilet training and diapers to your child.

Once your child is comfortable sitting on the potty chair, has observed other family members using the toilet, and can show or tell you when she is aware that she needs to "go potty," you can start toilet training in earnest. Begin by noting the times of day when your child normally eliminates. Then let her get used to sitting on the potty during these times. You may want to begin scheduling times each half hour or hour when you expect she might make use of the bathroom. Some child-care books recommend taking your child to the bathroom every ten minutes, but this can be exhausting for you and tiresome for your child. Each time your child urinates or has a bowel movement in the toilet, praise her enthusiastically. When accidents occur, treat them lightly and teach her to help you clean up if you like. Be aware, too, that if left alone, your child may play with whatever she's produced. If this happens, don't overreact, but firmly and calmly have *your child* help clean up.

Never force, scold, or punish your child into toilet training. You just cannot rush this process. If your child is not yet developmentally ready for this skill, or if she feels pressured, she may seem to be afraid to sit on the toilet or refuse to eliminate, even through you feel she needs to. Your child might also let you know she is not ready by refusing to sit still long enough or by otherwise "misbehaving." She may also regress, or appear to lose toileting skills at times, but this is normal for any child. If you are patient and consistent and give your child ample doses of praise, she *will* become toilet trained. For children with mental retardation, as for all children, a relaxed approach to toilet training works best.

In the very beginning, he balked at the potty seat because he has such problems with bowel movements. So we left the potty seat out and he walked by it for months, never saying a thing. But once he got over the balking stage, he had no problem sitting down. He usually did nothing, but he sat there. Now he is able to control his muscles, so he's beginning to be able to do it, but we'd probably be farther along if we spent more time on it. I intend to work with him this summer. . . . It's just that he's an only child, and there are always disposable diapers, so I don't find it a big problem.

We could have forced potty training more, but we're working on it and it's going to come. Today he was dry from 8 o'clock this morning until 12:30, and he sat down on that potty seat and he actually went. He was just elated. He hasn't learned to *not* go, but he has learned to go when he sits on the potty seat if he has to.

Bath Time

Most children like bath time, and children with mental retardation are generally no different. If the transition from another fun activity to the tub is a problem, try asking your child to help you prepare the bath and round up all the soap, shampoo, and other essentials. This is a signal to your child that bath time is about to begin and lets her get used to the idea little by little. Next, let your child get used to the feel of the water just as gradually. Sit on the side of the tub beside your child, supporting her back, and gently wash her toes, feet, ankles, and knees. Talk to your child in a calm, soothing manner or sing a song as you wash.

Afterwards, try to ease your child into the tub. Never force her, as this may increase her resistance and fear of the water. If she does resist, you may have to just give her a sponge bath. Another simple trick is to try using less water, adding a little more every night until you reach the level you want. To help your child feel more secure, you might also bathe with her and support her in the tub. Some parents bathe their child with siblings or toys to help distract her from her fears and make the process more enjoyable.

Once your child is in the tub, she may enjoy having her hair shampooed or may resist it mightily. If your child reacts this way, try using a washcloth to wash her hair or an empty plastic bottle to rinse. If your child won't lie back in the tub, ask her to look up at the  ceiling or light to keep the soap from trickling into her face and eyes. In any case, don't dawdle over washing hair. The quicker you finish up, the less time your child has to fuss about it.

If your child seems to be especially alarmed or uncomfortable during bathtime, it may be because she has sensory integration problems. Children who are hypersensitive to touch and textures may find it upsetting to have their clothes taken off, or may only tolerate the water if it's a specific temperature. Many children with these problems especially dislike having their face, ears, and neck washed and their hair shampooed. Do as much as you can to respect your child's fears, and get her through the hard parts as gently but firmly as possible. An occupational therapist or a teacher experienced in working with children with sensory integration problems may be able to suggest tips to make bathtime more tolerable for your child.

Other tips that can help keep bath time a positive experience for everyone include:

1. On bath days, try to schedule bath time at approximately the same time of day.

2. Use bubble bath sparingly. Although bubbles are fun for younger children, they sometimes cause skin irritation or urinary tract infections.
3. Just as you do at other times of the day, reward your child for her self-help skills and good behavior—for example, praise her when she lets you rinse her hair or washes herself.
4. Apply a mild lotion to your child's skin after her bath. This will help her relax.
5. Try a hot bath yourself at the end of a trying day. You deserve it!

As your child grows, you can phase in independent bathing as you would for any other child (unless she has seizures, motor imbalances, or another condition that requires monitoring). Let your child take over parts of the bathing process as she demonstrates she can do them herself. If she becomes too independent too fast, and insists on doing steps you know she can't do well, compromise—let her do what she can, and then help with the rest. For example, if your child can't clean herself well enough, let her have a washcloth, but keep one for yourself, and take turns washing her.

Bedtime

In general, children with mental retardation are no more likely to have problems with bedtime than are other children. If you can establish an orderly, predictable bedtime routine, your child's bedtime should be a pleasant experience for both of you. Remember, all young children like to know what to expect—especially at the end of the day. The fewer surprises there are, the more likely your child's bedtime will go smoothly.

Your family's routine will, of course, be different than any other family's routine, but many families find that certain activities make for a more successful bedtime. First, it often helps to give your child a play period after dinner so she can unwind. You can talk together about the day's events, and create a valuable sharing time for the whole family. Second, you may find that a warm bath relaxes your child and prepares her for sleep. (Then again, some parents report that baths excite their children, so if this is the case with your child, be sure to give her a bath earlier in the day.) Third, cuddling up with a favorite stuffed animal or blanket can help to put your child in the mood for bed. Finally, a nightly routine of reading a book, singing a familiar song, or gently rocking your child can all help her feel more relaxed and secure.

Sometimes young children with mental retardation have trouble separating from their parents and try to stay up late so that they can spend more time with their parents. But whatever your child's bedtime routine includes, you should make sure it begins about the same time every night. If you do not stick to a consistent bedtime, your child will most likely become overly tired. And if bedtime doesn't begin the same time every night, you are obviously not laying the foundation for a routine. If your child has trouble separating or falling asleep, it is therefore better to provide security by staying in her room until she falls asleep than it is to delay her bedtime.

If your child has autism, pervasive developmental disorder (PDD), sensory integration problems, or ADHD in addition to mental retardation, calming her down and establishing a bedtime routine may pose special problems. Children with these conditions are more likely to wake up during the night or have problems falling back asleep. In this case, the best solution is often to seek suggestions from a pediatrician, teacher, or school psychologist, or from other parents of children with similar conditions.

He was having a lot of problems with sleeping before we moved to our new house. It was because we were in a townhouse and the bedrooms were all upstairs, so when it was time for him to go to bed, he was separated and he did not like that. We moved into this house, and the first night we were here, that kid put himself to bed. We were just astounded. He could hear everybody—everybody was on the same floor.

Grooming

Like other children, your child can begin learning how to wash her face and hands, brush her teeth, comb her hair, and stay neat during the preschool years. As with other skills, however, it will take your child longer to learn good grooming habits and she may never be able to do some skills entirely on her own. Your child may have special problems with grooming if she is hypersensitive to touch.

For example, she may cry every time her hair is combed or gag when her teeth are brushed.

To help your child become more and more independent in grooming herself, you must look at what she can do now, and build onto that in small steps. Give her clear, consistent directions and provide reminders when necessary. For example, after your child puts her hands under the running water, help her do the next step, either by telling her, showing her, or helping her to rub her hands together.

Also keep in mind that delays in motor or sensory development may contribute to problems in mastering grooming skills. Help your child out by keeping things as simple as possible. For example, give her a hairstyle that is easy to keep neat and combed. Use liquid soap rather than a bar of soap if that is easier for your child. Buy her shoes with Velcro fasteners and jackets with zippers if she has trouble tying shoelaces or fastening buttons. And set up a large mirror so that your child can see herself as she brushes her hair, wipes her face with a washcloth, or cleans her teeth. Being able to see what they are doing often makes grooming easier for children with mental retardation.

One of the most important lessons for any child to learn is that she should use only her own grooming articles. To help your child learn this lesson, always keep her hairbrush, toothbrush, comb, etc. in the same easily accessible place. It may also help if you replace worn-out brushes with similar-looking brushes. For example, if your child is used to having a red toothbrush, don't replace it with a blue one.

If your child is hypersensitive to touch, you will likely need to work with a therapist or teacher to learn how to adapt grooming routines to your child's needs. They may discover, for example, that it is better if you stand in front of your child to comb her hair or brush her teeth, instead of leaning over her from behind. Or they may show you how to use a washcloth wrapped around your finger to gently brush your child's teeth.

His coordination wasn't all that great, so brushing his teeth was kind of tough. Also, he just didn't <u>want</u> to brush his teeth for the longest time. He hated the way it felt.

Giving Your Child Responsibilities

Chores are an integral part of daily life for most children. Doing tasks around the house helps children develop a sense of responsibility and allows them to feel like valued and respected members of the family. Your child with mental retardation, like all children, deserves to reap these rewards. And like all parents, you deserve to have your child help around the house.

When choosing chores for your child, keep in mind her attention span and abilities. Decide what she can accomplish with minimal effort and then gradually challenge her with more responsibilities. For example, you may want to begin by asking your child to help dust the furniture or wipe the table after a meal. You will probably

also want to teach her to put her toys away and straighten her room. Your child will do as you ask if you help her and make the task seem enjoyable. You might say, "Let's put this puzzle away so we don't lose the pieces." Or, "Let's pretend we work in a toy store and we want to have a clean store." Remember the power of praise!

To increase your child's chances of success, do not overwhelm her with a job that is too large, too complicated, or too imprecisely defined. For example, don't simply tell your child, "Clean up your room" or "Make your bed." Specify exactly what you want her to do—for instance, "Put the pillow on the bed" or "Put your shoes on the shelf." To help your child understand, use gestures or physically guide her through steps she has trouble with.

Finally, remember that your child will complete tasks at her own pace and in her own way. Often, you might be able to do something more quickly or more efficiently than your child can. For example, you may be able to place a spoon at every plate in seconds, while your child takes several minutes to do the same task. But you must allow her to move at her own rate—which *will* likely be slower than yours—or she will never master the job. You must also allow her to complete the task in her own way rather than expecting her to perform up to your adult standards. Don't say, "Good job, except you put the spoons on the wrong side." Focus instead on what she did right and reward her with unqualified praise. For example, "I'm proud of you. You put out two spoons. One for me, one for you."

Table 1 gives some examples of common household chores, together with the developmental ages at which children with mental retardation are often ready to start doing them *with adult supervision*. Remember that the ages suggested for these goals are *developmental*, and may or may not occur at the same chronological ages. That is, a child with mental retardation may not be developmentally ready to handle a typical three-year-old skill until her chronological age is five or more. Also remember that children vary in their readiness, ability, and motivation to perform these tasks. Do not rush your child if she is not quite ready to learn a particular chore at the suggested time, or hold her back if she is ready earlier than suggested.

If you are patient and accept your child's individual differences, she will learn to accept responsibility. Over time, she will become more skillful at household tasks. This in turn, will help her independence grow.

Julie has good days and bad days. Sometimes she could empty that whole dishwasher and put the items on the table. She has the cognitive ability to do that. But if I catch her at a bad time, she starts pounding the dishes and she can't do it. I know to back off, that this is not the right time.

Teaching Your Child

A major part of daily care is teaching your child to gradually take on responsibility for some of her own daily care. Most parents don't

Table 1

Task	Approximate Age
• Dusting furniture	2
• Wiping table with sponge	2
• Sweeping floor (child-sized broom)	3
• Feeding family pet	3
• Cleaning up room (picking up belongings and putting them away)	3
• Clearing the table (one item at a time)	3
• Shopping at grocery store (helping take packages from shelves)	3–4
• Unloading dishwasher	3-4
• Vacuuming rugs	5-6
• Folding laundry (small towels, washcloths, socks, handkerchiefs)	4–5
• Matching socks; identifying clothing to be put away (sister's drawer, own drawer)	4
• Putting groceries away at home	4-5
• Straightening pillows on bed	4-5
• Meal preparation (helping make a salad, dessert, drink)	4–6
• Setting the table	4-6
• Loading dishwasher	5-7
• Pulling up covers on bed	5-6

think twice about teaching their children daily living skills. As soon as their children show an interest or seem ready, they let them try to eat with a spoon, brush their teeth, dress themselves, and use the toilet. But when your child has mental retardation, you may think it takes special talent or training to help your child master self-help skills. This is simply not so. True, your child *will* need some special attention and more deliberate teaching in order to reach her maximum potential. But it is also true that she will basically follow the normal course of development—*just at a slower rate.* You can help her learn at her own pace and take that learning as far as possible. Even without formal training, you can easily incorporate learning experiences into many of your daily care routines. And as you observe your child take even small steps toward independence, your confidence in your abilities to teach her will grow.

As a parent, you are your child's first teacher. And you can often be her best teacher. After all, you will probably spend more time with her than anyone else will—at least during the first three years of your child's life. You may also continue to spend the most time with her for several years after that, depending upon your child's school program and your other obligations. Since young children learn best through imitation, you can help your child develop by being her model—that is, by demonstrating how to complete a task and encouraging your child to imitate each step. Because you know your child so well, you are also more likely to know what skills she needs and is ready to learn. Another advantage you have in teaching your child is that she may be more relaxed and ready to participate at home than she is in the busy, less familiar environment of a school. In addition, your house and your daily routine are filled with teaching opportunities. For example, you or other family members may lead your child along beside you as you collect soiled clothes from the laundry hamper. You introduce your child to daily living chores as well as basic language concepts when you talk about dirty clothes, washing or cleaning the clothes, putting them IN the machine, how soft they feel, or how good they smell. If she is willing, you can also encourage her to fold her clothes and put them in the correct drawer once they are dry.

Although the idea of making teaching a part of your routine may seem overwhelming, it really isn't. Just because the opportunities are there does *not* mean that you need to devote every spare moment to teaching your child. Teaching your child to handle a daily care routine herself does not take much longer than doing it for her. Furthermore, you won't need to spend a lot of time preparing formal "lessons." Most parents teach constantly and naturally without even realizing it. For example, every time you speak to your child, you are assisting her language development by providing a model for her and giving her practice in language comprehension. You strengthen her reasoning ability and problem-solving skills when you include her in family decisions or in planning daily activities. You enrich her reading and math readiness skills when you let her help you make a dish from a recipe, watch the traffic signal and tell you when to go, buy groceries, or run errands at the library, mall, or post office. You teach her sign/symbol relationships when you read a book to her or point out the logo on the supermarket or gas station. And you encourage independence when you let your child participate—at whatever level possible—in daily routines.

Of course, not every parent has the time or inclination to become actively involved in teaching their child. Especially if you work full time or have other children, you may feel you do enough just managing your day-to-day tasks. If so, you may need to seek help in teaching your child. As Chapter 5 explains, there are many educational professionals who can teach your child the skills she needs to become independent. At first, you may feel more comfortable consulting these professionals from the sidelines rather than working side by side with them. Or you may be content just to help out as the professionals request. After you have gained confidence in your abilities, you can then decide when to take a more active part in teaching your child.

No one expects you to automatically know what your child needs to learn or the best way to teach her. Your child's therapists and teachers can help you by giving you information on normal development, teaching strategies, and goals. These professionals will most likely welcome your participation. No doubt, they too would like help achieving their goals for your child. And they will be eager to help you because *your* work with your child helps *them*.

There are also a number of strategies you can learn on your own that should make teaching daily living skills easier. The methods below can be used to teach any child—not just a child with mental retardation. The main difference in applying these methods will be the size of the challenge you will face and the extra amount of patience and diligence you will need. Your child with mental retardation *will* progress, but more slowly than other children, and she may sometimes "forget" what you expect of her. Consistency will therefore be especially important in your family's daily life.

Setting Goals

Before you can teach your child, you must naturally know what you want to teach her. It is not enough to have a general idea that you would like your child to acquire skills that will help her to learn and become more independent. You must decide on the smaller, more specific goals that are most important for your child to achieve *at this time.* For example, your ultimate goal may be that as an adult, your child will be able to handle every aspect of mealtime on her own—shopping for the food, preparing the meal, eating it, and cleaning up. But for now, it is enough to teach her to help clear the table. If you work on one small step at a time, your child will gradually achieve success.

One of the simplest ways to choose an appropriate goal for your child is to watch for signs that she is interested in learning a particular skill. For example, your preschooler may try to help you dust the furniture or sweep the floor. You can also observe your child more formally to find out which tasks she might be ready to try. Watch her play and interact with family members and other children. Keep a daily journal and record her activities to discover her interests in learning. Here is an actual observation that could be entered into a daily journal:

> Joshua watched his older sister pour her own juice today. He immediately reached for the pitcher to help himself to juice, and I was pleased that he was able to lift the juice pitcher by himself and steady the cup. His older sister helped him pour the juice, and he smiled as she told him what a great job he did.

This parent observed her son show an interest in pouring his own juice. Consequently, this would be a good self-help skill for her to begin working on with him.

Over time, you may observe that your child is more receptive to learning at some times than at others. For example, you may notice that your child sometimes sings while she helps with simple chores. This may be a sign that your child is in the mood to help and is motivated to participate.

Aside from teaching your child the skills *she* wants to learn, you will also want to teach her skills *you* want her to learn in order to become more independent. Often these are skills that can make your daily routine easier as well. For example, perhaps you are always pressed for time in the morning because it takes so long to dress your child. If so, learning to dress independently may be an important goal for your child. Independent toileting skills, behaving properly at mealtime, sharing with siblings, and taking responsibility for her own belongings are other long-range goals for your child that reduce direct parent involvement and help you balance the needs of all members of your family. These types of goals are also vital to your child's future independence.

Whatever goals you choose for your child, it is important that they be realistic. Before attempting to teach a skill, consider your child's ability level and attention span. For instance, your goal may be for her to completely dress herself with little assistance. But what if she lacks the motor ability to fasten buttons or zippers or has difficulty putting her arms through her shirt sleeves? If so, it would be wise to rethink your goal so it is within your child's present abilities. You might instead set a goal for your child to help choose her own clothing and lay it on the bed, and then continue to help her dress while her motor skills improve to the point where you can set higher goals. You might also adapt clothing to make dressing easier for your child. Velcro shoes, elastic shoe strings, or pull strings on zippers can be useful modifications. Ask your child's occupational therapist for other modifications that might help.

An important corollary to setting realistic goals is to *start small*. Young children with mental retardation often become overwhelmed or confused if they are asked to do too many things at once. Perhaps there are four goals you would really like your child to accomplish. But your child may only be ready to handle two goals. If so, prioritize your goals and begin with the two you consider most important. Gradually introduce new goals only as your child masters previous ones.

Guard against setting goals that are too high by: 1) consulting with professionals; and 2) being sensitive to signs that you are asking too much (irritability, excessive crying, unwillingness to attempt a task, and defensive behavior such as hitting).

If you are unsure where or how to start, consult with your child's teacher or therapist. As a general guideline, Table 2 lists some typical goals appropriate for children with mental retardation of various ages. Once again, the ages suggested are developmental, not chronological ages. Bear in mind that there is no one "right" time for children to reach these goals; some children may be ready to learn a specific skill earlier and some may be ready later.

═══ ※ ═══

Typically, at a certain stage, children are willing to do certain things for themselves on their own. Relative to his biological age, I guess our son was later than most. But in terms of his mental age, he was probably at about the same age as a standard child when he decided that "yeah, I'm going to do this now."

═══ ※ ═══

He just learned to tie his shoes this summer, which was a big feat. We've been working on that for years. He really never had a whole lot of problems with self-care, except that he was just slow. He was like slow motion in terms of his growth and in terms of his ability to do certain things.

Your Expectations

As you narrow down your selection of goals, keep one final consideration in mind: your expectations can have an enormous effect on your child's progress. Although you may have accepted the notion that your child will develop more slowly than other children, you must never accept less from your child simply because she has mental retardation. Remember, children pick up subtle cues such as parents' facial expressions, tone of voice, and gestures. If you genuinely believe in and support all of your child's efforts, your child will get the message that she can do it. She will keep trying to reach the realistic goals you and her therapists and teachers set for her, and continue to progress along the road to independence.

Table 2

Age	Goals	People Who Help Teach*
	General Goals	
1+	Following directions, answering questions	Family members, teachers, speech/language pathologists (SLP)
2-3	Gross motor skills (jumping, running, throwing, climbing)	Family members, teachers, physical therapists (PT), occupational therapists (OT)
3	Fine motor skills (cutting, manipulating objects, pre-writing activities such as scribbling)	Family members, teachers, OT
	Toileting Goals	
2-3	Telling or indicating to parent the need to use the toilet	Parents, teachers, OT
3-4	Independently using the toilet	Parents, teachers, OT
	Eating Goals	
1-2	Using utensils	Parents, teachers, OT
ongoing	Sitting at table during meals	Parents, teachers
3-4	Demonstrating appropriate manners	Parents, teachers, SLP
	Dressing Goals	
2-3	Undressing self	Parents, teachers, OT
3-4	Dressing self without buttons or zippers	Parents, teachers, OT
4-5	Dressing self with buttons or zippers	Parents, teachers, OT
	Verbal Expression	
1+	Imitating speech of those around them	SLP, parents, teachers
2+	Responding to questions/directions ("What's that?")	SLP, parents, teachers
2+	Singing songs, doing rhymes, verbal games ("Ring around the Rosie"; "Eensy Weensy Spider")	SLP, parents, teachers

* To ensure effective planning, teaching, and reinforcement, everyone involved in teaching the child must communicate among themselves about goals, techniques, and progress.

On the other hand, if you have good intentions but low expectations, you will probably catch yourself doing things for your child instead of encouraging her to do them herself. For example, if you don't really believe your child can learn to make her bed, you may constantly take over as soon as she gets distracted from the task or leaves wrinkles. Your "help" can end up preventing her from getting the practice she needs to learn to do it right.

Thinking through the Steps

Once you have decided on a goal for your child, you must break down the skill you want her to learn into small, manageable steps. Your child's teachers or therapists can show you how to walk through the activity yourself, writing down each step you do in the order you complete it. They can also help you plan out how you will demonstrate and explain each step to your child. For example, if you intend to teach your child how to put on a pullover shirt, you might actually want to write down the following steps:

1. Check to see that the shirt is right side out. "The tag goes inside."
2. Find back of shirt.
3. Locate the neck hole. "Your head goes here."
4. Gently pull the shirt over your head. "Pull it down."
5. Place right arm into right sleeve. "Push your arm out."
6. Place left arm into left sleeve. "Push your arm out."
7. Pull the shirt down in front. "Down over your tummy."
8. Pull the shirt down in back. "Now down over your back."
9. "You did it! What a big girl!"

After each step is clear in your mind, one way to begin is by teaching your child the step closest to the goal. That is, start by encouraging your child to complete the *last* step independently. This way your child can learn one step that leads immediately to the goal you are working on. In the example above, you would first work on step 8 with your child. You would praise your child for each attempt she made to learn this step. Only after she was able to pull her shirt down would you work on step 7. Likewise, you would not move on to step 5 until she mastered step 6.

For an older child, the process is basically the same. But you might want to supplement your verbal instructions with picture cards illustrating each step involved. This not only helps your child learn the steps involved in the new task, but also helps teach the concept of sequences. To make the cards, cut pictures out of magazines or take real photos of your child. Then paste them to index cards and label them with a few simple words or symbols. For example, if you wanted to teach your child to set the table, you might plan it out this way:

1. Put one place mat in front of each person's place at the table.
2. Count out four napkins.
3. Put one napkin on the left side of each place mat.
4. Count out four knives, four forks, four spoons.
5. Put one fork on each napkin.
6. Put one spoon on the right side of each place mat.
7. Put one knife on the inside of each spoon.

If desired, you could make the drawings lifesized outlines, so your child could simply match the correct number of objects to the shapes. Or you could draw outlines on the place mats, indicating where the napkin, knife, fork, and so forth should go.

How long it takes your child to master each step will, of course, depend on your child's abilities and the complexity of the task. But in general, parents who work with their child on a consistent schedule, "doing it the same way each time," will teach their child how to plan out and complete the steps involved in the task.

No matter how long your child takes, try not to get impatient and complete a particular step for her. Granted, it will be quicker, but to encourage or teach independence, you *must* give your child the opportunity to try. By the same token, if time genuinely *is* limited, it may be better to do something for your child rather than rush her through the steps and leave her frustrated. Look for a more relaxed time to work on the skill. It is also usually not a good idea to try to abbreviate an activity to save time, since your child may not be willing to do a shorter version. Work with your child when you have the time to let her practice and get it right.

Motivating Your Child

If your child is interested in learning what you are teaching, it will naturally be much easier to teach her. Consequently, you may have to help motivate your child to learn whatever skill you are working on.

One key to motivation is to make sure your child feels involved in the learning process. She needs to feel as if she has some say in what she is being asked to do—not as if this is a demand being imposed on her. If you are teaching your child to complete a four-piece puzzle, for example, you might give her a choice of two puzzles. Show enthusiasm as your child first takes the puzzle apart, piece by piece. Encourage your child to name the colors on each piece, if possible, and to tell you where one piece goes in relation to another. Tell your child you are proud of her for working so hard to finish the puzzle. Not only do these strategies help motivate your child, but they also encourage making choices, solving problems, and completing tasks.

Another way to motivate your child is to make a game out of the skill you are teaching her. For example, if your child is learning to dress, you might play a tickling game with each body part before you cover it up. Or if she is learning to use the toilet, stuffed animals might be used as onlookers to cheer her on. "Let's show the bear how well you can use the potty!"

Some children with mental retardation are more willing to learn if they can imitate the behavior of a sibling, rather than a parent. For example, your child might not be too impressed if she sees you sweeping the kitchen floor, but if you "let" her younger brother do it, she might demand to share in the fun. Imitating a sibling's behavior can be especially motivating if the sibling praises your child or shows admiration for a job well done.

He'll make a mess and then expect somebody else to pick it up. So, over time, we have learned to make him become more involved in cleaning up, to the point where we will turn off the television. If we want it done quickly, then we have to be in there and have to sort of organize the picking up.

Reminding

As mentioned earlier, it is important not to take over completely when your child is having trouble with a task. But sometimes you may need to help her complete a step or understand what she needs to do. Especially in the beginning, you may need to physically guide your child through a task. (This is one method of "prompting.") For example, she may be learning to do puzzles. She tries to push a piece into a hole, but doesn't yet know how to twist the piece back and forth to make it fit. To help your child learn to make the necessary movement, you might hold your hand over your child's hand and physically twist the piece back and forth. Or if your child is learning to cut with scissors, you might use teaching scissors with two sets of finger-holes so you can guide your child's movements. As your child learns to do the skill independently, you should gradually phase out your physical help.

Once your child has mastered the movements involved in a particular skill, you may still need to provide reminders through more subtle types of prompts—namely, through gesturing, giving directions, or being physically present. For example, your child may be able to eat independently, but forgets to wipe her mouth with the napkin. Prompts such as "Wipe your mouth" or pointing to the napkin will remind her to do this step.

Sometimes your child may seem to ignore your reminders. Most often, this means she is "processing" or thinking through what you've said or done to remind her. Give your child *time to respond*. Don't prompt her constantly; instead, reward her with plenty of praise when she does respond.

Beware of letting your child rely too heavily on your prompts to remind her of what the next step is. Otherwise, she may become "prompt-dependent," or incapable of doing something without your reminders. To prevent prompt-dependency, provide suggestions or reminders intermittently. You might also try varying the way you phrase your reminders. For example, instead of always saying "Turn the light on," you could sometimes say "Let's turn the light on so we can see." This will help your child understand how things function and *why* she needs to do certain tasks.

As your child becomes more successful at a skill, taper off the number of reminders you give. Without your prompting, your child may at first hesitate to try or may ask for your help. Don't give more

help than you know she needs. Instead, encourage her independence. "You can do it!" or "Your turn now!" or "Do it by
yourself!"

═══ ※ ═══

**You just have to kind of give him what task he needs to do first. He likes
to have somebody else in the room, even if you're just sitting there. I
think he likes knowing that someone is there who knows what they are
doing, so to speak, and can direct him.**

Giving Directions

Whether you are prompting your child to do something she has
done many times before or telling her to do something for the first
time, your directions must be precise. Your message should be clear
and simple. Children with mental retardation rely on language that
is predictable, specific, and concrete, and learn to expect this as part
of their routine. For example, instead of saying "Make your bed,"
be more specific. Say "Time to make your bed. Let's pull the sheet
up first."

At the same time you are being specific, you must also try not
to overwhelm your child with too many details. Because mental
retardation affects her abilities to process information and to think
abstractly, your child will be perplexed if you give her several
instructions at once. This is especially the case if instructions are
unfamiliar or she is learning something new. And she will have
difficulty filtering out the unimportant details if you give too much
information. Rather than saying "Hang your coat on the peg over
there next to the door before you go upstairs," it is better to say
simply "Hang up your coat," gesturing toward the peg if she doesn't
already know where her coat goes. Then, after your child hangs up
her coat, you can say "Now let's go upstairs." Your child will
understand directions better if you present them one step at a time.
Too many demands may confuse her, and she may react by
withdrawing or misbehaving.

If your child does not immediately respond to your instructions,
don't get frustrated. Give her time to think through what you asked
her to do. The amount of time will vary, but children with mild to
moderate mental retardation can usually process a single verbal
direction within ten to thirty seconds or less.

Some children with mental retardation follow directions better if they are first walked through the steps and given a demonstration. For example, you might take your child through the whole process of brushing her teeth before backtracking to work on one step at a time. Afterwards, it helps to give verbal reminders until she is able to follow the direction independently. Before your child will be able to do as you ask when you say, "Brush your teeth," you may work with her on the reminders, "Brush up, brush down," "Spit the water out," "Turn the water off," and the like.

Of course, it doesn't matter *how* clear your directions are if your child is not paying attention to them. This means it is a good idea to reduce distractions to a minimum when you are giving a direction. Some children with mental retardation are distracted when people are talking or a television or radio is playing in the room. Others are distracted by faint sounds such as the hum of an air conditioner or the ticking of a clock. Visual distractions are common too. For example, if your child is assembling a stacking ring at a table cluttered with other toys, she may be unable to focus on what she is doing. You may find her looking at the floor, playing with other toys, or getting up from the table.

To get your child's attention, have her look at you or at the activity you want her to focus on. You may need to touch her chin or shoulder or physically turn her toward you. Saying "Look at me" and gesturing toward yourself teaches your child to pay attention and expect communication. Naturally, it is easier to get your child's attention if you are close to her—for example, if you face her on the floor or sit beside her at a table. This is especially important if you need your child's attention for ten or fifteen minutes or more. It also helps to bring yourself down to your child's eye level. For example, if you are both standing, squat or bend down to reach your child's eye level.

Rewards

Rewarding your child for a job well done is a crucial part of the learning process. If you reward your child at every step along the way to achieving a goal, you can keep her interest and motivation high. In addition, by rewarding only good behavior, you help your child learn age-appropriate social skills. And by encouraging and rewarding your child's progress towards independence, you increase her own interest in reaching this goal.

The best reward you can give your child is enthusiastic praise. Praise your child whenever she listens to directions and does as you ask. "I like the way you put away your drum!" Also praise your child when she does the right thing without a reminder. "Hey, you put all your dirty clothes in the hamper. I'm proud of you!" Reward the smallest indications of growth and continually raise your expectations. For example, praise your child for learning to zip her coat up half way, and praise her some more when she learns to zip her coat to the top.

Sometimes it is helpful to give your child tangible rewards such as food, stickers, or small toys. Relating the reward somehow to the goal is also effective. For example, you could let your child choose a new toothbrush for doing such a great job with dental care. But because your goal is for your child to eventually respond to praise alone, always pair tangible rewards with praise. And always make sure you tell her what she is being rewarded for.

If your child can understand the system, you may wish to use a chart system to reward her. The chart can be as elaborate or as plain as you care to make it. Basically, all you need is a piece of paper or cardboard with space for you to paste a sticker or draw a happy face each time your child does something you wish to reinforce. For example, if you are toilet training your child, you can make a chart to keep in the bathroom. Each time your child successfully uses her potty seat, give your child another happy face. After your child has earned a predetermined number of happy faces, you may want to give her a treat (a tangible reward or an activity she enjoys).

Another way to reward your child for progress toward a goal is to create a chart with a visual image of the goal your child is working on. For example, if you are trying to teach your child to brush her teeth independently, you could decorate a chart with a large toothbrush and mark off a predetermined number of spaces. Each time your child masters a step in brushing her teeth, allow her to color in one space or paste a sticker in it. Once all the spaces have been filled in, give her a reward that you and she have previously agreed upon. Or if your child is working on hanging up her coat, you could draw a picture of a coat with eight buttons down the front and tell your child that once she has colored in each button, she can have a special treat. For parents who are not especially artistic, magazines are a great source of photographs of children engaged in daily living skills such as tooth brushing. Photos of your child demonstrating the skill are also excellent reminders.

Whatever your child's age, be sure to include her in the selection of appropriate rewards. You can narrow down the possibilities by observing what kinds of treats or activities please her most. Then give your child a choice among two or three. Not all children are excited by stickers or the like, so find out exactly what your child *does* like. Maybe she has a favorite cassette of songs that you don't play much anymore because you've heard it 40,000 times. Or maybe she really likes to play a particular game, but it has so many pieces that it's a bother to put away. Other treats might include a visit to the local zoo, a trip to the park with Dad, a new outfit for a favorite doll, going to the library, eating out with Mom and Dad, or any other activity or tangible object your child likes.

However you reward your child, be sure other children in the family also have the chance to earn rewards. Including all siblings in a program like this teaches your child that all family members' contributions are important. It can also prevent siblings from resenting "special" treatment of your child with mental retardation.

In determining how much a particular reward should "cost," think about how often you would like your child to receive it. Also consider how often *you* would like to do the activity in question with your child. Keep in mind that children often enjoy simple activities such as being read to by an older sibling or visiting a friend. Rewards do *not* have to be elaborate!

When the time comes to redeem your child's reward, be sure to include your child in the exchange process. Counting happy faces or stickers on a chart is an excellent way to help her understand why she is being rewarded.

Repetition and Routine

Long after parents have become bored with an activity, their children often plead with them to "do it again!" This love of repetition serves young children well when they are learning daily living skills. Not only do children get much-needed practice when they complete a task many times in the same manner, but their confidence in their abilities also grows—especially when their parents praise them. Repetition is especially important for children with mental retardation because they sometimes need a great deal of practice to master a skill, and also because repetition strengthens their long-term memory. Children especially enjoy repetition during social, play, and language activities. Singing songs, playing simple games, experimenting with arts and crafts materials, and imitating actions (as in Simon Says) are activities you can enjoy with your child.

You can capitalize on your child's love of repetition to help her adjust to her daily care routine or to changes in it. Once she learns the sequence of her daily schedule, she will come to expect what will happen next. She will feel more comfortable, too, since having a predictable environment will make her feel secure. In addition, as your child becomes aware that not all activities, events, and daily tasks are repeated at the same interval, she will gradually begin to understand concepts of time such as "right now," "in a minute," "wait a little bit," "today," "tomorrow," and "later."

To help your child learn about her routine and understand it at a more abstract level, you may want to compile a photograph book or use a video camera to record her daily activities. Photograph or film your child engaged in daily activities such as:

1. dressing for the day;
2. eating breakfast;
3. brushing teeth;

4. toileting;
5. playing alone and with others;
6. eating lunch;
7. napping;
8. working with books, puzzles, or other learning aids;
9. eating dinner;
10. having a bath;
11. getting ready for bed.

Refer to the video tape or photograph book often to give your child the opportunity to remember special events such as a family vacation, a birthday party, a visit with Grandma. You can also use the photos or video to help you talk about the routine of your child's day. Depending on the level of your child's understanding, you might simply want to name the activities with comments such as: "Joey is having fun in the bathtub" or "Debbie has juice in her cup." Or you can name concepts demonstrated—for example, "a big splash," "a dark room," "a messy floor." You could also use the photos to quiz your child about her own routine: "Who's taking a bath?" or "What's Aaron doing?"

A fringe benefit of photographing or videotaping your child from year to year is that you can observe and appreciate the progress she has achieved. As your child gets older, you can show her photos or videos from her younger years. She'll love seeing what she used to do and how she used to look.

She functions by routine. She knows what the routine is like. When she was an office aide at school, she knew her job was to make the coffee and to do this and to do that, and don't get in her way if she has to do something. She knew exactly what she had to do. Some teacher came by to use the Xerox machine and our daughter told her that <u>she</u> was using the machine.

You have to be very careful about what you tell Daniel. If you tell him that something is going to be done by this day, it better be done by that day because he knows when that day comes. He literally follows it on a calendar.

We show her on a calendar when something is coming up. She's developed a grasp of the concept of "a day" now. She even understands "a week" and perhaps even "a month."

Our son has his own routine. It takes him a long time to be ready to deal with the world at large. He works into it over a relatively long span of time each day. It's a good thing he gets up early in the morning, because by the time he gets to school, he's barely focused.

Our daughter has a lot of programs taped from television. And we tape a lot of other stuff so that she can see it over and over again. She has her own VCR and TV in her room.

Helping Your Child Generalize Skills

Once your child has mastered a skill, your next job is to help her *generalize* it. That is, you need to work with her until she is able to perform the skill in various settings and with different people. For example, if your child learns table manners at home and then also uses good table manners in a restaurant, she has generalized this behavior to a new setting. If your child can use the toilet independently at home, school, and in public restrooms, she has generalized this skill, too.

Children with mental retardation often have a harder time than other children in seeing similarities among situations. As a result, they may be unable to generalize skills to a variety of settings, and problems can arise. For example, your child may have no trouble playing beside another child at home. But when she is at school, she may be aggressive with other children, may not share easily, or may stand back and watch others play.

To help your child generalize behaviors and skills, allow her to practice her daily life skills with different people and in varied environments. You should also teach these skills in settings where your child will naturally use them. For example, it is natural for your child to work with markers or playdough at a table. If she sits at a table when she uses them at school with the teacher and also sits at a table to use them at home, it will help your child realize that the table is the appropriate place to use these materials.

Using appropriate teaching materials also makes generalization easier for children with mental retardation. They learn best when they are taught with the actual objects used in carrying out daily living skills. For example, if the goal is to teach your child to unzip her jacket, why practice unzipping on a form board or doll? Your child will have less trouble generalizing when you teach her by putting her jacket on her and helping her learn to unzip it herself. The key is to involve as many of your child's senses as possible by creating a real experience. Let her hear the noise the zipper makes and talk about how much cooler she feels when her jacket is unzipped.

Another way to help children with mental retardation generalize is to make sure everyone who teaches them always uses more or less the same words when giving directions. For example, if you are teaching your child to eat with utensils, everyone at home and school could remind her by saying "Use your spoon, please," rather than "Don't use your fingers," or some other phrase. You have probably already settled on the phrasing to use in many situations without even realizing that you are teaching generalization. Most parents instinctively find the way that gets the best response from their child and stick to it.

Nonverbal responses to your child's behavior should also be consistent. For instance, if you want to break your child's habit of throwing a tantrum whenever she doesn't get her way, everyone at home and at school must respond the same way when she acts up. Perhaps your child does not have tantrums at school because the teachers always ignore her when she does. But if *you* continue to tell her to stop or otherwise pay attention to her when she has a tantrum, she will have a hard time transferring her good behavior at school to home. The same would hold true if one parent consistently ignores their child when she has a tantrum, but the other doesn't.

To limit the problems of generalization, you need to communicate with teachers, relatives, neighbors, and others involved in your child's care. If they are to treat your child with the consistency she needs in order to learn, they must have basic information about the methods and strategies you use to deal with her. Setting goals and planning how to teach them is useless if each person uses different methods or does not reward your child for the behaviors you are trying to encourage. For example, if your child wanders over to your neighbor's house without your knowledge, your neighbor should know how you would like her to deal with this behavior and react consistently. You might, for example, request that your neighbor always ask your child if she has permission to leave home and to send her back if she does not. Or if your child does have your permission, you might ask your neighbor not to let your child in the house unless she first asks the neighbor if it's OK to come over for a visit. Remember, consistency is the key to helping children with mental retardation learn new skills and behaviors and then generalize them to new settings.

She can learn things. She knows where everything is. You teach her, she'll learn. However, take her somewhere she's never been before, and she's lost.

He likes pizza, but it's funny because it's only in the last year or so that he has been willing to eat it outside the house. It's not so much that there are only certain kinds that he likes, but that he likes it to be cut up a certain way.

Uncooperative Behavior

Children with mental retardation (and "normal" kids too!) sometimes deliberately refuse to follow directions or to have anything to do with their parents' teaching efforts. Although this may be frustrating, it is a sign that you need to stop and think. You should review the following questions whenever this happens.

1. What time of day does my child refuse my requests—morning, before a nap, after dinner? Could she be acting up because she is tired or over-stimulated?
2. Has she been ill? Is she tired or just waking up? Is she still upset by a previous incident?

3. With whom is she acting this way: everyone, one parent, a sitter? Is a specific situation or person the source of the problem?
4. Am I pushing my child too hard? Do I want her to advance too quickly? Am I giving her the time she needs to respond and to gain confidence one step at a time?
5. When I am not pleased with my child's behavior, do I deliver the message clearly? For example, "I am not happy when you hit your brother." "You will *not* hit."
6. Am I being firm enough?
7. Can I anticipate undesirable behavior before it occurs and redirect my child or change the situation to avoid it?
8. Do I reward my child sufficiently when she shows small signs of even trying? Do I need a written record of my child's successes so I can track her progress?
9. Is my child refusing my requests because she enjoys or is intrigued by my reaction? Is she testing me?
10. Is my child imitating the behavior of a sibling, friend, or someone else she sees regularly? For example, is a younger sibling going through the "Terrible Twos" and yelling "no" to every request?
11. Is she bored by the activity or situation?
12. Can my child hear me adequately? Is she due for a hearing test? Has she had ear infections or fluid build-up that could affect her ability to understand verbal requests?
13. Are sleep problems at night interfering with daytime alertness, behavior, or energy?
14. Can teachers/therapists offer any useful solutions? Do I need to set aside more time to learn how to help my child by observing her teachers/therapists working with her?
15. Would it help to consult other parents of children with mental retardation for support or practical suggestions?

By using these questions to troubleshoot, you may discover that there is a reason behind your child's seemingly "unreasonable behavior." For example, you may be inundating her with requests when what she really needs is a nap. You may also find that a change in your own behavior can lead to major changes in your child's behavior. For example, if you have just changed jobs, are ill, or have recently added a child to the family, the stress of adjusting to the change in your life may affect how you behave and how you relate to your child.

Perhaps you have read through the questions above and still can't isolate a reason for your child's uncooperative behavior. If so, it may be time to seek guidance from the professionals working with your child or from a psychologist. But you should also be aware that sometimes parents do all the "right things" in response to a particular behavior, but still do not get the desired change. Sometimes there's no clear-cut answer as to why your child has begun scratching others or is suddenly refusing to walk when she can't have her way. This is when everyone has to make sure they work together to prevent the behavior and to be consistent and firm in their reactions. Be ready to jump at the smallest change in frequency or intensity of the behavior, and then try again to have an impact on it.

I was going out of my mind. I didn't know what was going on, what I was doing wrong. It seemed like nothing I had tried in the past worked. So I had to go in and talk with the teachers. Nobody really gave me any miracle answer, but they helped me figure out how to begin again.

Philip is in a beautiful stage right now. He's been home from school for the past three weeks and he has just fit in so nicely and gone along with the flow. But six months ago, Philip was going through a real rough period. He was running into the street, he was really regressed in his potty training, he was just screaming and mouthing, and going through something. I think it had something to do with where his youngest brother was developmentally.

Getting Help

Children with mental retardation are not the only ones who can be overwhelmed when they receive too many directions at once. After reading everything in the preceding sections about what you should and should not do when teaching your child, you may be at a loss as to where to begin. Or you may try to follow directions exactly as given here and discover that you still cannot teach your child a specific daily living skill. If so, don't hesitate to ask for help.

Teaching a child with mental retardation is rarely as simple in practice as it is on paper.

You certainly do not have to teach your child all her daily living skills on your own. Professionals such as the special education teacher, occupational therapist, and speech/language therapist will also work with your child on these skills. They should routinely let you know how the teaching process is going so you can reinforce and build on their teaching at home. Asking them to jot down notes about your child's progress in a notebook and send it home with your child on a weekly or daily basis is a good way to communicate about what does and does not work. You can also ask them to observe you and your child at home or at school as you help her with dressing, grooming, or some other daily living skill. Afterwards, the teacher or therapist may offer helpful guidelines and you can ask questions and express concerns. This gives you immediate feedback and is more valuable than just talking about what you should do and why.

Often a professional can come up with a solution to a problem that may have you baffled. For example, one little girl screamed every time her mother put her socks on. She would become enraged and tear them off screaming, "No socks!" Finally, her mother gave up in frustration, and the child wore shoes with no socks in the winter. Then, through trial and error, the teacher discovered that the girl simply didn't like *white* socks, but didn't have the language skills to explain her objections to her mother. Needless to say, this child now has a rainbow assortment of socks!

Not only can teachers and therapists solve problems unique to your child, but they can also offer solutions to problems that may be shared by many children with mental retardation. For example, they can show you where to put your child's hands to help her most easily pull off her socks and shoes. Or, if they are knowledgeable in sensory integration principles, they can help you understand why your child doesn't like to play in the sandbox or go barefoot, and teach you ways to help her overcome those hypersensitivities.

Even with the advice and help of professionals, you may sometimes become frustrated or angry at your child because she cannot or will not do as you wish. If so, you might benefit from seeking a support group for parents of children with mental retardation. It can be a comfort to know that other parents experience similar feelings.

In addition, members of support groups may suggest strategies that have worked in teaching their own children. There are also professionals such as social workers, counselors, and psychologists who specialize in seeing families with children with developmental disabilities. These professionals are trained to help parents figure out the best ways to manage problem behaviors and to learn to set limits and become more organized.

Occasionally you may feel the need to "take a break" from the constant routine of working with your child. Many parents of children with mental retardation feel more prepared, emotionally, to resume their responsibilities as parents after taking a vacation from their routine. To obtain temporary relief from full-time caregiving, you may want to seek out respite care providers. These are often people described as "specialists," "trained sitters," or "informed persons" who will watch your child for an hour, a day, overnight, or even longer. Respite care is discussed in detail later in this chapter.

For help locating a support group, counselor, or respite care provider, consult the Resource Guide or your phone book for the ARC chapter nearest you.

Discipline

All children need to know that there are right and wrong ways to behave. They need to learn, for example, not to run up to strangers for hugs or to dart into the street after a toy or pet. If they do not learn these lessons, their safety will be jeopardized and they will have difficulty adapting to community life and being independent.

The key to proper behavior is, of course, discipline. Most parents instinctively discipline their children when they do something dangerous or inappropriate. But when your child has mental retardation, you may hesitate to discipline her when she misbehaves. Perhaps you are reluctant to discipline her because you think she is incapable of learning, she doesn't understand what she did wrong, or you feel you are being too harsh. But if you do not teach your child proper behavior, she will have a great deal of difficulty functioning in society as she grows older.

It is true your child may have a harder time understanding the reasons she is not allowed to do certain things. She may need more reminders and explanations from you before she learns how to behave. But if you are firm and consistent, your child *will* learn better behavior—no matter how slowly. The following sections describe strategies that are often effective in disciplining children with mental retardation.

I think now there is really no difference in the way you discipline or praise a kid with mental retardation. Once upon a time, I probably thought there was a difference. Philip gets as much love, or probably more, than the other kids, but other than that, I see no difference.

Saying "No"

The foremost issue in disciplining any child is safety. And the best way to ensure your child's safety is to teach her the meaning of "no."

You can let your child know what activities are unsafe just as you would any young child. If your child is reaching for the stove, hold her hands, have her look at you, and firmly tell her, "No! It's hot!" Never assume that warning your child once is enough. You may need to repeat your warnings many times before she learns, so be consistent in telling her "no" each time she does something she shouldn't. By the same token, remember also to catch your child when she is being *good*, and reinforce her behavior with praise or other rewards.

Sometimes saying "no" may not stop your child. A shouting match probably won't stop her either, even if you enumerate your reasons for saying "no" in the first place. So, in some cases, you may need to go one step further and physically remove your child from the danger or divert her attention to something else. For example, if your child is hitting another child in the head with a shoe, you should step in and take the shoe away, and tell her, "We don't hit. We wear shoes on our feet!"

Of course, even if your child understands and responds to the word "no," you can't be with her every minute of every day to warn her away from every dangerous situation. But if you *aren't* around, your child may not have the judgement to avoid danger. Some parents report that their children just can't seem to understand the rules of safety. Particularly if they are impulsive or have sensory problems, children with mental retardation may seem fearless and unaware of danger. They may climb on an unstable piece of furniture, or put their hand into the dog's mouth. Until your child has the sophistication to anticipate the consequences of her actions, you may need to alter her environment to help ensure her safety. For example, you can teach her the meaning of "Mr. Yuk" and put stickers on anything you don't want her to taste or touch. You can also use painted lines, stakes and twine, or the like to mark off her play area or bike-riding area.

If your child seems determined to test her limits, you may have to let her learn on her own. For instance, if she continually plays rough with the family cat and ignores your pleas to be gentle, she may get the message more clearly when the cat scratches her. Experience *is* sometimes the best teacher, but never forget to keep the safety and welfare of your child—as well as those around her—a main priority.

She could get lost around the neighborhood, wandering. One time we had a group of people looking for her because she took the dog for a walk and made a wrong turn.

Ignoring Negative Behavior

If your child is misbehaving but is in no danger of hurting herself or others, you can try ignoring the behavior to see if it will go away. You may, for example, be able to reduce your child's tantrums by ignoring her whenever she has one. Tantrums are primarily attention-getting behavior and if your child can't get your attention this way, she will have to find another way.

If you have previously paid attention to your child's tantrums and now decide to ignore them, expect things to get worse before they improve. Your child will most likely throw even bigger tantrums to get your attention, but don't give in to her negative behavior. Do not even look in her direction. You may want to leave the room for a few minutes until the tantrum is over, making sure first that she is safe. Take care that you do not unconsciously signal your child that you are aware of her behavior by frowning, sighing, or some other gesture. Above all, be sure all family members understand and use this strategy or your child will seek out new targets for her tantrums or other misbehavior.

If misbehavior occurs outside the home, use discretion in deciding whether to ignore what your child is doing. For example, if you are driving in the car and your child acts up, gets out of her seatbelt, or distracts *you*, you may need to pull off the road to straighten the situation out. If you have the patience, you can simply refuse to drive on or to turn on the radio unless your child is properly buckled up. Your child must learn that a car is *no place* to act up! Likewise, in settings where your child's behavior is an embarrassment or interferes with others' enjoyment, ignoring her may not be the best course. For example, if you're at the movie theater or church, you will probably wish to remove your child from this setting to save yourself the embarrassment. Chapter 7 offers additional strategies for handling public misbehavior.

She will look at my face and try to read me. She is very much a people pleaser. She doesn't care about me as much anymore as she used to, but she does care about other people. She wouldn't want you to think badly of her.

Sometimes when my son's squealing, I get stares because I'm not "correcting" him. But I feel like I can't be telling him to stop all the time—sometimes it's when he's overstimulated. But I don't really know. Maybe I'm making excuses for myself . . . or for him . . . or maybe this is the right thing to do. I never know.

Rewarding Good Behavior

It is all well and good to ignore bad behavior in hopes that your child will learn that she won't get her way by misbehaving. But what if she gives up one type of misbehavior only to try a new one? For example, if your child learns that tantrums are ineffective because you ignore her whenever she has one, she might decide to try getting your attention by hitting you. To keep your child from trading in one negative behavior for another, you must teach her an acceptable alternative.

The best way to teach your child to behave is to praise and encourage her when she is on her good behavior. It's more important to teach her what *to* do than what *not* to do. For example, if she yells whenever she wants your attention, ask yourself how you would like her to communicate instead. Most likely, you would prefer her to address you in a normal tone of voice. So, to help her learn not to yell, first try to reward her when she is *not* yelling. Say to her, "I like it when you talk nicely (or quietly) to me." Praising your child each time she speaks in a lower tone of voice will decrease the possibility that she will yell at you or others. To make doubly sure your child learns that yelling is unacceptable, you can also use the ignoring technique described above. Cover your ears, turn your head, refuse to listen, or leave the room whenever she yells.

Remember, any child who does not receive praise or encouragement from her parents will "act out" to earn any form of attention, even if it is negative. As a parent, your goal is to build on your child's strengths and positive behaviors, not just to focus on her misbehaviors.

Catching the Behavior Before It Occurs

Remember the old saying, "an ounce of prevention is worth a pound of cure?" If you can prevent your child from beginning a problem behavior, discipline becomes much easier.

To effectively prevent misbehavior, you must learn to predict when it is likely to occur. Sometimes your child will give you clues that she is about to act up. For example, she may whine, tense her muscles, pace the floor, even hold her breath. In general, the telltale signs are no different than they are for other young children. Other times you might notice that your child's misbehavior is usually triggered by a specific event. For example, your child may begin running aimlessly through the house whenever she knows it's just about bathtime. Many children misbehave when there is a sudden change of routine and they feel uncertain about what happens next and what is expected of them. They may re-test old limits, trying to find out if the usual rules of behavior still apply.

To better predict when your child is going to misbehave, you may want to keep notes on your child's episodes of problem behavior, as well as the events immediately preceding them. For example, you may notice that she only bites other children when she wants the toy they are playing with.

Keeping track of your child's behavior this way can not only help you predict when she will misbehave, but can also help you evaluate the effectiveness of your discipline. For example, if you notice that your child continues to bang her head at bedtime despite your discipline of removing her from her bed whenever she does so, you might conclude that this method of discipline is not effective. In fact, if your child learns she can get out of going to bed by head banging, you are actually encouraging that behavior.

The Value of Distraction. If you can predict when your child's misbehavior will occur, you can use several strategies to distract her before she has a chance to act up. Many young children with mental retardation will stop misbehaving if their parents move them to another area of the house—that is, away from whatever is triggering their behavior. For example, if your child prefers to play with the knobs on the TV instead of putting on her shoes, you should either move to a room without a TV, place the TV in another room, or cover it up. When your child is older, you will most likely be able to explain, "You may watch TV after you put on your shoes."

Offering an alternate activity can also distract your child from misbehaving. For example, if your child persists in riding her tricycle after you've told her not to, say "Put your trike in the garage. It's time to go pick up Eric." Yet another way to distract your child is to begin giving her verbal directions. For example, if your child starts to tear a page of a book you are reading, you might say, "Wow, look at the fuzzy caterpillar," pointing to a picture in the book. At the same time, you could gently pull her fingers down to her lap. With her attention on the caterpillar, your child may "forget" to misbehave and is less likely to lose control. If your child is older (at least three or four), you may be able to keep her from getting upset simply by changing the topic of conversation. Timing is tricky, because if you wait until your child is in a full-blown tantrum it may be too late to distract her.

Sometimes you may want to completely avoid known problem situations as a way of preventing bad behavior. For example, if your child screams or begs for candy or ice cream, you may choose to keep these treats out of your child's sight, avoid checkout lines with candy displays, and take a route that doesn't go past the ice cream store.

252 ※ Daily Living

Or you can organize space in your home to prevent misbehavior. For example, if your child continues to ride her bike without supervision in the street, you might want to keep all bikes locked in the garage and have a specific time set aside for riding them when someone can watch. Or if she writes on walls with her crayons, keep them on an upper shelf out of her reach. Although you cannot—and should not—prevent all misbehavior this way, sometimes avoidance is a viable means of handling your child's behavior and making everyone's day go a bit easier.

Anticipate Change. When there is a change in routine, your child may misbehave out of uncertainty about what is going to happen next. To try to forestall this kind of behavior, let your child know ahead of time whenever you anticipate a change in routine. For example, after the family has been out to the movies, there might not be enough time to give your child her customary bath before bed. Tell your child several times that evening that she will have her bath in the *morning*, so she can get used to the idea. Or perhaps you are aware that your child's regular teacher will be out one day. That morning before school, prepare your child by talking to her about her teacher's absence. Tell her the substitute teacher's name, if you know it, and let her know that her regular teacher will be back soon.

Time Out

"Time out" refers to the strategy of temporarily removing a child who is misbehaving from an activity or situation she enjoys. It is especially useful when your child is in danger, or is out of control and cannot be distracted.

When you are giving your child a time out, you can either leave her in the room where she misbehaved, or take her to a separate "time out room." Find a place where your child can't see what others are doing or try to get their attention. Don't choose a place where there are toys or other fun things, but don't choose a dark or enclosed place, either. Children should usually remain in time out for as many minutes as they are years old. For example, if your child is two, give her a time out of one to two minutes; if she is five, give her a time out of five minutes. While she is having a time out, ignore her, or at least give her the impression you are ignoring her.

Ideally, this is how a time out is used to manage behavior: Two-year-old Sara sits on the floor playing with plastic pop-beads. Soon she discovers that she gets a reaction out of Ryan every time she hits him on the head with a string of beads. When Dad sees what Sara is doing, he promptly picks her up. He then places her in a small chair located away from the activity and tells her, "No hitting, Sara! You sit here." He walks away and ignores Sara. Dad returns after two minutes and tells Sara to "Go play nicely." Then Dad watches Sara for an opportunity to praise her for good behavior and says, "I like the way you're playing with Ryan."

Although this time-out procedure may seem relatively simple, there are many ways it can backfire. For example, your child can refuse to sit in the chair. She may "test" you by getting out of the chair to see if you are watching. In these instances, you may need to firmly hold her in the chair or make it impossible for your child to leave the time-out room—for instance, by putting a gate across the doorway. Your child might also fall limp to the floor and refuse to be led to the time-out area. If so, carry or physically guide her to the chair.

Time outs also may not work if you allow your child to find the soft spot in your heart—if, for example, you end her time out early if she begins to cry. In addition, time outs can become ineffective if you use them each and every time your child misbehaves. Furthermore, if you leave your child in the time-out chair too long, you may discover that she actually enjoys this little game. She may talk to herself, play with her buttons, take her shoes and socks off, or amuse herself in some other way. She may also tease you until she gets a harsher reaction.

Because becoming a skillful "time-out" artist can be challenging, you may want to resort to time outs only when and if other forms of discipline do not work as well. Remember, time outs *can* have a lasting impact on negative behavior if they are used wisely and with discretion. Here are some guidelines to help you manage time outs:

1. When misbehavior occurs, identify it. For example, tell your child, "We do not fight." Do not converse further with your child.
2. Gently, but firmly, lead your child to the time-out chair. If she physically resists, you may carry her to it.

3. Once your child is in time out, set a timer. It is helpful for your child to see you set the timer and learn that its bell signals the end of time out.
4. If your child does not remain in time out, be prepared to use a back-up consequence. For example, you may have to physically hold her in the chair until she gets the idea that you mean business. Stand behind her and don't talk to her or respond to her pleas, whines, or threats.
5. When the time out is up, have your child clean up any mess made while in time out. Then lead her back to the activity. Never comment on how well your child behaved in time out.
6. If she is screaming, whining, kicking, or otherwise misbehaving when the bell rings, time out begins again. Do not let your child leave time out while her behavior is out of control.
7. If it seems time out has stopped working, try keeping a record of when, how often, and in what situations you use time outs, so you can evaluate whether you are using them too often or need to change them in some way.

I heard him say, "I'm going back into my room. I need to cool off." So he knows that now. He knows when he gets tired, too, and he will put himself down for naps.

He used to spend a lot of time in his room. He ate in his room until about a year and a half ago. That was because he was more comfortable there. He would come out and do things with everybody, but then he would just remove himself when he felt overloaded. It was neat that he knew to do that instead of getting so worked up.

Keeping Your Perspective

Even if you always discipline your child for the right reasons using appropriate methods, your child may sometimes make you feel like a rotten parent for disciplining her. She may cry, scream, whine, act hurt, or otherwise send the message that you are being excessively harsh. But no matter how hard a lesson you must teach your child, do not feel guilty. Unless you set limits early and consistently, she will never learn the social skills she needs to become independent. It is better that she learn discipline from parents she knows love her, than from someone she doesn't know or feel sure about. For example, it is better that your child learn from you not to pick flowers without permission, than from an angry neighbor who may have little patience with your child.

On the other side of the coin, it is equally important not to feel guilty if you sometimes give up and let your child have her way. No parent can be consistent 100 percent of the time, and you should not consider yourself a failure if you occasionally take the path of least resistance. It is true that your four-year-old will need to know how to behave properly when she grows up. But four-year-olds do not become adults overnight. Now and then you *can* take a break from drilling her in good behavior. Use your discretion, as you would with any other child.

──── ※ ────

When we started out, we thought we were going to make him the best child with Down syndrome who ever lived. I, for one, have now decided that that should not be a goal. We want to do well for him and we want to give him what we can, but we're not going to keep him inside studying eight hours a day. He needs to be happy. Part of happiness is being able to be productive and feeling good about yourself, and that's where the training comes in. But he doesn't have to be the first child with mental retardation to become a brain surgeon or whatever. It's not that we're shirking off, but I don't really feel that we should push and push and devote our lives just to making him the best ever.

Finding Sitters and Respite Care

Parents of children with mental retardation sometimes feel guilty at the thought of leaving their child with a baby sitter. But you, like all parents, need a break from the relentless routine of daily care. For the sake of your own mental health and your marriage, you need to have time to yourself—both as a parent and a couple. Sometimes, too, distancing yourself from your child can give you the extra energy to cope when times seem burdensome, as well as a fresh perspective on the situation.

Needless to say, you don't want to leave your child with just anyone. But you can take a few precautions to make sure your child's sitter is competent and caring. First, ask prospective sitters for references and a description of related experiences. To further reduce anxieties, always invite your child care provider to your home to get to know your child before you leave him or her alone with your child. Explain your expectations and household routines, and answer any questions or concerns the sitter might have. Let the sitter spend some time playing with your child, and watch how he or she interacts with your child.

To locate a sitter trained in caring for children with mental retardation, you can contact your local ARC. These agencies sometimes provide training for teenagers, college students, and other reliable people interested in caring for children with special needs. Another source of referrals is your local university or public school. Special education teachers in training or in practice have the skills to look after your child on a daily or overnight basis. Parents or older siblings of other children with mental retardation are another valuable resource.

An alternative to hiring a private sitter is to look for *respite care*. As mentioned earlier, respite care offers temporary relief from the day-to-day routine of caring for your child. Care is given by licensed day care providers or others specially trained in caring for children with special needs. Respite care providers may come to your house, provide care in their own home, or operate a group home for overnight respite care programs. Fees are usually kept to a minimum and you can be certain your child will receive specialized attention. You may feel more comfortable leaving your child at a respite program if you first pay several announced or unannounced visits to the program to watch it in action.

Separation from your child can be hard, but it is something all members of your family can benefit from. Finding a capable sitter or respite care program is a crucial step to independence for both you and your child.

We had to find someone who wasn't going to "spaz out" if our son had a seizure. Luckily, Anna was willing to take the risk that this was a possibility. We took the time to explain things to her, like, "OK, this is

what happens when a seizure occurs. And this is what you do." She was pretty mature; she was responsible.

═══ ※ ═══

Before we found a babysitter, we didn't have anybody. I guess we had my mother. It was hard.

Conclusion

Caring for a child—any child—is an enormous challenge. When your child has mental retardation, the challenge may seem even more formidable. As you will discover, however, caring for a child with mental retardation is not really that different from caring for any other child. All children have the same basic needs, and these needs can usually be taken care of in pretty much the same ways— with love, perseverance, practice, and skill. Likewise, all parents have questions and need expert advice—whether from friends and family members, or from teachers, therapists, and other professionals who understand their child's special needs.

If you are patient and persistent, your child *will* learn daily care skills that will enable her to take care of her own needs, now and in the future. No matter how slow her progress or how small her gains, each step she makes will move her further down the road to becoming an independent adult. With guidance and encouragement from the whole family, your child will make you proud.

Seven

=== ※ ===

Family and Community Life

Judith Z. Krantz, Ph.D.*

Any time a child joins a family, there are bound to be changes. On the practical side, other children may need to double up in bedrooms to make room for the new family member, and there may be less money to spend on everyone's favorite activities. Almost certainly, parents will have less time to devote to one another and to their other children. On the emotional side, both parents and siblings may have trouble adjusting to any of these practical considerations, as well as to the new child himself.

Most parents expect these kinds of changes, and accept them as an inevitable part of raising a family. But when you have a child with mental retardation, your outlook on change may darken. You may have some pretty strong concerns about how this child will affect your life and your family's life. Must you give up your own hopes and dreams? Will your other children feel ashamed, burdened, resentful, or neglected? What will happen to your marriage and to your relationships with relatives and friends? Does this mean the end of normal family life?

There is a widespread belief—among professionals as well as the general public—that having a child with mental retardation usually or often leads to marital disruption, divorce, and emotional problems in both parents and siblings. But recent research, ex-

---

* Judith Krantz is a psychologist with the public schools in Montgomery County, Maryland, has a private practice, and is the mother of two teenage boys, one of whom has a disability. She knows about balancing acts.

perience, and common sense provide strong evidence that "it ain't necessarily so!"

How you, your spouse, your kids, friends, relatives—and people in the grocery line—respond to your child with mental retardation will depend a lot on what sort of person you (or they) are to begin with. Compassionate people react compassionately; friendly people remain friendly. Having a child with mental retardation does not alter your personality or your innate ability to cope.

Of course, there are some ways of viewing your child's mental retardation and some things to do that promote an easier, smoother adjustment. Some attitudes reduce emotional pain, while other points of view can actually cause more difficulty than is really necessary. For example, viewing your child with mental retardation as a negative reflection of your own worth will lead to endless pain and suffering for everyone. Viewing your child as a complete person who is "normal" for himself will give you the serenity to enjoy him for who he really is. To help you and your family find the path of least resistance, this chapter points out some of these attitudes— both harmful and helpful. It also explores some issues likely to confront you over the years as you adjust as a parent (biological or adoptive) and as a spouse, plus issues that can affect the adjustment of the brothers and sisters of your child with mental retardation. Finally, the chapter discusses how to deal with relatives and friends, as well as strangers who encounter your child.

Your Role as a Parent

Like all parents, you and your spouse set an example for the rest of the family. How you treat your child with mental retardation and the feelings you show toward him will profoundly influence how his siblings relate to him. Others outside your immediate family— grandparents, uncles, aunts, friends, department store cashiers— will often pattern their behavior and attitudes after yours, too.

If you are still having trouble adjusting to your child's mental retardation yourself, you may not exactly welcome the knowledge that what you do and say can shape so many people's behavior toward your child. But having to set an example also has its good points: for one thing, it gives you an awesome amount of power. You can use your natural influence on others to ensure that your child will grow up surrounded by loving, welcoming family and friends.

At this point, you may very well be thinking, "That all sounds very nice, but how do *I* know how to act with my child?" Generally, you should try to treat your child with mental retardation pretty much like any other child, making allowances for his learning style and level of development when necessary. Since this, too, is often easier said than done, the following sections provide some guidance on dealing with the pleasures and pitfalls that come with being the parent of a child with mental retardation.

I take Kyle to the barbershop and they all come up and say, "How are you doing today?" and "Give me five" and they are great with him. That's because of my attitude toward Kyle.

Our attitude is "Isn't she super?" and I honestly think it makes a difference in how people see her.

It's OK to Be an Ordinary Parent

When parents become aware of their child's "special" status, few of them know much about what that really means. Most of us begin with a vague mental image of "The Mentally Retarded Child," and can picture only children with the mildest of impairments or profound disability, with little in between. Somehow, in our minds, the parents of such children are endowed with special, saint-like qualities that enable them to deal with emotions and stresses that ordinary mortals could not. But what happens if a "special" child is born to an ordinary parent like you?

If you truly believe that it takes some special talent to raise a special child, your confidence and sense of competence may be at a low ebb—at least in the beginning. If there are other problems—such as seizures or cerebral palsy—associated with your child's mental retardation, raising your child may seem even more complicated. Many parents think that the usual methods of teaching a child to feed himself, use the toilet, and so forth won't work with a child with mental retardation. You might feel as if your fears are confirmed when other children who don't have mental retardation consistently outdo yours in the skills department. You may think you have adjusted just great to having a child with mental retardation, only to be shocked at your tears when you notice that the neighbor's three-year-old is riding a trike while yours is just learning to walk. Other especially vulnerable times are at the ages when "other kids" take major developmental steps: learning to read at age six, dating and driving in adolescence.

How can you help yourself get over these feelings that you are not a "good enough" parent? One of the most important steps is to get together with other parents of children with mental retardation. You'll slowly realize that *they* have no special talents as parents. They are just taking it one step at a time, the same as you. If you have other children, it also helps to realize that you have already proven your parental competence. Sit down and take an honest look at yourself as a parent. What are your strengths? Don't forget to count just hanging in there day by day.

As time goes by, it will probably occur to you that children with mental retardation really aren't so different from other children and can probably get by with ordinary parents. Children with mental retardation just learn more slowly or differently—that's what mental retardation is. As Chapter 4 discusses, the regular methods of child-rearing work just fine. It just takes more time, more repetition, and some extra patience. Your child will go through roughly the same developmental steps in pretty much the same order as other kids. While it's true that the "terrible two's" last longer, so do the "terrific three's."

Slower development also means you don't have to be so quick on the draw, either. You can take your time looking at and evaluating the various child-rearing techniques. You can choose the methods that best suit your child—the unique person, only part of whose makeup is mental retardation. You will probably get some ideas from the regular parenting books on the market. As for "special techniques," reading this book is a good start. The "special techniques" will be effective with your other kids as well. Kids are kids.

As for the shock when you periodically realize that your child with mental retardation really is developing at a slower rate than other children his age, I can only offer this comfort: no child lives up to all the hopes and expectations of his or her parents. These fantasy scenarios are developed when we ourselves are children and know little about real life. The pain is the result of the wrenching away of a big chunk of illusion. It is the same feeling any parent has when he or she is confronted with the independent reality of their child.

No child measures up to parental daydreams. Yet every child, in his own way, is much more complicated, interesting, and satisfying than we could ever have imagined. The feeling of a sudden, heartfelt hug from your child is proof enough of that. The only "special" parenting skill your child with mental retardation needs is your ability to totally accept all that is contained in that hug.

We ought to be able to have some enjoyment, too. We ought to have some time to ourselves. It's okay to let him sit down and watch The Lady and the Tramp on the VCR instead of sitting him down to say his alphabet.

I think that being a little older helps a bit. You don't panic quite so much. You know that despite things that you did or didn't do with your other kids, they turned out all right. Maybe it's wrong to have this mellow outlook sometimes, but I don't think so.

Accepting Your Child

For many parents, the initial feelings of grief, loss, guilt, and anger discussed in Chapter 3 linger on, complicating later adjustment to their child. Despite their best efforts, they may be unable to shake the feeling that things are not as they should be—that their child's mental retardation is all some horrible mistake. This couldn't possibly be happening to *them*. Yet despite these feelings, day by day most parents fall more and more in love with their child. Day by day, that love displaces the negative feelings, so that parents begin to give up their earlier ideas about how things "should" be. Slowly they begin to accept what *is*, changing their ideas about who they are in the process. Slowly they begin to see themselves as parents of a child who has mental retardation. Somehow life goes on, and it's not so bad after all. In fact, sometimes it's terrific.

A wise mother once confided that for years she had been subtly annoyed with her daughter's behavior. The child seemed to need constant prodding in every undertaking. "Then one day," this mother continued, "I realized I have a four-year-old daughter in a six-year-old body. Now her reactions make sense. I expect her to behave like a four-year-old, and now I can enjoy her achievements with her. We're not mad at each other any more."

This mother's poignant observation is at the heart of how parents overcome their negative feelings. By slowly giving up *your* ideas of who this child is and how he should act to satisfy you, you become open to who your child *really* is.

To get a sense of what your child is capable of, it may help to talk to medical personnel, therapists, and teachers. Remember, however, that they are human too, and sometimes project their own unrealistic hopes and wishes as if they were scientific predictions. Others may project their ignorance or fear by underestimating what can be achieved by determination and effort. Probably the best way to know what your child is ready and able to do is to *let him tell you*. Your child will let you know what he's ready to tackle next. Which toys delight him? Which experiences excite him? When does his face light up? These are a child's way of saying, "This is just what I need!" Focus your attention on each small step, one at a time, without worrying too much about where all this will eventually lead.

Of course, accepting your child does not mean you have to be thrilled that she has mental retardation. By the same token, defeated resignation will lead you to underestimate what your child can do. Because a child with mental retardation learns more slowly, new experiences and skills have to be presented over and over before he gets used to them. More practice is needed before mastery is achieved. Your child may need to be specifically taught to generalize—for example, to understand that red is red, whether it's a ball, a block, a flower, or hair. All of this takes extra work, and it's usually easier and more fun to participate in early intervention programs and special education and follow up at home, rather than trying to do it all yourself. This will also put you in contact with other parents of children with mental retardation and a whole army of people eager to work with your child.

Mental retardation is not reversible. Your child will always learn more slowly and have more trouble with abstract thinking than he would have otherwise. But children can be taught ways to compensate for some weaknesses. Accepting your child for who he is includes encouraging him to do what he can for himself while recognizing that there are limits to what hard work can accomplish. It's a fine line, but one that *all* parents walk.

Mental retardation does not wipe out personality. Each child has his own way of seeing the world, his own responses to those around him. Anyone who spends time with children with mental retardation knows that there are happy and there are unhappy kids with the same degree of retardation. Self-confidence, optimism, and eagerness to relate are qualities that come from experiencing acceptance of who we are. Some kids are natural huggers and snugglers. It's easy to express physical affection to them—they reach out for it. Other children, because of temperament or because they often don't feel well, seem unresponsive to physical affection. But remember, there are many ways to express love. Hugs and kisses may be secondary for your child (although these should be a regular part of his life, anyway).

Look your child in the eyes when you talk to him; let your voice express your tenderness. Have a special time every day just for him—for rocking or back rubbing or singing a song he likes. If there is an activity he really enjoys, such as swimming or riding on the back of your bike, do it regularly. When he's tired, sick, or just grumpy, let him have your permission to be less sociable. We all need this sometimes. Make sure that your child can be an active participant in at least some family activities—eating watermelon on the back porch, sledding down a snowy hill, sleeping in a tent on a camping trip.

Some children reject the usual forms of affection. It is very important to remember that they are not rejecting you or your love—it's the *form* that doesn't "speak" to them. Try different kinds of touches. What is soothing to you may be irritating to your child. Often a firm touch will be accepted where a gentler one is shrugged off. Perhaps massaging tight muscles with lotion will be what your child remembers as love. Don't forget sound. Sing different songs (make up your own if you're so inclined) to go with different activities such as bathing, dressing, distracting attention from a bumped knee. Leave an audio cassette playing quietly to help him fall asleep. As these sounds are associated with "feeling better," they will carry your message of affection and love.

Once I was talking to a teenage girl with mental retardation. She told me she knew her Mom loved her. I asked how she knew. "Because she always hugs me so good!" she replied with a laugh. Later, I passed this story on to her astonished mother. "That child is all bones and squirming muscles. Hugging her is something I've had to teach myself to do. She never seemed to like it particularly, but it seemed like the right thing to do. It paid off; it really paid off!" Sometimes we just have to operate on faith and good intentions.

As a parent, you do not have the choice of whether your child will be one with special needs. What *is* within your power is to choose whether this child will be one who always senses his own inadequacy and the disappointment his very existence arouses in those he loves, or whether he is secure in his place in the world, knowing he is welcomed with love.

I wish he wasn't retarded, but I love him as he is.

I remember saying, after the first day of class, "Well, she's in a special ed. program, but she's at the top of her class." I still wasn't ready to accept in reality that she was just about at the bottom. It's just that I went in there thinking that they were going to cure it.

———— ※ ————

I feel very, very lucky to have him. I feel sad, though, that he won't be able to marry and everything.

===== �֍ =====

I try to let Paige know that Daddy loves her all the time, whereas I think my other kids know that already. I try to keep instilling that in Paige—that I'm always there for her.

===== ✖ =====

My reaction is "Yes, he does have mental retardation, but isn't he cute, isn't he great?"

Striving for Balance

Loving and accepting your child does not mean spoiling him rotten. Accepting your child does mean you don't expect him to "make up" for anything. For example, you don't expect him to make up for having mental retardation by being super well-behaved. It also means your child is a part of the family, not the center of it.

It's not good for the growth and healthy development of *any* child to be the one who always gets what he wants, *or* the one who always has to share or compromise. All children must learn to negotiate, tolerate frustration (and thus discover it's not lethal), and have an opportunity to give as well as receive. This means that you, the parent, must balance the unique needs of all family members to make sure no one is shortchanged.

In deciding which of the needs of your child with mental retardation merit attention, it is often helpful to think about his mental age. The mother mentioned earlier found that her expectations and behavioral demands of her daughter were much more on target if she used typical four-year-old skills as a guide. Her daughter could not tolerate frustration like a six-year-old, but neither did she need to be treated like a two-year-old. Four-year-olds need brief, directed, activity-oriented playtime with friends, not the all-day, independent play of six-year-olds. It's not at all unusual for four-year-olds to wet the bed, and they need a response appropriate to a four-year-old, even if their body is six or eight years old.

If you let your child's mental age guide your treatment of him, it can make it easier for siblings to grasp the fairness of parental decisions. On a day-to-day basis, they will sense the consistency, even though it is guaranteed that they will whine, complain, and protest at your "unfairness." In smaller families, it's sometimes hard for parents to realize that these protests are normal sibling behavior and have nothing to do with the actual situation. No child thinks it's fair to go to bed earlier than a sibling. When you split the last brownie between two children, *both* will complain that the other's piece is bigger. In fact, when siblings obey you too readily, it is a sign of excessive pity and patronization.

Don't let any of your children "push your guilt button." Your children—with and without disabilities—will seek it out and try to work it to their immediate benefit. Your child with mental retardation may pull his "I'm just a helpless little baby" act to avoid putting real effort into a job. If you fall for it, he's just found a great way to get out of whatever is too difficult or unpleasant. Children without mental retardation try this too, but are usually not as successful. More likely, they'll try saying "The Forbidden": "She *always* gets to watch that dumb show. Do you have to be retarded to get any attention around here?" Don't fall for this one either. They both just want what they want when they want it. Children only see immediate consequences. Do they get to watch "their" show right now or not? As a parent, you must keep in mind that the way you handle your children's daily needs and wants can have long-range effects on their self-esteem and emotional maturity.

True, because you have a child with mental retardation, you may find this balancing act harder than usual. Children with special needs require more time and energy than other children. There are the extra medical appointments, therapies, and special classes, the sheer physical labor of packing and unpacking equipment and little bodies, driving, parking, etc., etc. In addition, you or others might expect that you will work on developmental goals at home, as well as provide any nursing care needed. There is also the undisputed fact that children with mental retardation take longer to grow to independence and therefore need more parental supervision. And even when a child with mental retardation is able to take care of some of his own daily needs, often he still takes longer to do everyday activities such as washing his hands, eating, dressing or undressing, and moving from one activity to another. Although the extra time spent on each of these activities doesn't seem like much, the accumulated weight of *all* of them, day after day, every day, can really stretch a parent's patience.

Financial realities may also be burdensome and inequitable. Special programs, equipment, and services are expensive, even if much of the cost is absorbed by the schools or your insurance. How do you pay for speech/language therapy without depriving Mary Anne of her beloved ballet lessons? At what point does an "adults only" vacation take priority over special day camp?

The emotional costs are also higher when there is a child with mental retardation in the family. The simple extra concern you feel for your child is a slow but steady drain on emotional energy. Being your child's advocate with various institutions and programs can be exhausting. Then there is the emotional drain of taking your child to therapies. To expect you not to resent the invasion, the loss of personal freedom, and the changes in plans would be unrealistic. To expect your other children to "understand" and not resent this is also unrealistic. Your other children are still children and will not see your point of view as a parent until they are parents (if you're lucky). If they feel free to do so, siblings will complain, sometimes bitterly. Frequently, their gripes are legitimate, but you feel caught in the middle. One way to step out of the middle is to accept your own negative feelings as normal. Then you will be able to agree with your children that it's a first-class pain, and you hate it too, but it has to be done. Quite often when we complain, we just want someone to really hear us and agree that our feelings are valid. This can free up the energy to get on with whatever must be done.

Sometimes these extra demands are absolutely necessary, and you just have to write them off as one of the hidden costs of parenthood. After all, you *are* the one getting the big, slurpy kisses and sticky hugs in return. But sometimes parents cave in to demands because of nagging guilt or unresolved anger about their child's mental retardation. It's as if they provide their child with more than he can use, at the expense of the rest of the family, in the hopes of "curing" the retardation. When you do this, all you end up with is a spoiled child and resentful family. Be careful that the needs you are trying to balance are really needs and not just preferences.

═══ ✳ ═══

If he is being naughty, then he ought to sit in the corner or whatever like some other child would have to do. He ought to be told "no" even if he gets upset.

As much as possible, I intend to treat Ryan just like I treated the other two kids. If he acts up, I intend to give him some kind of discipline unless it becomes obvious that it's not effective.

It takes more time to parent our daughter with mental retardation than it does our other kids. What they learn incidentally and what they do incidentally is so much more than what she does. They were more independent earlier.

I was spending so much time with Paige when she was in the infant/toddler program. I was working part-time, and I had a very understanding boss, but it got to the point where I had to quit because it was too much.

That was part of the need, to feel like you were doing as much as you possibly could. So I dragged her to a lot of medical appointments and different kinds of therapy.

One thing you do as parents of young babies is that you spend a hell of a lot of money. I thought I would try anything that came up. I took her to a treatment center for speech therapy because I thought she could really use more concentration on speech.

Having enough time and energy are definitely problems.

Avoiding the Overprotection Trap

Sorting out needs from preferences is equally important in setting expectations for your child. When a child with mental retardation is treated as "too sick" or "too disabled" to do things for himself, not only will others come to see him in this light, but so will the child himself. When everything is done for a child, he is deprived of a basic right: the right to struggle, to learn. Overprotection silences the little voice inside that says, "I am! I will! I can!" It is this little voice that is the seed of self-esteem and self-confidence.

How do you find the courage to let go and let your child try things on his own? This is a question that confronts the parents of all children, with or without disabilities. With non-disabled children, it's easy to use chronological age or the experiences of friends and family members as a guide. Letting them wander the neighborhood at two is negligent; at six, with intermittent checking and clear limits, it's an important step toward independence. A ten-year-old whose mommy is trailing him is headed for major problems. In the case of children with mental retardation, this is another area where mental age can be a helpful guide. While it is certainly possible for a child with mental retardation to learn self-care and safety rules beyond his mental age, this is usually not accomplished reliably until well into the elementary school years.

When it's time to let go, you instruct your child, practice with him, watch him practice, and—gradually—begin stepping back. You take a deep breath, trust your child, and hope for the best. To do less is disrespectful of the person your child is.

══ ※ ══

It bothers me that he will sometimes be hurt. I'm not going to be smiling when he comes home and says, "Somebody called me a retard."

══ ※ ══

One thing we have said at Sunday School is that we don't want special treatment for our son. If he acts up or he is supposed to be doing something like other kids are doing, we want them to have him do it. Yes, maybe he's not going to learn the same things, but don't treat him special because he has mental retardation.

══ ※ ══

She has become very dependent on people because everybody has allowed her to. So I need to pull away and we have to try. Sometimes we fail, but she is learning. And as time goes on, I am hoping to do more.

Your Marriage and Yourself

Unless you are a single parent, you do not have to shoulder the extra demands of raising a child with mental retardation alone. You and your spouse can share both the added responsibilities and the extra worries and concerns. Together you can work to help your entire family adjust. That is, at least in theory you can. First, though, you and your spouse may need to confront and work through some problems that may put increased stress on your marriage.

Potential Marital Stresses

One of the earliest stresses to arise often results from differences of opinion about the existence or extent of a child's delays. Usually, it is the mother who first experiences doubt about her child's rate of progress. This is because the mother is usually in closest contact with the child. Classically, it is the mother, then, who first voices concern to the father. In a sense, the father is in a no-win situation: if he agrees with his wife (perhaps relieved at the chance to express a deep uneasiness in himself), they share the moment. But it is a moment of fear; even the first prickle of panic. If he disagrees and reassures (whether sincerely or as a defense against his own fear), a division occurs. In the most intimate matter between them, there is a disruption in the flow of communication. If the disruption continues and grows, the father can feel "pushed out" of parenting this child and begin to ignore the child, the mental retardation, or both. The mother can feel abandoned and stuck with the full weight of responsibility. Husband and wife can end up living in different worlds, emotionally and physically.

Later on, similar problems may arise if one or both disagree with one another or with "the experts" about the magnitude of their child's delay and its impact on the future. Friction may also develop if parents can't agree on the right treatment or educational program for their child.

Aside from having differences of opinion about their child and his potential, spouses may also disagree—silently or out loud— about the division of child care responsibilities. Often, mothers end up carrying the major load of both physical care and emotional repercussions. This can lead to resentment on the part of the mother and guilt on the part of the father. These feelings, in turn, make it more difficult to change the situation.

Not surprisingly, many of the extra needs that complicate your family's balancing act can also lead to marital stress. Taking your child to special classes and therapies and expending extra worries on him may leave you too exhausted to pay much attention to your relationship with your spouse. It may seem easier to ignore minor difficulties in hopes that they'll go away. The trouble is that many problems don't just disappear, but grow larger.

Despite these additional stresses that a child with mental retardation *may* bring, it is important to remember that there are many possible sources of stress on a marriage, and a special-needs child is only one of them. It is more the cumulative number and intensity of stresses—financial, emotional, social, legal—that threaten a marriage, not the source of any one stress. Don't forget, too, there are many steps you as a couple can take to reduce the stress. Some useful strategies are outlined below.

======= ※ =======

My wife said, "I do all this stuff all day long, and so you are going to do this." So I said, "All right." But then it got to a point where I felt like Kyle hated me. When I walked in the house, he went, "AHHHH! This is the man who makes me eat things I don't want." Mealtimes was all I was doing. I didn't see Kyle in the morning except maybe if he happened to wake up. I would come home at dinner time and feed him, and then it was bed time. So all I would do would be forcing him to eat things he didn't like. He was really combative for a while.

What Helps

It seems almost too simple, but if you and your spouse are at odds about your child's abilities and potential, ask an expert what he or she thinks. Researchers have demonstrated that accurate assessment of a child's cognitive abilities and accurate feedback about those abilities can help couples see their child in a more realistic and similar light. And the more information couples receive, the greater their agreement usually becomes. Parents who are well informed also tend to be more accepting and less likely to be frustrated at unmet expectations. Information is also helpful in resolving other types of stresses, such as those caused by worries about what will happen in the future or conflicts over whether your child will benefit from a certain treatment.

Open communication is vital to conveying the information that can resolve stresses. For instance, if one spouse thinks she's doing too much of the childcare or resents being the one who had to give up her job to care for the child . . . or if one spouse still harbors lingering feelings that the mental retardation was the other spouse's fault . . . or if a spouse is consumed with worry about the future, it is important to share these concerns openly and work on solutions together. A counselor familiar with these issues can be a tremendous help in getting things rolling.

Talking things over with people besides your spouse is also important. Obviously, when both partners in a marriage have many people to turn to, both individually and as a couple, the marital bond carries a lighter burden than if spouses have only each other. *All* parents experience less stress when they get support from a variety of relatives or friends. This is especially true for mothers, who often feel they carry the bulk of the burden.

If you live in a small town, where most of both sides of the family also live, it can be tough to find a wide range of support. If the woman sitting next to you in the support group is your next-door neighbor's sister-in-law, and your pediatrician's receptionist is your mother's best friend, and your clergyman's brother is your husband's bowling teammate, chances are they will share opinions and observations about you, your child, and your family with each other. A tantrum in the grocery store can be expected to result in a knowing smile at church.

Sometimes you need to talk in the complete assurance of privacy. Sometimes you need to be able to say what you feel without worrying that it will come back to haunt you. As loving and supportive as they are, friends and family may not know that blurting out, "I *hate* her!" is sometimes the first step toward loving commitment.

You may want to consider professional counseling when negative inner feelings seem to keep intruding. It may be anger, or depression, or numbness, or despair. Perhaps it's an ache between you and your spouse that won't go away. To find someone knowledgeable about the adjustment process you're going through, you can try several avenues. Your local ARC may have a list of professionals they've dealt with. If your school district has school psychologists who are also in private practice, you may find someone this way. Most child psychologists have some knowledge or experience with children with disabilities and their families. Your pediatrician may have a name or two. The important thing is that the counselor and you "click." This doesn't necessarily mean that you fully agree with everything he or she says, but that you like the counselor enough to risk considering the ideas being offered.

Most likely, you and your spouse will let your social life slide during the early stages of coping with the news of your child's mental retardation. Once the routine of daily life sets in, however, you and your spouse need to re-vitalize your social lives—both individually and as a couple. Just because you have a child with mental retardation does not mean that a sense of isolation is inevitable. Most families with children with disabilities have social contacts that are quite similar to those of other families. Try activities where mental retardation is the focus (for example, P.T.A. and ARC groups) and activities where it is not (bowling league, book club, neighborhood cook-outs). Do things with groups and by yourself. After all, you don't stop growing as an individual just because you have a child with mental retardation. Being a parent is not your only identity.

Lastly, don't forget to have some fun together, even if you have to force yourselves. Your child needs happy, relaxed parents much more than grim ones. Start dating again. Take a class together, or share a pizza. There are cheap, fun things to do anywhere. (My husband and I once spent a beautiful fall afternoon in rural Illinois visiting a pig farm. It was neat!)

I sometimes think it might be easier for a couple to cope if they have a normal kid first and then a retarded kid. We had a retarded child first and then normal children, and I'll tell you, we had to grow up quick, real quick.

Brothers and Sisters

One of the most frequently voiced concerns among parents of children with mental retardation is "What about my other children? How will this affect *them?*" They worry that normal sibling relation-

ships are impossible because their child with mental retardation is so clearly "different" from his brothers and sisters. He learns more slowly and with greater difficulty; sooner or later younger siblings will easily surpass him in most skills. In addition, his judgement is poorer, and he may often have trouble "catching on" to what is going on around him.

It is unlikely that you will ever be able to overlook these differences completely. Your other children's achievements may be a constant reminder of "what might have been" if mental retardation had not "cheated" your child of some of his intellect. These comparisons may be a source of recurring emotional pain over the years. But it is important to recognize that however your child's differences may limit him in other areas, they do not mean he cannot become a loved and accepted part of his siblings' lives. Nor do they mean he and his siblings will never be able to enjoy companionship or that he will never feel like an important member of the family.

In fact, studies show that having a brother or sister with mental retardation often has a positive effect on other children over both the short and long term. For one thing, siblings of children with handicaps tend to have a wider variety of friends than other children. Children who are close to a brother or sister with mental retardation are also more likely to embrace humanitarian life goals—to be concerned with issues like justice, equality, and compassion. Older sisters in particular are often inspired to go into one of the helping professions and devote their lives to working with people who have special needs. There is an excellent movie, available on video, about the relationship of two adult brothers, one of whom has mild mental retardation. *Dominic and Eugene* is worth looking for.

Still, there is no denying that your child's mental retardation can pose special challenges for *all* your children. Like you, siblings may have problems accepting your child's mental retardation or coping with their emotions about it. Remember, children are, by their nature and stage of development, self-centered. All kids can only take so much (and shouldn't be pressured to be more accepting than it is in their power to be). You can't expect siblings to be saints—to ignore differences, to always keep your child's best interests in mind, or even to understand. Your child with mental retardation may also have trouble resolving differences between himself and his brothers and sisters. Then, too, his mental retardation may affect his ability or desire to interact with or care about his siblings. In addition, problems can arise if you devote too much time to your child with mental retardation and neglect the emotional needs of your other children. To help you ease the adjustment process for your children, some of the most important sibling issues are discussed below.

Lynn and Jessica share a bedroom. That was one of the best things I ever did. Every once in a while, Jessica will jump in bed with Lynn. They sit in there and giggle and laugh.

Eventually Jessica will have her own room, but for now I think it's kind of nice. They miss one another when they're apart.

Our son has always known that his sister's handicapped, but he's never quite known what to say about it.

When we were at my mother's house and my mother said that Phillip couldn't open the door, Jennifer said, "Come here, Phillip. Let me help you." Jennifer is taking the role of the older sister and is starting to help him out.

Your Children's Emotions

Just as you do, your other children will notice that something is "different" about their brother or sister with mental retardation. A three-year-old may wonder why her big brother wears diapers or still eats baby food, while a six-year-old may be frustrated that her sister "doesn't talk right" and can't play with her as she would like. Also like you, your children may react to these differences with emotions running the gamut from anger, resentment, and guilt, to grief, worry, and embarrassment. Because it can help both you and your children to realize that these emotions are completely normal, here are some thoughts and feelings siblings typically feel at different ages.

Preschool. Siblings who are under five can be quite perceptive. They may sense your anxiety about your child with mental retardation, even if they are not sure of its source. They may resent the extra time you spend with their sibling in therapy or in an early intervention program, and may regress to try to recapture your attention. For example, they may suddenly "forget" how to use the toilet or put on their jacket so that you have to help them. On the positive side, young children are usually anxious to help, and are often eager to do things with and for their sibling with mental retardation. If they are praised for their helpfulness, they are not only likely to feel good about themselves, but also about their sibling.

School-Age (6–12). School-aged children may wonder what's wrong with their sibling with mental retardation and worry about "catching" it. They may feel embarrassed by their sibling, at the same time they feel guilty for having these feelings. They may try to overachieve to compensate you for what they perceive as your "loss" or to make it abundantly clear that *they* are not retarded and thus distance themselves from their sibling. They may be enraged at having to "explain" their sibling to their friends, perhaps risking rejection or being seen as an object of pity. They may even fear that they somehow caused the mental retardation by some negative thought of their own. For example, at some point most kids wish that the new baby would die or would just go away. Children of this age typically have "magical thinking." They believe that they—like the wicked witch in so many fairy tales—have the power to cast an evil spell on the baby. To a school-age child who is just discovering the concept of personal responsibility, the idea of causing Martin's mental retardation by wishing he would die is just as logical as causing bad grades by not doing homework.

Adolescence. In adolescence, a child who was eager to help when his sibling was little may explode in rage or smolder ominously when requested to do one thing. Of course, teenagers spend major portions of their time exploding or smoldering, and most parents learn not to take it personally. But when parents have worked hard to encourage their child to help out with a sibling with mental retardation, and may really be counting on this help, this seemingly sudden switch can be deeply shocking and puzzling. Have you been living in a fool's paradise all these years? No, you just have a teenager on your hands. It helps if you know a little about adolescent development.

Teenagers suddenly become embarrassed at facts of life they never minded before. Striving to be "perfect" to their peers, they don't even want to acknowledge that they have *parents*, let alone a sibling with disabilities. They are often convinced that "everybody" will think they are weird, and that they will be socially unacceptable and rejected by anyone who sees or even knows they have a sibling with mental retardation.

Besides feeling embarrassed, adolescents usually have a real fear of responsibility for their brother or sister with mental retardation. Teenagers are struggling hard to master *self*-responsibility; they sense that being responsible for anything or anyone else will overwhelm their meager resources. They are afraid that somehow, their sibling is going to sidetrack them from their main job of growing up successfully. They worry that their obligation to their brother or sister will keep them tied to their mother and father—that true independence will be beyond their reach.

Of course, just because your teenager is embarrassed and fears being overwhelmed by responsibility does not mean you should cease to expect some help from him. You will, however, get more cooperation if you acknowledge these concerns out loud. You should also sometimes allow your teenager to choose not to accompany the rest of the family on an outing. ("I know Susan's table manners embarrass you in public. You don't have to go with us to McDonald's if you don't want to. There's stuff in the fridge if you'd rather eat here.") This will make it easier to demand participation on other occasions. ("We are *all* going to your grandmother's for Thanksgiving, and that includes you.")

Sometimes it's tempting to expect your "normal" adolescent to bring his sibling along to the movies or the mall or whatever. Teenagers with mental retardation often yearn for the active social life they see their siblings enjoying. Their friends from school often live beyond walking distance, so an adult's help is usually needed for them to have even the simplest social contact. It seems so logical for a sibling to let him "tag along," at least once in a while.

Your other children may offer to take their sibling along without any prompting from you, but don't count on it. Family relationships will probably go a lot smoother (now and later) if you confine your requests to things your children can do together at home. This means including the sibling with mental retardation in Sunday afternoon games of Monopoly or Nintendo, watching sports on TV, going along with the sibling's choice of video, and so forth. Most of all, it means that your other children should keep promises made to their sibling with mental retardation. A date to play Barbies should not get cancelled because of homework or a more appealing invitation.

One activity that helps everyone build skills is cooking together. Whether it's brownies from a mix or a whole meal, all your children can benefit from the experience. You may even talk with your other children about setting up some regular (daily or weekly) activity with their sibling with mental retardation. Teenagers want to help, and can contribute a lot, if they are not asked to do it in front of their peers, and if it's something they feel they can handle. Don't forget to let your teenager know that you appreciate whatever efforts he makes on his sibling's behalf.

Every once in a while his younger sister will ask a question, but it's more like "that's the way it is." We are letting her grow into it. Once in a while, we'll explain something to her about mental retardation, but I have never sat down and had a long, hard-pressed talk about it.

People say really rude things to our older son about "your retarded brother," essentially making fun, kind of, or not respecting differences or remembering that they're talking about a human being.

It has sometimes been hard for our other two kids that they have a sister who is different from somebody else's older sister. But it is great that they have really kind of ridden along with it. They have never stopped having friends over. She's a puzzle to the friends, too. They know that she has mental retardation—that has never been a question—but they also see her doing these other things. Sometimes I'll overhear our son say, "If you think I'm a good speller, or whatever, then you won't believe how my sister can spell."

When we talk about the future, Katie's brother always says, "Of course she would stay with me and she wouldn't be sent anywhere." Katie's sister is not as decided. She says, "I'm going off to college. I don't want to have to give up college. I love her, but I don't want to take care of her in the next couple of years. I don't think I can; I don't think it's fair to me." We said that's right. We told her we wanted truthful answers, and that's what she gives us.

Helping Your Children Adjust

As mentioned earlier, your other children will, to a large extent, follow your lead. If you treat your child with mental retardation with love and concern, his siblings are likely to pick up this attitude, too. Still, there will probably be times when your mere example is not enough to help your children cope with their emotions. They may have worries—expressed or unexpressed—that they cannot solve on their own. Or they may be ambivalent; on the one hand, they may care deeply for their sibling with mental retardation, but on the other hand, they might resent the extra time you seem to spend with him. Although there is no one best way to help your children cope, here are a variety of strategies that often help:

Communication. A standard technique in psychotherapy that is used to help people of any age deal with an upsetting experience is to have them tell the story over and over. It seems that simple repetition slowly dissolves the painful, negative feelings, leaving the event to be incorporated as just one of many events in the person's life. Repetition seems to take away the power of the event.

Thus, listening to your other children talk about their sibling with mental retardation is extremely helpful to them. Ask questions about how they feel and what they think. Share with them some of your own thoughts and feelings. For example, "You know, before we had Eric I thought children with mental retardation had to live in a hospital their whole life." "I used to be scared Jennifer's mental retardation was my fault, too. It took me a long time to stop trying to make up for it."

Praise your children for sharing their private thoughts and feelings with you. As you know from your own experience, it takes tremendous courage and trust to do so. Praise yourself as well. It also takes courage and trust to listen without judgement or defensiveness.

Information. In communicating with your children, you will naturally want to supply them with accurate information appropriate to their age level. This becomes especially important as your children grow and begin to pick up misinformation from other children or even other adults. Answer their questions as honestly and completely as you can, but don't overload them with too much information. Stress that you don't know all the answers, but you are prepared to try to find out. If you willingly volunteer information and answers to their questions, your children are less likely to get the message that mental retardation should be kept a secret because it is something to be ashamed of.

For help answering or anticipating your children's questions, you may want to turn to some of the excellent children's books on mental retardation that may be available at your library. Some books are geared to younger children, and generally carry the global message, "Kids with mental retardation are nice too." One such book is *Don't Forget Tom*, by Hanne Larsen. As siblings get older, they may want more information about what life is like for a child with mental retardation. *We Laugh, We Love, We Cry*, by Thomas Bergman, uses both photographs and brief text to describe the daily lives of sisters with mental retardation. Late elementary and middle-school age siblings may want to understand on a more abstract level. *Like It Is: Facts and Feelings about Handicaps from Kids Who Know*, by Barbara Adams, is helpful at this age. One advantage of this book is that it places mental retardation in the context of several other common handicaps, each of which is explained by a child who actually lives with that handicap.

These are by no means the only good books on the subject. Ask the children's librarian to help you find others. Your local ARC, too, may have suggestions. Also consult the Reading List at the back of this book. The important thing is to read these books together with your children, including your child with mental retardation. Discuss how the ideas presented do or do not relate to their own perceptions. For example, "Susan, do you feel like that sometimes? John, can you think of a time Susan seemed to feel that way? How did it make *you* feel?"

When your children are older, it may even be interesting to check out a book or two written a number of years ago, to help them grasp how much has changed in the field of mental retardation. This can be helpful for parents, too! New laws, new educational practices, and new research make the situation much more hopeful and exciting than you or your children may realize.

Getting Your Children Involved. When your other children are at certain ages and stages, letting them help "teach" your child with mental retardation is an excellent way to foster understanding. It can also be great fun for everyone involved if you incorporate these learning opportunities into playtime. Children with mental retardation often allow siblings to teach them without the competitiveness that usually accompanies sibling play. Your child with mental retardation may even let his brother or sister read to him when he doesn't seem to have the attention span to sit still for you to do it.

Keep two important limits to sibling teaching in mind. First, make sure that the activity is within the grasp of your child with mental retardation. If his mental age is three, he will not be able to understand and follow the rules of Chutes and Ladders or Candyland, no matter how patiently his siblings explain them. He may be able to *pretend* to play for five or ten minutes, though. Be sure you make this clear to his sibling, or it's a set-up for frustration and failure for everyone.

Second, make it clear that it is not your other children's *job* to teach their sibling with mental retardation. Your child with mental retardation already has parents and doesn't need more. If your other children resist playing with or teaching their sibling, don't force the issue. The resistance may be temporary, anyway. It's a parent's job to raise each of his or her own children, not to police the relationship between them.

If your child with mental retardation complains about being left out, handle it the same way as you would with any other child. Be sympathetic with the child who is left out, but remind him that brothers and sisters sometimes need to play with their friends, and find something else for the "left-out one" to do.

Organization. As discussed earlier, it is essential that you juggle all the competing demands on your attention so that no one in your family feels slighted. None of your children should feel as if his needs are unimportant or secondary to those of your child with mental retardation. But given the extra time it probably takes to look after your child with special needs, how do you ensure that each of your children gets his fair share of your attention? The answer lies in organization.

Staggered bedtimes are a big help. While an older child is in the bath, a younger child (or one who needs an earlier bedtime) can be having his "talking time" with one parent all to himself for ten full minutes. Children generally love this so much you may need a clock or timer to exit gracefully. Most of the time, a child who *knows* he has ten minutes will get in what he wants to say before the time is up. If not, there's always tomorrow night. This is also a nice opportunity for some casual affection: back rubbing or hair smoothing. If I had to choose between reading a story and "talking time," I'd choose the latter. Stories can be read at other times; this special intimacy between parent and child seems to happen mostly when the covers are pulled up and the lights are off. Some switching off between parents gives each child a chance to have a real relationship with each parent. This kind of intensive, consistent, predictable attention goes a long way toward smoothing feathers that were ruffled during the day.

In addition, be sure that choosing the destination of family outings gets rotated. (You and your spouse each get turns, too!) Once in a while, get a sitter for your child with mental retardation if he's really not able to participate in a particular activity. Or get a sitter for your other kids while your child with mental retardation gets to go with both parents to an activity he would enjoy but the others would not.

Making other family choices should be rotated as well: which carry-out place gets called, which TV show or video gets watched, whose turn it is to have a sleep-over, and so forth. You may end up keeping a chart or occasionally getting fed up with the whole thing and exerting your parental right to rule by fiat, declaring martial law as needed.

Individuality and Specialness. Most of the ideas suggested above have the nifty side-effect of giving *everyone* a turn at feeling special. Naturally, your other children need your support and blessing to develop lives outside the family as well, and to be recognized for what they accomplish. *Everybody's* artwork and "A" papers should be displayed on the refrigerator; everybody should be encouraged to develop their special talents and pursue their special interests. Just as you shouldn't be limited solely to being the parent of a child with mental retardation, your other children need to feel that they are more than just siblings of a child with mental retardation.

Be sure also to recognize your other kids for the effort they make to be "good siblings" to your child with mental retardation. No one ever overdosed on sincere compliments. Ask, "Was it hard to bring Amy home and have her meet Jonathan? I'm proud you had the courage to try it." Or, "It's neat the way you play with Pam on Saturday mornings. It lets me sleep a little longer, and I know she's thrilled at getting all her big sister's attention. You really know how to play with her!"

Adopting a Child with Mental Retardation

Up to this point, everything that has been said applies both to biological parents of children with mental retardation and to adoptive parents who did not initially know that their child had handicaps. Most of it also applies to parents who deliberately set out to adopt a child with mental retardation. But in some important ways, the planned adoption of a child with disabilities is easier. A couple has the opportunity to consider the effects on themselves, their family, and the child in advance. The freedom to say "no" can result in a wholehearted "yes." The guilt and shock do not have to be worked through. Denial may be present to some degree, but there is usually less, and it is less intense. Furthermore, adopting a child with mental retardation does not arouse worries or concerns that future children will also have mental retardation.

Yet, once the decision to adopt is made, the feelings and experiences of adoptive and birth parents is much the same. All parents must adjust to the demands of daily and long-term care, and in the process, come to care deeply about their child's accomplishments. All parents are concerned about their child's happiness and future, and desire what is best for him.

Siblings, too, generally experience similar feelings and conflicts whether their brother or sister with mental retardation is adopted or not. But there may also be important differences. Often, parents make the decision to adopt a child with mental retardation a family matter, and let older siblings take part in discussions. The older siblings have thus helped to make the decision and have chosen their role much as the adults have. In a sense, the child with mental retardation joins an intact family that has chosen to include him. Certainly, this is the easiest situation in which to deal with the initial feelings of siblings.

Of course, when siblings are too young to participate in the decision, they should be told as much in advance as possible. It's a good idea to explain that this child will need lots of extra love. Love is amazing: the more you use it, the more there is. It is important that the brother- or sister-to-be understands that love "rightfully" theirs is not going to be taken away to give to the new child. Tell them so in straightforward language. You might also use the example that turning on the light in the kitchen does not make it darker in the living room. Also make sure your other children understand that regressing or "acting like a baby" is not the way to get extra attention.

If the adopted child is older than your other children, your oldest birth child may feel he is being replaced, and this should be addressed directly with him. You might say something like, "Steve, you know that Mikey is two years older than you, so he will be your older brother. But he also has mental retardation and can't yet do all the things you can do. So in some ways, he'll be more like a younger brother. What do you think about that?"

Whatever the adopted child's age, the issues will probably be much the same as when parents are expecting a new baby. At first there is limit testing and ambivalence. Rules you thought were cast in stone will be ignored. There will be burping at the table, tantrums at bedtime, bathroom "accidents," whining, announcements that the new member of the family is not wanted after all, and so forth. Whatever limits you have set up in your household will be tested by someone. Basically, your other kids are asking, "Can I get away with murder?" Your calm, firm assurance that indeed they cannot—that the old rules will continue to be enforced in the usual manner—will be very reassuring to all of your children, including the new one. It helps everyone understand that "this family is going to go right on being this family, only now we have Catherine in it, too."

In general, you can smooth out problems if you keep the lines of communication open. Ask your children for their feelings and reactions. Listen carefully, and correct straightforwardly any misunderstandings. If you and your children are honest with yourselves and one another, everyone usually adjusts, and it seems as if the family has always had a child with mental retardation.

Friends and family, too, will generally adjust to your decision to adopt a child with mental retardation—but it may take some time. Whatever their attitudes, remember: you have the right to make decisions in your own life that may not be what others would have chosen for themselves or for you. Also remember that misgivings others have are often out of concern for you and other members of your immediate family. Then, too, you should realize that they may be wondering what this means for their lives. Most parents don't choose to be "special parents." Grandparents may not choose to be "special grandparents" either. They might avoid your child with mental retardation, or give preferential treatment to your other children. This is primarily the grandparent's loss. Once you have stated your concerns, you have no real control over the behavior of another person. Give friends and relatives time to get used to the idea, and to get to know this new family member. If you have confidence in your decision, so will most others.

We were told there's a waiting list for people wanting to adopt children with Down syndrome. I went to ARC and asked if I could read some books on Down syndrome so I'd know a little about it. That helped a lot because, before that, I would say that I was afraid of people with mental retardation. Then I visited him every day for a couple of weeks. That's how I got to know him. The foster mother told me he was just a normal baby. But I felt that he was a baby who would need care for much longer than a "normal" child.

We have Kyle because he has Down syndrome. If he was a perfect, regular child, he would not have been given up. So we are blessed or thankful—it's very hard to explain—that he has this handicap. We don't want him to have this handicap, but if he didn't have it, we would not have <u>him</u>. It is very, very weird to look at . . . it's very hard to explain to somebody.

We didn't have a doctor walk in and say to us, "Your healthy child is retarded," and I feel that that must be terrible, terrible. . . . I can't imagine it, even though I feel that I can imagine it better than most people, because I deal with a lot of the other emotions.

If you look at what we face, we probably face everything everybody else does except for this one issue. We knew he was going to be retarded when we took him. Maybe it's something we shouldn't be proud of, but I do say he is adopted if somebody asks, maybe too easily.

My mother said, "Why take on another child, first of all, and secondly, yes, he's real cute, but why take on a handicapped child?"

I think our parents were concerned because they thought we were getting ourselves into something that we might later regret, not because they had a bad reaction to him.

My mother has said, "And I'm the grandmom that said maybe you shouldn't take him," meaning like "Wasn't I stupid?"

Our son is included in everything. We haven't had any real problems as a family. I mean, it's crazy around here with all of them . . . but that's what having three kids is like. I think they all complement each other.

Community Life

Not so long ago, having a child with mental retardation in the family was considered a socially embarrassing tragedy. Even when the rest of the family went on an outing, the youngster with handicaps was often left at home. Today, due to incredible effort on the part of parents, community life is much more open to family members with mental retardation. Now you are likely to see other families with a child with mental retardation at nearly any public gathering, be it an amusement park, church service, or local mall. This is as it should be. People with disabilities really are a part of the community, and have the right to participate in it as much as anyone else. In addition, including *all* your children in community activities can help the whole family—as it really is—strengthen their feeling of "family"—as it really is.

Of course, just because you would like to include your child with mental retardation in all family activities doesn't necessarily mean that you will always feel comfortable doing so. Especially in the beginning, you may feel as if you and your child are too conspicuous. You may worry that others' comments may wound family members, or that your child may embarrass you in front of legions of strangers. But the fear of embarrassment and hurt feelings only grows if

catered to. It may take some firm self-talk, but once you've confronted and conquered this fear, you and your family will be much stronger. You will also have learned that your fears are usually worse than the reality. Before you know it, you'll be an old hand at handling situations as they arise.

Handling Reactions from Others

There is no denying that your child probably *will* attract notice. Children with mental retardation may be obviously different from other children in a variety of ways and may therefore inspire questions or comments from others. Sometimes it may be simply your child's appearance which causes notice. If your child has one of the better-known syndromes such as Down syndrome, adults may be *less* likely to ask questions because they realize your child has mental retardation. If your child has a condition that fewer adults are familiar with, or that is less noticeable physically, you may get questions or odd comments that can sometimes be awkward. Don't feel you have to respond. A look of stunned amazement at such poor manners may be enough. Or, if you feel comfortable, just saying, "He's mentally retarded" may have the desired effect.

Your child's communication skills—unclear speech, signing, and so forth—may also attract attention. A child with few physical signs of mental retardation may surprise others with her immature sentence construction or articulation. For example, an impulsive announcement, "Me wan' ha'buh'guh!" on entering a fast-food restaurant will certainly draw some notice. At the park, any delays in motor skills, too, will be apparent. Your child may not be walking yet, or may not use the playground equipment in the same way as others his age. At elementary school age, he may prefer sitting in the sandbox or still need help swinging. Even when using age-appropriate equipment, his play may be noticeably less sophisticated than other children's. For example, he may still prefer to play *beside* other children, rather than *with* them.

You may get questions from both children and adults about why your child is not yet wearing "big kid's" underwear. Changing diapers in a public restroom can be a real adventure! In addition, if your child uses special equipment such as hearing aids, orthotics, or communication boards, others will naturally be curious about their function.

Your knowledge of your child's differences can help you prepare for others' questions and comments. It is often helpful to plan and rehearse a general explanation in advance. For example, you might decide to respond to a child who loudly asks, "What's wrong with *him*?" by saying, "He has mental retardation, and that means he learns more slowly than others." If the situation allows, you may follow up by suggesting a more appropriate way for the person to talk or act with your child in the future. For example, "Her name is Veronica, and she came to the store with her mommy, too. Why don't you tell her *your* name?"

Decide in advance what label you prefer to use for your child's handicap, be it mental retardation, handicap, developmental delay, multiple handicap, disability, or whatever you feel comfortable with. The label may change as your child changes, or as your feelings about your child's retardation change. The label might also change according to the situation. For example, an explanation in a clinic waiting room may be much more specific and detailed than one in the drugstore.

Remember that you need only deal with the question asked. A comment about your child's delayed motor skills does not obligate you to describe the effect retardation has on abstract thinking. A question about your child's prominent ears does not need to be answered with an explanation of the genetics of fragile X syndrome. Just answer questions matter-of-factly.

You can teach your other children these principles as well. It may be helpful to actually rehearse the scene in advance, switching roles each time, so everyone gets a chance to be the "questioner" and the "answerer." As your child with mental retardation is able, include him in the practice.

Being well prepared helps to remove the anxiety and worry so that you and they *can* be casual and matter-of-fact. If a comment is hurtful (for example, "What an ugly kid!"), teach your family to state directly, "That hurts my feelings." Certainly this is something a child can say, even to an adult. When the purpose is clearly aggressive, no explanation is needed. Your child with mental retardation, if she has sufficient speech, and her siblings can state the truth: "You don't know what you're talking about," and *leave*. Sometimes it's a good idea to just leave.

Perhaps you are wondering why you should respond to comments and questions from strangers in the first place. Why should your child be any of their business? There are three major reasons. First, an explanation may make expectations more realistic and appropriate for your child. For example, at a fast food restaurant, you might want to tell the cashier, "Beatrice has trouble talking, but she would like to place her own order using her book." In a public women's restroom, if someone objects to your bringing your seven-year-old son with you, you may respond with, "Samuel learns more slowly than other children. He needs help using the toilet." On the whole, once you have given them an explanation, most people are quite understanding of your child's special needs.

The second reason follows from the first. When others have realistic expectations of your child, he is more likely to find socializing pleasant and fun. Your child learns that he can indeed participate fully, taking pride in his own accomplishments (don't forget the compliments!).

The third reason also follows from the first. By giving strangers brief explanations, you are helping to educate the world about mental retardation. Answering a question now may radically change that person's viewpoint. After all, mental retardation is a natural, normal situation. Nobody did anything wrong, so there's nothing to be ashamed of. Most people ask or comment only out of curiosity or simple ignorance. They do not mean to intrude, and are glad to understand better. Sometimes, though, people can be straight-out rude and hurtful. They don't want to be educated. Unless you have infinite time and the skin of an armadillo, don't try. Just go about your business, knowing that being a jerk is a bigger handicap than having mental retardation.

A final tip on dealing with the reactions of strangers: never assume you know the motivation. The woman at the next table may be staring at your child because she runs the local early intervention program and is wondering why she doesn't recognize your child (this has happened to me). She may volunteer at your child's school and think she recognizes him, but has never met you. Perhaps the man behind you at the bank is a plastic surgery resident, admiring your child's scars. It may be that the child with the loud question has a cousin with mental retardation, and is trying to understand how all of this is connected.

There are many reasons for staring, commenting, or questioning. Make life easy for yourself; assume most people are good at heart and just want some information. The way others treat your child will usually reflect the way you treat them. If you are calm, pleasant, and friendly, they will walk away from the exchange more knowledgeable, accepting, and open than when they first approached you. You will have accomplished something important.

For about the first year, many people stopped me and said, "Isn't he cute?" Then about stroller-age, people would come up and say "hi," and I could see them stop because he would turn around and they would realize that he was a handicapped child. I saw them stop in mid-sentence, almost, as through they were going to say "cute." But then they would say "How are you" instead of "Isn't he cute," or something.

I don't think anybody in the neighborhood ever required a label for Andrea's disability. We've been living here for seventeen years, so Andrea was born after we were already here. Nobody ever really asked for a specific explanation.

When people ask what's the matter with her, we've just learned to use the term "retarded." Our little girl Paige is retarded. She doesn't look it, but she is. I think usually when you think of retarded you think of Down syndrome or something else that you can see in a child's features. Now if I look long and hard at Paige, I guess I could see some abnormalities in some of her features, but at first glance you don't see that. So yeah, we say she's retarded.

Our son has always had a funny gait. It looks like shuffle-hop-skip, and people make fun of that. I keep hoping that junior high is the age where people are the most obnoxious and that in high school there will be more maturity and a willingness to accept differences.

A lot of people ask, "Why does he use sign language? Is he deaf?" And I say, "No, he has Down syndrome and they use it with that." The response is usually "Oh, I didn't know that." Some people are interested; others are like, "Uh-oh, I stepped into something I wish I hadn't" and so they walk off. I have never had a bad reaction. But I definitely bring sign language into it, because people are more interested in a deaf person or a person with sign language than a retarded person, as far as I'm concerned. Maybe it doesn't scare them as much.

We can go to a grocery store and he'll go up and start talking to someone. We get various reactions. We've had some really good reactions and we've had some really horrendous reactions. He doesn't seem to pick up on the negative in the bad reactions, though.

Sometimes someone will see him having trouble walking and ask, "What's wrong?" I just usually say he has cerebral palsy. People have heard of that and they'll just say "Oh." Sometimes it's more of an "Oh, that's sad" kind of an "oh." I don't go into the mental retardation.

Before our daughter came along, if I saw a child who was obviously retarded I'd be curious and I'd be looking because this person was different. But I didn't want to stare. Now when I go out and see a retarded child, I want to see how this child is doing and everything, but I still don't want to stare. There's a totally different reason for my curiosity. I want to understand how this person is different and the same as my child.

═══ ※ ═══

I was at the check-out counter in a toy store and the cashier turned to me and said, "Oh, does he have Down syndrome?" I said, "Yes, he does." I didn't have to go any further than that because she told me she had a seven-year-old son who was retarded.

═══ ※ ═══

You want to go up and talk to other people who have kids with mental retardation. You want to say something like "Hey, we've got something in common." But then you know that they probably don't want to be treated differently than anybody else, so it's a little confusing as to what to do.

═══ ※ ═══

I want everybody to like my son.

═══ ※ ═══

All the neighborhood kids just accept Aaron.

The Public Tantrum

Most parents, whatever their child's age or ability/disability, dread one thing above all others: the big, fat, public temper tantrum—especially the elaborate luxury model complete with kicking, screaming, tears, and hitting. It may be hard to remember at the moment it is happening to you, but every parent within earshot will be sending you waves of sympathy. Naturally, you will be most acutely aware of noses in the air and looks of disapproval. These people are not parents, and know nothing about children. Do not waste one drop of energy worrying about these people.

Deal with public tantrums or other misbehavior much the same way you do at home. Your child may simply be trying to find out how you deal with these behaviors away from home, anyway. There is no other way to find out if the limits are consistent, except by pushing them to see if anyone pushes back. That someone does push back can be a huge relief to an overtired, overstimulated little guy. It also lays the groundwork for the rules on future outings. Now he *knows* you really mean it.

If one verbal reminder is not effective, giving your child a time out is possible in almost any situation. (See Chapter 6 for an explanation of how a time out works.) I know one mother who enlisted her children's help in choosing a "time out place" each time they entered a new public environment. This was always the first order of business in a new mall, park, museum, swimming pool, or the like. If the family has been there before, she immediately reminds everyone of the specific place they will have to sit in for five minutes following any misbehavior. I don't know if she brings her kitchen timer with her or not. I do know that time out in a public place has actually been required only twice. I also know that the kids remember the designated spot, though months may have passed since the previous visit. They also know that the rules follow them wherever they go.

If a time out is ineffective or inappropriate, remove your child (and possibly the whole family) from the scene. Leave your grocery-laden cart in the aisle, pick up your child (thereby alerting all spectators that this *is* your child—feel the sympathy waves if you can), march straight to the car, and drive straight home. When you have yourself in hand, state the rule firmly and calmly: if you cannot behave yourself at the grocery store (or whatever), you cannot stay there.

Remember, it is your job to raise this child. Ignore the reactions of others. If your child behaves like an obnoxious little brat, he desperately needs you to help him learn to behave properly. Otherwise, he will grow up to be a big obnoxious brat. Make it clear before leaving home exactly which (if any) treats your child may expect. Unless you are training him to be a street beggar, do not succumb to wheedles and whines for anything not agreed upon in advance. Granted, these situations can sometimes be tough, especially when your imagination runs wild. Even if people *are* clucking their tongues at your "cruelty" to "that poor little retarded child," parents are the only people who can teach their children to behave properly in public. The "cluckers" will cluck just as loudly at her *in*appropriate behavior a few years from now if you give in at the critical moment.

In the car, there may be no "cluckers," but misbehavior must be dealt with in much the same way. If you are still close enough, you may choose to turn around and go home. You should remind your child of this possibility and what could cause it *before you leave.* In any event, you can usually pull over to the shoulder and stop the car. Wait until behavior conforms to the rule. Announce that you see he is obeying the rule, and you are glad because now you can continue on your journey. The rules should be very concrete, like "Everyone must have their seatbelts buckled (or be in their safety seats)." "No fighting" is a workable rule for short distances only. I once spent nine hours on a trip from Louisville to St. Louis: a total of four hours were spent sitting on the shoulder.

Of course, in planning any excursion, keep your child's limitations in mind. The visit may have to be kept quite short to prevent exhaustion, hunger, or other factors from making your exit a hurried one. Reminders and time outs are effective only when your child has the physical and emotional capacity to do as you ask. Otherwise, they are cruel.

—— ※ ——

When we go to a restaurant or something like that and Kyle acts up like any child might act up, my wife especially becomes concerned that people are going to say, "Look at that little retarded boy acting up" as opposed to "Look at that little two- or three-year-old acting up," so she's extra careful that he doesn't act up. She's almost overly careful.

—— ※ ——

Some people said "Hi." And I said, "Say hi, Sonny," and Sonny spit. Inside I was thinking, "Oh my gosh, they're going to think he's retarded," and it was not that at all—he was just being a brat.

—— ※ ——

In my mother's church, there are several adults with mental retardation. Some of them know how to act, but at least one of them knows that she can get her way because she has been allowed to manipulate people for her entire life. That's wrong. I don't want my son to be like that.

—— ※ ——

We take something for him to draw on in restaurants. If we can keep him occupied and if he's not so overwhelmingly hungry that he's going to die in the next five minutes, he's really not too bad.

He's much more patient in restaurants than he used to be. It used to be that you had to have something for him to eat immediately. I mean, before you did anything else, you had to order him something that they could get to him quickly.

If we give her a spanking because she's being bad, we worry that people will say, "Look at them—they're abusing that little retarded kid." We don't think of him as a little retarded kid, but we are conscious of others' perceptions.

If he is brought up to be polite and know appropriate behavior, then if people don't like him, that's their problem.

Socializing with Other Families

It *is* important for your family to know that they have a life outside the home and can do anything "normal" families can do. You need to take your children shopping and on other errands; go for family walks, picnics, bike rides, and camping trips; and have fun at the movies, the bowling alley, or the skating rink. But not all community activities need to be carried out alone on center stage, before curious strangers. Many families make a point of doing things with friends who already accept and welcome their child with mental retardation. Others find that doing things with families who also have a child with disabilities makes going out in public easier. There really is strength in numbers. Doing things with friends (whether or not they have a kid with mental retardation) is a less anxiety-ridden, more natural way to teach children social skills.

Your county parks and recreation department may provide especially valuable opportunities for socializing. Some offer programs especially for families which include a member with mental retardation. Participating in one of these programs puts families in touch with similar families, but the focus is not on the disability but on activities such as arts and crafts, softball, swimming, nature walks, campfires, and holiday parties. Taking part in these programs allows siblings to realize that their family is not unique, and gives everyone a chance to see how others handle various situations.

——— ※ ———

We pay a lot for her to be a social person. She belongs to whatever teen club is around. What we pay out for a weekend for her is phenomenal. You pay the registration for all these things, and every time they go somewhere, it's $25 or $30.

——— ※ ———

Sometimes we have to decide what she can do; whether to go to Harper's Ferry or King's Dominion. Sometimes it is repetitive. She and her friends keep going to the same places because there's not a whole lot we can think of that's clever or new. I sometimes think she should be more integrated into the community, but you've got to be realistic. Most teenagers are not going to be real helpful to her because they can do things a lot more on their own. At least if our daughter goes with a group to King's Dominion, they usually walk around together so they don't get ripped off and don't get lost.

Community Safety

Letting your child do things alone or with other children outside the house is also part of community life. The degree of supervision needed depends on the level of your child's functioning (mental age). A child of six whose mental age is more like a three-year-old's should not be allowed to roam the neighborhood at will with the other kids. But he is quite capable of playing with neighborhood friends at their house. Invite friends with mental retardation from your child's school or your parent support group. Neighbors whose social and play skills are around the same level can also be invited.

Carefully watch interactions between your child and children who are at a much higher developmental level. Well-meaning children may make your child into a kind of pet or living baby doll. A little of this goes a long way. Older children may inadvertently or intentionally victimize him, or may make fun of him by playing on his eagerness to please and to be accepted.

Many adults in your child's life may know your child's name, although he may not recognize them. For example, the director of the nursery school, the speech therapist, or an aide from another class may all have a legitimate relationship with your child, but may not be well-known to him. Children quickly learn to go with people who call them by name. Thus, it may be wise not to have your child's name printed on backpacks, T-shirts, and the like, so strangers cannot pick up on this clue. Even so, you probably want some assurance that if your child gets lost, someone will be able to help him. You might consider having your phone number engraved on a disk that your child can wear on a chain around his neck, inside his shirt. Your child knows it's there, and can be taught to show it to an adult if he gets lost. Until your child is able to do this, he should not be allowed outside without supervision.

Your child's level of understanding is an important indicator of when he is ready to learn safety skills. You can teach him how to safely cross streets or whatever just as you would any child, but your child will require more practice. Have him tell you when it's safe to cross as you go for walks in the neighborhood. Decide on landmarks beyond which he is not to go, and point these out to him. Point out berries, toadstools, crab apples, and flowers and tell him clearly, "We *never* eat anything from outside; it will make us very sick." Don't expect him to discriminate poisonous from non-poisonous plants.

Sometimes she is real babyish and that throws you off and takes a couple years off your life when you think of her as an adult.

If he goes to the tot lot, his older brother's there. We never allow him to go into a situation where one of the three of us is not there.

He doesn't understand concepts of good people/bad people, so we have to be very careful. He would talk to anybody and he would go with anybody, just about.

Conclusion

Having a child with mental retardation can change your family's life in many ways. Some of these changes will be easier for you than others; some stages and situations more comfortable than others. There will be times you wish you could pull the covers up over your head and make it all go away. Often these times are just before a period of major growth, when everything seems chaotic and hopeless. At other times you'll wonder what had you so worried. Eventually, a time will probably come when you couldn't conceive of life without your child—a time when you are able to objectively add up all the pluses and minuses and realize just how much your child brings to your family. Your child can help to keep you focused on what is really important in life: love and laughter; friendship and caring; tenderness and trying your best. Differences between people and the importance of meeting some impossible standard will fade into the background and take their proper place as trivial in the scheme of things.

Be kind to yourself. Go at your own pace and refuse to be overwhelmed. As both research and experience show, having a child with mental retardation may be the end of a fantasy or of blithely taking things for granted. But it is not the end of the world. True, your world may be different than you expected. But it does not necessarily stop you from having a happy marriage, a happy family, and a happy life.

Eight

=== ※ ===

Legal Rights and Hurdles

James E. Kaplan and Ralph J. Moore, Jr.*

Introduction

Now that you have a child with mental retardation, it is worthwhile to learn about some of the more important laws that apply specifically to people with disabilities. There are laws guaranteeing your child the right to attend school and to live and work in the community. Other laws grant your child financial and medical assistance, if she qualifies. Still other laws govern your long-term planning for your child's future.

It is vital for you as a parent to understand the workings of these laws. If you know what your child is entitled to, you can help ensure that she receives the education, training, and special services she needs to reach her potential. You will also be able to recognize illegal discrimination and assert your child's rights if need be. Finally, if you understand how laws can sometimes work against families of children with disabilities, you can avoid unwitting mistakes in planning for your child's future.

There are no federal laws that deal exclusively with mental retardation. Rather, the rights of children with mental retardation are provided in the laws and regulations for children and adults with

* Ralph J. Moore, Jr., and James E. Kaplan are both active in the area of the legal rights of children with disabilities. They are the co-authors of the "Legal Rights and Hurdles" chapters in Woodbine House's parents' guides to Down syndrome, epilepsy, autism, and cerebral palsy. Mr. Moore, a partner in the law firm of Shea & Gardner in Washington, D.C., is the author of *Handbook on Estate Planning for Families of Developmentally Disabled Persons in Maryland, the District of Columbia, and Virginia* (Md. DD Council, 3rd edition, 1989). Mr. Kaplan is an attorney in private practice in Maine.

disabilities generally. In other words, the same laws that protect all children with disabilities also protect your child. This chapter will familiarize you with these federal laws so you can exercise your rights effectively and fully to protect your child.

It would be impossible to discuss here the law of every state or locality. Instead, this chapter reviews some of the most important legal concepts you need to know. For information about the particular laws in your area, contact the national office of the ARC or your local or state ARC affiliate. And remember, consult with a lawyer familiar with disability law when you have questions or need specific advice.

Your Child's Right to an Education

Until relatively recently there was no law in the United States ensuring that children with disabilities receive *any* education at all. Until the middle of this century, children with disabilities were usually excluded from public schools. They were sent away to residential "schools," "homes," and institutions, or their parents banded together to provide private part-time programs, frequently in church basements. In the 1960s, federal, state, and local governments began to provide educational opportunities to children with disabilities, and have continually improved these opportunities to this day.

Perhaps nothing has done so much to improve educational opportunities for children with mental retardation as The Education for All Handicapped Children Act of 1975, better known as Public Law 94–142. In 1990, Congress changed the name of this law to the Individuals with Disabilities Education Act (the "IDEA") and renumbered it Public Law 101–476. This comprehensive law, along with some recent amendments, has vastly improved educational opportunities for almost all children with disabilities. Administered by the U.S. Department of Education and by each state, the law works on a carrot-and-stick basis.

Under Public Law 94–142, the federal government provides funds for the education of children with disabilities to each state that has a special education program that meets federal standards. To qualify for the federal funds, a state must demonstrate, through a detailed plan submitted for federal approval, that it has a policy assuring all children with disabilities a "free appropriate public education." What this means is that states accepting federal funds under Public Law 94–142 must provide both approved educational services and a variety of procedural rights to children with disabilities and their parents. The lure of federal funds has been attractive enough to induce all states to create special education plans that can truly help children with mental retardation.

The IDEA, however, has its limits. The law only establishes the *minimum* requirements in special education programs for states desiring to receive federal funds. In other words, the law *does not* require states to adopt an ideal educational program for your child with mental retardation or a program that you feel is "the best." Because states have leeway under Public Law 94–142, there are differences from state to state in the programs or services available. For example, the student-teacher ratio in some states is higher than in others and the quality and quantity of teaching materials also can vary widely from state to state.

States *can* create special education programs that are better than those required by Public Law 94–142, and some have. Indeed, some state laws impose a higher standard than does the federal law itself. Check with the placement or intake officer of the special education department of your local school district to find out exactly what classes, programs, and services are available to your child. Parents, organizations, and advocacy groups continually push states and local school districts to exceed the federal requirements and provide the highest quality special education as early as possible. In addition, these same groups continually urge the federal government to raise the requirements for states under the IDEA. These groups need your support, and you need theirs.

What Public Law 94–142 Provides

Since Public Law 94–142 was passed in 1975, it has been amended many times. Today the IDEA and its amendments make up a large volume of laws and regulations. The Resource Guide at the back of this book tells you how you can obtain copies of these laws and regulations from the U.S. Senate or House of Representatives. The summary below highlights the provisions most important for parents to know about.

Coverage. The IDEA is intended to make special education available to all children who have a condition that "adversely affects" their "educational performance." As Chapter 4 explains, the law specifies a number of "handicapping conditions" that automatically qualify a child for special education. Mental retardation is one of these conditions. A diagnosis of mental retardation or other similar condition is therefore enough to establish that the IDEA applies to your child. Regardless of whether your child's mental retardation is labelled "mild," "moderate," "severe," or "profound," she qualifies for services because her condition hinders her learning.

"Free Appropriate Public Education." At the heart of Public Law 94–142 is the requirement that children with disabilities receive a "free appropriate public education." Like every other child, children with mental retardation are entitled to receive an education at public expense. They are also entitled to an appropriate educational program—one that takes into account their

special learning needs and abilities. To help clarify what your child is and is not entitled to, this section examines more precisely what each of the elements of "free appropriate public education" means.

"Free" means just that—regardless of the parents' ability to pay, every part of a child's special education program must be provided at public expense. Often this requirement is satisfied by placing a child in a public school, but the school district must pay the cost of all the necessary services your child will receive there. And if no suitable public program is available, the school district must place the child in a private program and pay the full cost. Remember, the IDEA does not provide for tuition payment for educational services *not* specifically approved for your child by the school district or other governing agency (unless, as explained later in this chapter, the decision of your school district is overturned). If you place your child in a program the school district does not approve for your child, you risk having to bear the full cost of tuition.

It often is difficult for parents to accept that the "appropriate" education mandated by the IDEA does not guarantee for their child either the best possible education that money can buy or even an educational opportunity equal to that given to nondisabled children. The law is more modest; it only requires that children with disabilities be given access to specialized educational services individually designed to benefit the child. In interpreting the IDEA, the United States Supreme Court has stated that a "free appropriate public education" need not enable a child with disabilities to maximize her potential or to develop self-sufficiency. Instead, a school district can meet the law's requirement of providing educational opportunity in a wide variety of ways. For example, a school district may not be required to provide an individual teacher for each student with mental retardation or provide every child with mental retardation year-round education even though doing so would maximize that child's educational opportunity. The nature and extent of services provided, however, typically depends on the nature and extent of the need. The law in this area is constantly evolving as new lawsuits based on these issues are decided. Check with your local ARC for information about the current state of the law regarding what is considered an "appropriate" educational program.

Only you can assure that your child receives the most appropriate placement and services. Under the IDEA, parents and educators are required to work together to design the individualized education program for each child. But if you feel that a school district is not making the best placement for your child, you must demonstrate to school officials not only that your preferred placement is appropriate, but that other placements the school district might prefer are not. The goal is to reach an agreement on the appropriate placement. If agreement cannot be reached, there are procedures for resolving disputes. These procedures are discussed later in the chapter.

"Special Education and Related Services." Under Public Law 94–142, an appropriate education consists of "special education and related services." "Special education" means specially designed instruction tailored to meet the unique needs of the child with disabilities, including classroom instruction, physical education, home instruction, and—if necessary—instruction in private schools, hospitals, or institutions. Special education teachers, therapists, and other professionals—all provided by the school district at its expense—are responsible for delivering these educational services. "Related services" are defined as transportation and other developmental, corrective, and supportive services necessary to enable the child to benefit from special education.

"Related services" are often a critical part of a special education program. Services provided by a trained speech/language therapist, occupational therapist, physical therapist, psychologist, social worker, school nurse, aide, or any other qualified person may be required under Public Law 94–142 as related services. Some services, however, are specifically excluded. Most important among these exclusions are ordinary medical services provided by a physician or hospital. For example, medical treatment for attention deficit/hyperactivity disorder (ADHD) or immunizations cannot be provided as related services under the IDEA.

"Least Restrictive Environment." Public Law 94–142 requires that children with disabilities must "to the maximum extent appropriate" be educated in the *least restrictive environment.* The least restrictive environment is the educational setting that permits your child to have the most contact possible at school with children who do *not* have disabilities. Under Public Law 94–142, there is therefore a strong preference for mainstreaming children with disabilities, including children with mental retardation. Some school officials may simply assume that all children with mental retardation—or all children with moderate or severe mental retardation—should be educated in a separate special setting. This generally is not true. Most children with mental retardation, including those with severe mental retardation, can receive at least some of their instruction with their nondisabled peers, with proper in-classroom supports and therapy. In some localities, all children with disabilities are educated in regular classrooms.

In practice, the IDEA requires that children with disabilities be integrated into their community's regular schools and classes as much as possible. Some children with mental retardation receive most or all of their instruction and services in regular classes with nondisabled classmates, going to a separate classroom only to receive special services that cannot be provided in the regular classroom. Other children may require more instruction and services in special classes, but nevertheless join the rest of the school for many subjects, such as physical education and music, and for assemblies and lunch. The law is intended at least in part to end the historical practice of isolating children with disabilities either in separate schools or out-of-the-way classrooms.

The IDEA also recognizes that regular classrooms may not be suitable for all educational and related services some children require. In these cases, the federal regulations allow for placement in separate classes, separate public schools, private schools, or even residential settings if the school district can demonstrate that this kind of placement is required to meet the child's individual *educational* needs. The determination must be individualized, however; it cannot be based only on the type or severity of the child's disability. When placement within the community's regular public schools is determined to be not appropriate for a child, the law still requires that she be placed in the least restrictive educational environment suitable to her individual needs. This can include some participation in regular school or regular classroom programs and activities.

Neither mental retardation itself nor the level of mental retardation is a sufficient basis for a school district to refuse to provide opportunities for your child to learn with her nondisabled peers. Because some of the most important learning in school comes from a student's peers, it is important to observe your child's placement closely to make sure that she is receiving the greatest possible opportunity for involvement with nondisabled students regardless of her level of mental retardation.

When Coverage Begins under Public Law 94–142. The IDEA requires all states to begin providing special education services from the age of three. In addition, in 1986 Congress enacted Public Law 99–459, a program of grants to states that create an approved program for providing early intervention services to infants with disabilities from birth through age two. The law allows states to take several years to develop a program for providing early intervention services. Some form of early intervention services under this program is now available in each state. But because the process of developing early intervention programs under this law is not complete, there is wide variation in what services are provided,

in how and where those services are provided, and in which government agency provides them. By 1993, it is expected that all states will have completed the process of developing early intervention programs under this law. Because each state may decide for itself which state agency will provide these early intervention services, you need to check with your local school district, the state education agency, or local ARC about where to go to get them. Early intervention services can include speech/language, physical, or occupational therapy to help young children with mental retardation maximize their early development. Chapter 5 discusses the types of early intervention services your child may receive.

Under the IDEA, special education services must continue until children reach age eighteen, and in some cases, age twenty-one. If a state offers education to regular education students until age twenty-one, it must do the same for its special education students.

Length of Services. Currently under Public Law 94–142, states must provide more than the traditional 180-day school year when the unique needs of a child indicate that year-round instruction is a necessary part of a "free appropriate public education." In many states, the decision to offer summer instruction depends on whether the child will lose a substantial amount of the progress made during the school year without summer services. If so, the services must be provided at public expense. Because some children with mental retardation can regress without year-round services, their parents should not hesitate to request year-round instruction.

Identification and Evaluation. Because the IDEA applies only to children who are found to have a disability, your child must be evaluated before she is eligible for special education. Public Law 94–142 requires each state to develop testing and evaluation procedures designed to fairly identify and evaluate the needs and abilities of each child before she is placed into a special education program. Areas of development suspected to be delayed must be tested: health, vision, hearing, social and emotional development, general intelligence, academic performance, communication ability, and motor skills. Each professional who evaluates your child must take your input into account. This means that parents—who understand their child's developmental needs best—should take an active role in the evaluation. You should gather as much information as you can to establish what special educational services your child needs. The evaluation process is explained in detail in Chapter 4.

"Individualized Education Program." Public Law 94–142 recognizes that each child with a disability is unique. As a result, the law requires that your child's special education program be tailored to her individual needs. Based on your child's evaluation, a program specifically designed to address her developmental problems must be devised. This is called an "individualized education program" or, more commonly, an "IEP."

The IEP is a written report that describes:

1. your child's present level of development;
2. both the short-term and annual goals of the special education program;
3. the specific educational services that your child will receive (for example, class and curriculum);
4. the date services will start and their expected duration;
5. standards for determining whether the goals of the educational program are being met; and

6. the extent to which your child will participate in regular educational programs.

Under federal regulations, educational placements are supposed to be based on the IEP, not vice versa. That is, the services your child receives, and the setting in which she receives them, should be determined by your child's individual needs, not by what happens to be available in existing programs. "One size fits all" is not permitted by the IDEA. Services and placements should be tailored to your child, not the other way around.

A child's IEP is usually developed during a series of meetings among the parents, teachers, and representatives of the school district. Even your child may be present. School districts are required to establish committees to make these placement and program decisions. These committees, which are called by different names in different areas, are sometimes referred to as Child Study Teams or Administrative Placement Committees. They decide what services your child will receive in addition to deciding where she will receive them.

Writing an IEP is ideally a cooperative effort, with parents, teachers, and school officials conferring on what goals are appropriate and how best to achieve them. Preliminary drafts of the IEP are reviewed and revised in an attempt to develop a mutually acceptable educational program.

The importance of your role in this process cannot be over-emphasized. You cannot always depend on teachers or school officials to recognize your child's unique needs as you do. To obtain the full range of services, you may need to demonstrate that withholding certain services would result in an education that would *not* be "appropriate." For example, if you believe that a program using augmentative communication methods is best for your child, you must demonstrate that failing to provide these services would not be appropriate for your child's specific needs. Or if you want an academic-oriented program for your child, you must demonstrate that a program that emphasizes only vocational or functional skills is not appropriate given your child's skills, abilities, and needs.

IEPs should be very detailed. You and your child's teachers should set specific goals for every area of development, and specify how those goals will be reached. Although the thought of specific planning may seem intimidating at first, a detailed IEP enables you to closely monitor the education your child receives and to make sure she is actually receiving the services prescribed. In addition, the law requires that IEPs be reviewed and revised at least once a year (or more often if necessary) to ensure your child's educational program continues to meet her changing needs.

Because your child has special needs, it is essential that her IEP be written with care to meet those needs. Unless you request specific services, they may be overlooked. You should make sure school officials recognize the unique needs of your child—the needs that make her different not just from other children with disabilities, or from other children with mental retardation, but even from other children with her level of mental retardation.

How can parents prepare for the IEP process? First, explore available educational programs, including public, private, federal, state, county, and municipal programs. Observe classes and see for yourself what different programs have to offer. Local school districts and local organizations such as the ARC can provide you with information about programs in your community. Second, collect a complete set of developmental evaluations to share with school officials—get your own if you doubt the accuracy of the school district's evaluation. Third, give thought to appropriate long-term and short-term goals for your child. Finally, decide for yourself what placement program and services are best for your child, and request them. If you want your child educated in her neighborhood school, request that, and request the services necessary to support her in that setting. If no program offers everything your child needs, you should request that an existing program be modified to best meet your child's particular needs. For example, if your child would benefit educationally from learning sign language, but no programs currently offer such instruction, request it anyway and offer suggestions about how the school district can efficiently meet your child's specific needs in its existing programs.

To support placement in a particular type of program, you should collect "evidence" about your child's special needs. Then back up your position that a particular type of placement is appropriate by presenting letters from physicians, psychologists, therapists (speech/language, physical, or occupational), teachers, developmental experts, or other professionals, as the case may be.

This evidence may help persuade a school district that the requested placement or services are the appropriate choices for your child. A few other suggestions to help parents through the process are:

1. Do not attend IEP meetings alone—bring a spouse, advocate, physician, teacher, or whomever you need for support;
2. Keep close track of what everyone—school district officials, psychologists, therapists, teachers, and doctors—involved in your child's case is doing;
3. *Get everything in writing;* and
4. Be assertive. Children with unique developmental challenges need parents to be assertive and persuasive advocates during the IEP process. This does not mean that school officials are always adversaries, but does mean you are your child's most important advocate; you know her best.
5. Read Chapter 10 for more information on advocacy.

"Individualized Family Service Plan." Parents of children from birth to age two use a plan that is different from the IEP used for older children. Under Public Law 99–457, states receiving grants to provide early intervention services must draft an "individualized family service plan" (IFSP). This plan is similar to the IEP, but reflects the different focus of Public Law 99–457. Unlike the IDEA, which focuses primarily on the needs of the child, Public Law 99–457 emphasizes services for the family. In other words, the law recognizes that families with young children with special needs often have special needs themselves. Consequently, IFSPs do not just specify what services are provided for the child with mental retardation. They also describe services that will be provided to: 1) help parents learn how to use daily activities to teach their child with mental retardation; and 2) help siblings learn to cope with having a brother or sister with mental retardation. The procedures and strategies for developing a useful IFSP are the same as described above for the IEP.

The school system has been good about doing what they're supposed to. But you almost have to have an answer for every one of their arguments.

If you walk into the IEP meeting having done your homework, they will just about do anything reasonable you request.

Once there was no county official at the IEP meeting to approve it. That ticked me off. They were saying, "Well, just make a deal with the school your daughter attends." I said, "Look, that takes time. I don't want my daughter starting OT and PT in December or January. I want services to start with school day number one."

You get butterflies when spring comes and it's time to plan for the next school year. The school's job is to provide for those kids as best they can while saving the county as much money as they can. They don't want to waste money if it's not needed. They have to question some people's requests. They do <u>their</u> job, and you have to be prepared to put up an argument, if necessary.

Mainstreaming is so important because not only does it help our son, but it will help the other people he is in contact with now. Someday, these people are going to be his doctor, his surgeon, his teachers, his baker, his grocer . . . whatever. So many people nowadays don't know how to act with a mentally retarded person—but they can learn.

Resolution of Disputes under Public Law 94–142

Public Law 94–142 establishes a variety of safeguards to protect your rights and the rights of your child with mental retardation. For instance, written notice is always required before any change is made in your child's identification, evaluation, or educational placement. In addition, you are entitled to review all of your child's educational records at any time. Further, your school district is prohibited from deceiving you and from making decisions without consulting or notifying you first. School officials must state in writing what they plan to do with your child, how, where, when, and why.

Despite these safeguards, conflicts between parents and school officials sometimes arise. When they do, it is usually best to resolve disputes with your school district over your child's educational program *during* the IEP (or IFSP) process, before hard positions have been formed. Although Public Law 94–142 establishes dispute resolution procedures that are designed to be fair to parents, it is easier and far less costly to avoid disputes by reaching agreement during the IEP process or by informal discussions with appropriate school district personnel. Accordingly, you should first try to accomplish your objectives by open and clear communication and by persuasion. If there is a dispute that simply cannot be resolved through discussion, however, there are further steps you may take under Public Law 94–142 and other laws to resolve that dispute.

First, the IDEA allows parents to file a formal complaint with their local school district about *any matter* "relating to the identification, evaluation, or educational placement of the child, or the provision of free appropriate public education to such child." This means that you can make a written complaint about virtually any problem you perceive with any part of your child's educational (or early intervention) program if you have been unable to resolve that problem with school officials. For example, if school officials insist on placing your child in a self-contained, functional curriculum class, you can file a complaint about that placement if you think she should be in an integrated or more integrated academic program. Or, if after evaluation, the school district decides that your child does not need special education, this too can be challenged. This is a very broad right of appeal, one that parents have successfully used in the past to correct problems in their children's special education programs.

The process of challenging a school district's decisions about your child's education can be started simply by sending a letter of complaint. This letter, which should explain the nature of the dispute and your desired outcome, typically is sent to the special education office of the school district. You have the absolute right to file a complaint—you need not ask the school district for permission to do this. For information about starting appeals, you can contact your school district, your local ARC, local advocacy groups, or other parents.

The first step in the appeal process is usually an "impartial due process hearing" before a hearing examiner. This hearing, usually held on the local level, is your first opportunity to explain your complaint to an impartial person, who is required to listen to both sides and then to render a decision. At the hearing, you are entitled to be represented by an attorney or lay advocate; you can present evidence; and you can examine, cross-examine, and compel witnesses to attend. Your child has a right to be present at the hearing as well. After the hearing, you have a right to receive a written record of the hearing and the hearing examiner's findings and conclusions.

Just as with the IEP process, you must present facts at a due process hearing that show that the school district's decisions about your child's educational program are wrong. To overturn the school district's decision, you must show that the disputed placement or program does not provide your child with the "free appropriate public education" in "the least restrictive environment" that is required by the IDEA. Evidence in the form of letters, testimony, and expert evaluations is usually essential to a successful challenge.

Parents or school districts may appeal the decision of a hearing examiner. The appeal usually goes to the state's educational agency or to a neutral panel. This state agency is required to make an independent decision upon its review of the record of the due process hearing and of any additional evidence presented. The state agency then issues its own decision.

The right to appeal does not stop there. Parents or school officials can appeal beyond the state level by bringing a lawsuit under the IDEA and other laws in a state or federal court. In this kind of legal action, the court must determine whether there is a preponderance of the evidence (that is, whether it is more likely than not) that the school district's placement is proper for that child. In reaching its decision, the court must give weight to the expertise of the school officials responsible for providing your child's education, but you can and should also present your own expert evidence.

During all administrative and judicial proceedings, Public Law 94–142 requires that your child remain in her current educational placement, unless you and your school district or the state education agency agree to a move. If you place your child in a different program without an agreement, you risk having to bear the full cost of that program. If, however, the school district eventually is found to have erred, it may be required to reimburse you for the expenses of the changed placement. Accordingly, you should never change programs without carefully considering the potential cost of that decision.

Attorneys' fees are another expense to consider. Parents who ultimately win their dispute with a school district may recover attorneys' fees, at the court's discretion. Even if you prevail at the local or state level (without bringing a lawsuit), you likely are entitled to recover attorneys' fees. A word of caution: A court can limit or refuse attorneys' fees if you reject an offer of settlement from the school district, and then do not obtain a better outcome.

As with any legal dispute, each phase—complaint, hearings, appeals, and court cases—can be expensive, time-consuming, and emotionally exhausting. As mentioned earlier, it is wise to try to resolve problems without filing a formal complaint or bringing suit. For example, you should consult with other parents who have filed complaints and talk to sympathetic school officials. When informal means fail to resolve a problem, however, formal channels should be pursued. Your child's best interests must come first. The IDEA grants important rights that you should not be bashful about exercising.

The IDEA is a powerful tool in the hands of parents. It can be used to provide unparalleled educational opportunities to your child with mental retardation. Using it effectively, however, requires an understanding of how it works. The Reading List at the end of this book includes several good guidebooks to Public Law 94–142 and the special education system. The more you know about this vital law, the more you will be able to help your child realize her potential.

Programs and Services When Your Child Is an Adult

Some children with mental retardation grow to live independently or semi-independently as adults. Many, however, will have varying needs for special services depending on their skills. These services include employment, job-training, and residential or community-living programs. Regrettably, these services are often unavailable because there are very few federal laws requiring states to offer programs for adults with disabilities. And what programs exist typically are underfunded and have long waiting lists. As a result, many parents are left to provide the necessary support and supervision on their own for as long as possible. The sad truth is that under Public Law 94–142 thousands of children receive education and training that equip them to live independently and productively, only to be sent home when they finish schooling with nowhere to go and nothing to do.

Now is the time to work to change this sad reality. The unemployment rate for people with mental retardation and for all disabilities is appallingly high, especially for young adults. As waiting lists for training programs grow, your child may be deprived of needed services, and, consequently, of appropriate employment opportunities. Programs sponsored by charities and private foundations are limited and most families do not have the resources to pay the full cost of providing employment and residential opportunities. The only other remedy is public funding. Just as parents banded together in the 1970s to demand enactment of Public Law 94–142, parents must band together now to persuade local, state, and federal officials to take the steps necessary to allow adults with disabilities to live in dignity. Parents of *children* with disabilities should not leave this job to parents of *adults* with disabilities, for children become adults—all too soon.

Vocational Training Programs

There is one educational program supported by federal funding available to most adults with mental retardation. Operating much like Public Law 94–142, several federal laws make funds available to states to support vocational training and rehabilitation programs for people with disabilities who qualify. As with the IDEA, states that desire federal funds must submit plans for approval. Unlike the IDEA, however, these laws do not grant people with disabilities enforceable rights and procedures.

Under federal law, adults must fulfill two requirements to qualify for job-training services: 1) they must have a physical or mental disability that constitutes a "substantial handicap to employment"; and 2) they must be expected to benefit from vocational services. In the past, some people with mental retardation were denied vocational training services because they likely could not meet the law's second requirement of being able to perform competitive full-time or part-time employment. Recent amendments to the law, however, require that services and training be provided to people even if the most they will achieve is "supported employment." This term means employment in a setting with services such as a job coach or special training which allows an individual to perform work. No longer can people with mental retardation be deprived of job training and services just because of the severity of their condition.

The state Departments of Vocational Rehabilitation, sometimes called "DVR" or "Voc Rehab," are charged with carrying out these laws. Adults who apply for Voc Rehab services are evaluated, and an "Individualized Written Rehabilitation Plan" (IWRP) or an "Individualized Habilitation Plan" (IHP), similar to an IEP, is developed. The IHP sets forth the services needed to enable a person with a disability to work productively. Under these programs, adults with mental retardation can receive vocational education after they reach age twenty-one, if there is room in the program. You should contact your state vocational rehabilitation department, the ARC, or local ARC affiliate for specific information on services available to your child. Despite shrinking federal and state budgets, some states and communities offer their own programs, such as group homes, supported employment programs, and life-skills classes. Other parents and organizations will have information about programs available in your area.

I don't want my son to be given a job just because he's retarded and this is the job the work program placed him in. If he doesn't do it well, he should be replaced. My mother has complained about the bag boy in her grocery store. I said, "You need to go and tell the manager that the bag boy needs to go through a work program or something." Otherwise, it's not fair to the retarded person, my mother, or anybody else to expect him to handle the job.

The older she gets, the more time I want her to spend learning an actual job and the less time at school. The future is so uncertain, the least we can do is make sure she gets good job training.

Developmentally Disabled Assistance and Bill of Rights Act

Under a federal law called the Developmentally Disabled Assistance and Bill of Rights Act, states can receive grants for a variety of programs. Important among them is a protection and advocacy (P&A) system. A P&A system helps protect and advocate for the civil and legal rights of people with developmental disabilities. P&A offices have been leaders in representing institutionalized people with mental retardation seeking to improve their living conditions or to be placed in their community. In addition, P&A offices can represent you if you cannot afford an attorney for a Public Law 94–142 due process hearing or a discrimination suit. Because people who are disabled by mental retardation may not be in a position to protect their own rights or speak out for themselves, it is important that each state's P&A system offer adequate protection. Consult the Resource Guide at the back of this book for information on locating your state's P & A office.

Anti-Discrimination Laws

In a perfect world, no one would be denied opportunities—discriminated against—solely on the basis of disability, race, sex, or any other factor beyond her control. Unfortunately, our world remains imperfect, and the federal government has enacted several laws to ensure that children, adolescents, and adults with disabilities be given the right to live and work in the community to the fullest extent possible. This section reviews the highlights of the landmark Americans with Disabilities Act (ADA) and the Rehabilitation Act of 1973, both of which prohibit discrimination against your child with mental retardation.

The Americans with Disabilities Act of 1990

The Americans with Disabilities Act (ADA) prohibits discrimination against people with disabilities, including children and adults with mental retardation. It is based on and operates in the same way as other well-known federal laws that outlaw racial, religious, age, and sex discrimination. The law applies to most private employers, public and private services, public accommodations, businesses, and telecommunications.

Employment. The ADA states that "no . . . [employer] shall discriminate against a qualified individual with a disability because of the disability of such individual in regard to job application procedures, the hiring or discharge of employees, employee compensation, advancement, job training, and other terms, conditions, and privileges of employment."

This means that private employers cannot discriminate against employees or prospective employees who have a disability. The law defines "qualified individual with a disability" as a person with a disability who, with or without reasonable accommodation, can perform the essential functions of a job. "Reasonable accommodation" means that employers must make an effort to remove obstacles from the job, the terms and conditions of employment, or the workplace that would prevent an otherwise qualified person from working because she has a disability. Accommodations can include restructuring the job, shuffling schedules, adapting training and policies, and providing readers or interpreters if necessary. Failing to make reasonable accommodations is itself a violation of this law.

The law, however, does not *require* employers to hire people with disabilities or to make accommodations if doing so imposes an "undue hardship" on the employer. Rather it prohibits employers from refusing to employ qualified people with disabilities solely because of the existence of the disability. For example, if a person with mental retardation applied for a job as a file clerk in an office, it would be discriminatory for the employer to refuse to hire her if she was as qualified as or *more* qualified than other applicants to perform the job's duties, if the employer's refusal was based on the applicant's mental retardation. The employer is not required to always hire qualified people with mental retardation, but cannot use the existence of mental retardation to refuse to hire a person who otherwise can perform the job. The employer is prohibited from either inquiring whether the applicant has a disability or from refusing to make some reasonable accommodation such as minor scheduling changes or providing extra training.

The employment discrimination provisions of the ADA took effect in July 1992. During its first two years, this section will apply to employers with twenty-five or more employees. After July 1994, it will apply to employers with fifteen or more employees.

The ADA specifies procedures to follow for people who believe they have been the victim of employment discrimination. You must first file a complaint with the federal Equal Employment Opportunity Commission (EEOC). This agency is responsible for resolving employment discrimination complaints. If the agency does not satisfactorily resolve the dispute, a lawsuit may be brought for an injunction prohibiting further discrimination and an order requiring affirmative action. If you prevail in court, you will be entitled to attorneys' fees. Your local ARC may be able to provide you with basic information about how to challenge discriminatory employment practices, but a lawyer may eventually be required.

Public Services. This part of the ADA prohibits discrimination against people with disabilities by state and local public agencies that provide public transportation. It is a violation of the ADA for agencies to purchase buses, rail cars, or other conveyances that are not accessible to people with disabilities. Likewise, all architectural barriers in state and local government buildings and facilities must be removed to "the maximum extent feasible," and new buildings and facilities must be constructed without them. The ADA also requires that private companies providing transportation services make their buses, trains, or rail cars accessible.

Public Accommodations. One of the most stunning and far-reaching provisions of the ADA is its prohibition of discrimination in public accommodations. Mirroring the approach of the civil rights laws of the 1960s, the ADA bans discrimination against people with disabilities virtually *everywhere*, including hotels, inns, and motels; restaurants and bars; theaters, stadiums, concert halls, auditoriums, convention centers, and lecture halls; bakeries, grocery stores, gas stations, clothing stores, pharmacies, and other retail businesses; doctor or lawyer offices; airport and bus terminals; museums, libraries, galleries, parks, and zoos; nursery, elementary, secondary, undergraduate, and postgraduate schools; day care centers; homeless shelters; senior citizen centers; gymnasiums; spas; and bowling alleys. The list is practically endless: any place open to the public must also be open to people with disabilities, unless that is not physically or financially feasible. No longer can businesses exclude people with disabilities just because they are different. The excuse that people with disabilities are "not good for business" is now unlawful thanks to the ADA.

The great promise of the ADA lies in its provisions that define the failure to make public accomodations accessible to people with mental retardation as discrimination. For example, a theater, restaurant, or museum cannot exclude people with mental retardation from their facilities, cannot restrict their use to certain times or places, and cannot offer them only separate programs, unless to do otherwise would impose unreasonable cost on these facilities. The end result is that the new law is not simply neutral; it does not merely prohibit active discrimination, but rather imposes duties to open our society to all people with disabilities.

Like the civil rights laws of the past, the ADA also requires integration. It bans the insidious practice of "separate but equal" programs or facilities which offer separate services to people with disabilities, rather than access to programs offered to everyone else. The law prohibits the exclusion of people with disabilities on the grounds that there is a "special" program available for them. For example, a recreation league (public or private) could not uniformly

exclude people with disabilities on the ground that it offers a comparable separate league for them.

People who are the victims of discrimination can ask the court for an injunction prohibiting further discrimination. And if the U.S. Attorney General brings a lawsuit to halt a pattern and practice of discrimination, monetary damages and civil penalties may be imposed. Again, your local ARC and your state's P&A office will be able to provide you with information and assist you in challenging discrimination.

The ADA has the potential to provide extraordinary freedom and opportunity to people with mental retardation. By prohibiting discrimination and requiring reasonable accommodation, the ADA stands as the Bill of Rights for people with all disabilities, including mental retardation.

The Rehabilitation Act of 1973

Before the ADA was enacted, discrimination on the basis of disability was prohibited only in certain areas. Section 504 of the Rehabilitation Act of 1973 continues to prohibit discrimination against qualified people with disabilities in *federally funded programs.* The law provides that "No otherwise qualified individual with handicaps in the United States . . . shall, solely by reason of his handicap, be excluded from the participation in, be denied the benefits of, or be subjected to discrimination under any program or activity receiving federal financial assistance. . . ."

An "individual with handicaps" is any person who has a physical or mental impairment that substantially limits one or more of that person's "major life activities," which consist of "caring for one's self, performing manual tasks, walking, seeing, hearing, speaking, breathing, learning, and working." The United States Supreme Court has determined that an "otherwise qualified" handicapped individual is one who is "able to meet all of a program's requirements in spite of his handicap." Programs or activities that receive federal funds are required to make reasonable accommodation to permit the participation of qualified people with disabilities. This can include programs like day care centers and schools and jobs in programs receiving federal funds.

Health Insurance

Often a child's mental retardation, or the condition that causes a child's mental retardation, can cause serious problems for families in finding and keeping health insurance that covers their child. Unfortunately, most insurance companies do not offer health or life insurance at a fair price, or sometimes at any price, to people with conditions such as Down syndrome, fragile X syndrome, cerebral palsy, and epilepsy that often accompany mental retardation. This practice results from the belief that these children and adults are likely to submit more insurance claims than others. Until they become adults, children who are covered from birth by their parents' insurance face fewer problems, but this depends on the particular terms of the insurance.

About half the states outlaw handicap-based discrimination by prohibiting insurance companies from using a condition such as mental retardation as an excuse to deny coverage. The drawback to all of these laws, however, is that they still allow insurance companies to deny coverage if the denial is based on "sound actuarial principles" or "reasonable anticipated experience." Insurers rely on these large loopholes to deny coverage. In short, the laws are ineffective in protecting families from insurance discrimination. Even the ADA does not prohibit these same "sound actuary" practices that frequently result in denied coverage.

A few states have begun to lessen the health insurance burdens on families with children with disabilities. Some states offer "shared risk" insurance plans. Under these plans, insurance coverage is offered to people who could not get coverage otherwise. The added cost is shared among all insurance companies (including HMOs) operating in the state. To be eligible, a person must show that she has been recently turned down for coverage or offered a policy with limited coverage. The cost of this insurance is usually higher and the benefits may be limited, but it is usually better than no health insurance at all. Some laws also cover people who have received premium increases of fifty percent or more. In addition, Medicare and Medicaid—discussed below—may be available to help with medical costs. Check with your state insurance commission or your local ARC for information about health insurance programs in your area.

Driver's License

People with mental retardation have the same right as everyone else to obtain a driver's license. If they can pass the written test and the driving test, people with mental retardation can and do obtain licenses. In addition, if your child knows how to drive and understands the rules of the road, but cannot read well enough to pass the written test, the test may be given orally. No state is entitled to deny a person with mental retardation the opportunity to obtain a driver's license simply because of the condition. But if your child's mental retardation is accompanied by seizures or another condition that would make it dangerous for her to drive, a driver's license may be denied.

Planning for Your Child's Future: Estate Planning

Although some children with mental retardation grow into independent adults, others are never able to manage completely on their own. This section is written for parents whose children may need publicly funded services or assistance, or help in managing their funds when they are adults.

The possibility that your child may be dependent all of her life can be overwhelming. To properly plan for your child's future, you need information in areas you may never have considered before, and you must find inner resources you may not believe exist. In most families, parents remain primarily responsible for ensuring their child's well-being. Consequently, questions that deeply trouble parents include: "What will happen to my child when I die? Who will look after her? How will her financial needs be met? Who will provide the services she will need?"

Some parents of children with mental retardation delay dealing with these issues, coping instead with the immediate demands of the present. Others begin to address the future when their child is quite young. They add to their insurance, begin to set aside funds for their child, and share with family and friends their concerns about their child's future needs. Whatever the course, parents of children with mental retardation need to understand in advance of any action some serious problems that affect planning for the future. Failure to avoid these pitfalls can have dire future consequences for your child and for other family members.

There are three important issues that families of children with mental retardation need to consider in planning for the future. These are:

1. the potential for cost-of-care liability;
2. the complex rules governing government benefits; and
3. the child's ability to handle her own affairs.

Of course, there are many other matters that may be different for parents of children with mental retardation. For example, life insurance needs may be affected, and the important choice of trustees and guardians is more difficult. But these types of concerns face most parents in one form or another. Cost-of-care liability, government benefits, and the inability to manage one's own affairs, however, present concerns that are unique to parents of children with serious disabilities.

Cost-of-Care Liability

Some people with mental retardation reside in state-run facilities. When a state provides residential services to a person with disabilities, it usually requires her to pay for them if she has the funds to do so. Called "cost-of-care liability," this requirement allows states to tap the funds of the person with disabilities herself to pay for the services the state provides. States can reach funds owned outright by a person with disabilities and even funds set aside in some trusts. A few states go further. Some impose liability on parents for the care of an adult with disabilities; some impose liability for other services, like day care and vocational training, in addition to residential care. This is an area parents need to look into early and carefully.

Parents should understand that payments required to be made to satisfy cost-of-care liability do *not* benefit the person with disabilities. Ordinarily they add nothing to the care and services the individual receives. Instead, the money is added to the general funds of the state to pay for roads, schools, public officials' salaries, and so on.

It is natural for you to want to pass your material resources on to your children by will or gift. In some cases, however, the unfortunate effect of leaving your child with mental retardation a portion of your estate may be the same as naming the state in your will—something most people would not do voluntarily, any more than they would voluntarily pay more taxes than the law requires. Similarly, setting aside funds in your child's name, in a support trust, or in a Uniform Transfers to Minors Act (UTMA) account may be the same as giving money to the state—money that could better be used to meet the future needs of your child.

What, then, can you do? The answer depends on your circumstances and the law of your state. Here are three basic strategies parents use:

First, strange as it may seem, in some cases the best solution may be to disinherit your child with mental retardation, leaving funds instead to siblings in the hope that they will use these funds for their sibling's benefit, even though they will be under *no* legal obligation to do so. The absence of a legal obligation is crucial. It protects the funds from cost-of-care claims. The state will simply have no basis for claiming that the person with disabilities owns the funds. This strategy, however, runs the risk that the funds wiil not be used for your child with mental retardation if the siblings: 1) choose not to use them that way; 2) suffer financial reversals or domestic problems of their own, exposing the funds to creditors or spouses; or 3) die without making arrangements to safeguard the funds.

A preferable method in many cases, in states where the law is favorable, is to leave funds intended for the benefit of your child with mental retardation in what is called a "discretionary" trust. This kind of trust is created to supplement, rather than replace, money the state may spend on your child's care and support. The trustee of this kind of trust (the person in charge of the trust assets) has the power to use or not use the trust funds for any particular purpose as long as it benefits the beneficiary—the child with mental retardation. In many states, these discretionary trusts are not subject to cost-of-care claims because the trust does not impose any *legal* obligation on the trustee to spend funds for care and support. In contrast, "support" trusts *require* the trustee to use the funds for the care and support of the child and can be subjected to state cost-of-care claims. Discretionary trusts can be created under your will or during your lifetime; as with all legal documents, the trust documents must be carefully written. In some states, to protect the trust against cost-of-care claims, it is necessary to add provisions stating clearly that the trust is to be used to supplement rather than replace publicly funded services and benefits.

A third method to avoid cost-of-care claims is to create a trust, either under your will or during your lifetime, that describes the kind of allowable expenditures to be made for your child with mental retardation in a way that excludes care in state-funded programs. Like discretionary trusts, these trusts—sometimes called "luxury" trusts—are intended to supplement, rather than take the place of, state benefits. The state cannot reach these funds because the trust forbids spending any funds on care in state institutions or programs.

In using these estate planning techniques, parents should consult a qualified attorney who is experienced in estate planning for parents of children with disabilities. Because each state's laws differ and because each family has unique circumstances, individualized estate planning is essential.

We've gone to talks by lawyers about financial planning for the handicapped. I know all the ins and outs. We just haven't done it yet. At this point, most of our financial worries are about our other son, who will probably be going to college and that sort of thing. He's a junior in high school, so the obvious financial requirements for him are more immediate. Peter, on the other hand, is going to be at home for a long time, certainly into his twenties. He's very dependent; not emotionally capable of spending a lot of time away from family or parents.

We've been told that we can't have anything in his name, because if we did, any adult services he's eligible for would use his money first. We do have a very small trust for him, but basically, we don't want him to be in the will or things like that. It's just impossible.

I said, "I'm talking my pennies and I'm going to open a bank account for Eric." And my wife said, "You can't do that, because he can't have any money to his name." And I said, "What? He <u>can</u> have at least a couple hundred dollars." I want him to start learning what money's all about, so when he's nine years old he can go to the store and buy bubble gum and a comic book, just like any other kid. So, now my son has this bank account with maybe $21 in it. I'm not going to add to it in leaps and

bounds, but my other children have accounts, so I want Eric to have that too.

Government Benefits

A wide variety of federal, state, and local programs offer financial assistance for people with disabilities. Each of these programs provides different services and each has its own complicated eligibility requirements. What parents and grandparents do now to provide financially for their child with mental retardation can have important effects on that child's eligibility for government assistance in the future. In addition, the complex rules governing some programs—such as Medicaid—can have far-reaching effects on your child's life.

SSI and SSDI

There are two federally funded programs that can provide additional income to people with mental retardation who cannot earn enough to support themselves. The two programs are "Supplemental Security Income" (SSI) and "Social Security Disability Insurance" (SSDI). SSI pays monthly checks to senior citizens and to children and adults with serious disabilities who lack other income and resources. SSDI pays a monthly check to adults disabled from work who are either covered by Social Security based on past earnings, or whose disability began before age eighteen and who are the children of deceased or retired persons who have or had Social Security coverage. Both SSI and SSDI are designed to provide a monthly income to people with disabilities who meet the programs' qualifications. Both programs are administered by the Social Security Administration. There are additional programs that may provide financial assistance to people with disabilities, including children of deceased federal employees and military personnel.

Qualifying for SSI. If your child qualifies for SSI, she will receive monthly payments from the Social Security Administration (SSA) to "supplement" your family's income. As of 1992, the *maximum* payment provided through SSI was $422 per month. In order to receive SSI benefits, an applicant must establish that she is "disabled." To qualify as "disabled," the applicant's condition must be so disabling that she cannot engage in "substantial gainful activity." This means that she cannot perform any job, whether or not a suitable job can be found. The Social Security Administration regulations prescribe a set of tests for making this determination. The test of severity is somewhat different for children and adults.

Recently, the SSA has changed its regulations to allow more children to qualify as disabled. This is because the U.S. Supreme Court held in 1990 that the rules for determining which disabilities qualify children for SSI benefits were too restrictive and discriminatory. SSA is now attempting to notify the almost 450,000 children who were wrongly rejected that they may reapply for benefits. Therefore, if your child's application for SSI has been rejected in the past, you may want to consider reapplying. The same is true if you have been considering applying but have doubted that your child would qualify.

SSI's eligibility requirements do not end with the test of severity. Eligibility for SSI is also based on financial need. An applicant is ineligible to receive SSI benefits if her assets (including property owned in her own name and income she is entitled to receive under a trust) exceed a certain level. Currently, that level is $2,000. In addition, for children under eighteen years of age who live at home, the resources of the parents are also considered. In general, children who come from a family of four with income exceeding $25,000 per year are not eligible for SSI payments.

Many people with mental retardation work. In fact, for most parents, finding a job for their child with mental retardation is a goal they strive hard to achieve. It is an unfortunate irony that earning a salary can affect eligibility for SSI and SSDI. Under the rules governing SSI benefits, earning income can reduce your child's benefits or disqualify her altogether. This is because, as presently administered, SSI is intended to provide income to people whose disabilities prevent them from working. This rule is unfair to people with mental retardation who are able to perform work because it can force a choice between work in the community at reduced pay and needed SSI benefits. People receiving SSI, however, *can*, under the statutory work incentive program, earn up to a certain amount (now $821 per month) and still keep *some* SSI benefits; the benefits will be reduced by the amount of excess income earned. In addition, under the PASS program (Plans for Achieving Self-Support), a recipient can receive income or assets in her own name, provided the funds will be used to make it possible for the SSI recipient to work in the future or to establish a business or occupation that will enable her to become gainfully employed (and get her off SSI).

Unless she participates in the PASS program, however, your child will be ineligible for SSI if she has assets in her own name greater than a prescribed level (now $2,000). The assets of parents are deemed to be assets of their children under age eighteen in determining eligibility, so most children with disabilities become eligible when they reach age eighteen. It is vital to properly plan your child's financial future to avoid jeopardizing her right to receive SSI benefits. You should check periodically with the Social Security Administration to determine the current rules that apply to your child.

Qualifying for SSDI. People with disabilities may also qualify for SSDI—disability benefits under the Social Security program. The test for disability is the same as it is for SSI. People do not have to be poor to qualify for SSDI, unlike SSI, however; there are no financial eligibility requirements based on resources or unearned income. To be eligible, an applicant must qualify on the basis of her own work record for Social Security purposes, or she must be unmarried, have a disability that began before age eighteen, and be the child of a parent covered by Social Security who has retired or died.

As with SSI, your child's employment can cause serious problems. The work incentive program under SSI does not apply to people on SSDI, who lose eligibility if they earn more than a certain amount per month (now $500), because they are deemed not to be disabled. Again, this rule places an unfair burden on recipients of SSDI by forcing them to make a choice between work and financial security. Recently, however, a new program under SSDI allows recipients to work for one year on a trial basis without losing eligibility to determine their ability to work (and get off SSDI). Advocacy organizations, such as the ARC, are trying to secure further changes in the present work disincentives.

Medicare

Medicare is a federal health insurance program that helps pay for the medical expenses of people who qualify. People who are eligible for SSDI benefits, either on their own account or on a parent's account, will also be eligible for Medicare, starting at any age, after a waiting period. These persons will automatically receive Part A (hospital) coverage, and they can elect Part B (medical) coverage, for which they will pay a premium (If a person can also qualify for Medicaid, discussed below, Medicaid may pay the Medicare Part B premium.) In some cases, children or adults with disabilities who would not otherwise be eligible for Medicare may qualify if a third party—parents, relatives, charities, or even state and local governments—pay into Medicare. Called "third party buy-in," this works very much like purchasing private health insurance. Check with your local Social Security Administration office for details.

Medicaid

Medicaid, a federally funded program, is also important to some people with mental retardation. Medicaid helps pay for the medical care of people who are eligible for SSI or who have incomes insufficient to pay for medical care. In most states, if your child meets the eligibility criteria for SSI, she will qualify for Medicaid when she reaches age eighteen. Because eligibility is based on financial need, however, placing assets in the name of your child with mental retardation or providing her with income through a trust can disqualify her.

Community-Based Services. Under current law, Medicaid pays for medical and personal care services (feeding, grooming, transportation) for people with disabilities, including people with mental retardation, only under certain conditions. Specifically, services can be provided only in Medicaid-certified residential institutions, called "intermediate care facilities" (ICFs). This law is behind the times; most people with disabilities such as mental retardation are best served where they live—in the *community*, not in institutions. Nevertheless, families today face the prospect of having to institutionalize their child in order for her to receive vital services. Currently, the Secretary of the federal Department of Health and Human Services has the authority to waive the ICF requirement on a case-by-case basis, but these waivers are limited. Congress recently enacted a limited program to allow eight states to be reimbursed for providing community-based supported personal living arrangements (CSLA). Obviously, more needs to be done so that all states can provide medical and personal care services outside of institutions. Advocates continue to press Congress and state and local officials to bring Medicaid into the present, so that people with disabilities can live as full a life as possible in their communities.

It is important for parents to become familiar with the complex rules governing SSI, SSDI, Medicare, and Medicaid. Always feel free to contact your local Social Security Administration office, or call their national toll-free number (800/2345–SSA). And as discussed below, it is even more important to avoid a mistake that could disqualify your child from receiving needed benefits.

Competence to Manage Financial Affairs

Even if your child with mental retardation may never need state-funded residential care or government benefits, she may need to have her financial affairs managed for her. Care must be exercised in deciding how to make assets available for your child. There are a wide variety of trusts that can allow someone else to control the ways in which money is spent after you die. Of course, the choice of the best arrangements depends on many different circumstances, such as your child's capacity to manage assets, her relationship with her siblings, your financial situation, and the availability of an appropriate trustee or financial manager. Each family is different. A knowledgeable lawyer can review the various alternatives and help you choose the one best suited to your family.

Need for Guardians

Parents frequently ask whether they should nominate themselves or others as guardians once their child with mental retardation becomes an adult. The appointment of a guardian costs money and may result in the curtailment of your child's civil rights—the right to marry, to have a checking account, to vote, and so on. Therefore, a guardian should be appointed only if and when needed. If one is not needed during your lifetime, it usually is sufficient to nominate guardians in your will.

A guardian will be needed if your child inherits or acquires property that she lacks the capacity to manage. Also, a guardian may be required if a medical provider refuses to serve your child without authorization by a guardian. Occasionally it is necessary to appoint a guardian to gain access to important legal, medical, or educational records. Unless there is a specific need that can be solved by the appointment of a guardian, however, a guardianship should not be established simply because your child has mental retardation.

We've thought about naming our friends as Kyle's legal guardians for a period of four or five years, but we don't know what'll happen if our other two kids don't want to take over come the end of that period. We want to leave it in such a way that his guardians get to make the decision as to what happens then. We trust them to make the best decision.

Recently we sat down with our older son and said that we needed to update our wills. We asked him if he thought he'd be available to be Kelly's guardian sometime in the future. First he said "yes" right away, and then he said, "Let me think about it a little bit." Then he came back and said that definitely he would do that. But we're really hoping this won't happen until our son is much older and has gotten his own life going.

Life Insurance

Parents of children with mental retardation should review their life insurance coverage. The most important use of life insurance is to meet financial needs that arise if the insured person dies. Many people who support dependents with their wages or salaries are underinsured. This problem is aggravated if hard-earned dollars are wasted on insurance that does not provide the amount or kind of protection that could and should be purchased. It is therefore essential for any person with dependents to understand basic facts about insurance.

The first question to consider is: Who should be insured? Life insurance deals with the *financial* risks of death. The principal financial risk of death in most families is that the death of the wage earner or earners will deprive dependents of support. Consequently, life insurance coverage should be considered primarily for the parent or parents on whose earning power the children depend, rather than on the lives of children or dependents.

The second question is whether your insurance is adequate to meet the financial needs that will arise if you die. A reputable insurance agent can help you determine whether your coverage is adequate. Consumer guides to insurance listed in the Reading List of this book can also help you calculate the amount of insurance you need.

The next question is: What kind of insurance policy should you buy? Insurance policies are of two basic types: term insurance, which provides "pure" insurance without any build-up of cash value or reserves, and other types (called "whole life," "universal life," and "variable life"), which, in addition to providing insurance, include a savings or investment factor. The latter kinds of policies are really a combined package of insurance and investment. The different types of insurance are described in more detail in the consumer guides to insurance listed in the Reading List of this book. Whether you buy term insurance and maintain a separate savings and investment program, or instead buy one of the other kinds of policies that combines them, you should make sure that the insurance part of your program is adequate to meet your family's financial needs if you die. A sound financial plan will meet these needs and will satisfy savings and retirement objectives in a way that does not sacrifice adequate insurance coverage.

Finally, it is essential to coordinate your life insurance with the rest of your estate plan. This is done by designating the beneficiary—choosing who is to receive any insurance proceeds when you die. If you wish any or all of these proceeds to be used for your child's support, you may wish to designate a trustee in your will or in a separate revocable life insurance trust. Upon your death, the trustee will receive the insurance proceeds and use them to benefit your child. If you do not have a trustee, your child's inheritance may be subject to the cost-of-care claims, or may interfere with eligibility for government benefits, described earlier.

A Guide to Estate Planning for Parents of Children with Mental Retardation

More than most parents, the parents of a child with mental retardation need to attend to estate planning. Because of concerns about cost-of-care liability, government benefits, and competency,

338 ✳ Legal Rights and Hurdles

it is vital that you make plans. Parents need to name the people who will care for their child with mental retardation when they die. They need to review their insurance to be sure it is adequate to meet their child's special needs. They need to make sure their retirement plans will help meet their child's needs as an adult. They need to inform grandparents of cost-of-care liability, government benefits, and competency problems so that grandparents do not inadvertently waste resources that could otherwise benefit their grandchild's future. Most of all, they need to make a will so that their hopes and plans are realized and the disastrous consequences of dying without a will are avoided.

Proper estate planning differs for each family. Every will must be tailored to individual needs. There are no formula wills, especially for parents of a child with mental retardation. There are, however, some common mistakes to avoid. Here is a list:

No Will. If parents die without first making wills, state law generally requires that each child in the family share equally in the parents' estate. The result is that your child with mental retardation will inherit property in her own name. Her inheritance may become subject to cost-of-care claims and could jeopardize eligibility for government benefits. These and other problems can be avoided with a properly drafted will. Parents should never allow the state's laws to determine how their property will be divided upon their deaths. Estate planning can make you feel uneasy, but it is too important to ignore.

A Will Leaving Property Outright to the Child with Mental Retardation. Like having no will at all, having a will that leaves property to a child with mental retardation in her own name may subject the inheritance to cost-of-care liability and may disqualify her for government benefits. Parents of children with mental retardation do not just need any will, they need a will that meets their special needs.

A Will Creating a Support Trust for the Child with Mental Retardation. A will that creates a support trust presents much the same problem as a will that leaves property outright to the child with mental retardation. The funds in these trusts may be subject to cost-of-care claims and jeopardize government benefits. A will that avoids this problem should be drafted.

Insurance and Retirement Plans Naming the Child with Mental Retardation as a Beneficiary. Many parents own life insurance policies that name a child with mental retardation as a beneficiary or contingent beneficiary, either alone or in common with siblings. The result is that funds may go outright to your child with mental retardation, creating cost-of-care liability and government benefits eligibility problems. Parents should designate the funds to pass either to someone else or to go into a properly drawn trust. The same is true of many retirement plan benefits.

Use of Joint Tenancy in Lieu of Wills. Spouses sometimes avoid making wills by placing all their property in joint tenancies with right of survivorship. In joint tenancies, property is owned equally by each spouse; when one spouse dies, the survivor automatically becomes the sole owner. Parents try to use joint tenancies instead of wills, relying on the surviving spouse to properly take care of all estate planning matters. This plan, however, fails completely if both parents die in the same disaster, if the surviving spouse becomes incapacitated, or if the surviving spouse neglects to make a proper will. The result is the same as if neither spouse made any will at all—the child with mental retardation shares equally in the parents' estates. As explained above, this may expose the assets to cost-of-care liability and give rise to problems with government benefits. Therefore, even when all property is held by spouses in joint tenancy, it is necessary that both spouses make wills.

Establishing UTMA Accounts for the Child with Mental Retardation. Over and over again well-meaning parents and grandparents of children with disabilities open bank accounts under the Uniform Transfers to Minors Act (UTMA). When the child reaches age eighteen or twenty-one, the account becomes the property of the child, and may therefore be subject to cost-of-care liability. Perhaps more important, most people with disabilities first become eligible for SSI and Medicaid at age eighteen, but the UTMA funds will have to be spent before financial eligibility for these programs can be established. Parents should *never* set up UTMA accounts for their child with mental retardation, nor should they open other bank accounts in the child's name.

Failing to Advise Grandparents and Relatives of the Need for Special Arrangements. Just as the parents of a child with mental retardation need properly drafted wills or trusts, so do grandparents and other relatives who may leave (or give) property to the child. If these people are not aware of the special concerns— cost-of-care liability, government benefits, and competency—their plans may go awry and their generosity may be wasted. Make sure anyone planning gifts to your child with mental retardation understands what is at stake.

Children and adults with mental retardation are entitled to lead full and rewarding lives. But many of them cannot do so without continuing financial support from their families. The *only* way to make sure your child has that support whenever she needs it is to plan for tomorrow today. Doing otherwise can rob her of the future she deserves.

The one thing we're absolutely adamant on is that our other children should not be obligated to care for our son for the rest of their lives.

We've had to plan for Cindy's future differently than we have for our other children. We have pretty much dispossessed her at this point.

═══ ✳ ═══

We just haven't gotten around to estate planning yet. It's embarrassing, but that's the truth.

═══ ✳ ═══

We don't want our son to end up living somewhere where he is "taken." We want him to go somewhere where he is "wanted."

═══ ✳ ═══

When she grows up, her skills will probably be good enough that she can hold down a job and stuff like that. When I think about her future, I'm more worried about what's going to happen when we die. That's why I've been looking into estate planning.

═══ ✳ ═══

I would hope that our other children would kind of keep an eye out for her and I think that they probably would, but I would never want them to feel burdened or obligated—that they are expected to take their sister

to live with them. That could break up somebody's marriage. I would
never expect that.

═══ ❊ ═══

I wouldn't want to burden our other kids, but I have a feeling, and this
is something that I'm not saying that I will instill in them, but I have a
feeling that just the way their hearts are now, we won't have to ask them.
I think they would say to us, "We'll take care of our brother whenever
he needs us." I think that it's in their hearts that they would say, "Don't
worry about it, Mom and Dad; we've got it."

Conclusion

Parenthood always brings responsibilities. But extra responsibilities confront parents of a child with mental retardation. Understanding the pitfalls for the future and planning to avoid them will
help you to meet the special responsibilities. In addition, knowing
and asserting your child's rights can help guarantee that she will
receive the education and government benefits to which she is
entitled. Being a good advocate for your child requires more than
knowledge. You must also be determined to use that knowledge
effectively, and, when necessary, forcefully.

Nine

== ※ ==

When Mental Retardation Isn't the Only Problem

D. Michael Rice, Ph.D.*

Mental retardation is not an illness. It doesn't affect your child's health, just his ability to learn. Yet children with mental retardation often spend more time in doctors' and therapists' offices than other children do. This is because there are a number of conditions often associated with mental retardation that may require professional diagnosis and treatment. For example, children with mental retardation are more likely to have hearing and vision problems, attention disorders, and seizures.

Some disorders that *may* accompany mental retardation occur more often in children who have certain syndromes. For instance, heart problems are especially common in children with Down syndrome. Other disorders such as seizures are more likely in children whose mental retardation is linked to brain damage. Still other conditions occur with about the same frequency, regardless of the cause of mental retardation.

Of course, just because there are certain conditions that children with mental retardation are more likely to have, it doesn't mean that your child will have them all. In fact, your child may not have any

---

* Dr. Rice is currently School Psychologist at the River Street School, which provides services for children with a wide range of developmental disabilities from throughout central Connecticut. He holds an M.A. from the University of North Carolina at Greensboro and a Ph.D. from the University of Rhode Island.

of them, or he may have only a few. If your child *does* have other conditions associated with mental retardation, though, there are medical, therapeutic, or educational strategies that can help. Although specialists can't "cure" most of these conditions, they can usually reduce their effects on your child's growth and learning.

Generally, the sooner that physical or developmental problems are diagnosed and treated, the better for your child. These conditions often need to be taken into consideration, along with your child's mental retardation, in making educational and other decisions. Because you can play a crucial role in identifying potential problems, this chapter provides an overview of conditions frequently associated with mental retardation. And because you and your child's doctors and therapists will often be making joint decisions about your child's treatment, this chapter also discusses ways to develop good parent-professional relationships. Armed with this information, you can not only take an active, knowledgeable role in your child's treatment, but also ensure that he receives the best possible care.

Attention Deficit Hyperactivity Disorder (ADHD)

Attention Deficit Hyperactivity Disorder (ADHD) is a condition that disrupts the ability to focus and maintain attention, effectively consider choices, and benefit from teaching. Symptoms include: 1) the inability to sit still or to control the urge to be physically active; 2) *impulsivity,* or acting without thinking—for example, constantly interrupting others or being bossy; 3) difficulty paying attention, together with rapid loss of interest in the topic of conversation and in activities; and 4) sometimes aggressive behavior—for example, hitting, kicking, or throwing tantrums. In the past, ADHD was known as "hyperactivity" or "minimal brain dysfunction."

About 3 to 5 percent of all children with "normal" intelligence have Attention Deficit Hyperactivity Disorder. It is diagnosed about six times as often in boys as in girls. Although researchers have not yet determined how common it is in children with mental retardation in general, studies have shown that it occurs more often in children with particular types of mental retardation. For example, about 20 percent of children with cerebral palsy have some type of attention deficit disorder. Children with fragile X syndrome, too, are especially prone to the symptoms of ADHD.

Key to the diagnosis of ADHD is a child's age. Most children are impulsive, inattentive, and overactive at some time in their lives. Younger children are usually more active and less attentive than older children. ADHD is diagnosed in an otherwise normal child *only* if his activity level and inattentiveness are greater than average for children of the same age. For children with mental retardation, this means that activity levels and attentiveness should be compared with those of children with the same mental age, rather than chronological age.

Typical children with ADHD may blurt out answers before a question is completed, talk excessively, have trouble following directions, seem very restless, or persistently be unable to focus their attention. Especially if they are very "impulsive," they may behave dangerously or recklessly—running into the street or grabbing a pot on the stove even though they know about "hot" and "danger." Parents of children with ADHD are likely to describe them as "climbing the walls," or "driven." Children with mental retardation and ADHD may have a great deal of perseverative behavior—performing the same action over and over.

Actually, hyperactivity is not always the primary symptom of ADHD. In some children, the only major symptom is inattentiveness. They may simply be unable to focus their attention and effort or may give up when an activity becomes slightly difficult. They may often miss much of what is said or shown to them. Most of these children, however, are able to focus their attention for longer periods of time if they find an activity especially interesting.

When a child has mental retardation and symptoms of attention deficit, diagnosis can be complicated. Technically (according to the "official" definition of ADHD), children with more significant mental retardation are not considered to have ADHD, although they may show many apparent symptoms. And sometimes doctors and psychologists cannot be sure whether a child's symptoms of ADHD are the result of ADHD or of the condition causing mental retardation or of the mental retardation itself. Consequently, your child may not be labelled as having ADHD even though he appears to have similar symptoms.

When a child has mental retardation in addition to symptoms of ADHD, social and learning problems are compounded. Children with mental retardation *and* ADHD often miss out on opportunities to interact with other children and expand their social skills. For example, because of their problems with attention, they may not realize that another child is talking to them unless they are addressed by name. And because of their inattention, they may have greater difficulty sticking with a task long enough to learn how to do it.

If you think your child may have ADHD or behavior like it, you should consult a pediatrician, preferably a "developmental" or "behaviorial" pediatrician who specializes in child development or behavior. Alternately, you may wish to consult a psychologist if your child's behavior problems are your main concern.

Whatever type of professional you consult, you can expect the diagnostic process to include a thorough medical evaluation. This is because hyperactivity can sometimes be a symptom of lead poisoning, diabetes, hyperthyroidism, or other conditions that require treatment. Hyperactivity and inattention can also be side-effects of some medications, such as those used to treat seizures or allergies. In addition, anxiety or agitation due to depression may cause an increase in activity level and drops in attention span.

As part of the evaluation, the doctor will ask a variety of questions to find out about your child's developmental history: Have you just recently begun to notice attention and behavior problems in your child, or has he had them for months or years? Does your child behave inappropriately in all situations, or only a few? For example, does he seem to have trouble focusing his attention while doing schoolwork but not while watching television? Does your child have any known allergies that could produce hyperactivity? As mentioned earlier, the doctor should also consider your child's "mental age" or "developmental age" in arriving at a diagnosis. As discussed in Chapter 1 and 4, mental age refers to the age level most like that at which a child actually functions. If your child has a chronological age of seven but a mental age of four, he would not be diagnosed with ADHD unless his symptoms were excessive for a four-year-old, rather than a seven-year-old.

In the past, professionals often didn't treat ADHD because they believed that children outgrew their symptoms of inattention, hyperactivity, or impulsivity once they reached adolescence. Today specialists know that ADHD usually continues into adulthood. Consequently, they have developed several methods of treating the symptoms. These methods most often include medication and behavior management strategies.

Research has shown that specific medications can dramatically benefit many children's behavior. In fact, medication for ADHD was first used successfully in the 1950s in an institution for children with mental retardation in Providence, Rhode Island. These medications can greatly improve many children's ability to attend and focus their attention on learning tasks. Although parents are sometimes apprehensive about using any medications with their children on a long-term basis, most physicians consider drugs the primary treatment when a child has a clear diagnosis of ADHD.

The most effective treatment for controlling symptoms of ADHD is usually a form of stimulant medication called Ritalin™ (methylphenidate). According to some researchers, however, a more effective medication for children with mental retardation may be Dexedrine™ (dextroamphetamine). Other medications that may be prescribed if Ritalin or Dexedrine do not help your child include Cylert™ (pemoline) and Tofranil™ (imipramine). As beneficial as these medications can be, they also have a range of potential side effects to watch for. Medication may cause loss of appetite, sleep disturbances, headaches, irritability, moodiness, weight loss, insomnia, and increased heart rate. In addition, some researchers believe that if the dosage is too high, it may adversely affect cognitive abilities. For example, a child may become withdrawn or emotional or get "stuck" on a particular task. This belief is currently being challenged, however, as a recent study has shown that high dosages do *not* affect cognition.

Because of the potential side effects, medications are usually used only when a child's behavior interferes with his overall functioning. For example, they are often recommended when a child has trouble getting along with peers, a decreased learning rate, or difficulty responding to discipline. If your child is prescribed any medication, it should first be evaluated on a trial basis. The physician should weigh the positive effects of medication on your child's behavior against any negative side effects. You will probably be asked to observe your child at home while teachers observe him at school. Both you and the teachers should record changes in your child's behavior, as well as any side effects such as changes in appetite, irritability, or moodiness. You should then give the physician your observations, being as specific as possible. To help teachers make observations, be sure they know what medication your child is taking, along with the dose and time it was given.

As with all medications, the goal is to produce the maximum benefit with a minimum of side effects. To arrive at the optimum dose for your child, your physician will probably vary the dose over the course of a few weeks and ask you and your child's teachers to report on changes in your child's behavior. If the medication is beneficial to your child, you should see improvement right away.

If medication is prescribed for your child, he should be re-evaluated yearly to determine whether his medication should be withdrawn or the dosage changed. Should your child's behavior worsen after discontinuing medication, the medication may be re-started after a few days.

Medications should *always* be used together with behavior management strategies, the second major treatment for attention deficits or hyperactivity. Chapter 6 discusses behavior management strategies in detail. Briefly, behavior managment strategies involve analyzing behavior problems and then developing plans to change them. For children with mental retardation and ADHD, the key to behavior management is "positive reinforcement"—rewarding appropriate behavior. Many children with ADHD thrive on attention, highly stimulating activities such as video games, and physical games, which can be used to reward gradual improvements in behavior. Parents know what their children enjoy most and can often come up with a whole menu of rewards to use with their children. Another important aspect of behavior management is to make changes that make it more likely that your child will succeed and not become overly frustrated. For example, shortening work periods and allowing for breaks between work periods, gradually increasing the amount of time you expect your child to concentrate, and allowing him more time to learn from consequences can all help in behavior management.

Behavior management strategies can not only help your child improve his behavior but can also help you regain a feeling of control. Often parents of children with ADHD feel like failures, or feel frustrated, inadequate, or embarrassed by their child's behavior or lack of attention. Learning behavior management and motivational strategies can help you conquer these feelings.

For guidance in learning behavior management strategies, consult your child's school psychologist or special educators. You might also investigate whether your school agency employs a "behavior specialist" who could help you develop methods to improve your child's behavior.

Attention deficits and symptoms of ADHD *can* affect everyday life and further impede the learning and development of your child with mental retardation. But with early and proper diagnosis, learning and behavior problems can be minimized through appropriate medical and educational intervention.

ADHD seems to run in my family. My son with Down syndrome and ADHD has an older brother who also has some ADHD symptoms. But only my son with Down syndrome gets medication to help eliminate ADHD. Why? I figure that my son with Down syndrome has enough obstacles in the way of his learning that he does not need another problem. He is less able to overcome challenges, so I am willing to help remove them. But I think that my older son can and should learn how to cope with his ADHD. I'm not trying to make his life more difficult, but I think he can learn things by overcoming this challenge that my other son would not learn.

Ritalin has made a huge difference in Mandy's education, in her ability to receive education. It has enabled her to be "available" cognitively for learning. She can focus long enough to learn, follow directions in class, and keep up with what is going on in and out of the classroom.

Doctors in this area seem too quick to push medications on kids. You really need a kid with a firm diagnosis of ADHD to justify putting your kid on these drugs, not just a little behavior problem that a bit of parental effort might control. It is easy to convince yourself of a "medical" cause of all behavior problems and then to expect a pill to cure them.

Seizures

Seizures are temporary states of abnormal electrical activity in the brain. They occur when brain cells discharge or "fire" when they aren't supposed to. These discharges are stronger than required for normal brain activity and can cause a variety of symptoms. Some result in almost no observable changes in behavior, perhaps causing the child to blink his eyes or stare off into space for several seconds. These are called absence or petit mal seizures. Others last several minutes and may produce considerable muscular jerking, confusion, pale or bluish skin color, loss of consciousness, drowsiness, and sometimes loss of bladder or bowel control. These are referred to as generalized tonic-clonic or grand mal seizures. Still others may be preceded by an "aura"—a strange smell, sound, visual sensation, or emotion such as fear or anxiety—after which the child suddenly stops his activity and may engage in repetitive, purposeless behavior. These are known as complex partial or temporal lobe seizures. When seizures occur repeatedly over a period of months or years, they are diagnosed as *epilepsy.*

Epilepsy is one of the most common disorders associated with mental retardation. This is because it is caused by many types of injuries to the nerve cells of the brain or by problems in the way they interact. In other words, a brain injury or disorder that causes mental retardation can also produce seizures. Some causes of mental retardation that can also contribute to the development of seizures include maternal drug or alcohol abuse, hypoglycemia, complications of prematurity, anoxia or hypoxia, and head injuries.

Children with mental retardation are thought to be from five to twelve times more likely to have a seizure disorder or epilepsy than other children. Studies of children with mental retardation between the ages of five and sixteen have found ranges of 7 percent for children with mild mental retardation, to as high as 67 percent for those with severe mental retardation. Three times out of four, these seizure disorders begin before age nineteen. And when epilepsy is caused by prenatal factors or birth injuries, seizures usually begin within the first twenty-four hours of life, and almost always before the age of five.

Although seizures can be alarming to watch, they are not painful and your child will not remember them. Once a seizure has begun, there is nothing you can do to stop it. It is understandable to feel helpless and frightened, but if you don't panic, you can help make your child more comfortable. Here are some steps to take:

1. Keep calm, loosen your child's clothing, and put something soft under his head. Turn your child to one side, but do not try to restrain him. Do not put anything into his mouth; he *cannot* swallow his tongue.
2. Remove hard, sharp objects from the area so that he won't hurt himself if he moves around.
3. After the seizure is over, keep your child lying on his side and allow him to rest. He may be confused, so you may need to help him get his bearings again. Tell him specifically where he is and suggest a quiet activity for him to do until he is re-oriented.
4. If the seizure lasts more than five minutes, or if your child appears to pass from one seizure to another without regaining consciousness, call the doctor or an ambulance. (Be sure that your physician gives you specific written instructions beforehand as to when to have your child taken directly to the hospital.)

Although seizures are not painful, they *can* further delay your child's development. They can interrupt learning opportunities and interfere with socialization. They can also lead to mental disorganization—day-to-day confusion and loss of skills previously learned. Especially when children have very frequent seizures or poorly controlled seizures, they may forget or have trouble recalling information, learn skills at a slower rate, or score lower on intelligence tests over time. In short, poorly controlled seizures can lead to decreased learning and reasoning skills. For children with mental retardation, this can translate into greater delays in development than they would otherwise have.

Because seizures can have such a pronounced effect on learning, it is important that they be diagnosed and treated as early as possible. To determine whether your child has seizures, he should be evaluated by a neurologist. The neurologist will conduct a thorough evaluation and may also administer one or more tests to measure the electrical activity in your child's brain. The primary test he will use is the electroencephalogram (EEG). He might also use MRI (Magnetic Resonance Imaging) or a CT scan. See Chapter 1 for a description of these tests.

If your child is diagnosed as having seizures, he will most likely be prescribed one or more types of *anticonvulsant* medications. These medications are often highly effective in preventing or reducing the number of seizures. Over 50 percent of people have no seizures when taking medication and another 20 to 30 percent have fewer or less severe seizures. They may, for example, have absence seizures rather than grand mal seizures.

There is no "best" type of anticonvulsant to control all types of seizures, nor a "best" dose. Too little medication may have no effect on your child's seizures. Too much medication may produce side effects such as nausea and vomiting, drowsiness, dizziness, irritability, headache, changes in the blood, and even liver disease. Excessive medication may also decrease your child's ability to do schoolwork or other daily activities due to drowsiness or changes in activity level or mood. Your child's neurologist will work to find the lowest dose which controls your child's seizures with a minimum of side effects. He should carefully evaluate the effects of medications on your child's learning and behavior before, during, and after medication is prescribed. Your child's teachers should also be aware of medications your child is taking and their potential side effects, and should let you know how they are affecting his learning and behavior. Often, more than one medication is needed to bring seizures under control.

Some physicians do not like to "tinker" with medications once they have discovered a combination that controls seizures. But as your child grows, it may be necessary to adjust the types and doses of medications he receives. If your child has no seizures for two years, the physician might also consider discontinuing medication. In the past, many physicians thought that epilepsy in children with mental retardation was a permanent condition requiring lifelong treatment, but that view is changing. Recent studies have shown that children with mental retardation who do not have seizures for two years while on medication may remain seizure-free without medication. Discuss this issue openly with your doctor and obtain a second opinion if your questions are not answered or your doctor's responses don't satisfy you.

If medication cannot effectively control your child's seizures or if he has so many seizures that they impair his learning, he may be considered to have a "dual disability." If so, he may need additional life skill training or more repetition of previously taught material to help him maintain his skills. You may also have to work closely with both medical and educational professionals to reduce the impact of your child's seizure disorder on his development.

Rarely, surgery is considered when seizures cannot be controlled by medication and they occur with great frequency. Surgery can sometimes reduce seizures or prevent them from spreading to other areas of the brain. Your neurologist can advise you whether surgery might help your child, and also explain the possible risks and benefits. You can also consult the Epilepsy Foundation of America, at the address in the Resource Guide, for information on the latest treatments for seizures.

Our son started having seizures at about the age of three, but he only had one a year for the first three years. He had one at three, one at four, and had just turned five when he had another grand mal [tonic clonic] seizure. Then he started having petit mal [absence] seizures all the time.

The worst situation for her is to be in a highly stimulating environment in the middle of summer when it's hot and humid. That throws her on the edge of a seizure faster than anything else.

His CAT scan came back okay, but he had abnormal EEGs. They've just recently diagnosed him with a lesion on the left-hand side of his brain. They started him on seizure medication, and that seems to help.

Vision Problems

The IDEA defines "visual handicap" as a visual impairment which, even with correction, impedes a child's ability to learn. According to this definition, a number of visual problems can be considered handicaps, including:

1. nearsightedness (*myopia*): inability to see distant objects clearly.
2. farsightedness (*hyperopia*): inability to see nearby objects clearly.
3. strabismus: a condition that results when the muscles controlling one eye are stronger than the muscles controlling the other, which causes an eye to turn in (*esotropia*) or out (*exotropia*). Eyes do not focus together, and problems with depth perception or double vision can result.
4. cataracts: clouding of the eye lens due to genetic causes or infections.
5. amblyopia (lazy eye): a condition in which the brain turns off or suppresses the eye with relatively weaker vision to prevent the child from having blurred or double vision. Amblyopia can develop as a result of cataracts, strabismus, or nearsightedness. If suppression of vision continues too long, the weaker eye can lose its ability to see.
6. low vision: a catchall phrase used by school systems to describe children with vision of 20/70 or less in the better eye. (20/70 vision means that, even with eyeglasses, a child sees objects that are twenty feet away only as clearly as someone with normal vision would see them from seventy feet away.)
7. total blindness: corrected vision of 20/200 or less in the better eye or a field of vision of 20 degrees or less.

Depending on the cause of his mental retardation, your child may be more likely to have one or more of these vision problems. For example, children with cerebral palsy, fragile X syndrome, and Down syndrome have a greater risk of being nearsighted or having strabismus. Children with cerebral palsy and Down syndrome are also more likely to have cataracts. But remember: even though children with mental retardation are more likely to have vision problems, the incidence of serious visual handicaps is still quite low. Although children with mental retardation are about twenty to thirty times more likely than other children to have total vision impairment, this still only amounts to about 2 to 3 percent of all children with mental retardation.

Obviously, vision impairments can hamper a child's ability to learn and adjust to his environment. Vision problems reduce the amount of information children are able to take in by limiting input they get from their sense of sight and by making it harder for them to explore, and learn from, objects around them. Learning about spatial concepts and relationships such as "under," "above," and "behind" is especially hard. Since understanding these concepts is already more difficult for children with mental retardation, having a vision problem can greatly add to their difficulties.

Early detection of problems is essential. Watch your child for signs of vision problems: squinting or blinking, difficulty focusing on objects or following them with the eyes, complaining of eyes hurting, frequently rubbing the eyes, bloodshot or tearing eyes, tilting the head to look at things, seeming to prefer one eye over the other, irritability or short attention span during activities calling for close-up work. If you suspect a vision problem, consult an *ophthalmologist*—a medical doctor trained to diagnose diseases of the eye, perform eye surgery, examine vision, and prescribe glasses.

To ensure that your child's vision is accurately evaluated, it is best to find an ophthalmologist or optometrist who is experienced and comfortable with treating the vision problems of children with special needs. These professionals can assess your child's vision even if he does not know his letters or is nonverbal. For example, they might use vision charts that depict "hands" pointing in various directions, and ask your child to point in the same direction as the hands. Charts showing shapes or blocks of colors of various sizes might also be used. In addition, the ophthalmologist can use a test known as an *evoked potential* to measure your child's vision. This test requires absolutely no response from your child. Electrodes are attached to your child's scalp; then lights are flashed in various parts of the visual field for each eye. A computer detects and monitors how much of this stimulation is received by your child's visual cortex—the part of the brain that processes visual information. Another way to test vision is to use an *autorefractor*. This device simply requires that your child track a colorful object as it appears to float across his field of vision. The measurements taken with the autorefractor can tell the eye specialist what prescription is needed to correct your child's vision with 80 to 90 percent accuracy.

Once the eye specialist has determined the nature and extent of your child's vision problem, he can recommend appropriate treatment. Glasses can improve nearsightedness and farsightedness in most cases. It can, however, be a struggle to get your child with mental retardation (or any child, for that matter) to wear his glasses. Consequently, you may have to be creative in devising rewards that will encourage him to wear them. You may also find it helpful to attach an elastic strap such as athletes use to the earpieces of the glasses to keep them on your child's head. Be sure also that the glasses fit comfortably with no pressure points and that the lenses are clean enough for your child to see out of.

Corrective glasses may also be prescribed to treat strabismus. Or, a patch may be worn over the stronger eye to force the child to use, and strengthen, the muscles of the weaker eye. If these treatments don't correct the muscle imbalance, surgery may be necessary.

Surgery is always necessary to remove cataracts from the eye lens. The procedure is usually quite successful on children and requires only a short hospital stay. If the lens is removed from your child's eye, he will be prescribed a contact lens to replace it.

Treatment for amblyopia depends on the underlying reason that the brain is suppressing vision to one eye. For example, if suppression is due to extreme nearsightedness in one eye, then glasses can correct the nearsightedness and the amblyopia. If it is due to strabismus, then patching may help both problems.

If your child has low vision or total blindness he will probably be enrolled in a program for children with multiple handicaps. Here he will work with vision and mobility specialists, teachers trained in educating children with visual impairments. These specialists can help him use his available vision, teach him to compensate for lack of vision, or help him build on information he acquired before the vision problem developed.

Besides helping children to compensate for their vision loss, educational programs for children with multiple handicaps should also offer experiences that foster normal growth and development—for example, field trips to "hands-on" locations such as petting zoos or museums that allow touching and doing, contact with sighted children, and other tactile (touch) and hearing activities. These programs should also have a variety of special instructional materials, including "talking books," pop-up and other "touch" books, cassettes, large-print materials, and computer games and educational programs.

If your child has a significant vision problem, his teachers and therapists should suggest ways to adjust your home environment to make learning easier. For example, they will help you learn to use light and sounds to enable your child to get along in different settings. They should recommend ways to keep your child safe without overprotecting him and inadvertently limiting his learning.

Basic guidelines on teaching a child with vision impairment include:

1. Make verbal directions specific. Don't say "over there"; instead say, "on top of the table."
2. Try to use verbal guidance rather than physical guidance as much as possible. For example, rather than guiding your child's hands to a toy, say, "Use your hands to find the barn. Can you find the cow? The cow is thirsty. She needs a drink." (But when your child is young and is exploring a new environment, you may want to comfort him by holding his hand.)
3. Since facial expressions provide very little feedback to a child with a vision impairment, *pay attention to your voice tone* and *use plenty of verbal praise.*
4. Do not set lower limits for "inappropriate behavior" for your child with vision impairments than you would for a sighted child. Permitting misbehavior certainly will not benefit him, especially when he is around other people, who will be less tolerant.
5. People often raise their voices to talk to children with vision impairments. It's a natural impulse but totally unnecessary.

6. Prepare your child ahead of time for any changes in his environment. Tell him, for example, if you are going to move a chair from one side of the room to another, or if the rug in the hallway has been removed for cleaning.
7. Encourage your child to use his hands to explore new objects and areas as you explain and describe what you see. Be patient with his questions about new places and things, explaining in as much detail as he can grasp.

Last, but not least, be aware that children with visual impairments—even those with mental retardation—may develop unusually keen sensitivities through other senses. For example, your child may be extraordinarily good at deducing your emotional state simply by listening to your voice intonations, or unusually good at remembering people by their voices. With the help of medical and educational professionals, you can help your child's talents bloom.

Stephen is very, very farsighted. He's good about wearing his glasses, but I can't really tell if they make a difference for him. But we just feel like he's already got enough to handle with his mental retardation. We want to give him whatever advantage we can, so we'll keep having him wear them until we get a clearer picture of what glasses do for him.

When she was two, we took her to a bunch of ophthalmologists. One said she wouldn't wear glasses, one said it wouldn't make any difference if she wore glasses, and one said, "Well, if you want them, we'll get them for you." Those doctors made a lot of assumptions—like she's going to pull them off and flush them down the toilet. They couldn't seem to relate to the fact that this could be a kid with some learning problem on top of mental retardation, and that glasses could help. It certainly couldn't hurt.

Hearing Problems

Good hearing is crucial to the development of a variety of skills. Learning to speak hinges on being able to hear and imitate others; learning to understand language depends on the ability to hear and decipher what others say. And the development of language skills is crucial to the development of cognitive skills. Not only do children learn by paying attention to the sounds around them, but they also learn by asking how, what, when, and especially *why*. Obviously, for children with mental retardation, hearing problems can further impede development of these important skills.

Hearing problems occur in less than 2 percent of normally developing children aged birth through fourteen. In general, children with mental retardation are more likely to have hearing problems than other children are. The likelihood that your child will have a hearing impairment may depend on the cause of his mental retardation. For example, about 40 percent of children with Down syndrome have at least a mild hearing impairment, and up to about 15 percent of children with cerebral palsy have hearing problems. Children with more severe mental retardation are also more likely to have hearing impairments.

The sooner hearing problems are diagnosed, the sooner you can reduce their impact on your child's learning. You should therefore watch your child closely for signs of a hearing impairment. These signs include, first of all, not responding to sounds—particularly to new sounds or to sounds associated with something he likes. Other signs can include holding back and not participating in activities, appearing withdrawn, and having more delays in language development when compared to skills in other areas. For example, your child might have the cognitive skills to follow simple directions when you point to something you want him to get or do. But when you give him simple directions orally, he may not be able to do what you ask.

If you suspect a hearing impairment, consult an *audiologist*—a professional who is trained and certified to identify and measure hearing loss or impairment and who is also knowledgeable in the use of hearing aids. If possible, try to find an audiologist experienced in working with children with developmental disabilities. Ask your physician, school speech-language therapist, or local ARC for recommendations.

How the audiologist will evaluate your child's hearing often depends on your child's age. Children younger than two or two and a half are usually tested through a procedure called "soundfield audiometry." The child is seated between two loudspeakers in a darkened or dimmed sound-proof booth. The audiologist channels his or her voice through one of the two speakers and then watches whether the child turns toward the sound.

For his hearing to be measured more precisely, your child needs to be able to wear earphones and to respond to tones heard through them. Headphones enable the audiologist to isolate the hearing of one ear from the other and determine how much hearing a child has in each ear. Often children can be tested using this method by the time they are two and a half. But many children, especially children with mental retardation, may resist wearing earphones until they're older. They may find that the earphones look frightening or feel funny covering their ears. They may be extra sensitive to touch around their head or face, or frightened if people put their hands close to their face. If your child is scheduled for an audiological evaluation, the process may go more smoothly if you have him practice wearing earphones at home. Try letting him listen to music or a story through a portable cassette player for just a few minutes several times before the appointment.

If your child is able to wear earphones, the audiologist will begin by evaluating your child's ability to hear sounds through "air conduction." She will test your child's ability to hear tones of different frequencies (pitches) that are important in the production and understanding of speech sounds. The audiologist will try to find the softest level at which each tone is just barely audible in each of your child's ears. This level is known as the "hearing threshold."

After measuring your child's air conduction, the audiologist will measure his bone conduction, which is another important element of hearing. Through bone conduction, sounds are transmitted to the inner ear when soundwaves cause bones of the skull to vibrate. To measure bone conduction, the audiologist will place an instrument called a bone oscillator or bone conduction vibrator on the mastoid bone (the bony prominence on the skull) just behind your child's ears. Then she will again measure the softest level at which your child can hear tones of various frequencies. By comparing your child's bone conduction measurements with his air conduction measurements, the audiologist can determine whether any hearing loss is due to an outer or middle ear problem, or to a problem further up the auditory pathway.

One other test the audiologist may do is a test of acoustic immittance or tympanometry. This involves putting an earphone into your child's ear to measure movement of the eardrum. The basic idea is that if the middle ear cavity has abnormal pressure or contains fluid, then the eardrum won't move the same way it would otherwise. Although tympanometry is not painful, your child may cry if he thinks the mechanism looks frightening, he doesn't like having things placed in his ears, or because he doesn't understand what is being done to him.

The audiologist charts your child's hearing on a form called an "audiogram." This is really a graph that shows how your child's hearing at each sound frequency compares to the normal ability to hear. The degree of hearing loss your child has at each frequency is expressed in *decibels (dB),* a unit of measurement referring to the loudness of sound. If your child has no hearing loss (zero decibel loss) at a given frequency, his level of hearing would be charted as 0. In other words, the closer your child's hearing is to 0 level at each frequency, the closer it is to normal. Most audiologists consider anywhere from 0–15 decibels to be within the normal range of hearing, and 15–25 decibels to be a slight hearing loss.

If the audiologist does not find a hearing problem, you should ask her when and if you should bring your child back for additional evaluations, since hearing losses can develop at any time. Just because a problem is not diagnosed when your child is young does not mean he won't develop a condition later on that affects his hearing. Because your child's hearing is so important, you will want to know if it changes in the future. Also, be sure to check with the audiologist any time *you* suspect any changes in your child's hearing.

Types of Hearing Losses. If the audiologist does detect a hearing problem, it will be one of two types: *conductive* or *sensorineural.* Conductive losses are the most frequent kind of hearing loss in children, and especially in children with mental retardation. A conductive hearing loss occurs when the transmission of sound waves is impaired as they travel through the child's ear canal, across the eardrum (tympanic membrane), and along the chain of tiny bones in the child's middle ear. This type of hearing loss is often temporary and intermittent, and is usually the result of fluid in the middle ear. This fluid may or may not be caused by an infection. Children with certain types of mental retardation, including Down syndrome and fragile X syndrome, are more likely to have middle ear fluid. So, too, are children who have allergies.

Children with frequent or prolonged episodes of middle ear fluid often have language learning disabilities. Some scientists believe that this is because when middle ear fluid comes and goes, the messages a child receives through his sense of hearing are so variable. In other words, a particular word or phrase heard through fluid may sound very different than when it is heard through the usual dryer environment of the middle ear. You can see how confusing this would be for a child just learning language. Then imagine if that child had mental retardation as well.

One other occasional cause of conductive hearing loss is a condition known as *stenotic canals*. In this condition, the ear canals are narrower than usual. If the narrowing is serious enough, the flow of sound waves can be impeded. Children with Down syndrome often have some stenosis or narrowing, but the narrowing is usually not enough to impair hearing.

Sensorineural hearing losses are the result of damage to the inner ear, auditory nerve, or both. These structures ordinarily convert sound pressure waves to nerve impules and send those impulses to the brain. Damage to the inner ear or auditory nerve can occur as the result of prenatal exposure to rubella, toxoplasmosis, mumps, cytomegalovirus (CMV), and certain antibiotics. It also occurs in about 1 percent of children with cerebral palsy. Sensorineural hearing losses are permanent and do not get better with age. They may, however, worsen and should therefore be carefully monitored by your child's audiologist.

Treatment of Hearing Loss. In theory, treatment of hearing problems depends on their source, the degree of impairment, and whether both ears have a loss. Problems resulting from middle ear fluid are generally treated by an ear, nose, and throat specialist (ENT). The ENT prescribes antibiotics if the fluid is due to infection, and antihistamines or decongestants if the fluid is not due to infection. A fairly new treatment is to use steroids to clear up the fluid. If medication cannot control episodes of middle ear fluid or if they happen frequently, the ENT may recommend that tiny tubes known as pressure equalization (PE), myringotomy, or ventilation tubes be surgically inserted in the eardrum. These tubes equalize the pressure of the middle ear and often alleviate fluid build-up and reduce the number of infections.

If your child has a significant hearing loss due to stenotic canals or some other cause, an audiologist will probably recommend hearing aids to amplify sounds. A "significant" hearing loss is generally considered to be one that will impede language development or affect his education.

In practice, several factors besides the cause and extent of your child's hearing loss may affect treatment. These include your physician's opinions about what constitutes a significant hearing loss for your child with mental retardation. For example, if your doctor feels that a child with mental retardation needs every advantage possible to augment his learning and development, he may immediately prescribe medications for your child's problem with middle ear fluid even though he might not prescribe this treatment so quickly for a child who doesn't have mental retardation. Some physicians feel that a little fluid will not have a major impact on a child's development and may stop at prescribing antibiotics. Others show great concern for a child's language and learning development and may be concerned that even a slight, temporary hearing loss in one ear can have a major educational impact.  Consequently, they may be quicker to prescribe myringotomy tubes.

If hearing aids are recommended for your child, it may be only a temporary measure until middle ear fluid clears up or until tubes are inserted in his ears. If he has a permanent hearing loss, he will need to wear hearing aids all his life. In either case, it may be difficult at first to get your child to wear them. Because hearing aids increase the volume of all sounds (not just speech), they can be annoying to the wearer. They can also be annoying because they feel strange in your child's ear or because he doesn't like having someone's hands near his head when the aids are inserted or adjusted. In addition, the quality of sound heard through a hearing aid is different and can frighten or confuse your child at first. Consequently, you will need to gradually increase the time your child wears his hearing aid, starting with only a few minutes at a time per day. Praise is important, and you may also need to use other rewards to increase your child's cooperation in wearing his aids.

If, even with a hearing aid, your child seems to understand visual information much better than auditory information, the speech-language pathologist will probably suggest that he learn to use augmentative communication methods. He will likely begin by learning to use manual sign language or a language board with symbols or pictures for words or phrases. If it seems likely that your child will not develop useful speech for a period of several years, the speech-language pathologist may recommend an electronic language board with a voice synthesizer.

If your child needs to learn one of these alternative methods of communication, it goes without saying that you will, too. Your child's school may offer classes, or you can take a class through local community colleges or universities or through schools for the deaf. Your child's speech therapist can acquaint you with other methods of communication, and also teach you communication strategies to use with your child at home. Together, you can minimize your child's hearing problems to help him learn and grow socially, emotionally, and academically.

Jarrell had recurrent ear infections. His eardrum had even ruptured a few times, but we didn't know that he had the infections because they weren't painful for him and he never spiked a fever. We couldn't even get the doctors to test him. I kept saying to them, "This child does not hear," and they told me, "You're just overwrought parents. Come back in another three months." So we finally got an appointment, and inside of a month the doctor had gotten him into a hospital to have his adenoids removed and tubes put in his ears.

═══ ※ ═══

The first difference we noticed about Peter was that he wasn't hearing properly when he was very young. He has a permanent hearing loss that he got primarily from having middle ear problems over and over again.

We were lucky. Our doctor took the position that if Lynn had any problems, we had to give her any help we could. He drained her ears because he said you can't let a kid like her have any kind of a hearing loss, even marginal, if it makes a difference.

The doctors still don't know if his hearing problems are only from the chronic ear infections. There could be some structural anomaly in his ear canal. He wears a hearing aid now.

Autism and Pervasive Developmental Disorder

"Pervasive developmental disorder" (PDD) is the diagnostic term for any condition that begins before the age of about four or five and includes some or all of the following symptoms:

1. delays and difficulties in social skills (lack of eye contact, lack of interest in people, and indifference or aversion to being touched);
2. distorted development of communication (abnormal use of facial expression, gestures, and spoken language, sometimes including nonsensical language, or *echolalia*—parrot-like repetition of other people's words or phrases);
3. limited range of interests (the desire to repeat activities over and over again, fascination with one particular object);
4. over-sensitivities to touch, sounds, smells, or other sensations (crying when touched, sitting with fingers in the ears to block out noises);
5. resistance to changes in the environment.

A child who has some, but not all of these symptoms may be diagnosed as having "pervasive developmental disorder - not otherwise specified (PDD-NOS)." A child who has all of these symptoms—at least to some degree—is usually diagnosed as having autism. This section will focus mainly on autism for two reasons. First, autism and PDD-NOS share the same symptoms; the distinction lies in the number, not the type, of symptoms that a child has. Second, much more information has been gathered on children with autism, because autism has been used as a diagnosis longer than PDD-NOS has. Bear in mind, however, that most of the information that applies to children with autism also applies to children with PDD-NOS.

Autistic symptoms definitely interfere with the development of relationships with others and with overall learning. Yet despite its adverse affects on learning, autism is not the same as mental retardation. Mental retardation generally causes delays in most areas of development, whereas autism primarily affects development of communication and social skills. Some children with autism have average or above average intelligence, while all children with mental retardation, by definition, have below average intelligence.

Although there are clear distinctions between mental retardation and autism, the two conditions often overlap. About 1 in 1,000 children has autism, and about 70 to 89 percent of children with autism also have mental retardation. The number of boys diagnosed with autism outnumbers the number of girls by two or three to one. Autistic-like symptoms are especially common in boys with fragile X syndrome and in girls with Rett syndrome.

The earliest signs of autism or PDD often include extreme anxiety, delayed language, resistance to change, and unusual responses to touch, smell, or other sensations. These symptoms usually appear before the age of two, but can sometimes begin as late as age five or six. If you think your child shows autistic tendencies, he should be examined by a multidisciplinary team consisting of a pediatrician, speech-language pathologist, psychologist, and possibly also an occupational therapist. A good developmental evaluation can often be obtained at a hospital (especially a major medical facility), pediatric clinic, or regional Developmental Evaluation Clinic. Many cities also have evaluation clinics.

To diagnose your child, the multidisciplinary team will rely heavily on information you provide about your child's behavior and abilities at home. The team members should also give your child a meticulous physical exam, examine his chromsomes for evidence of a genetic disorder, and perform an EEG and brain imaging test. (See

Chapter 1 for a description of these tests.) This is because autism is often a symptom of an underlying disorder which may also require treatment. For example, autistic symptoms may be signs that a child has fragile X syndrome.

If your child has autism and mental retardation, you may very well consider autism to be his primary disability. That is, his difficulties in relating to you and returning your affection may seem like a bigger handicap than the learning delays caused by mental retardation. Medical and educational professionals, however, don't generally make a distinction between primary and secondary disabilites. Instead, they respond to the needs of a child based on his symptoms, problems, or delays. Knowing that your child has autism, will, however, affect how they work with your child to overcome his delays. For example, the speech-language pathologist will recognize that your child will have more trouble learning to use language socially than he would if he just had mental retardation. She will therefore spend more time concentrating on helping your child learn to communicate appropriately with others than she would otherwise.

As yet, there is no "cure" for autism. Various medications are sometimes prescribed to reduce some of the symptoms of autism, such as anxiety, physical restlessness, compulsions, wide variations in mood, and self-injury. The medications most often prescribed include Haldol™ (haloperidol), Lithium, Tegretol™ (carbamazine), Trexan™ (naltrexone HCL), Buspar™ (buspirone HCL), Depekene™ (valproic acid), Anafranil™ (clomipramine), and Catapres™ (clonidine). These medications are effective in controlling symptoms in some children, but they can also cause side effects ranging from sleepiness, constipation, and blurred vision to restlessness, allergic reactions, and changes in liver function.

Your physician should discuss potential benefits and side effects of any medication with you. Although the benefits for your child may clearly outweigh the drawbacks, you should make an informed decision. Once a medication is prescribed, you, your physician, and your child's teachers should carefully monitor its effects and side effects. It may take several days or even weeks of gradually adjusting the dosage to arrive at the level that produces the most benefits and the fewest undesireable side effects for your child.

Usually, educational strategies are far more effective then medications in treating autistic symptoms. Speech-language pathologists can provide ideas to help children with autism learn language skills. Occupational therapists can work with them to improve their over-sensitivities to touch and other sensory problems. Psychologists and special education teachers can teach social skills and offer suggestions for handling behavior difficulties. They can also help you learn the best ways to interact with your child and to motivate him to learn and to behave appropriately.

Whatever the degree of your child's autism, you can expect it to add to the challenges posed by his mental retardation. Difficulty organizing and making sense of his world and limited language skills will combine to create a situation ripe for behavior that is difficult to manage and understand. Children with autism *and* mental retardation often have peculiar habits. For example, they may have unusual sleep patterns or sleep very little; have preoccupations with certain objects—for instance, with unplugging all the electrical appliances or closing all the doors in the house; or have self-injurious behavior such as pulling out their hair or banging their head.

Your child may need constant monitoring, as well as very precise limits for behavior. To help him adjust to everyday life, you will need to carefully observe his habits, interests, and sensitivities to touch, sound, and other sensations. Because most children with autism have great difficulty communicating, you may need to use your child's behavior for clues as to what he is thinking or feeling. For example, your child might become self-injurious when he has an earache or is not allowed to do something he wants to do. Or, take the example of a young student with autism who entered the classroom one morning, turned, and walked back into the hallway. This child had very limited language skills and couldn't tell anyone what was wrong. Instead, he walked from one end of the building to the other and back, and wouldn't even walk outside, an activity he usually enjoyed. During his trips down the hallway, he often stopped to get a drink of water. A call to his mother revealed no out-of-the ordinary behavior that morning or the night before. Then, within six hours, the boy vomited and became pale. That evening he developed a fever and came down with the flu.

The point is, never assume that a child with autistic symptoms is behaving oddly for no good reason. He may be trying to communicate what he feels, what he needs, or how he sees the world. Also remember that children with both autism and mental retardation do attend school and learn self-help and academic skills. As with any child with mental retardation, your knowledgeable assistance is very important to your child's adjustment, learning, and overall happiness.

Learning Disabilities

Sorting out the difference between mental retardation and learning disabilities can be confusing. As explained in Chapter 1, mental retardation causes general delays in all areas of learning—motor skills, language skills, social skills, self-help skills, and cognitive skills. Learning disabilities, on the other hand, cause learning difficulties in only one or a few very specific areas. For example, a preschool child with learning disabilities may have extra trouble remembering what he's seen but not what he's heard. An older child with learning disabilities might have great difficulty with spelling and writing, but no problems mastering mathematical or scientific concepts. When children have learning disabilities, they do more poorly in an area than expected, given their overall level of intelligence. By definition, learning disabilities are not the result of other causes such as mental retardation or hearing and vision impairment.

Like other children, children with mental retardation may sometimes have more problems in one area of learning than another. But for the most part, experts do not classify these problems as learning disabilities. This is because it is impossible to say whether or not the extra difficulties are caused by mental retardation—and, as explained above, bona fide learning disabilities are *not* caused by mental retardation. Instead, a child with mental retardation may be described as having specific strengths and weaknesses, or specific learning difficulties. For example, some children with mental retardation may have greater-than-expected difficulty with eye-hand coordination and may therefore have extra problems with handwriting or completing puzzles. Or a child with mental retardation may learn to count but have great difficulty following the teacher's directions to count more quietly. Often, children with Down syndrome learn to read fairly well, but have great difficulty acquiring basic math skills.

There is no medical treatment for learning difficulties of this nature. But being aware of their existence can help you and your child's teachers plan ways to help your child overcome his learning weaknesses. For example, if your child has extra trouble writing, he might have more success with a computer. If he has difficulty following spoken directions, the teacher might try communicating with pictures or manual signs and gestures. Teachers can give special emphasis to your child's problem areas, and together you can work to discover how your child learns best.

Paul has terrible visual perception. But he can spell and he can memorize telephone numbers. He knows everybody's telephone number.

He's much more into drawing then sports. Drawing is something he can do well. But he's always had a hard time throwing, kicking, or catching a ball.

═══ ※ ═══

She does things that surprise us, but she also does things that are really lower than we think they should be for somebody who has these other abilities.

Cerebral Palsy

"Cerebral palsy" is a catchall term for a variety of disorders of movement, balance, and coordination. It occurs in about 1 to 2 births out of a thousand, and is caused by damage to the brain before birth, during birth, or within the first three years after birth. This damage may be due to premature birth and associated complications such as brain hemorrhage, or to head injury, stroke, or infections such as meningitis. In some cases, the damage may be traced to a genetic condition in the fetus that prevents the brain from developing normally. In 20 to 30 percent of children with cerebral palsy, there is no known cause. Brain damage does not worsen over the course of a child's life; that is, cerebral palsy is not a progressive disorder.

The precise symptoms produced by cerebral palsy depend on the location of the brain injury. Brain injuries may affect movement on one or both sides of the body, in one, two, three, or all limbs. They also cause a variety of problems with *muscle tone*—the amount of tension or resistance to movement in a muscle. Muscle tone may be abnormally high (*hypertonic*), so that movements are harder to make, or it may be abnormally low (*hypotonic*), so that movements are floppy and difficult to control. Cerebral palsy may also cause jerking and other involuntary movements of parts of the body. Frequently, muscle tone problems affect the muscles needed for speech; 75 to 90 percent of children with cerebral palsy have some delays or difficulties with speech. They may have problems with articulation of sounds or with rhythm, or have a harsh or breathy voice quality.

Because of these problems with movement and speech, it is often hard to evaluate the cognitive abilities of children with cerebral palsy. They may be physically unable to point to the correct response on an IQ test or even to indicate a "yes" or "no" response. As a result, in years past many children with cerebral palsy were mistakenly diagnosed with mental retardation. With improved communication technology, this is less likely to happen. Today, researchers think that about 25 percent of children with cerebral palsy have some mental retardation.

If your child has cerebral palsy in addition to mental retardation, his delays will be compounded. As mentioned earlier, your child will probably have special difficulties with speech. He may also have additional cognitive delays if he is unable to move around and explore his world. For example, he may have trouble learning the concepts "around," "over," and "through" if he is unable to crawl over or around objects, and he may have problems learning about cause and effect if he is unable to knock down a tower of blocks or otherwise try out the concept. In addition, it may be hard to determine which of your child's motor delays result from his cerebral palsy, and which from his mental retardation.

Because the movement problems of cerebral palsy can influence your child's development so profoundly, it is essential to minimize them as much as possible. From an early age, your child should be seen by a team of medical and therapeutic professionals in addition to his special education teacher. As your child grows older, the physician and physical therapist may recommend casts, splints, or special molded devices (*orthotics*) to make movements easier for him. An orthopedic surgeon may suggest operations on your child's bones or soft tissues (muscles, tendons, ligaments) to ease or prevent movement problems. The speech pathologist will work to improve your child's speech or to develop alternate means of communication, and the physical or occupational therapist will use exercises and therapeutic techniques to enhance your child's movement skills. Particularly if your child has mild retardation, he may also see a psychologist or psychiatrist to help him deal with frustrations at not being able to control his movements and speech. Last, but not least, you as a parent will play an essential part in helping your child reach his full potential and maturity. You may need to coordinate the services from the professionals on your child's team, and you will most certainly be asked to work on movement, communication, and other goals at home with your child.

—— ✳ ——

There was a time when I worried that maybe she would never walk, although nobody ever said that to me. It was just sort of inconceivable that maybe she **wouldn't** walk. I felt impatient to have that happen. Now she can walk with a walker, although she's never walked by herself. My new worry is her speech.

Dealing with Medical Professionals

Whatever your child's special needs, enlisting the aid of caring, competent medical professionals is the key to helping him make the most of his abilities. To ensure that your child receives the best possible care, both you and the medical professionals must be sensitive to the unique needs of your child and your family. For example, a child who has moderate mental retardation and epilepsy will have different needs than a child who has mild retardation and speech problems. And a family that has limited funds to spend on medical specialists will have different considerations than a family with ample funds. Finding affordable medical professionals with the training and understanding to work with your child may not be easy. Unlike other parents, you can't simply look for someone who is "board certified" or licensed in his or her area of practice or specialization. Here are some suggestions to get you started on your search:

1. Ask other parents of children with mental retardation about medical professionals their child has seen. The grapevine, while not always accurate, may be useful in narrowing down the field.
2. Try contacting a university-affiliated medical school in your area. They often have top-notch professionals with years of experience in their field of expertise. Make sure when you make an appointment, though, that your child will actually see the physician you requested and not a resident or medical student.
3. If your area has a children's hospital or regional developmental evaluation clinic, check into the services they provide. These facilities offer a wide range of professional services, often for a fee based upon family income. (Look under "Public Health Clinic" or "Physicians/Pediatricians: Developmental Pediatricians" in your phone book.)
4. Your physician or your child's pediatrician can be a good source of names for specialists such as neurologists and ophthalmologists. So, too, can the local ARC.

Once you have set up an initial appointment, your search is not necessarily over. You will want to determine as quickly as possible whether the physician will be responsive to your needs, or whether you should keep looking. In general, it may help if you think about what you value in *your* physician—whether it's technical skills, personality, demeanor, or availability—then use these values as your guides.

You may want to begin by asking the professional what kind of training and experience he or she has had with children with mental retardation or any other disabilities your child has. Next, try to get a feel for his attitude toward you and your child. Does he show respect for your child as a person, spending time talking with him, explaining or demonstrating what will take place before doing a medical procedure? Can your child communicate with him and vice versa? Does he treat you as an expert with knowledge about your child that only you could have? Does he seem to value your opinion?

While you are trying to gauge the suitability of the physician, pay attention to the kinds of explanations he offers you. It is very important that the physician speak in a language you can understand, and not withhold any information vital to the well-being of your child. Whenever a test is to be performed, he should carefully explain the procedure and any risks involved and let you know if there may be side effects of medications. He should welcome your questions and make sure you understand the answers. Just as importantly, he should show respect for your feelings and those of your child, no matter what news he has to tell you. He should be able to explain information humanely, never in an off-hand or cruel manner. In short, he should treat you like a real person with real feelings, not like just another $100 office visit.

Of course, you may not be able to make a judgement about all these factors on your first visit. And there are other questions that it may take you several weeks or months to find the answers to. For example, there may be some times when it is more critical for your child to receive immediate medical care than others. How responsive is the physician in emergency situations? Does he make room in his schedule to see you and your child right away?

Remember that no two physicians, psychiatrists, neurologists, or other specialists are alike. If you have had a difficult or bad experience before, explain the problem to the professional who will see your child. Also explain what you expect from *this* evaluation or visit. Tell the doctor when you are pleased and thankful for the services you have received, and also tell him when you are not pleased.

Above all, be honest with yourself and the physician. Be honest about things that are happening at home, your lifestyle, and practical limitations on your time and energy. For example, let the doctor know if you cannot afford a particular test for your child because you have just lost your job, or if you would like help breaking your child of the habit of sleeping with you. Be honest about how much time you can devote to your child's education and treatment. (Remember, the rest of your family needs you, too.) Also try to be honest with yourself about your child's skills and limitations so you can have realistic expectations about how much the physician or specialist can do for your child. And if, in all honesty, you do not think the physician or specialist is doing a good enough job, go elsewhere. After all, it's your child and your money!

Even if you are basically satisfied with your physician, you should never hesitate to ask for a second opinion. Feel free to consult another doctor whenever you have any questions about other treatment options, or are unsure that your child's progress or improvment is as great as it should be. You should also seek another opinion when your current physician is unwilling to change your child's treatment or try another approach when the current approach is ineffective or unsuccessful.

As you begin to assemble a team of competent, compassionate professionals to care for your child, you may find that you need to take on the role of a *case manager.* That is, it may be up to you to make sure that all the various professionals on your child's team are kept informed about your child's problems and treatments. You may also need to juggle the many logistical and scheduling problems associated with coordinating medical and other professional consultations. You will need to keep track of when your child needs to be seen again by a given specialist, and also follow any recommendations he or she may make for you and your child's regular pediatrician to carry out. Be sure to keep a file with copies of reports from each evaluation performed on your child. That way you will always have this information at your fingertips whenever educational or medical professionals are making plans for your child. Finally, every time that professionals meet to discuss your child and his treatment, you should see that they use the opportunity to plan and make sure that your child receives all the evaluations and professional consultations he needs.

Besides acting as your child's case manager, you should also do what you can to make sure doctor visits or hospitalizations are as pleasant as possible for your child. If your child is to have a potentially traumatic test or procedure, it often helps to visit the doctor's office in advance to let your child get accustomed to the surroundings and the people. You can also prepare him by telling him a simple story with a happy ending about the upcoming visit or procedure. To minimize waiting time, try to schedule appointments for periods when the doctor is less busy. And before you leave the house, always call ahead to find out if the doctor is behind schedule. Finally, be prepared to explain your child's special needs not only to the doctor, but to his staff. For example, if your child becomes very uneasy in a crowded, noisy waiting room, ask the receptionist if you can wait in an examination room instead. If your child is very sensitive to touch around his face, tell the audiologist *before* she tries to put earphones on your child's head.

The pediatrician and neurologist we have now are great. Anything that I have every requested that they do for him they have done. He's had CATs, MRIs. Anytime I've read about a new procedure and said to them, "Well, let's see if this shows anything," they've done it. They have never questioned my judgement.

I got really angry with a doctor once when Paul was two. First the doctor was about an hour and a half late seeing us. Then when we got in, he hadn't read the records, so he started to read them in front of us. Paul was already tired.

We always had to go from one professional to the next and try to put everything together ourselves. We were really the case managers. No one else would assume the responsibility for it.

From the beginning, we've always <u>felt</u> privy to what is in Kathleen's records, although most doctors don't automatically share it all. So I used to sneak a look when the doctor walked out instead of saying "Give me a copy of this."

The best doctors we've found are the ones who'll just say, "Okay, I'll go along and support the parents because I don't know if it will work, but maybe it's worth a try."

Conclusion

Children with mental retardation, like all children, have a wide range of physical and emotional needs. It is true that the disorders mentioned in this chapter may limit your child's abilities and skill development. But it is also true that these disabilities do not place any set limitations on your child's potential. It is impossible to predict a child's potential at a very early age, especially when the child has handicaps that make assessment of abilities more difficult. Talk to all the professionals who know and work with your child, as well as to other parents, and then set realistic, yet optimistic goals. Reach for the next skill without undue worry about where your child will be ten years from now.

If your child has other disorders in addition to mental retardation, learn all you can about them. The Reading List at the back of the book lists useful publications that can help you get started. If there are new treatments that may help improve your child's symptoms, discuss them with the appropriate professional and decide if they might benefit your child. Evaluate these treatments on the basis of gains or improvement you see in your child, and periodically ask his doctors and teachers about trying different strategies.

You cannot cure your child's disabilities. You cannot make his disorders go away or prevent them from influencing his growth, learning, or development. Nor can you sacrifice your family or yourself by dedicating all of your hours to your child. But you *can* develop a positive attitude toward life and living and communicate this attitude to your child. With professionals, you can become a partner in your child's treatment and education and see that his medical and educational problems are minimized. Most importantly, you can be a loving and supportive parent and appreciate your child for what he *can* do, rather than what he cannot do.

Ten

=== ❊ ===

Advocacy: Fighting for Your Child—Fighting for What is Right!

Helen Reisner *

When I was asked to write a chapter about advocacy for this book, I said I'd think about it. I didn't want to agree to write about something so important without first giving it some serious thought. I wanted to make sure I had something helpful to say on the subject and that I could actually put it into words. After weeks of thinking about what to write, throwing away page after page, doing a lot of reading, and struggling with the message of advocacy, I realized I was going about it all wrong. What parents need is not a step-by-step, cookbook approach to advocacy, but an understanding of the philosophy of advocacy. Publications on the nuts and bolts of asking questions, going to IEP meetings, and fighting for integrated day-care and school placements abound. So this chapter will focus primarily on how to feel powerful and how to feel right about speaking up for your child.

Of course, if you have recently learned that your child has mental retardation, you might not be feeling especially powerful right now. In fact, you might be feeling helpless and bewildered and downright incapable of taking decisive action. How do you get to

* Helen Reisner is an Information and Referral Specialist for the United Cerebral Palsy Associations, Inc., in Washington, D.C. She is the editor of *Children with Epilepsy: A Parents' Guide* (Woodbine House, 1988) and the executive producer of a documentary film about epilepsy, *Just Like You and Me*. Ms. Reisner is the mother of three children, one of whom has mental retardation.

the point where you're ready to stop grieving over the parts of your child's life you can't control so you can begin to take control of the parts that you can? Here's my story:

About seven years ago, my perfect baby developed a devastating type of seizure called infantile spasms. Naturally, I didn't know a thing about seizures and had never even heard of infantile spasms. As the doctors explained what infantile spasms would mean to my son, I heard only two words: "mental retardation." I was scared—for him. I only knew what I could recall about the astonishingly few people I had ever known who had mental retardation. One was a girl named Maureen who lived in the country near us when I was growing up. When she was outside, we would sometimes stop by her yard and swing with her. Her mother was always beside her. Maureen didn't talk, and sometimes when she bit or pinched us, we ran away from her. Then one day Maureen disappeared. She just ceased living at home and none of us ever knew where she went. Her mom was still in the yard sometimes when we went by, but Maureen was not.

Many years later, I went to a concert at a college in central Pennsylvania that happened to be near an institution. That night the institution bought tickets for about fifty or so residents, who came to the concert in a large group accompanied by the institution staff. They sat together and seemed to enjoy themselves, but to everyone else there, they were different and separate. An amazing thing happened to me that night. When I went to the rest room during intermission, I saw Maureen. I recognized her immediately, even after all those years. I spoke to her and she responded, but I was obviously a stranger to her. I left the concert feeling a strange mixture of curiosity, wonder, compassion, and deep regret that we used to run away from Maureen.

So, when the doctors told me that infantile spasms usually meant mental retardation, memories and emotions came rushing back. But it took me years to learn what mental retardation really is, and even after seven years, I don't consider myself an expert on the subject. Sure, you can read books on mental retardation, consult "experts," and have your child tested, but these things can never really show you what mental retardation is truly about. Each person—each child—is so different and unique that no professional, test, or book can reveal who they truly are. In the end, I came to realize that only people with mental retardation can teach us what mental retardation is. They are people first. And that, I think, is what the doctors left out on that unforgettable night when they explained to me that my baby would develop mental retardation.

They also left out a lot of other information. I have since realized that I turned to them for information and direction that they simply did not possess. I needed other parents to show me the way in the world of disability. The doctor did give me one piece of advice, though, which I resented at the time. Now I thoroughly understand what he meant. He told me, "I cannot answer your questions. I cannot tell you what to expect or what he will become. You'll just have to go home and live it."

Well, we went home and our whole family went through major adjustments living it. In some respects, my story is probably similar to many; in other respects, dramatically different. But it's not my story that is important for me to share here; it is the number one lesson I learned about being the mother of a child with mental retardation. The lesson I learned is that *I* have to work to make sure my son's life has dignity and that he has the chance to make it in this world to the best of his ability. Nothing matters more to my child's future than defending his rights as a citizen of the United States and his right to live and participate fully in the community. And it is through advocacy—the topic of this chapter—that his rights and his future can be protected.

What is Advocacy?

Technically, advocacy means pleading another's cause or speaking up for the rights of others. But what it boils down to is nothing more than believing in yourself and your child—and speaking up. That is all. The first part, believing that what you know about your child is true, is easy. If you have faith in your intuition, if you recognize that common sense often makes good sense, then there is a strong foundation for advocacy. The second part, speaking up effectively, usually has to be learned. Most parents have no trouble getting motivated to learn advocacy skills, however, when they realize that advocacy means speaking up for their children and ultimately, sticking up for their children's right to live, work, and play in the community right along with everyone else. Period.

Most likely, you have already engaged in advocacy. When you began to realize that something was wrong with your child's development, perhaps you spoke up. Maybe you had to convince the doctor or teacher to do something different, or to look at your child another way. Maybe you've had to educate the parents of other children in the neighborhood, people in the post office, or your own parents. Maybe, like me, you didn't know too much about mental retardation and had only some vague recollections from your past. Now that you have a family member who has mental retardation, you've silently taken the vow to defend her. I stood beside my innocent, sleeping child and swore to myself that I'd protect him, fight for him, defend him, and love him—no matter what.

The role you'll play as an advocate will vary and you'll have highs and lows, ups and downs, successes and failures. Expect that. But never give up. Regardless of what happens today, this month, or this year, we are all in for the long haul. We won't always get exactly what we think is best for our children, but at least we'll be striving toward it.

Becoming an Advocate

There are no special requirements for becoming an advocate. It does not require a college degree or years of training. There are really just three steps. The first step is believing in your child. The second step is believing in yourself and your intuition. The third step is educating yourself. From there you can move on to actual advocacy—to educating others. Because your life will naturally provide you with plenty of practice in speaking up, anguishing over how you come across is not one of the steps to advocacy. As long as you take the first three steps and then "speak from the heart," you'll come across just fine.

If you stop to notice, you will be amazed at how many different forms advocacy can take. You will have to speak up for your child with medical professionals, insurance agents, teachers, babysitters, friends, relatives, and the general public. You've probably already had that universal favorite—the grocery store encounter, in which you explain your child's behavior, language, or appearance to a complete stranger. Yes, even there you were an advocate for your child. You were educating others about mental retardation.

Some Advocacy Basics

Here are some suggestions about following the three steps to becoming an advocate:

Step 1. It's worth repeating: Believe in your child! Always. As your child grows up, you'll watch her develop skills and acquire knowledge that may never be revealed by tests. Write her achievements down in a journal. Keep it simple, but write it down.

Step 2. Believe in yourself. You are your child's best advocate and best friend. You know her better than anyone else. You are the constant in her life. Professionals will come and go during your child's lifetime, but you will remain. You have the big picture gathered from years of living with and observing your child. You have the long-term interests of your child in mind. Because of this, you have very important information to share that no one else has. Sharing it is advocacy. Writing it down is good sense.

Step 3. Educate yourself about mental retardation, disability programs, laws, and advocacy procedures. Reading this book is one step toward becoming an advocate. Call the ARC, your local federally funded parent training and information center (PTIC), Parent-to-Parent organizations and support groups, and the National Information Center for Children and Youth with Disabilities (NICH-CY). Contact information for these organizations can be found in the Resource Guide at the end of this book. Send away for free information from the national organizations, subscribe to parent magazines, and make a point to meet other parents. Nobody can give you as much education as another parent.

You do not have to know everything to be your child's advocate. Being an informed advocate or an informed consumer does not mean that you have to become a walking encyclopedia of disability law. Far from it. It is much more important to know where to find information than it is to know everything. There are disability advocates and information providers all over the place. They can be found at the organizations mentioned above and in this book's Resource Guide. Remember *your* role: know your child and become a part of the team that advocates for her. That's the key.

When you ask for information, consider the source. Learning from another advocate is not the same as learning from the agency administering or delivering a service. For example, if you call the teacher, special education director, or the Department of Education, you're likely to get information that has a slightly different twist to it than if you call an advocate at the ARC, PTIC, or Parent-to-Parent program. When someone has worked the system to get services, their perspective is a little bit different from that of the person responsible for administering a program. You want to learn from people who have walked the path before you and have some experience. Often, staff members at the ARC, PTIC, and Parent-to-Parent are parents themselves. They have a child in the system. They know the ropes. They are there to help newcomers, share their experience, and give you insight. Talk to them.

As you educate yourself, you'll soon discover that systems have evolved over the years to meet the needs of children with disabilities. Although this chapter focuses mainly on the educational and medical systems, be aware that helping your child receive the best educational and medical services will be just the beginning. Your child also has other program options such as SSI and Medicaid, which are covered in Chapter 8. Your child may be eligible for services that can be explained to you by the ARC or the PTIC. Down the road, after the school years are over, housing, vocational education, employment, and community living will become priorities. But the key to your child's eventual participation in all these programs is you, for now.

Whether you are trying to learn about SSI, Medicaid, or special education and related services (speech/language therapy, occupational therapy, physical therapy, transportation, recreation, counseling), the way you'll go about finding the information is the same. Different federal agencies oversee the many programs that are regulated by federal law. Each state writes up its own state plan for administering the service in the state. For example, states submit special education plans for approval to the federal Department of Education. The state plan is actually a contract with the federal government about how the state will spend the federal dollars that it receives. The way services are delivered may vary slightly from state to state and county to county; federal law, however, is the backbone of each system. (This is explained more in Chapter 8.)

The best and most complete information you'll ever get about your child's rights is from the law itself. For example, get a copy of the laws that provide for special education. You can do this by calling your congressman or your local PTIC. You can also call or write the U.S. Senate or House of Representative document rooms at the addresses given in the Resource Guide at the back of this book. To find out the names of the laws, their numbers, and a general summary of what they provide, call NICHCY and ask for the pamphlet called "The Education of Children and Youth with Special Needs: What Do the Laws Say?" Another important resource, although somewhat dated, is called *Summary of Existing Legislation Affecting Persons with Disabilities* (1988. Publication No. E-88-22014, U.S. Department of Education, Office of Special Education and Rehabilitative Services, Clearinghouse on the Handicapped, Washington, DC 20202-2524). Call your local ARC or PTIC for a copy of the State Plan for implementing special education in your state. Then call the Special Education Director at your local school district and ask for a copy of the school district's policy for implementing special education.

One truly outstanding book about advocacy is *Educational Rights of Children with Disabilities: A Primer for Advocates*, by Eileen L. Ordover and Kathleen B. Boundy (For ordering information, contact the Center for Law and Education, 955 Massachusetts Avenue, Cambridge, MA 02139, 617/876-6611.) Read it.

Also consider signing up for parent training at the ARC or PTIC. These organizations offer courses that train parents in using federal and state special education laws to their fullest and in protecting their child's rights. The courses are usually free. Still more help is available from two federally funded agencies charged with protecting the rights of people with disabilities. One is often referred to as the DD Council, which stands for the Developmental Disabilities Council, and the other is referred to as the P&A, or Protection and Advocacy agency. Both are strong, advocacy-oriented agencies and can give you information about your state's services. You may call them any time you like and ask them any question you have. Both agencies are there to help you and to advocate for you. Information on contacting your state DD Council and P&A can be found in the Resource Guide of this book.

Wherever you turn for answers, don't be shy about asking questions. You are entering what is called "the service delivery system." Think of yourself as a customer. You are going to buy something and you want to know as much as possible before you buy it. For example, let's say that your child is about to begin going to school. You wonder if she could go to the neighborhood school with her older brother. You could ask the teacher or principal. And he or she could say "no" or "she would learn better in a special school" or give any number of reasons. However, if you understand that going to the neighborhood school is permitted today, you can begin to gather facts to support your request. Read books and articles. Ask whatever questions pop into your mind. And remember: *There are no stupid questions.* If you get the feeling that your child's program just isn't meeting her needs or could be improved, listen to your intuition, gather information, and speak up. You are not alone.

When my son first entered an early intervention program, I was naive. I didn't really know the law, and I floated through his first placement meeting blindly. The placement I requested for my son was denied. Rather than giving him the home-based program he needed due to a seriously diminished immune system, he was placed in a center-based preschool education program. I was told he'd spend a year there being evaluated. Not knowing any better, I went along.

On his first day, we arrived at a school for children and young people with special needs up to twenty-one years of age. For the first time in my life, I saw lots and lots of people who all had mental retardation. I was numb from the shock. My son was only thirteen months old. He hadn't even received a definite diagnosis of mental retardation then, so why was he supposed to go to this school? Did somebody forget to tell me something? I felt angry and betrayed. To top it off, the rest of the little children in his class were all walking and sort of talking. They sat in chairs and in a circle while the teacher sang songs and played games with them. My son sat on my lap and watched. When the other children painted or played with toys, he lay on the floor like a little slug. The physical therapist spent short amounts of time with all the children. The speech/language therapist wasn't available for a few weeks, and, I was told, there wasn't an occupational therapist yet. I was confused. The document I was given at the placement meeting said he was supposed to receive therapy every day. I knew something wasn't right but I didn't know who to talk to about it.

When I left that little classroom and walked through the school with all the older children and young adults, my intuition screamed at me to do something and do it quick. I believed I was right—I believed my child needed something different—but the other parents seemed happy. The teacher wasn't too concerned, either. However, she did tell me about a parent training class. Rather than let self-doubt take over, I went to the class.

I was right. I learned that my son's IEP was a contract with the school district and that the services indicated on it were to be provided, no ifs, ands, or buts. I learned all about special education law and how it was implemented in my state and school district. I learned that a form of protection called "due process" is built into the law. I learned that I could appeal his placement if I felt it was inappropriate. I learned that parents are granted the right to be a part of the team that writes the IEP. I learned that all I had to do was gather information and speak up. Mostly I learned that the squeaky wheel really *does* get the grease.

I appealed my son's placement, following the due process procedure outlined in the law, and the home-based program was approved. Eventually, my son's health improved and his special education program was changed to reflect his individualized special education needs. But it was what *I* learned that enabled me to stand up effectively for him.

If there's one thing I could wish for parents who are at the beginning stages of all this, it would be assertiveness. You've got to be assertive, because you're it. You've got to trust your own information and trust your own judgment. You know your kid better than anybody else.

If I think that his home school is the best place for him and they don't allow him to go there, I will probably fight them. But if I lose, I wouldn't want the teachers to hold it against him.

The school is going to get a physical therapist and she is going to observe our daughter and then make a recommendation on how many minutes of therapy per week she thinks our daughter needs. But I'm going to be right there, and we have always gotten what we wanted our daughter to have. You have to be a lawyer for your child: if you can prove that this is the best thing for your child, the school system goes along with it.

The Future

Another important part of your personal education, which is often overlooked, is to take a good look at your child's future. Just do it. Go with your parent support group, or another parent, and visit an institution and a group home. This is important to do because your child will be thrust out of the special education system when she reaches twenty-one years of age. You need to find out what will be there for her when the yellow school bus stops coming each morning.

My visits provided me with a new perspective and gave me the commitment to help my child gain as much as possible toward independence now. Just as with other children, our children's special education is the foundation of their future independence. Carefully look at your child's strengths and preferences and build her program around them. Just as you ask other kids what they want to be when they grow up, you should think along the same lines with your child with mental retardation. Time passes quickly. Building your child's future into today's programming is not only essential, but required by law. The IDEA requires transition planning for all

children in special education. But transition to what? Go and see what exists now and you'll get a clear view of the services that are available today for adults with mental retardation. You'll understand why parents feel committed to advocate. You'll understand why parents band together and speak up.

═══ ※ ═══

Our daughter's future is very scary because we are very aware of the lack of adult services. We don't know how independent she will be. She needs a lot of support, but she also has some very interesting skills.

═══ ※ ═══

We feel we need to fight for Carl's rights so he can reach his absolute potential. Otherwise, we're afraid he might be stagnating with a box of cookies in front of the TV set when the school system isn't there for him any more.

Being a Smart Advocate

Before you charge full steam ahead, here are some tips I have learned from experience. You can use these tips as a starting point until you learn your own style of advocacy and develop your own tricks for making the job easier and more successful.

Get Help

For parents, it often seems easy to advocate for someone else, as long as that someone else is not your own child. When faced with a conference room full of professionals all focused on your child, you may feel caught between wanting to come across effectively and wanting to protect your child by not saying anything that might upset "them." You may bite your tongue instead of saying what you really want to, because you may fear that your child might be treated differently. You are also very emotionally involved with your child and it's hard to put that parental love and concern aside even temporarily.

The answer to this universal dilemma is easy. Take along someone who can keep you from losing your temper or becoming too emotional, and can help you say what you mean tactfully. Take a friend, your spouse, another parent of a child with disabilities, or an advocate. Again, call the ARC, the PTIC, the Parent to Parent, the P&A, or the DD Council. There are professional advocates you can hire to help you and there are people who volunteer with organizations as advocates. Try not to wait until the last minute before an important meeting to ask for help. Being well prepared is essential. But sometimes you just won't have the time or any forewarning. You might get a disturbing note in your child's backpack and you'll need to act immediately. Even at the last minute, you may still be able to find help from the organizations and agencies mentioned above. Ask for help.

If you look for help in advocating for your child, be choosy and follow your intuition. If you get an uneasy feeling about the person who will be helping you advocate, find someone else. Finding someone you trust who is on the same wavelength as you is essential. Working with someone who shares your drive to get what you want for your child is better than working with someone who might know the ropes but comes across like a cold fish. You want to find someone who can arouse respect, as well as an emotional response in others. Trust *your* instincts.

Develop Relationships

Developing relationships throughout your child's life is important to both you and your child. It will help you immensely to get to know people like teachers, therapists, administrators, government officials, medical professionals, and advocates and to keep them up-to-date on how you and your child are doing. The flip side of the coin is that you'll discover that many people are genuinely concerned and interested in you and your child. They welcome your communication. You are sharing important information. For example, you can tell school administrators how their programs are actually being implemented. And you can give teachers the "home picture" of your child—what she can and cannot do at home.

It is important to get to know the people who work with your child. First and foremost, teachers, teacher's aides, therapists, cafeteria workers, bus drivers, and others have an interest in your child. Just as we respond to friendliness, so do they. I'm not saying that you are supposed to befriend everyone in your child's world; rather, let people get to know you. They are there to help and they spend a great deal of time with your child. They observe her when you are not around and may have valuable information to share with you about her. These little tidbits add to the picture of your child and her behavior. They help you learn what your child is capable of out of your sight, and help you better gauge her educational and other needs. Help open the doors to communication. Keep people up-to-date and let them know that you appreciate their insight.

Get It in Writing!

This is the most important tip. Whatever you do, do not fail to *take notes*. Sometimes you might balk at writing down one more thing, but do it anyway. You don't have to keep anything fancier than just a running record. What works best for me is a composition-style notebook that is sewn together rather than spiral bound. (I prefer this type because if I rip out a page, it begins to fall apart, so I don't rip out pages!) Every time I talk to someone, I write down the date, the name and number of the person, and where they work. I jot down what I asked and what they answered. If I think that what they are saying is important, I ask them to put it in writing. If you follow this procedure, it will help you put your efforts into an organized, chronological order. You can go back through your notebook and build a case if you need to.

Don't stop writing just because you are on the phone. It is especially critical to document important phone conversations. Remember, too, that the old-fashioned method of writing to people instead of calling them makes a great deal of sense if you're not in a crisis. True, sitting down and writing a simple, straightforward letter takes a few minutes, but then you can mail away your letter and forget about it for awhile. (Be sure to keep a copy!) No children will be scrambling for your attention as they do when you're on the phone, and you can take the time to put your thoughts in order. Writing is far less stressful, and you're usually guaranteed a response, which, by the way, is your solid documentation. A phone conversation can be forgotten, misinterpreted, or denied. A letter is proof. If your child is being denied a service, you'll know precisely why and you'll have it in writing. NICHCY has a good publication called "A Parent's Guide—Special Education and Related Services: Communicating Through Letter Writing." It is a sensible how-to guide that can also be used as a guide for writing letters about any subject.

If you are writing a letter to express an important complaint about inappropriate services or to request services that are being denied, you should send copies of it to other people and note that on the letter itself. For instance, if the school bus is repeatedly late, even after you've made many phone calls and verbal complaints, a letter to the director of transportation, with copies to the special education director, the superintendent of schools, the school board president, the ARC, the P&A, and the Department of Education will usually solve the problem. In some cases, you'll want to send a copy of your letter to local, state, and national elected officials. Don't forget that federal representatives want to hear what is going on in their jurisdictions.

When you write or speak to someone, anecdotes are one of the most useful tools you have. Using your own personal experiences to illustrate your point will help officials empathize with your problem. I clearly remember trying to find a playgroup/nursery school for my son to go to on days he didn't have regular school. I was trying to integrate him with non-disabled kids his own age. It was not easy. I went from program to program alone, without support and guidance from knowledgeable advocates. Eventually, I discovered an advocacy agency that helped parents locate integrated child care, and found an integrated setting for my son.

Not long afterwards, my county council began considering cutting funds for this agency. I was able to share with the council a specific example to try to persuade them to reconsider. I told them that I had spent about six weeks visiting schools. I had taken my son along each time and he had been expected to immediately join in, play, and follow instructions while the teachers watched his every move. We faced rejection after rejection. The repeated rejections sapped my energy and will, and sometimes it seemed easier just to give up. One school director took my son and me into her office and tried to be nice when she told us that my son didn't fit in. She said that he had too many needs and that they didn't have enough staff to help him. This was all baloney. It was a co-op school where mothers routinely helped out. My child was actually more cooperative, congenial, and less of a behavior problem than some of the other two-year-old terrors in the class. It was his lack of language, his mental retardation, and his potential for seizures that scared them. But she wouldn't tell me that. As I got up to leave, I picked up my son and he looked over my shoulder and smiled at her. She said, "He has such a pretty smile, though."

I think that the people on the council listened to my story and put themselves in my shoes for a minute. They felt the unnecessary rejection we had experienced. They funded the agency to help parents find integrated child care.

Don't forget people after the fight is over. Thank you letters are important. Let teachers, administrators, elected officials, and others know when things are going well. You never know when you might need their help again.

Rather than pushing her to do her best, the teachers clung to their notions about mental retardation. I tried to convince them not to pay so much attention to the label. So what if kids with that label aren't expected to make so much progress in reading? I thought my daughter could make greater progress, so I spoke up.

From the time she was two years old, we have advocated for every placement that she's had. Had we let the system decide, who knows where she would have ended up? Sometimes we had to battle it through, but at least we had support. We used whatever help was available.

Advocating in the Medical Community

Making sure that your child's medical needs are met is an important form of advocacy. It is also a potential source of extreme frustration. For example, how many times have you called the pediatrician or gone to the office with your child, knowing full well something was very wrong, only to be told that the only thing wrong is your own stress and that your child "looks fine." And how hard did you have to work to convince doctors to finally get serious about delays in your child's development? Challenging doctors about their science is more difficult than challenging educators about their programs. Although parents can learn the rules of education, learning medicine isn't as easy.

Despite the differences between educational and medical advocacy, this is an arena in which you can still rely on the basics of advocacy outlined earlier. Believe in your child and trust and educate yourself. Speak up: If you can do it with teachers, administrators, lawyers, and elected officials, you can do it with doctors.

Frankly, I had to become a nuisance to my son's pediatrician to get him to examine my son for epilepsy. I knew he was having seizures, yet the doctor never saw one and for some reason was not familiar with the kind my son was having. I took my son and literally sat in the doctor's office all day so the doctor could actually see a seizure for himself. And that was just the beginning. Since then, I've had my work cut out to convince the doctors to assist me with speech/language therapy, occupational therapy, and the prescriptions for orthotics and other devices. Frequently they have given me the impression that they just did not want to put themselves on the line.

Here are some suggestions about advocating in this field. First, talk with other parents to find physicians who have interest and expertise in working with children with mental retardation. Otherwise, you'll end up wasting your time while *you* educate your child's doctor. Second, get in touch with the Association for the Care of Children's Health (ACCH), which is a policy and advocacy organization for families with acute or chronically ill children. This association publishes books and pamphlets that can help you explain illnesses and medical procedures to your child, as well as help you become an effective medical advocate. ACCH also has a national parent network that can put you in touch with parents who can help answer your questions. The address and telephone number for ACCH are listed in the Resource Guide in this book.

One useful book that can help you learn about medical advocacy is called *Special Needs—Special Solutions: How to Get Quality Care for a Child with Special Health Needs, A Guide to Health Services and How to Pay for Them*. It is written by Georgianna Larson and Judith A. Kahn (1990. Lifeline Press, 2324 University Avenue West, Suite 105, St. Paul, MN 55114). This book covers many important issues, from working as a team member with medical professionals, to types of health care coverage, to record keeping.

If you run into health insurance problems, you can request guidance from the consumer advocate in the office of your state's Insurance Commission. Insurance Commissions are found in different departments in different states: call the state government information number listed in your phone book to request the number. In addition, each disability organization and most of the PTICs have insurance and medical systems experts. Their services are usually free, so take advantage of them. The P&A system mentioned earlier can also help with insurance coverage or Medicaid reimbursement issues.

When submitting health insurance claims for a child with special needs, documentation is essential. Services such as speech/language therapy, physical therapy, and occupational therapy, and items such as augmentative communication devices and other durable medical equipment must all be documented as medically necessary. Keep copies of all correspondence and insurance claims forms. Get in touch with the advocacy agencies named earlier for more information on how to document medical necessity. Ask your doctor, too.

In educating yourself, remember one of the most forgotten resources—the library. You can find a wealth of information about your child's medical condition at the public library, and also at the medical library of nearby teaching hospitals. You can work closely with the reference librarian at your local public library to find out what books or journals would be most useful.

Other important resources are the many University Affiliated Programs (UAP) located in universities around the country. UAPs can provide you with information and referral to other programs in your state. Individual UAPs have staff with expertise in a variety of medical and developmental areas, and can provide information, technical assistance, and inservice training to agencies, service providers, and parent groups, to name a few. To locate a UAP in your state, contact NICHCY, your local PTIC, or the National Association of University Affiliated Programs (listed in the Resource Guide). Feel free to call them to find help.

Ensuring that your child receives quality medical care can tax even the most intrepid and assertive parent. But the ultimate decisions about your child's treatment are in your hands. So, like it or not, you are an equal partner of your child's medical team. Act like one: get the facts and speak up.

Power in Numbers—Class Advocacy

You might be the most informed and skilled parent-advocate, backed up by an array of professional advocates, and still have no power to get what you know is best for your child. Why? Because what you want is simply not available. Why? Because no law or government regulation requires it. In the areas of education, day care, vocational training, employment, health care, community living, and discrimination, there are many gaps and inadequacies in federal, state, and local laws and regulations. If laws do not provide for services or mandate fairness or access, you can be sure they won't magically appear.

You can also be sure that local, state, and federal elected representatives do not spend every waking moment thinking of new ways to help people with disabilities. Usually, they have to be pushed— sometimes quite hard—to do the right thing. And the more people who push, and the more effectively they work together to push, the greater the chances are that our representatives will respond. This is class advocacy: speaking up for a group of people.

Too often in the past, people with disabilities and their families have failed to speak up. That has been changing over time, but the need for advocacy on behalf of people with disabilities will never end. So, while you learn to advocate specifically for your child, do not neglect to learn about advocating for the group of people to which your child belongs. If parents do not band together to fight for the rights of all children with disabilities, no one else will.

Why should you get involved in group advocacy? Working just for the betterment of your own child is shortsighted. The programs, benefits, and rights you want for your child when she is older will come into existence *only* through class advocacy. Working for others is truly working for yourself and your child. Break down the barriers and eliminate the stigma hindering all people with disabilities and you have done the same thing for your child.

Parents *can* effectively change laws and society. We have done it before. In the early 1970s, for example, parents banded together and pushed for the landmark legislation of Public Law 94–142, which guaranteed a free and appropriate education for children with disabilities. *Parents* did this. They wanted their children to live at home and go to school just like other kids do, and they didn't rest until they had achieved their goal. We can do it again. We truly do have the power.

Getting Started

The steps involved in class advocacy are nearly the same as they are in case advocacy (advocating for your child alone). The first step is to believe in your child, as well as in children and adults just like her—in their abilities, potential, and rights. Second, believe in yourself. You can be just as effective on a class level as you are on your own individual level. You don't need special training, college degrees, or experience in public speaking. Your personal knowledge of the concerns shared by families affected by disabilities qualifies you to speak up. You know more about how mental retardation affects lives than a boatload of "experts."

The third step—educating yourself—is, once again, crucial. You need to learn about the issues affecting people and families with disabilities. To do this, join local and national organizations such as the ARC, PTIC, and specific disability organizations. The newsletters these organizations issue often highlight the current government, legislative, and legal issues affecting your child. There are even more organizations listed in this book's Resource Guide. And do not hesitate to let your local and national organizations know what is going on in *your* area. For example, let the ARC know that your child's applications to SSI and Medicaid have been rejected because your income was just a bit over the legal maximum. Tell them the eligibility criteria are too strict. Start locally. Believe it or not, most "national" movements start out as local fights.

Advocating with Others

Once you know what the issues are, what laws or regulations are being proposed, or what legislation is needed, you can get involved in many different ways and on many different levels. Do just what you feel comfortable doing. If you prefer writing letters instead of meeting with legislators, that's fine. If you prefer speaking to writing, that's fine, too. If you prefer working out of your house alone to working in large groups, there will be plenty of ways you can help. Whatever level of advocacy you participate in or however you do it, you can be sure that your contribution will be needed and appreciated. The following sections explain some of the more common ways in which groups and individuals advocate.

Calling Legislators. Calling your state or federal representative is a lot easier than it sounds. After all, these folks are paid to listen to your concerns. It should not be any more intimidating than calling your dry cleaner. And, if you think elected officials are not really interested in the opinions of parents, you are wrong. With so many issues requiring their vote, representatives want and need input from citizens about what matters. Always assume that your legislators need to be educated about a bill or issue; it is very likely that they do. And remember, in the area of disabilities, *you* are an expert to your legislator. Many will vote according to what they hear from a remarkably small number of voters. So, speak up; you really can make a difference.

Before you call, write a few notes about what you want to say. That way you will be prepared to speak smoothly. Always mention that you are a constituent and that you vote. Often legislators (particularly federal representatives) will have their aides field phone calls and just tally what people say. State legislators, on the other hand, often will be available to speak directly with you.

It is as important to ask other parents to call their legislators as it is to call yourself. Numbers truly matter, and with some issues, you can be sure that any opposition (yes, believe it or not, there is often organized opposition) will marshal their telephone forces, too. Don't be outmaneuvered!

Writing Legislators. Writing to a legislator is even easier than calling, but does require thought and planning. And, believe it or not, your letter will be read. As with calling, there is power in numbers: Round up as many people as you can to write.

Your letters should be as persuasive as you can make them. Don't badger or threaten; use the facts to convince. Remind your representative subtly that you and people just like you vote and are watching to see what he or she does on the issues. Here are some suggestions about letter-writing:

1. Keep letters short and to the point.
2. Identify yourself as the parent of a child with mental retardation and as a member of a larger group.
3. Briefly explain the issue as you see it, and how it affects your own family.
4. Refer to specific legislation by bill number.
5. Do not hesitate to come right out and ask for their vote on the bill (after all, they feel free to ask for yours).
6. Do not send form letters. They are not as effective as personal letters.

What do you do *after* the vote? If your legislator votes your way (whether or not your side wins), send a letter of thanks. It is not too early to mention some upcoming issues that you hope will also merit his or her support. If your legislator voted against you, send a letter that expresses your disappointment clearly and unequivocally. Remind your legislator that your support in the future depends on his or her support of the issues critical to you. Hold out the hope that he or she can redeem your support by voting correctly in the future. Don't let your legislator write you off.

Above all, never forget that our government is a democracy. Everybody gets a vote. There is great power in numbers. As the parent of a child with mental retardation, you'll begin to understand that full participation in the community is the result of legislation that guarantees it. Those laws are constantly being changed or amended to provide fuller participation and more opportunities for all persons with all kinds of disabilities. Mental retardation is not easy for the general public to understand. Through knowledge comes understanding and through understanding comes acceptance. If our children are kept out of sight, they remain out of mind. It's up to us to help create understanding and change the world in which they will grow up.

Most of the parents in our group feel like we're all on the same side. We know that the school system will have to listen to us if we have seventy parents waving a petition around instead of just one parent fighting the battle alone.

I feel as if I am fighting as much for the rights of all kids with Down syndrome as I am for my son. I feel that you can get so much more accomplished as a group.

Keeping Perspective

My job in this chapter has been to motivate you to take action on behalf of your child and children like her. I hope you become a strong and effective advocate. But please do not feel you must devote your entire life to advocacy. All of us parents rely on each other to help with the fight for our kids, but if you burn out early, we all lose. If you pace yourself, give yourself breaks, and remember the real reason for your advocacy, you will be able to sustain your efforts over the long haul. Personally, I enjoy advocacy; it gives me energy. It makes me feel I can make a difference. It may *not* have the same effect on you, however, so think very carefully about what you are comfortable doing. Then do it.

Conclusion

It's been twenty years since I ran into Maureen at the concert. I wonder if she has moved out of the institution and into the community. I wonder if she lives in a group home or has her own apartment. I wonder if she goes to work. I wonder if she ever fell in love or got married. I wonder how her mom is doing. You see, Maureen is my age. She's got many years and a lot of life ahead of her. When we were kids, programs and services did not exist. The choice wasn't there. It's there now—but only because parents believed in their children, trusted themselves, spoke out, and educated the public. Parents and their advocacy allies changed the system so that it respects human dignity. Of course, we've still got a long way to go, but today the hope and promise are brighter than ever.

Today, we have choices. We can say "no." We can say, "Wait a minute, this doesn't seem right. We want something different." We can say that our children deserve the same opportunity to live, work, and play in the community as everyone else. Our children need not bear the outdated burden of shame, misunderstanding, or fear. As parents, we must see to it that they do not.

Glossary

Adaptive behavior: the ability to function independently and successfully in the world.

ADHD. *See* Attention Deficit Hyperactivity Disorder.

Advocacy: working to protect the rights and opportunities of someone who is unable to do so for himself.

Age equivalent score: the age at which the "average" child gets the same number of items correct.

Anoxia: lack of oxygen to tissues (including the brain), causing cell death or damage.

Articulation: the production of speech sounds.

Attention: the ability to focus on something and maintain that focus over time.

Attention Deficit Hyperactivity Disorder (ADHD): a disorder that causes excessive activity, impulsivity, and difficulties with focusing attention.

Audiologist: a professional trained in the diagnosis of hearing disorders and the use of hearing aids.

Auditory: having to do with hearing. "Auditory comprehension" generally refers to understanding spoken language.

Augmentative communication system: the use of manual signs, language (picture) boards, or computerized communication systems to aid the use and development of language.

Autism: a physical disorder of the brain that impairs a child's social and communication development, causes sensory problems, and unusual behaviors. Autism is frequently accompanied by mental retardation.

Bell curve: a curve on a graph that shows the distribution of characteristics in a population. These curves are used to show the range of human intelligence and developmental skill acquisition, as well as many other characteristics of populations.

Bilateral intgegration: using the two sides of the body together; for example, both hands.

Borderline: an IQ score that is not low enough to be within the range of mental retardation, but is also below the average range of scores. Borderline IQs are often considered to be between 70 and 79.

Central nervous system (CNS): the brain and the nerves travelling along the spinal cord to and from the brain.

Cerebral palsy: a disorder of movement, balance, and coordination caused by damage to the brain before three years of age.

Chromosomes: microscopic rod-shaped bodies located within the cells that contain genetic material.

Cognition (cognitive skills): thinking abilities; for example, understanding concepts, attending, remembering, reasoning, etc. Cognitive abilities allow us to organize and understand the world in order to respond to it.

Computerized Axial Tomography (CT Scan or CAT Scan): computerized x-rays used to visualize soft tissues of the body, such as the brain.

Conductive hearing loss: a temporary or permanent hearing impairment caused by a problem of the ear canal or the middle ear cavity.

Cortex (cerebral cortex): The area of the brain involved in thinking and learning.

Cost-of-care liability: the right of a state providing care to a person with disabilities to charge for care and to collect from his or her assets.

Development: the interaction between the biologic material with which a child is born and the physical and social environment surrounding her, and the resulting growth and learning.

Developmental delay: a condition that interrupts a child's development so that one or more areas of learning is behind where it should be for his age. There is no implication as to the cause of the delay and the child may or not "catch up."

Developmental disability: A lifelong condition that begins before adulthood and prevents a child from developing normally. Can refer to any delay in development regardless of cause, but often used to refer specifically to mental retardation and PDD/autism.

Developmental milestone: a developmental goal that acts as a measurement of developmental progress over time—for example, sitting up; speaking in two-word phrases.

Developmental pediatrician: a physician who has specialized training in the assessment and treatment of disorders affecting development.

Discretionary trust: a trust in which the trustee (the person responsible for governing the trust) has the authority to use trust funds for any purpose, as long as funds are expended only for the beneficiary.

Disinherit: to deprive someone of an inheritance.

Distractability: the inability to maintain attention on something to which one needs to attend.

Down syndrome: a common genetic disorder in which a person is born with forty-seven rather than forty-six chromosomes, resulting in developmental delays, mental retardation, low muscle tone, and other effects.

Due process hearing: part of the procedures established to protect the rights of parents and children with disabilities during disputes under the IDEA. These are hearings before an impartial person to review a child's identification, evaluation, placement, or special educational services.

Dyspraxia (apraxia): difficulty planning and executing movements.

Early intervention: specialized programs developed for children birth through two years to minimize the effects of conditions that interfere with normal development and learning.

Electroencephalogram (EEG): recordings of the electrical activity of the brain, usually of the cortex. Used in diagnosing seizures.

Encephalitis: inflammation of the brain: sometimes as a complication from certain viruses.

ENT (otolaryngologist): a medical doctor specializing in diagnosing and treating disorders of the ears, nose, and throat.

Epilepsy: a recurrent condition of abnormal electrical discharges in the brain, i.e., seizures.

Estate planning: formal, written arrangements for handling the possessions and assets of people after they have died.

Expressive language: using words, written symbols, and gestures according to a system of rules in order to express oneself.

Family coordinator: a professional whose role is to help parents locate and obtain services and the support they need to best parent their child with disabilities.

Fetal alcohol syndrome (FAS): a group of physical, developmental, and behavioral characteristics in a child resulting from maternal drinking during pregnancy. Often associated with mild mental retardation.

Fine motor: relating to the use of the small muscles of the body, such as those in the hands, feet, fingers, and face.

Fragile X syndrome: a group of physical, developmental, and behavioral characteristics resulting from a genetic condition in which the long arm of the X chromosome looks as if it has been partially broken off. Can cause mild to severe mental retardation or learning disabilities. Boys are usually more significantly affected.

Generalization: the ability to apply previous learning to new situations.

Genes: located within the chromosomes, genes contain the hereditary material that determines a person's physical, intellectual, and other traits.

Gross motor: relating to the use of the large muscles of the body, such as those in the arms, legs, and trunk.

Handicap: any disability that impedes a person's ability to perform a specific task.

Handicapping condition: an educationally and legally based term denoting that a child's areas of disability are being specified in order to determine his eligibility for special education or other services.

Hemispheres: the right and left sides of the brain.

Hydrocephaly: a condition in which excess cerebrospinal fluid collects in the ventricles of the brain.

Hypotonia: low (floppy, loose) muscle tone.

Hypoxia: insufficient oxygen to body tissues, including the brain. *See* Anoxia.

IDEA: Individuals with Disabilities Education Act. The reenactment of P.L. 94-142, the law guaranteeing children with disabilities a free, appropriate education in the least restrictive environment.

IEP (Individualized Education Program): a written report that details the special education program to be provided a child with disabilities.

IFSP (Individualized Family Service Plan): a written plan for providing early intervention services to children and their families.

Immittance (impedance, tympanometry): a test used to detect abnormal pressure or fluid in the middle ear by measuring movement of the eardrum.

Integrated: mainstreamed; refers to situations in which children with disabilities have at least some routine contact with children without disabilities.

Intelligence: thinking (cognitive) ability and its efficient use for taking in information and incorporating it into one's existing framework of knowledge.

Intelligence quotient (IQ): the score from a standardized test of intelligence indicating a person's overall level of cognitive function relative to other people the same age. IQ is one determinant for the diagnosis of mental retardation, with scores below 70 usually considered to be in the mentally retarded range.

IQ. *See* Intelligence quotient.

IWRP (Individualized Written Rehabilitation Plan; IHP-Habilitation): a plan describing the services a person with disabilities needs to work productively. Written through the state department of vocational rehabilitation.

Kinesthesia: awareness of movement of body parts.

Language: the system of rules by which we use words and gestures to express our thoughts and understand others; i.e. communicate. *See also* Expressive language; Receptive language.

Learning: taking in new information as the result of experience or practice and integrating it into the body of knowledge already owned.

Learning disability: a condition that causes someone to have more difficulty learning in one or more specific areas than would be expected based on that person's overall cognitive abilities.

Learning modality: the sensory systems or channels (visual, auditory, tactile, etc.) through which a child learns.

Least restrictive environment: the requirement under the IDEA that children receiving special education must be made a part of a regular school to the fullest extent possible. Included in the law as a way of ending the traditional practice of isolating children with disabilities.

Low average: a range of IQ scores at the bottom of the average range. Often considered to be between 80 and 89.

Luxury trust: a trust that describes the kind of allowable expenses in a way that excludes the cost of care in state-funded programs in order to aviod cost-of-care liability.

Magnetic Resonance Imaging (MR or MRI): a type of x-ray using magnetic fields.

Mainstreaming: involving children with special needs in situations in which they interact with children without special needs.

Memory: the cognitive ability to store and recall information from any of the sensory systems (visual, auditory, tactile, etc.) May be on a short-term or long-term basis.

Meningitis (viral): inflammation of the meninges (covering around the brain and spinal cord) as a result of certain viruses.

Mental age (MA): on tests of intelligence, the age at which an average child receives the same number of items correct.

Mental retardation: cognitive functioning (thinking abilities) below the normal range. Causes difficulties and delays in learning and adaptive functioning. Mild M.R.: scores on intelligence tests from 70 to 50 or 55. Moderate M.R.: scores from 50 or 55 to 35 or 40. Severe M.R.: scores from 35 or 40 to 20 or 25. Profound M.R.: scores from 20 or 25 and lower.

Microcephaly: smaller than usual, underdeveloped head and brain.

Midline: the vertical center of the body.

Motor development: acquisition of movement skills.

Muscle tone: the degree of elasticity or tension of muscles.

Myelination: the development of the covering around each nerve fiber.

Neurological: having to do with the nervous system.

Noncategorical: educational/developmental programs that include children with a variety of handicapping conditions.

Nondisjunction Trisomy 21: the common type of Down syndrome, caused by the failure of chromosomes to separate during meiotic cell division in the egg (female) or sperm (male).

Occupational therapist (OT): a therapist who is trained to treat disorders of fine motor and adaptive skills, and sometimes is also trained to treat sensory integration problems.

Ophthalmologist: a medical doctor trained to diagnose and treat eye diseases, perform eye surgery, examine vision, and prescribe glasses.

Oral sensory-motor (sensorimotor): having to do with the abilities of processing sensory information and using the muscles in and around the mouth.

Orthotics: lightweight devices designed to provide stability at a joint or stretch muscles. Used especially for children with cerebral palsy.

Otolaryngologist. *See* ENT.

Percentile score: the percentage of children the same age who would have scored lower on the test—e.g., 60th percentile means 60 percent have the same score or lower.

Perseveration: the act of continuing or repeating an activity or thought to the extreme.

Pervasive developmental disorder (PDD): a diagnostic term referring to a condition that seriously affects a child's social and communication development. Autism is a type of PDD.

Phenylketonuria (PKU): a metabolic disorder that can result in mental retardation if not treated early enough.

Physical therapist (PT): a therapist trained to treat disorders of movement or posture.

P.L. 94-142. *See* IDEA.

P.L. 99-457: An amendment to the IDEA encouraging states to provide special educational services for children under three.

Posture: the ability to maintain body positions. Requires the integration of information from the systems of balance (vestibular) and movement of body parts (proprioception).

Pragmatics: the rules underlying the social use of language.

Praxis: the ability to organize and execute a sequence of movements.

Problem-solving: one of the cognitive abilities important for intelligence. The ability to figure out ways to do something based on previous learning while taking new information into account.

Proprioception: the sense that provides input about where body parts are in relation to other parts and how the parts are moving.

Psychiatrist: a medical doctor specializing in the diagnosis and treatment of emotional and behavioral disorders that may have an underlying physical cause.

Psychologist: a professional trained in the science of human behavior and learning, who treats emotional and behavioral disorders, and does psycho-educational assessments which yield information about intelligence and the diagnosis of mental retardation.

Public Law 94-142. *See* IDEA.

Public Law 99-457. *See* P.L. 99-457.

Range of motion (ROM): the degree of movement a joint is capable of performing.

Receptive language: the ability to understand spoken, written, or gestural language.

Related services: transportation and other developmental, corrective, or supportive services needed to enable a child with disabilities to benefit from a special education program. Under the IDEA, a child is entitled to receive these services as part of his special education program.

Respite care: child care services provided by trained staff, designed to give parents a break from caring for their children with disabilities.

Seizure: temporary, abnormal electrical activity in the brain which results in involuntary changes in consciousness or behavior.

Self-contained classroom: a class of only children receiving special education services, and usually staffed by a special education teacher.

Self-help: relating to skills involved in caring for one's self, including eating, dressing, personal grooming, etc.

Sensorineural hearing loss: a hearing loss caused by damage to the inner ear and/or the auditory nerve; usually permanent.

Sensory integration: the ability to take in, process, and organize sensations.

Sensory-motor (sensorimotor) abilities: the ability to receive information through the senses and respond with appropriate movements.

Shared risk insurance: a type of insurance policy sometimes available to people who could not otherwise get insurance, made possible when all companies within the state share the extra cost of insuring "high risk" children and adults.

Special education: specially designed instruction tailored to meet the individual needs of each child with disabilities.

Special education teacher: a teacher trained in teaching children with various developmental disabilities and in designing instructional programs to meet each individual child's needs.

Speech: the process of producing and combining sounds into words in order to communicate.

Speech/language pathologist (SLP): a therapist trained to diagnose and treat disorders of communication, including those of speech, language, and oral sensory and motor deficits.

Standard deviation: on standardized tests of abilities and development, the amount of variability of scores within the representative sample on which the test was standardized.

Standard score: a test score based on the normal distribution curve—the "bell curve." In tests scored with standard scores, 100 usual equals exactly average, and there is a standard deviation of 15 (i.e., scores 15 points above and below 100 are also considered average).

Standardized tests: tests which are administered in exactly the same way each time; e.g., with the same directions, same materials, etc. A standardized test is developed by being administered to a representative sample and contains only items that reliably characterize responses over an age range and discriminate among a range of ability or skill levels.

Support trust: a trust that requires that funds be expended to pay for the beneficiary's expenses of living, such as housing, food, and transportation.

Syndrome: a group of characteristics that have been shown to have the same cause and to occur together, and may include aspects of physical appearance, behavior, and development.

Syntax: the system of rules governing the way words in a particular language are put together to form phrases or sentences.

Tactile defensiveness (hypersensitivity): an overreaction to or avoidance of touch.

Temperament: the emotional style with which one is born.

Toxoplasmosis: a disease caused by a parasite, common in mammals. It can result in mental retardation if a child contracts it before birth.

Tympanometry: a test that measures fluid that may be present behind the eardrum or detects a blockage of the eustachian tube.

Uniform Gifts to Minors Act: a law that governs gifts to minors. Under the UGMA, gifts to minors become the property of the minor at age eighteen or twenty-one.

Vestibular: having to do with the sense of body position in relation to gravity and movement.

Visual handicap: defined by the IDEA as a visual impairment which, even with correction, impedes a child's ability to learn.

Williams syndrome: a set of characteristics including some of the following: elfin facial features, low birth weight, or failure to thrive, heart disorders, and mental retardation or disorders of learning.

Reading List

Chapter One

Batshaw, Mark L. and Yvonne M. Perret. 3rd ed. *Children with Disabilities: A Medical Primer.* Baltimore: Paul H. Brookes, 1992. Includes a thorough chapter on the nature, assessment, and causes of mental retardation, as well as useful information on genetics and genetic disorders.

Diagnostic and Statistical Manual of Mental Disorders. 3rd ed. revised. Washington, DC: American Psychiatric Association, 1987. Defines mental retardation, intellectual and adaptive function, associated features, possible causes, prevalence, and differential diagnosis.

Krishef, Curtis H. *An Introduction to Mental Retardation.* Springfield, IL: C.C. Thomas. This is an introductory textbook so the writing is a bit technical, but the information is very good. It includes a chapter on the definition of mental retardation and on tests of intelligence, as well as chapters on classification and the pros and cons of educational labels.

Moore, Cory. *A Reader's Guide for Parents of Children with Mental, Physical, or Emotional Disabilities.* Rockville, MD: Woodbine House, 1990. An annotated bibliography of books on disability topics, including a section specifically on mental retardation, as well as listings on topics such as advocacy, planning for the future, and education.

Schopmeyer, Betty B. and Fonda Lowe. *The Fragile X Child.* San Diego: Singular Publishing Group, 1992. Written primarily for therapists, but also useful for parents. It contains a description of the genetic basis of fragile X, as well descriptions of children's behavioral and developmental characteristics and therapeutic interventions.

Stray-Gundersen, Karen. *Babies with Down Syndrome: A New Parents' Guide.* Rockville, MD: Woodbine House, 1986. A good introduction to the issues involved in raising a child with Down syndrome. Chapters discuss causes and characteristics of Down syndrome, emotional issues, daily care, education, family life, and legal issues.

Chapter Two

Seagal, Marilyn and Don Adcock. *Your Child at Play.* New York: New Market Press, 1985. Three separate books cover the years from one to two, two to three, and three to five. The series provides wonderful, readable information that helps parents understand how their young children experience the world. Gives useful insight into the development of thinking abilities, language, and play and exploration. Provides suggestions for parents to do with their children.

Schwartz, Sue and Joan E. Heller Miller. *The Language of Toys: Teaching Communication Skills to Special-Needs Children.* Rockville, MD: Woodbine House, 1988. Gives details on how to use toys to help develop your child's communication skills through play. Includes examples of conversations between parent and child.

Chapter Three

Buck, Pearl S. *The Child Who Never Grew.* 2nd ed. Rockville, MD: Woodbine House, 1992. Nobel prize winning author Pearl Buck reveals her struggle to understand the cause of her daughter's mental retardation (PKU) and the long road to acceptance of her daughter's differences. A landmark book in disability literature.

Dickman, Irving with Dr. Sol Gordon. *One Miracle at a Time: How to Get Help for Your Disabled Child.* New York: Simon & Schuster, 1985. Parents write of their experiences with their children and with getting services for their children's needs.

Dorris, Michael. *The Broken Cord: A Family's Ongoing Struggle with Fetal Alcohol Syndrome.* New York: Harper & Row, 1989. A powerfully written account of an adoptive father's feelings concerning the alcohol abuse that was the source of his son's disability. The author tells of his experiences in raising his adopted son and describes the boy's challenges in dealing with fetal alcohol syndrome.

Dougan, Terrell, Lyn Isbell, Patricia Vyas. *We Have Been There.* Nashville: Abingdon, 1983. Parent essays about topics ranging from getting the diagnosis, to deciding what to do next, to helping your child as she grows up. Excellent insight from parents who know.

Jablow, Martha Moraghan. *Cara: Growing with a Retarded Child.* Philadelphia: Temple University Press, 1982. A mother of a child with Down syndrome writes of the first seven years of her daughter's life. Much of the book focuses on the impressive progress Cara makes in her education and development.

Perske, Robert. *Hope for the Families: New Directions for Parents of Persons with Retardation and Other Disabilities.* Nashville: Abingdon, 1981. Written and illustrated by parents of a child with a developmental disability to give other parents an understanding of what their lives are like. Recognized are all parents' expectations and dreams for their children, as well as the struggle to get beyond the pain of realizing that raising your child is not going to be what you had thought it would be.

Simon, Robin. *After the Tears: Parents Talk about Raising a Child with a Disability.* Orlando, FL: Harcourt Brace Jovanovich, 1987. This short but helpful book written by a parent explores the process of learning to cope with having a child with a disability, from the early, floundering days when the disability is first diagnosed, through the beginnings of acceptance and a new way of life.

Trainer, Marilyn. *Differences in Common: Straight Talk on Down Syndrome, Mental Retardation, and Life.* Rockville, MD: Woodbine House, 1991. Essays on the realities of raising a child with Down syndrome. Trainer pulls no punches, frankly exploring what is right and what is wrong with the way society treats people with mental retardation today, as well as how that treatment affects children and families alike.

Turnbull, Ann and H. Rutherford Turnbull III. 2nd ed. *Parents Speak Out: Then & Now*. New York: Macmillan, 1985. In their own words, parents tell what it is like to raise a child with disabilities.

Chapter Four

Boehm, Ann E. and Mary Alice White. *The Parents' Handbook on School Testing*. New York: Teachers College Press, 1982. Explains common tests of intelligence and achievement, as well as tests for preschool readiness. There are chapters on questions to ask the school staff concerning assessment of children with special needs. Appendices explain various types of scores,including percentiles, stanines, grade equivalents.

Compton, Carolyn. *A Guide to 75 Tests for Special Education*. Belmont, CA: Fearon Education, 1984. Includes sections on assessment of specific areas of learning—e.g., visual-motor integration, auditory discrimination, reading, etc.—as well as on intelligence and developmental scales. Describes what each test is meant to measure and defines terms.

Chapter Five

Anderson, Winifred, Stephen Chitwood, and Deidre Hayden. *Negotiating the Special Education Maze: A Guide for Parents and Teachers*. Rockville, MD: Woodbine House, 1990. A road map for parents who discover there's a whole other world of education out there: special education. This book is designed to help parents obtain the most appropriate education for their child. Includes case studies to demonstrate how the system works.

Bennett, Tess, Barbara V. Lingerfelt, and Donna E. Nelson. *Developing Individualized Family Support Plans: A Training Manual*. Cambridge, MA: Brookline Books, 1990. Written to train professionals in writing IFSPs, but useful in helping parents understand the purposes and underpinnings of these documents. Includes a glossary, sample IFSP forms, and a list of possible skills the IFSP might include as goals.

Coleman, Jeanine G. *The Early Intervention Dictionary: A Multidisciplinary Guide to Terminology*. Rockville, MD: Woodbine House, 1993. Defines terminology, abbreviations, and acronyms parents and professionals are likely to encounter in the early intervention field.

Jordan, June B., James J. Gallagher, Patricia L. Hutinger, and Merle B. Karners, eds. *Early Childhood Special Education: Birth to Three*. Reston, VA: CEC-ERIC Clearinghouse, 1988. Describes model early intervention programs and approaches.

"A Parent's Guide: Accessing Programs for Infants, Toddlers, and Preschoolers with Disabilities." Free publication available from NICHCY at P.O. Box 1492, Washington, DC 20013.

Turnbull, Ann and H. Rutherford Turnbull III. *Families, Professionals, and Exceptionality: A Special Partnership.* Columbus, OH: Merrill, 1986. Discusses what is required for effective teaming of parents and special education professionals. Also reviews the history of parent-professional partnerships and describes how families can help make the partnership work.

Chapter Six

Baker, Bruce L., Allan J. Brightman, Jan B. Blacher, Louis J. Heifetz, Stephen P. Hinshaw, Diane M. Murphy. 2nd ed. *Steps to Independence: A Skills Training Guide for Parents & Teachers of Children with Special Needs.* Baltimore: Paul H. Brookes, 1989. An indispensable, step-by-step guide to teaching your child self-help, play, household care, and other skills essential to independence. Includes information on toilet training and behavior management.

Clark, Lynn. *SOS! Help for Parents.* Bowling Green, KY: Parents Press, 1985. A how-to book on managing everyday problems of children's behavior. Includes easy-to-apply strategies and illustrations that lend a bit of humor to frustrating situations. Order directly from publisher at P.O. Box 2180, Bowling Green, KY 42102.

Foxx, Richard M. and Nathan H. Azrin. *Toilet Training Persons with Developmental Disabilities: A Rapid Program for Day & Nighttime Independent Toileting.* Champaign, IL: Research Press, 1973. An older, but useful book.

Chapter Seven

Dougan, Terrell, Lyn Isbell, and Patricia Vyas. *We Have Been There: A Guidebook for Families of People with Mental Retardation.* Nashville: Abingdon Press, 1983. Includes essays and comments from parents about family life with their children with mental retardation. Also includes writings by the siblings of children with mental retardation.

Featherstone, Helen. *A Difference in the Family: Life with a Disabled Child.* New York: Penguin, 1982. The account of a parent who is also an educator and her life with her son with severe disabilities. This book has become a favorite of parents because it provides the chance to hear from another parent who has been there and knows what it's like.

Kaufman, Sandra Z. *Retarded Isn't Stupid, Mom!* Baltimore: Paul H. Brookes, 1988. A mother's account of raising a daughter with mild mental retardation to adulthood and the struggle to help her become an integrated, independent member of her community.

Perske, Robert. *Circles of Friends.* Nashville: Abingdon, 1988. A perspective on real friendships among people with disabilities and without, and how such relationships can enrich the lives of all involved.

Powell, Thomas H. and Peggy Ahrenhold Ogle. *Brothers and Sisters: A Special Part of Exceptional Families.* Baltimore: Paul H. Brookes, 1985. Words from siblings and experts on the experiences of being a brother or sister of a child with disabilities.

Chapter Eight

Commerce Clearing House Editorial Staff. *Americans with Disabilities Act of 1990: Law and Explanation.* Chicago: CCH Inc., 1990. The law itself, presented in as readable a form as possible.

Kaye, Barry. *Save a Fortune on Your Life Insurance.* New York: J.K. Lasser, 1991. How to determine the type of life insurance policy that is best for you, as well as how much life insurance you need.

Lieberman, Trudy. *Life Insurance.* New York: Consumer Reports Books, 1988. Includes explanations of the different types of life insurance policies, as well as tips on finding the right policy for your family.

Turnbull, H. Rutherford III, Ann P. Turnbull, G.J. Bronicki, Jean Ann Summers, Constance Roeder-Gordon. *Disability and the Family: A Guide to Decisions for Adulthood.* Baltimore: Paul H. Brookes, 1989. Discusses government programs (e.g., SSI and Vocational Rehab.), legal definitions, and rights of children with disabilities. It includes sections on financial planning, advocacy, and helping your child become a part of the community.

Chapter Nine

Batshaw, Mark L. and Yvonne M. Perret. 3rd ed. *Children with Disabilities: A Medical Primer.* Baltimore: Paul H. Brookes, 1992. Includes readable chapters on the diagnosis, causes, and treatment of autism, cerebral palsy, hearing and vision impairments, attention deficit disorders, and seizures.

Freeman, John M., Eileen P.G. Vining, and Diana J. Pillas. *Seizures and Epilepsy in Childhood: A Guide for Parents.* Baltimore: Johns Hopkins University Press, 1990. A first-rate overview of the nature, diagnosis, and treatment of seizures in children. Includes a chapter on raising a child who has seizures in conjunction with mental retardation or other disabilities.

Geralis, Elaine, ed. *Children with Cerebral Palsy: A Parents' Guide.* Rockville, MD: Woodbine House, 1991. Edited by a parent with chapters by experts, this helpful book gives parents a thorough understanding of the nature and treatment of cerebral palsy and includes valuable information on how to care for and raise your child.

Lukens, Kathleen. *Song of David.* Nanuet, NY: Venture Press, 1989. The story of a family's discovery that their child has autism and mental retardation. This is an account of their experiences raising their son and their thoughts on each individual's worth in the world.

McArthur, Shirley. *Raising Your Hearing-Impaired Child: A Guide for Parents.* Washington, DC: Alexander Graham Bell, 1982. Practical advice on teaching and caring for a child with a hearing impairment.

Parker, Harvey C. *The ADD Hyperactivity Workbook for Parents, Teachers, and Kids.* Plantation, FL: Impact Publications, 1988. Includes sections on possible "tools" for managing behavior that parents can use, as well as suggestions for classroom behavior management. Includes stickers, sample charts, and behavior contracts to use.

Powers, Michael D., ed. *Children with Autism: A Parents' Guide*. Rockville, MD: Woodbine House, 1989. Provides parents with a detailed explanation of their child's disorder, along with suggestions for teaching their child, managing behavior, integrating their child into the family, and finding educational programs.

Reisner, Helen. *Children with Epilepsy: A Parents' Guide*. Rockville, MD: Woodbine House, 1988. Gives parents a detailed understanding of the nature of seizures, what information the EEG can yield, how to develop your child's self-esteem, and how educational and medical professionals can help.

Ripley, Susan. "A Parent's Guide: Doctors, Disabilities, and the Family." Available free from National Information Center for Children and Youth with Disabilities (NICHCY) at P.O. Box 1492, Washington, DC 20013. Addresses common concerns of parents looking for physicians for their children with disabilities.

Schwartz, Sue, ed. *Choices in Deafness: A Parents' Guide*. Rockville, MD: Woodbine House, 1987. Presents the pros and cons of three communication methods used by children with hearing impairments: oral communication, cued speech, and total communication.

Scott, Eileen P., James E. Jan, and Roger D. Freeman. *Can't Your Child See? A Guide for Parents of Visually Impaired Children*. 2nd ed. Austin: Pro-Ed, 1985. Designed to help parents raise a child with visual impairments from infancy to adulthood. Includes a chapter on children with multiple disabilities.

Chapter Ten

Des Jardins, Charlotte. *How to Get Services by Being Assertive*. Chicago: Coordinating Council for Handicapped Children, 1980. This older book still offers much valuable advice on how to advocate for needed services for children with disabilities.

Des Jardins, Charlotte. *How to Organize an Effective/Advocacy Group and Move Bureaucracies*. Chicago: Coordinating Council for Handicapped Children, 1980. A must for parents interested in joining with others to advocate on behalf of all people with disabilities.

Ordover, Eileen L. and Kathleen B. Boundy. *Educational Rights of Children with Disabilities: A Primer for Advocates*. Cambridge, MA: Center for Law and Education, 1991. An easy-to-read book chockful of helpful information on educational advocacy. Gives parents the feeling that they are allowed to do what they have to do. Includes an excellent index.

Rosenberg, Bernard. *From Catastrophe to Help for the Retarded*. New York: Rivercross Publishing, 1989. Written by a parent who has done some of the "crusading" for the rights of children with mental retardation. A look at where we've come in our education, care, and efforts to meet the needs of children to help them be productive and included in society.

Schwier, Karin. *Speakeasy: People with Mental Handicaps Talk about Their Lives in Institutions and in the Community*. Austin: Pro-Ed, 1990. In their own words, adults with mental retardation tell of their experiences in institutions and other segregated settings. Their stories present a compelling case for integration of people with disabilities in all aspects of community life.

Turnbull, H. Rutherford III, Ann P. Turnbull, G.J. Bronicki, Jean Ann Summers, Constance Roeder-Gordon. *Disability and the Family: A Guide to Decisions for Adulthood.* Baltimore: Paul H. Brookes, 1989. Includes chapters on how to advocate for your child in her present educational placement, as well as to secure the services you anticipate her needing in the future.

Books for Children

Adams, Barbara. *Like It Is: Facts and Feelings about Handicaps from Kids Who Know.* New York: Walker and Co., 1979. Includes a chapter on developmental disabilities and mental retardation which explains terms, gives factual information, and answers questions such as what IQ tests are and whether people with mental retardation are dangerous or mentally ill. Most photos are of adolescents.

Bergman, Thomas. *We Laugh, We Love, We Cry: Children Living with Mental Retardation.* Milwaukee: Gareth Stevens, 1989. About the experiences of two sisters who have mental retardation, and are five and six years old. The text interprets how children with mental retardation might feel about their lives. Includes good photos of family life, school, and therapy.

Berkus, Clara Widess and Margaret Dodd. *Charlsie's Chuckle.* Rockville, MD: Woodbine House, 1992. The infectious laughter of a seven-year-old with Down syndrome brings a group of angry adults back to their senses. Illustrated with colorful, appealing photographs.

Cairo, Shelley. *Our Brother Has Down's Syndrome: An Introduction for Children.* Willowdale, Ontario: Anick Press, 1985. Two young sisters describe life with their little brother, Jai, who has Down syndrome. Charmingly illustrated with color photographs.

Emmert, Michelle. *I'm the Big Sister Now.* Niles, IL: Albert Whitman, 1989. A story written from the point of view of a younger sister of a girl with profound mental retardation and cerebral palsy. Includes wonderful drawings of the girls' family life.

Garrigue, Sheila. *Between Friends.* Scarsdale, NY: Bradbury Press, 1978. Written for older elementary school-aged readers. A young girl's friendship with a girl who has Down syndrome is tested by other friends and even by her mother, who seems afraid of her friend with mental retardation.

Larsen, Hanne. *Don't Forget about Tom.* New York: Thomas Y. Crowell, 1974. Written to illustrate what it means to have mental retardation and to show a day in the life of a nine-year-old with mental retardation.

Meyer, Donald J., Patricia F. Vadasy, and Rebecca R. Fewell. *Living with a Brother or Sister with Special Needs: A Book for Sibs.* Seattle: University of Washington Press, 1985. There are chapters written by siblings of children with mental retardation, cerebral palsy, epilepsy, and hearing and vision impairments. The book is written for children in early elementary school and up. Includes notes to adults giving examples of questions children sometimes ask and some of the feelings they express.

Moss, Deborah. *Shelley, the Hyperactive Turtle*. Rockville, MD: Woodbine House, 1989. Shelley and his friends learn why his behavior is sometimes out of control and what can be done to help him. Written for preschool and early elementary ages.

Prall, Jo. *My Sister's Special*. Chicago: Children's Press, 1985. Told from the viewpoint of a brother whose sister has cerebral palsy and brain damage and uses a communication board. It is appropriate for preschool and elementary school children. Includes good photos.

Thompson, Mary. *My Brother, Matthew*. Rockville, MD: Woodbine House, 1992. David describes what it's like to have a younger brother who doesn't move or talk like other kids. Although he finds life with Matthew frustrating and embarrassing at times, David also enjoys being looked up to by his brother and the warm feeling that comes from knowing he understands Matthew better than anyone else does.

Wartski, Maureen Crane. *My Brother Is Special*. Philadelphia: Westminster Press, 1979. Written for older elementary and middle school readers. An older sister enters her little brother, who has mental retardation, in an athletic event, even though her parents are against the idea at first.

Magazines and Newsletters

The ARC. News and information about mental retardation and the activities of the national ARC and its local chapters. Available from The ARC, 2501 Avenue J, Arlington, TX 76006.

Down Syndrome News. Information and news about issues related to Down syndrome in particular and disabilities in general. Available from National Down Syndrome Congress, 1605 Chantilly Dr., Atlanta, GA 30324.

The Exceptional Parent. Information and guidance for families of children with all disabilities. Publishes an annual resource guide. 1170 Commonwealth Ave., Boston, MA 02134.

Pacer Advocate. A newsletter for people with an interest in legislation and court rulings affecting individuals with disabilities, as well as in special education issues. Available from PACER Center, 4826 Chicago Ave. S., Minneapolis, MN 55417.

Pacesetter Newsletter. A quarterly newsletter for parents interested in special education issues. Available from PACER Center, 4826 Chicago Ave. S., Minneapolis, MN 55417.

Sibling Information Network Newsletter. Information about research, books, meetings, and other issues of interest to siblings of people with disabilities. Available from Connecticut's University Affiliated Program, School of Education, University of Connecticut, Box U-64, Room 227, Storrs, CT 06268.

FREQUENTLY USED EVALUATION INSTRUMENTS

NAME OF TEST	ADMINISTERED BY	AGES[1]	TYPE	SCORING
General Tests of Intelligence				
Wechsler Preschool and Primary Scale of Intelligence-Revised (WPPSI-R)	Psychologist	4–6½	general cognitive	standard scores
Stanford-Binet Intelligence Scale–4th Ed.	Psychologist	2–adult	general cognitive	standard scores
Kaufman Assessment Battery For Children	Psychologist	2½ –12½	general cognitive	standard scores
McCarthy Scales of Children's Abilities	Psychologist	2½–8½	general cognitive	standard scores
Bayley Scales of Infant Development	Psychologist	birth–2½	general cognitive	standard scores
Specialized Tests of Intelligence				
French Pictorial Test of Intelligence	Psychologist	3–8	non-verbal test	standard scores
Leiter International Performance Scale	Psychologist	2–18	non-verbal test	standard scores
Columbia Mental Maturity Scale	Psychologist	3–12	non-verbal test	standard scores
Adaptive Behavior Scales				
Vineland Adaptive Behavior Scales	Psychologist	birth–adult	interview checklist	standard scores
Developmental Profile (Alpern-Boll)	Psychologist	birth–12	interview checklist	age equivalents
Articulation				
Goldman-Fristoe Test of Articulation	Speech/Language Pathologist	2–up	observation of articulation	age equivalents
Language				
Bracken Test of Basic Concepts	Speech/Language Pathologist	2–8	receptive test of concepts	standard scores
Peabody Picture Vocabulary Test-Revised	Speech/Language Pathologist	2–adult	receptive vocabulary	standard scores
Nonspeech Test for Receptive/Expressive Language	Speech/Language Pathologist	5½–21	nonverbal communication	age equivalents
Receptive-Expressive Emergent Language Scale (REEL)	Speech/Language Pathologist	birth–3	observation checklist	age equivalents

1 Age ranges are the ages for which the tests have norms or age scores. Sometimes tests are used that do not have appropriate norms, but some information can be gained by using the tests, if not specific scores.

Instrument	Examiner	Age	Domain	Scores
Sequenced Inventory of Communication Development-Revised (SICD-R)	Speech/Language Pathologist	birth-4	general language	age equivalents
Test of Language Development-2 Primary	Speech/Language Pathologist	4-8½	general language	standard scores
Gardner Expressive One-Word Picture Vocabulary Test-Revised	Speech/Language Pathologist	2-12	expressive vocabulary	standard scores
Motor Functioning and Perception				
Bayley Scales of Infant Development—Motor Scale	OT & PT	birth-2½	gross & fine motor	standard scores
Peabody Developmental Motor Scales	OT & PT	birth-3	gross & fine motor	standard scores
DeGangi-Berk Test of Sensory Integration	OT	3-5	sensory integration	cutoff scores
Developmental Test of Visual-Motor Integration	OT	2½-18	fine motor/drawing	standard scores
Motor-Free Visual Perception Test	OT	4-8	visual perception	standard scores
Gardner Test of Visual-Perceptual Skills	OT	4-12	visual perception	standard scores
Earhardt Developmental Prehension Assessment	OT	birth-6	upper extremity use	age equivalents
Preschool Developmental Profiles				
Birth to Three Checklist of Learning & Language Behavior	Special Ed Teacher[2]	birth-3	general developmental levels[3]	age equivalents
Early Intervention Developmental Profile	Special Ed Teacher	birth-3	general developmental levels	age equivalents
Early Learning Accomplishment Profile	Special Ed Teacher	birth-3	general developmental levels	age equivalents
Learning Accomplishment Profile: Diagnostic Edition (Revised)	Special Ed Teacher	birth-6	general developmental levels	age equivalents
Woodcock-Johnson Psychoeducational Battery: Tests of Achievement	Special Ed Teacher	2-adult	academic and pre-academic skills	standard scores

2 Often administered by different members of team. Primarily used by Special Education Teachers to develop and assess IEP goals. Others who may use portions of these tests include the SLP, OT, and PT.

3 Usually includes preacademic or academic readiness skill areas such as counting, matching, knowledge of categories and concepts, as well as language, social skills, and motor development.

Resource Guide

National Organizations

The national organizations listed below provide a variety of services that can be of help to you and your child with mental retardation. For further information about any of these organizations, call or write and request a copy of their newsletter or other publications.

Accent on Information
P.O. Box 700
Bloomington, IL 61702
309/378–2961
For a nominal fee, this organization will perform information searches on topics such as daily care and products and devices for people with disabilities. They also offer useful publications, including a *Buyer's Guide* that lists equipment and devices as well as their manufacturers. Write and request information on Accent Special Publications.

Alexander Graham Bell Association for the Deaf
3417 Volta Place, NW
Washington, DC 20007
202/337–5220 (Voice/TDD)
Their Children's Rights Program conducts educational advocacy for deaf children and has consulting services for legal rights. The organization answers questions from families of hearing impaired children and publishes a journal and newsletter.

American Association of University Affiliated Programs
    for Persons with Developmental Disabilities
8605 Cameron Street, Suite 406
Silver Spring, MD 20910
301/588–8252
Many universities offer programs and services for children with disabilities and their families. Most University Affiliated Programs offer diagnosis and treatment of disabilities and conduct research on handicapping conditions and methods of teaching. For the location of the University Affiliated Program nearest you, contact the AAUAP at the address above.

American Council for the Blind
1155 15th St., NW
Suite 720
Washington, DC 20005
202/467–5081

The ACB serves people with blindness, visual impairments, and deaf-blindness. They advocate for civil rights, national health insurance, rehabilitation, eye research, technology, and other issues that concern blind citizens. You can call the toll-free number for information and referrals.

American Foundation for the Blind
15 West 16th Street
New York, NY 10011
212/620–2000; 800/232–5463
The Foundation is a national clearinghouse for information on all aspects of visual impairment. They can also refer you to services for your child and offer useful publications.

American Physical Therapy Association
1111 N. Fairfax Street
Alexandria, VA 22314
703/684–2782
The APTA has a free list of publications, "Publications of Interest to Parents and Educators of Handicapped Children." They can also direct you to the APTA chapter in your area. Call and ask for Information Central.

American Speech-Language-Hearing Association
10801 Rockville Pike
Rockville, MD 20852
301/897–5700 (Voice/TDD)
ASHA researches communication disorders. It has fifty state affiliates that can provide information about services available locally. The organization offers brochures on speech/hearing disorders and information on computer software and augmentative communication.

The ARC
500 E. Border St.
Suite 300
Arlington, TX 76010
A grassroots national organization of people with mental retardation and their advocates (formerly known as the Association for Retarded Citizens). Publishes information on all types of developmental delays and supports an extensive network of local associations.

The Association for Persons with Severe Handicaps (TASH)
7010 Roosevelt Way, N.E.
Seattle, WA 98115
206/523–8446
A professional/parent organization that advocates for a dignified lifestyle for all people with severe handicaps. Publishes a newsletter and other publications.

Association for the Care of Children's Health
3615 Wisconsin Avenue, NW
Washington, DC 20016
202/244–1801
Through education, advocacy, and research programs, ACCH meets the psychological and developmental needs of children with chronic illnesses or disabilities. They offer a bi-monthly newsletter and a Parent Resource Guide, as well as other publications.

Autism Society of America
8601 Georgia Avenue
Suite 503
Silver Spring, MD 20910
301/565–0433
A national organization for parents and professionals dedicated to promoting a better understanding of autism, encouraging the development of services, supporting research, and advocating on behalf of people with autism and their families. Provides information about autism through the ASA Information and Referral Service and publishes a newsletter. Contact the national ASA at the address above for the address of the nearest local chapter.

Children with Attention Deficit Disorders (CH.A.D.D.)
1859 N. Pine Island Road
Suite 185
Plantation, FL 33322
305/587–3700
Provides information and support to parents of children with attention deficit disorders. Contact the national organization for the address of the nearest local chapter.

Children's Defense Fund
25 E St., NW
Washington, DC 20001
202/628–8787
CDF is a legal organization that lobbies and brings test cases to court to expand the rights of children, including children with mental retardation.

Children's Hospital of St. Paul
345 North Smith Avenue
St. Paul, MN 55102
612/298–8504
Conducts research into and distributes information about cytomegalovirus (CMV) and its effects.

Clearinghouse on Disability Information
Office of Special Education and Rehabilitative Services
U.S. Department of Education

400 Maryland Avenue, SW
Room 3132, Switzer Building
Washington, DC 20202–2524
202/205–8241
This federal organization offers information on civil rights, federal benefits, medical services, education, and support organizations. It publishes *OSERS News in Print,* a newsletter regarding federal activities affecting people with disabilities, and *Pocket Guide to Federal Help for Individuals with Disabilities,* a summary of services and benefits available to individuals who qualify.

Cornelia de Lange Syndrome Foundation
60 Dyer Avenue
Collinsville, CT 06022
800/753–2357; 203/693–0159
Offers support and information to parents and teachers of children with Cornelia de Lange syndrome; publishes a newsletter, a membership directory, and fact sheets; supports research.

Council for Exceptional Children
1920 Association Drive
Reston, VA 22091–1589
703/620–3660
This organization focuses on the educational needs of exceptional children. It conducts computer searches for information and publishes journals.

Down Syndrome Adoption Exchange
56 Midchester Avenue
White Plains, NY 10606
914/428–1236
Helps prospective parents locate children with Down syndrome to adopt. Also helps parents who decide to give up their children with Down syndrome locate adoptive families.

Epilepsy Foundation of America
4351 Garden City Drive
Suite 406
Landover, MD 20785
301/459–3700; 800/EFA-1000
The EFA answers questions and provides information on seizure disorders and medications. The professionals on staff can also refer you to other organizations and agencies depending on your needs.

Fetal Alcohol Education Program
School of Medicine
Boston University
7 Kent Street
Brookline, MA 02146
Can provide information on the effects of fetal alcohol syndrome on cognitive abilities, as well as on effective teaching strategies for children with FAS.

The 5p- Society
11609 Oakmont
Overland Park, KS 66210
913/469–8900
Offers support and information for children with Cri du chat syndrome and their families. Publishes a newsletter.

Fragile X Southeast Network
Duke University Medical Center
Box 3364
Durham, NC 27710
800/654–FRAX
Publishes a newsletter, books, videos, and audiotapes on fragile X syndrome for families and professionals.

IBM National Support Center for Persons with Disabilities
P.O. Box 2150
Atlanta, Georgia 30301
800/IBM-2133 (voice); 800/284–9482 (TDD)
This is a clearinghouse for information on adaptive as well as technical equipment.

International Rett Syndrome Association
8511 Rose Marie Dr.
Fort Washington, MD 20744
301/248–7031
Collects and distributes information on children with Rett syndrome; offers support to parents; publishes a newsletter; promotes research related to Rett syndrome.

Lowe's Syndrome Association
222 Lincoln Street
West Lafayette, IN 47906
317/743–3634
A national nonprofit organization for parents and professionals. Can provide referrals to doctors experienced with Lowe's syndrome; publishes a newsletter and pamphlets; fosters communication between families; and supports research.

March of Dimes Foundation
1275 Mamaroneck Avenue
White Plains, NY 10605
914/428–7100
The March of Dimes is dedicated to preventing birth defects and publishes many brochures and fact sheets of interest to parents of children with special needs.

National Association for the Education of Young Children
1834 Connecticut Avenue, N.W.
Washington, DC 20009
800/424–2460; 202/232–8777
Publishes an *Early Childhood Resource Catalog.*

National Association for Parents of Visually Impaired
2180 Linway Drive
Beloit, WI 53511
800/562–6265
This national organization of parents promotes the development of parent groups, provides information and publications about visual impairments, publishes a newsletter, and sponsors workshops.

National Association of Private Schools for Exceptional Children
1522 K Street, NW
Suite 1032
Washington, DC 20005
202/408–3338
This association publishes a newsletter and a directory of private schools for children with special needs.

National Association for Visually Handicapped
22 West 21st Street
New York, NY 10010
212/889–3141
A national non-profit organization which serves partially sighted/low vision children and adults, this association distributes public education materials.

National Down Syndrome Congress
1605 Chantilly Road
Atlanta, GA 30324
800/232–NDSC
A national organization of parents and professionals. Provides information and support; publishes a newsletter and other publications; holds an annual convention. Contact the NDSC for the location of the nearest local chapter.

National Down Syndrome Society
666 Broadway
New York, NY 10012
800/221–4602; 212/460–9330
A national organization for parents and professionals dedicated to promoting a better understanding of Down syndrome; funding research related to Down syndrome; providing information and support for families and individuals with Down syndrome. Offers several helpful publications.

National Easter Seal Society
70 East Lake Street
Chicago, IL 60601
312/726–6200 (voice); 312/726–4258 (TDD)
The National Easter Seal Society helps people with disabilities and their families by offering screening, advocacy, public education, and other services. The society also publishes many informative booklets and pamphlets.

National Fragile X Foundation
1441 York Street
Suite 215
Denver, CO 80206
800/688–8765; 303/333–6155
Supports research into diagnosis, treatment, and education of individuals with fragile X syndrome; provides information on fragile X; publishes a newsletter.

National Information Center for Children and Youth
    with Disabilities (NICHCY)
P.O. Box 1492
Washington, DC 20013
703/893–6061; 800–999–5599
This clearinghouse provides free information on educational programs and other special services to parents of children with handicaps. You may call or send in questions. NICHCY also produces fact sheets, information packets, and "State Sheets," which list organizations in each state that can help people with disabilities.

National Information Center on Deafness
Gallaudet University
Merrill Learning Center, Room LE-50
800 Florida Avenue, NE
Washington, DC 20002
202/651–5051 (Voice); 202/651–5052 (TDD)
The NICD provides information and printed materials about deafness, and referrals to other resources. It also offers reading lists on topics in education of deaf children. Information services and single copies of publications are free.

National Organization on FAS
1815 H Street, N.W.
Suite 750
Washington, DC 20006
Can provide information and referral to families of children with fetal alcohol syndrome or fetal alcohol effects.

Parent Care
101½ Union Street
Alexandria, VA 22314
703/836–4678
For parents and professionals concerned about children with disabilities resulting from premature birth. Provides information, referral, and support for families of infants who require special care at birth. Publishes a newsletter and a *Resource Directory*.

Prader-Willi Syndrome Association
6490 Excelsior Boulevard
Suite E-102
St. Louis Park, MN 55426
612/926–1947
Distributes publications on Prader-Willi syndrome and a bimonthly newsletter. Can provide referrals to physicians with special knowledge about the condition. Local parent groups affiliated with the national organization provide support and information; contact the association at the address above for the location of the nearest chapter.

Rubella Project
Developmental Disabilities Center
St. Luke's Roosevelt Hospital Center
428 West 59th Street
New York, NY 10019
212/523–6280
Can provide information on rubella and its complications.

Rubinstein-Taybi Parent Group
414 East Kansas
Smith Center, KS 66967
913/282–6237
Provides information and publications on Rubinstein-Taybi syndrome, and helps parents make contact with other families with children who have the syndrome.

Senate Document Room
Hart Building
Washington, DC 20515

202/224–7860
and
House Document Room
Room B-18
House Annex #2
Washington, DC 20515
202/225–3456

To get a copy of a federal bill or law, you can call or write to either of the following offices. The bill or law will be sent to you via first-class mail on the same day your request is received.

Sibling Information Network
CT University Affiliated Program
991 Main Street, Suite 3A
East Hartford, CT 06108
203/282–7050

The Network is an organization for siblings of people with disabilities. Its quarterly newsletter contains resource information and addresses family issues.

Special Olympics
1350 New York Avenue, N.W.
Suite 500
Washington, DC 20005
202/628–3630

An international program of physical fitness, sports training, and athletic competition for children and adults with mental retardation. Open to competitors of all ability levels and ages.

United Cerebral Palsy Associations
Seven Penn Plaza
Suite 804
New York, NY 10001
212/268–6655; 800/USA-1UCP

UCP is a national organization for people with cerebral palsy and their families. Through its local chapters, it provides a variety of services, including information and referral, parent support, advocacy, and educational and work programs for people with cerebral palsy. A subscription to its *Family Support Bulletin* is free. Other publications are also available. Contact UCP at the address above for the affiliate nearest you.

Williams Syndrome Association
P.O. Box 3297
Ballwin, MO 63022–3297
314/227–4411

Provides support and assistance to families of children with Williams syndrome. Publishes a newsletter and brochures; encourages research.

Local Organizations

In addition to the national organizations listed above, there are also a number of public and private agencies in each state that provide certain kinds of assistance to people with disabilities and their families. Some of the types of state organizations that you may find helpful are listed below.

To obtain the most up-to-date listing of addresses and phone numbers of your state organizations, contact NICHCY at 703/893-6061 or 800/999-5599 and request a free copy of the "state sheet" for your state.

The State Department of Education is the agency responsible for providing education to school-aged children, including special education services to children with mental retardation. In many states, the Department of Education also administers early intervention programs for children aged 0-2, and preschool special education programs for those aged 3-5. If it does not, it can refer you to the agency that does.

The State Mental Retardation Program provides funding, in some states, for residential and day programs for children and adults with mental retardation. In other states, the State Mental Retardation Program can direct you to the appropriate funding agency.

The Developmental Disabilities Council provides funding for direct services for people with developmental disabilities. Most provide services such as diagnosis, evaluation, information and referral, social services, group homes, advocacy, and protection.

The Protection & Advocacy Agency is a legal organization established to protect the rights of people with disabilities. It can supply information about the educational, health, residential, social, and legal services available for children with mental retardation in your state.

ARC Chapters and their many programs are essential resources. ARCs can provide information and referral, put you in touch with other parents, and provide respite care. NICHCY will be able to provide you with the address of your state ARC, but there are also many local branches. To locate the branch nearest you, contact your state ARC or check your telephone book under "Association for Retarded Citizens" or "ARC," or look under the name of your city, county, region, state, or state capital (e.g., "Howard County ARC").

Parent Programs include privately and publicly funded groups that offer support, information, and referral services to parents of children with special needs. NICHCY's state sheet will provide you with contact information for some of the many parent programs in your state, but you will likely be able to locate others by contacting your local ARC, your child's school, a nearby developmental disabilities clinic, or your pediatrician.

State Easter Seal Societies carry out the work of the national society on a local level. State Societies offer a variety of services for children with disabilities and their families, including information and referral, advocacy, and support.

Index

definition of, 174–75
disputes about, 315–18
federal laws mandating, 304–18
parents' role in, 199–203
professionals involved in, 181–91
programs, choosing appropriate, 203–6
settings, 175–76
state laws concerning, 385
Special education teachers, 148–49, 182–84, 200–203, 245
Speech development, 58–59. *See also* Speech/language pathologists
Speech/language pathologists, 149–52, 188–91, 213, 245
Spoiling child, avoiding, 267–71
SSDI, 331–34
SSI, 331–34
Standard scores, 135, 136
Sterilization, 45
Strabismus, 354, 356
Strangers' reactions, 290–93
Sturge-Weber syndrome, 31
Supplemental Security Income, 331–34
Support groups, 117
Syndrome, definition of, 30
Table setting, 231
Tactile defensiveness, 77–78, 213, 219, 220, 360
Tantrums, 241, 248–49, 295–97
Task analysis, 230–31
Tay-Sachs disease, 27

Teachers. *See* Special education teachers
Teaching materials, 205
Teaching strategies for parents, 222, 224–44
Temperaments, 61–62
Teratogens, 31–32
Tests, scoring of, 135–36
Therapists. *See* Occupational therapists; Physical therapists; Speech/language pathologists
Time outs, 252–54, 296
Toilet training, 215–16
Touch, oversensitivity to. *See* Tactile defensiveness
Toxemia, 35
Toxoplasmosis, 34, 362
Triennial evaluations, 137–40
Trisomy 13, 29
Trisomy 18, 29
Trisomy 21. *See* Down syndrome
Trusts. *See* Estate planning
Tuberous sclerosis, 27
Tumors, 39
Uniform Transfers to Minors Act (UTMA), 329, 339
University Affiliated Programs, 395
Vestibular system, 153
Vision problems, 353–58
Vision tests, 355–56
Vocational training, 319–20
Williams syndrome, 31, 40, 70
Wills. *See* Estate planning

649   Children with mental
C   retardation.

10445

$14.95   10/14/1993

DATE			

BAKER & TAYLOR BOOKS